*Maurice Baring Restored*

# BY PAUL HORGAN

## NOVELS

The Fault of Angels

No Quarter Given

Main Line West

A Lamp on the Plains

A Distant Trumpet

Far From Cibola

The Habit of Empire

The Common Heart

Give Me Possession

Memories of the Future

Mountain Standard Time (*a collected volume
containing* MAIN LINE WEST, FAR FROM CIBOLA, *and*
THE COMMON HEART)

Everything to Live For

Whitewater

## OTHER FICTION

The Return of the Weed

Figures in a Landscape

The Devil in the Desert

One Red Rose For Christmas

The Saintmaker's Christmas Eve

Humble Powers

Toby and the Nighttime (*juvenile*)

Things As They Are

The Peach Stone: *Stories from Four Decades*

## HISTORY AND OTHER NON-FICTION

Men of Arms (*juvenile*)

From the Royal City

New Mexico's Own Chronicle (*with Maurice Garland Fulton*)

Great River: The Rio Grande in North American History

The Centuries of Santa Fe

Rome Eternal

Citizen of New Salem

Conquistadors in North American History

Peter Hurd: A Portrait Sketch from Life

Songs After Lincoln

The Heroic Triad: *Essays in the Social Energies of
Three Southwestern Cultures*

Maurice Baring Restored

# Maurice Baring Restored

*Selections from his Work, Chosen and Edited,
with an Introductory Essay and Commentaries
by*

# Paul Horgan

FARRAR, STRAUS AND GIROUX
*New York*

Printed in Great Britain

'Rien de trop!'
*– The favourite maxim of La Fontaine,
according to Maurice Baring.*

---

'Everything about him . . . gave one the
impression of centuries and hidden
stores of pent-up civilization.'
*– Maurice Baring, describing Altamura
in* The Coat Without Seam.

# Contents

## 6. Poems

Contents

# Introduction

*For Michael Wheeler-Booth, who gave me his copy of Dame Ethel Smyth's biography of Maurice Baring with the inscription, 'Paul Horgan – to start you on a book on M.B.?'*

THE HONOURABLE MAURICE BARING was born in 1874, a younger son of the first Lord Revelstoke. The Barings, like the Rothschilds, were prominent in international finance, and members of the family made careers in public affairs. He grew up in a world of great country houses, and town houses in London; of grand social style under Queen Victoria and King Edward; of opulence in the externals of life; of casual and habitual contact with royalty and its fringes; and of rigid adherence to a code of manners which seemed at times a conspiracy to maintain the visible structure of the upper class at the expense of individuals – both those within it and those without it.

Baring's world was defined for him by a succession of nannies and governesses, tutors at Eton, Cambridge, and Oxford, highly placed aunts and uncles and cousins, some of them gifted with intellectual as well as social pleasures. But more: he was close to parents whose interests transcended the usual upper-class concerns – hunting, shooting, 'society' as an end. From his Lutheran clergyman ancestor emerged bankers, cabinet ministers, and diplomats. Brilliant marriages produced an easy, thoughtless, conventional grace for the Barings, in a world where nobody seemed to work. Everyone went from house to house on visits, and from capital to capital, where everyone knew everyone else, lived on gossip, much of it penetrating and fateful, and where all kept alive a firm fabric of society behind which every variation of infidelity was arranged, and formally ignored, with every effect of joy or sorrow. At all costs convention was preserved, with all its faces of power, wealth, privilege and high style glistening in the afternoon light of the Victorian and Edwardian heydays.

In one of Baring's novels, a great lady 'divided people into those you know and those you didn't know'. She derived much of her attitude from the heritage of the eighteenth century, with, as he put it, 'its horror of enthusiasm'. The same peeress saw the Eton and Harrow match as 'one of the most sacred festivals of a well-spent life', and this hint of busy complacency suggests the society in its grand decline.

1

It was a period when it was, for a woman, a career to be an official 'beauty'. One such was so dazzling that, as someone in Baring said, 'you saw green after looking at her'. The society was erected to enclose and display the Victorian or Edwardian 'beauty'. Personal beauty was the supreme gift, and a poor young woman, if she had it, could go far, if she also had manner or the making of it. Every art of style, adornment, deportment, and setting was brought to enhance her effect. In his auto-biography, *The Puppet Show of Memory*, Baring set forth the institution uncritically and lyrically. Remembering young girls playing in the park, he spoke of them as 'the future beauties of England all at play in their lovely teens'.

It was a society and a period in which marriage was still described as 'a shock' for the young beauties who entered upon it. 'I had no idea what marriage meant,' said a brilliant European widow in a Baring novel, 'and it was a terrible shock to me. My husband was good, but he did not understand.' It was a world closed to all life unlike its own, and the key in the lock was indifference. 'What friends!' exclaims Lady Jarvis in Baring's first novel, *Passing By*, 'fast colonials, and the dregs of the Riviera!', and thus whole populations are shuddered off into oblivion.

[ ii ]

It was not just the world you'd think of in which to breed an artist of sensibility and justice. But Baring was fortunate in his father, who had charm and imagination, if no professional talents, and he must have given encouragement to his son's first revelations of these qualities. Lord Revelstoke was spoken of as 'a good humanist', who knew Latin, and was fluent in French, German, and Spanish.

One day he gave Maurice Baring a present which he never forgot, as an artist never forgets something which has powers for his work. Walking down a path in the park of his country house in Devon with his son, Lord Revelstoke said, 'This is your path; I give it to you and the gate at the end.' Delight in possession was crowned by a leap of the imagination. 'It was the inclusion of the little iron gate at the end,' wrote Baring, 'which made that present poignantly perfect.' It was a gate through which he could forever go. Another time his father evidently recognized the im-portance for children of providing them with wonders of gratification and fulfilment, if they were to trust life afterwards with an affirmative con-fidence. Baring loved a toy train in a shop window, but he knew it could never be his, for the price was fifty shillings, and who ever had fifty shillings? And then, one evening, the train was his – it was given to him at home. 'From that moment I knew for certain that miracles could happen and do happen,' he wrote, 'and subsequent experience has con-firmed the belief.' Powerful experience or open simplicity, and sometimes both, must underlie the impulse of the soul that finds itself in art or in faith, and in enduring experience, Baring always kept simplicity.

There was much light-hearted tradition all about as he grew up. Puns were a family tradition – he remembered the delight of all at the answer of a shooting guest at his father's country house when asked if he had shot any duck. 'Not even,' replied the guest, 'not even a mallard imaginaire.' His own wit, which a friend called 'fantastic and unaccountable', was nurtured by polite family prankishness with jokes, riddles, allusions, literary games with fashionable verse-forms such as the triolet. He carried his wit into action. Once as a small boy he asked a great-aunt ('she was old enough', he wrote later, 'to have played the harp to Byron') to give him an antique onyx ring with a pig engraved on it. She said, 'You shall have it when you are older.' An hour later he went back to her room and said, 'I am older now. Can I have the ring?' She gave it to him.

His appealing sense of fantasy, then, governed the reality of time in such a small episode as this; and his vocation was forecast early in the nursery atmospheres and occupations which were his daily pleasure. The family governess was a remarkable Frenchwoman whom the children called Chérie. To her Maurice Baring owed a life-long debt in the development of his affinity, and thus his sensibility, for the life of the imagination and many of its great embodiments in works of literature. Chérie – though, as he said, she was not a literary person – had a love of literature which she communicated by reading aloud to her small charges. He reciprocated by composing a story for her, 'La Princesse Myosotis et Le Prince Muguet, par O.M.G. (Reine de Beauté), Illustré par M.B. (Son Mari)'. The illustrations were done in pencil and water colour. Any gift for Chérie surely could not be purchased – must be made by hand, and so return her loving achievement to her from one whose imagination she had helped to release. She once brought Maurice Baring a toy theatre from Paris. It became France to him – he called it quite solemnly the Théâtre Français – and its toy characters made a population for his mind which must ever afterwards have held meaning for him as he regarded the real world and traced its patterns in his books – a Harlequin, a Columbine, a king and a queen, many princesses, a coarse ruffian with black eyebrows, a masked hangman, and various peasants, officers, Papal halberdiers, and loutish gendarmes with heavy moustaches. Many children have toy theatres and make up plays and stories – but most outgrow them. The destined artist among the generality of child-artists never does. The mystery and delight of creative expression lives on with him as he leaves childhood, and for Maurice Baring the slowly discovered real world always bore something of those early trials of the imagination and helped to animate his mature work and vision. Much of it seemed prophetic to him in a way which he could later identify. 'I have often noticed,' he wrote long afterwards, 'that any factor, feature or person, who or which is destined to play an important part in one's life, casts a shadow before, sometimes a long time before that part begins to be played. For instance, I spent many years of my life in Russia, and many months in St Petersburg; and my night nursery in London when I was a child was adorned with views of the Neva and other sights of St Petersburg, which were framed on the walls.' The principle of fate, often taking its energy from small causes, is a recurring motivation in his novels.

But the fateful was not always to be taken heavily, and he was quite willing to parody it with a lightness of mockery which if it teased others also suggested that he took himself mockingly.

At Oxford an Indian student clapped him on the back and said, 'Hullo, old chap!'

Baring turned and the Indian stammered his apologies. 'I mistook you for Mr Godavery.'

'But I *am* Mr Godavery,' Baring replied.

Calm, sudden fantasy marked his comic style. His aunt Lady Ponsonby said to him one day in his youth, 'I don't think I really like you in pince-nez; must you really wear them?'

'I won't,' he replied, 'if you don't like them, darling,' and at once threw his glasses into the fire. Poor Lady Ponsonby could only murmur afterwards, 'I wish Maurice didn't think it amusing to shy his pince-nez into the fire!'

When, after Eton, where he haunted the library and devoured books as other boys devour sweets and sticky messes, he entered Trinity College, Cambridge (he spent only one year there), he impressed an older student as 'an unremarkable youth, shy and shambling, with prominent blue eyes, and nothing to say for himself. . . . He sat on the edge of his chair, only uttering from time to time an abrupt high dry cackling laugh, between a neigh and a crow.' But very shortly, he was discovered to be 'a most amusing companion, with a genius for nonsense in word and deed'. Sir Edward Marsh wrote this impression years later. He remembered that Baring's humour 'was the most ridiculous thing in the world', and supported the remark with an anecdote of how Baring on buying postage stamps in the post-office at Florence 'sniffed them with an air of suspicion. "*Sono freschi?*" he asked.'

Such a talent for caprice had its first formal literary expression at the end of Baring's year at Cambridge, when, says Marsh, 'he brought out an elegant little daily called the *Cambridge ABC* in four numbers, with a beautiful cover by Aubrey Beardsley. . . . Three quarters of it was written by the editor. The feature was a charming series of "Immoral Stories for Children", exhibiting the triumph of Evil over Good.' He felt his path into writing by way of youthful perversity made innocent by the ridiculous.

He was always as ready to enact his absurdities as to write them. Later, living in Oxford, though not as a student, he took rooms above a chemist's shop, and he enjoyed it when he would 'slip down and pose as an assistant', prescribing plausible remedies for customers, with a professional air. Once on a moving train he could not fit 'a new and expensive overcoat into his suitcase', and solved the difficulty by throwing the coat out of the window without interrupting his stream of conversation. He once used a British battleship and its appurtenances, including the sea, as comic props. It was his habit to spend several weeks a year aboard H.M. ships, and throughout the fleet his nickname was 'Uncle'. After lunching on board with the admiral commanding, Baring, going ashore, deliberately stepped into the sea instead of into the admiral's barge.

His comic style took him to any limits, and sometimes, we uneasily think, somewhat beyond, to amuse friends. Lady Diana Cooper said that he would set fire to 'his sparse hair and it would fizzle a little and go out, and he would light it again with a match till it was all singed off, but his scalp never burnt, and he laughed uproariously as I did. . . . Next day he sent me a telegram every two or three hours.' But his gaiety was not always so self-punishing, and his humour often called forth responses in kind. One day while playing tennis with Sarah Bernhardt – a circumstance remarkable enough in itself – he drove a tennis ball directly to her and it struck her in the bosom. At once she 'died' in her best tragic manner – eyes rolled up out of sight, terminal sighs – while she was lowered to the lawn by horrified bystanders. And then silence, long enough to impress, followed by an immediate recovery.

His early verbal comedy is somewhat akin to the style of Ronald Firbank and Saki. Attending the first night of Madame Bernhardt in *L'Aiglon* (17 March 1900) he wrote that 'the theatre was paved with beaten celebrities' – with here an echo of Horace Walpole. After a visit to the Château of Coutances, with its aisles, avenues, canals and ponds, he said the park 'was inhabited by exiled peacocks and discredited white pheasants'. G. K. Chesterton said, 'the levities of Maurice Baring were worthy of some fantastic *macaroni* or *incroyable* of the eighteenth century'.

If his comedy enlivened his personality and his friends, it was not simply a superficial accomplishment but a true strain of his versatile character. In 1903 he wrote somewhat heatedly to a solemn friend: 'I think that the existence of merely frivolous people who are bent on amusement is a necessary element in this grey world, and that Helen of Troy, Mary Stuart, Ninon de L'Enclos, Diane de Poitiers, Petronius Arbiter, and Charles II are equally necessary in the scheme of things as St Paul, Thomas Aquinas, John Knox, Pym, and Lady Jane Grey'.

[ iii ]

Along with his sense of comedy, whether in the frivolous act or the parodistic vein (which presupposes a serious knowledge of the matter in

5

hand) Baring held a considerable store of learning in the lightest possible grasp – apart from any branch of mathematics, for, noted *The Times*, 'he had extraordinary incapacity to deal with figures'. In the face of the tasks of study he had been a wildly irreverent schoolboy, yet without visible effort he became one of the most deeply cultivated men of his time. Monsignor Ronald Knox, who knew him and all his works, said, 'There are . . . certain rare intellects which aspire to a sublime ignorance in vain. They cannot choose but learn.' Baring's nature, he went on, 'was one which constantly absorbed, as it constantly exuded, something which (for want of a less abused word) you can only label "culture".' Baring himself hit off this sort of character in one of his novels, as he described a certain Wilfred Abbey, 'who seemed never to have read, nor to read anything at all, as if a well-educated man knew all that was necessary without reading a book. He could always cap a quotation, and never missed an allusion. He seemed to have absorbed his culture from the air.' Indeed, it was possible, like the Virginian matron Grace Winslope in *Cat's Cradle*, to be 'rather too well read'. Again, of Charles Donne, an artist, in the novel *Comfortless Memory*, Baring wrote, 'I found he understood everything without being told. That although apparently he looked at nothing, he saw everything, and that he lighted firmly on the best.' Such observations could, under testimony by many who knew Maurice Baring, be taken as details from a self-portrait, despite his disclaimer of great learning, such as he made in the preface to *Have You Anything to Declare?* where he stated that though he had 'only a smattering of learning', he was 'fond of books and fond of reading'. Sir Edward Marsh said he thought he had never seen Baring 'actually reading a book – he would pick one up, peck at it like a thrush at a worm, and soon put it down again; but there must have been some process of "inward penetration".'

Literature and reality were for him the same. Looking out over Rome one day from the Janiculum, he spoke of memories 'from Macaulay' – and in the lightness of the reference he caught the sustaining power of literature to create reality, so that an artist's words once read become part of our own truth and of our own qualifying memory. As for Rome, its beauty entered into him 'like a poison', he said, and 'the delicious poison ran through my veins and the eternal charm sank deep'.

Places held him as people did, and he responded to their spirit with his own particular reflex – which was to produce his response in art. A sitting-room provided for him by Count Benckendorff at Sosnofka in Russia was his 'favourite room in all the world' and in all his life, he said, and 'at its big table I painted innumerable water colours, and wrote four plays in verse, two plays in prose, three long books in prose, besides translating a book of Leonardo da Vinci and writing endless letters and newspaper articles'. The versatility hinted at in this animated statement actually went farther. He loved music, could play at the piano scandalous impersonations of great composers, was adept at musical jokes, and was happy with musical people, like Donald Tovey and Ethel Smyth. Of his swift understanding of her music, Dame Ethel Smyth said, 'he always knew what one was aiming at', and though he could not read music, his pianistic parodies were accomplished enough to deceive Tovey.

He grew up during the period when Wagner was a cause and a battle-cry, a prophet or a false god, and he described at the time the odd double effect which the Wagnerian sounds still carry. He spoke of a 'quality of slowness and hypnotic mesmerism. . . . At its worst it is like the noise people make by rubbing the rim of a glass of water; at its best it is some-thing very mysteriously beautiful.' Both ecstasy and oppression came with it, and 'the feeling of being suffocated, like laughing gas'.

Personal discovery of the great artists and their work became in Baring's books as in his life a dominant power, and few novelists have made more real the private experience of an awakening to the sound, the humanizing force, of literature and music. Beethoven, Heine, Tennyson, Swinburne, Schubert, the Russian poets, novelists, and playwrights, all 'happen' to his fictional characters, as they did to him in life, as cata-clysmic events after which they are never again the same. For him the arts were not mere pastime or entertainment – they were profoundly effectual encounters in his own growth and discovery.

## [ iv ]

As a young man in London cramming for examinations leading to the diplomatic service, he made friends with various literary men of his time. Dining often at the house of Edmund Gosse, he met such men of letters as George Moore, who one evening was 'severe on Maupassant', whose stories he called 'merely carved cherry-stones', and Max Beerbohm, Arthur Symons, Rider Haggard, and Henry Harland. Other friends, early and late, were G. K. Chesterton, Hilaire Belloc, and Vernon Lee (Violet Paget), besides his natural company of acquaintances in the inter-locked world of the great families of his class whose members, wherever he went in the world, seemed to have representatives who governed and set tone and provided the comforts of recognition and the reassurances of familiar style.

'His genius for languages,' remarked a close friend, 'was greater than a natural gift,' for he 'could think and create in the mind of the language rather than translate it into words.' Perhaps like a character in his novel *The Lonely Lady of Dulwich* he 'spoke most languages and was silent in none'. In his opening page of *Have You Anything to Declare?* he referred to the literatures which had been his lifetime 'baggage', and mentioned the Greek, Latin, Persian, French, Italian, German, Spanish, Scandinavian, Sanskrit, Hebrew, Chinese, and Arabic, though he did not know the last four. Oddly, he did not list English and Russian language and literature, but these may by their very familiarity to him have slipped his mind.

Already mobile in thought, through his mastery of foreign literatures, he was to be for all his active life a great traveller. In the most off-hand manner possible, he would set out for Rome, Paris, Malta, Seville, Lisbon, Constantinople, Vienna, Berlin, St Petersburg or Mukden with the ease of one who felt at home in any land or language. Even in time of war, he gave the air of an experienced itinerant who composed himself in movement. In his diary of the 1914 War he wrote, 'A Frenchman sitting next to us in the train whom I knew said, "Il y a seulement quatorze personnes qui voyagent en temps de guerre et on est sûr de les rencontrer. Vous êtes l'une des quatorze".'

His gift of generosity and outgoing love of people, friends, or strangers, high or low, was a proper attribute for such a traveller. And yet about his ease of response to the incidental moment, place, or person of life, there was in spite of its light civility a deeper value. He put his finger on it in a letter from St Petersburg, in 1914, when he wrote, 'I see how I may be superficially influencible and influenced, but my inside *kernel* is very independent, very difficult to influence, and it takes a long time to form'.

The master of trivial drollery, who must often have seemed to protect himself by nonsense from engagement with life, was capable of deep and salutary realism when necessary. Writing to a bereaved friend, he said, 'You must make up your mind whether you wish to live or die, and as it appears that you are unable to die, you must now concentrate on living'. In this remark a number of possibilities are indicated about attitudes toward life's most formal realities; and we have a sense that he is speaking to himself as well as to another with a melancholy laid under courage which makes the gaiety of much of his writing account for more than drollery and games.

'What a blessing your friendship, your whole self, are, dear Maurice,' wrote Vernon Lee to him in 1908. It is a note we overhear throughout his days, and because he had so much to give, we realize that he had many selves through which to give it.

'Listen to me, Mr Trevenen,' says Madame D'Alberg to Christopher in the novel *The Coat Without Seam*, 'I am going to be quite frank with you. You are complicated, I am not.'

The character to whom this is said is a young man who repeatedly throws away chances for the very happiness he grudgingly longs for, and as we watch him grind his life away between his sense of his own worth and corroding self-doubt, we seem to hear an autobiographical undertone.

To a lady of the Russian Imperial Court whom he knew in Petersburg Baring seemed 'to be rather a freak'. But then she found that he had 'wonderful insight', in fact, 'almost uncanny', and if he was 'sometimes absurd', he was again 'and even always very lovable'. He had the gift of continuity in human relations, for, she said, 'one always met with him again as though one had only parted yesterday'.

In rounding off personal impressions of his quality and presence, we might look at a photograph of him playing solitaire at Half-Way House, Steyning Road, Rottingdean, where he spent the penultimate period of his life.

There is a plain card-table in a plain white room with a simple panelled fireplace. On the walls and the mantelpiece hang framed photographs of the famous and of friends – often one and the same – and framed caricatures by Spy out of *Vanity Fair*. Wearing a tweed suit, Maurice Baring is seated at the table, on which the cards are laid out. He is alone. He leans his head on the spread fingers of his right hand and holds the unused pack in his left. He is gazing thoughtfully at the pattern of cards. He seems to be brooding – in another context he might be praying. He has a great head, with a massive cranium, egg-shaped, entirely bald but for a grey fringe. His straight nose is finely chiselled, with a flared nostril, suggesting a strong, sensitive appetite for sensation, first of all for the breath of life. A small grey moustache is close trimmed. His large ears are set close. He wears a sober expression. He must be a tall man, and uses an eye-glass and is blue-eyed. His lower lip is pushed up against the upper in thought. He seems to be ruddy. In the comic gravity of a man regarding a game of patience, he is supporting the human condition alone, which is his life's way, in which he always gives forth more than he is given.

We know by other means various small traits which the photograph cannot show. His voice had a low register, for at Eton he 'sang among the baritones'. He took up painting water-colours at one period, 'which were very dreamy and romantic in their general effect, but a little on the messy side'. On being asked what they were like, a witty lady answered 'Penny-Whistlers'. He could be careless about his appearance – Arnold Bennett attending a debate in Queen's Hall between Shaw and Belloc saw him looking 'very shabby . . . with loose brown boots and creased socks'. Yet he was fastidious, though perhaps sometimes for comic effect. Still, he warned Edward Marsh against going to the Franz Hals room in the Hermitage Museum, St Petersburg, 'because the subjects of the portraits were so repulsive' that he 'hadn't dared go close up to them for fear of the smell'. He was indifferent to money and its power. He had not made a will, he said, 'because I practically have no property', and Marsh recorded that 'he was never one to take care of either pounds or pence'. In the strains of bucolic melancholy which he imitated in his little literary game-book of *Translations Ancient and Modern* (*With Originals*), he himself wrote, 'Riches I crave not, neither power, nor fame', wearing the air of a countryside Roman in the *Georgics*, and yet, we somehow feel, speaking directly for himself, 'nor even love, having tasted the sweetness and the bitterness thereof, but a farm where trees give shade in the summer and provide logs for the winter, enough for a blazing hearth'. It is a reflection of a sophistication beyond material interests, which with such difficulty escape the taint of vulgarity. No, 'I never really enjoyed mundanities for themselves', he wrote to Ethel Smyth from France in wartime, and went on to sound a note held steady all his life, 'but I am grateful to them as also to Diplomacy, which I *loathed*, for having given me the opportunity of making three or four great friends'. Many would have agreed with the conclusion of a recent scholar who said, 'If the term "genius" may be applied to the difficult art of friendship, Maurice Baring possessed it.'

We have much testimony of his high spirits with friends, and we think of how it is when this gray, bald, tall, lean, sober presence in the photograph, with a solicitor's face, must light up for the benefit of other persons, and how his animation must release the compunction and the love for others which made them declare him lovable and honourable, selfless, and good. Simply good. Goodness has often been regarded as a bore: but all evidence indicates that Baring was never a bore.

If we try to call alive the essential energy which the repose of the photograph cannot give us, we could do not better, I think, than to quote a friend who was asked whom he considered a man of genius in his generation. It was Herbert Asquith, later to be Prime Minister of Great Britain, who replied, 'For genius in the sense of spontaneous, dynamic intelligence, I have no doubt that I would say Maurice Baring.'

[ v ]

Let us now look a little more closely at the literary work of this personality, who was so observant of the universally human under the particular and transient style of his time.

He was a votary of a vocation all but vanished – that is, a writer accomplished and expressive in all literary forms, from poetry to drama, journalism to the novel, the critical essay to the learned literary spoof. With so much to cover, we have little opportunity to do justice to all these, and I shall give most of my attention to his pastiches and his novels, in which, I think, his most expressive work is to be found. But a word or two along the rest of the line will be useful in developing a view of his quality.

In 1904 he gave up what began as a career in diplomacy after holding junior posts in Paris ('having such fun here now,' he wrote from the British Embassy in 1900), Copenhagen, and Rome, and went as a reporter for the *Morning Post* to cover the Russo-Japanese War. His journey to war took him across Russia, and the whole episode was significant for him chiefly because it introduced him to the Russian people, whose language he had been studying for five years. His war-reports are full of a clear light and a warm heart – 'Bless you,' wrote Vernon Lee, 'for your courage of being capable of horror and pity and yet no sentimentalist, and for your passionate desire for good understanding between nations.' The life of every day glistens in his dispatches, and his zest for the arresting detail in man and human ways turns up again and again. But nothing in his early career as a journalist exceeded his interest in a discovery he made on the way to the theatre of war: his first dispatch came from Moscow and it introduced the art of Anton Chekhov to the general English world, for he saw a performance of *Uncle Vanya* at the Arts Theatre and immediately knew he had come into communion with a new literary vision. His review of the performance is the first chapter in his collected volume of reports and impressions called *With the Russians in Manchuria*. The pieces in general skilfully demonstrate his idea of his task: 'The essence of journalism,' he said, 'is sensation captured on the wing.'

In 1914 he came to war again, this time as a volunteer officer attached to the headquarters of the Royal Flying Corps, under the command of General Trenchard. Baring's calm in the face of unfamiliar military details led straight to comic improvisation, which the service bore with fortitude. Going out to France he found it impossible to cope with the wrap-puttees which were regulation for officers and men. Anyone who has ever tried to roll these up about the calves with spiral precision must sympathize when Baring discarded his and, instead, acquired and wore a pair of long pale gaiters. The regulars of his service frowned upon these, and he thought to improve matters by switching to the black gaiters worn by sailors, but these too were all wrong. In the end, it was General Trenchard himself who instructed his new staff officer in how to unroll the wrap-puttees about his calves.

Baring remained with Trenchard until the end and later spoke of him 'in the highest terms' to Arnold Bennett. All Baring's contemporaries, as he observed at a wartime reunion dinner of old Etonians, were lieutenant-generals – presumably as professional soldiers. He himself reached the rank of major. After the war he published a book called *R.F.C. H.Q.*, an excellent record of early air warfare. From its pages it is clear that he was incessantly busy at his staff duties, working long hours and always on the move. Yet a man of his gifts and temperament is not himself if he does not steal time to read, even in the busiest job. These are some of the authors and books, in a casual jumble representing both the haphazard and the selected, which he read at war: Paul Bourget, Jane Austen, Ann Douglas Sedgwick, Heredia, Lord Morley's memoirs, *Eminent Victorians* by Strachey, the *Mabinogion*, Paul Desportes, Anatole France, Heraclitus, Rider Haggard, Henry James, Alexander Pope, Faguet's *History of*

*French Literature*, Horace (he translated *Eheu fugaces*), Butcher and Lang's Homer, Wordsworth, Dante, La Fontaine, Racine, Molière, Edgar Lee Masters, the letters of Pliny the Younger, O. Henry, Barry Pain, *Coriolanus*, *Timon of Athens*, *Hamlet*, *Othello*, *Macbeth*, *Twelfth Night*, and *King Lear*.

All his grace and culture, his special wit, his mixture of preciosity, fastidiousness, and bland intellectual honesty, might, you would think, make him a figure of silliness once in uniform and confronting the rude life of men at war. But we have witnesses to the contrary. General Trenchard wrote, 'The very first day he showed me his complete lack of self-interest, his complete honesty, and his wonderful loyalty. . . . He knew more about what mattered in war and how to deal with human nature, how to stir up those who wanted stirring up, how to damp down those who were too excitable, how to encourage those who were new to it, and in telling me when I was unfair, than any other man I know. He was a man I could always trust. He . . . was almost my second sight in all the difficult tasks that came in future years. He was the most unselfish man I ever met. The flying corps owes to this man more than they know or think . . . this great man . . . words fail me in describing this man.' And the final word came from the Commander of all the Allied Forces, Maréchal Foch himself, who said, 'There was never a staff officer in any country, in any nation, in any century, like Major Maurice Baring.' Here we can leave the soldier resting in honour upon his arms and return to the man of letters.

[ vi ]

The theatre deeply engaged him, both as observer and as playwright. He delighted in great stage effects and persons. In particular, Sarah Bernhardt, Eleanora Duse and Feodor Chaliapin were objects of his fascinated worship. In essays and novels he tried with remarkable success to arrest on the printed page the exalting impact of their evanescent art. He caught the majesty of Chaliapin (who once told him he wanted to act in Shakespeare), and one feels that he admired Duse to the farthest limits of thought – but that he adored Bernhardt with both mind and heart. His monument to her consists of a biography (1933) and many pieces scattered through his essays and novels. She figures as Anaïs Dorzan in *Darby and Joan*, in *Cat's Cradle*, she appears by name, and in *C* and other novels she appears as Madame Lapara, always with electrifying effect upon the persons within the book – an effect conveyed so convincingly that the reader, too, is brought to feel it.

It was inevitable that he should write plays – ambitious, full-length pieces, meant to be acted. He wrote also many short and witty parodies and pastiches in dramatic form, but these were clearly meant only for the page and the eye. The earliest of his serious plays belong to a *genre* which, once respectable, now raises qualms, for they were poetic dramas, written in blank verse, full of studied archaisms, operatic situations, lost gallantries, over-significant incantations, and the rest.

He had somewhat better fortune with drawing-room comedies set in his own period and written in the almost telegraphic dialogue which he used in his fiction. Several of these plays had productions in respectable art theatres, but none succeeded, and what is probably his best play, *His Majesty's Embassy*, has never been produced at all – professionally, anyhow.

Max Beerbohm reviewed Baring's play *The Grey Stocking* in the *Saturday Review* on 6 June 1908, and came to the conclusion that this playwright was an 'adramatist' – that is, one who deals not with heightened life such as we generally associate with theatre – 'heroes, villains, buffoons . . . people who are either doing or suffering either tremendous or funny things' but rather was one who dealt 'merely in humdrum and you and me'. To be an adramatist, Beerbohm said, the playwright must be 'very much an athlete' if he is to bring enough energy into his non-happenings. *The Grey Stocking* gave Beerbohm the impression that Baring was 'very athletic by nature', but that he had 'not trained' quite hard enough. Beerbohm came to the play 'on the look-out for things happening; and the fact that nothing happened rather bothered me', he decided. He ended his review with the statement that 'Mr Baring gives us deliciously clever sketches of his characters; but he does not give us the full, deep portraits that are needed'.

Actually, in present reading, the play seems to present only one adequately drawn character, Miss Farrer, a novelist with a cult for saying flatly what she thinks, which on principle is the opposite of what everybody else thinks. She puts us in mind of Dame Ethel Smyth, as she weaves in and out of the main idea of the play without actually contributing to it. This is a limp exercise in unhappy marriage, with hopeless and muted love outside it, in a symmetry which seems contrived and undramatic, offering not one but two such situations. We are sure that Baring is referring to people he knows and can talk about; but to animate them on the stage is quite another matter. And yet, 'Some of the scenes in *The Grey Stocking*', wrote Bernard Shaw to Maurice Baring, 'show a very rare sort of dramatic talent', and we must agree that if there is not much action, there is genuine feeling within the materials of the play; and Shaw went on, evidently to console Baring for the play's failure – it had one performance – 'the real difficulty of course is that you show society as it really is and not as our good public conceives it'.

Another play, *The Green Elephant*, offers an entirely different tone and energy. It is designed after French farce – rapid entrances and exits, wildly involved plot, confusions, lies, intrigues of love and crime concerning jewels stolen at a weekend party in a country house – all laid on with a bare-faced air of plausibility which is naïvely theatrical. The play's action has rather the air of children acting – 'being' and 'declaring' – things patently unbelievable, and believed only through a conspiracy of politeness. If his earlier play was formless, this one is over-plotted and too rigidly formalized. Again, only one character, Lady Warburton, seems to contain the breath of life.

In *A Double Game* it is atmosphere which seems to consume the author's available vitality at the expense of other values. It is a play of the revolutionary movement of 1907 in Russia. While it has some dramatic tension, and certainly suggests Baring's love of the Russians and know-ledge of their style, the 'Russianism' of it seems synthetic, and the end is a finale in the manner of Chekhov, with a pistol-shot and suicide offstage. Again, the individual characters merely seem to have lines to speak, without the inner energies of life which would make them into genuine creations. Baring's feeling for the place and time of the play is better – indeed wonderfully – brought to page in *The Puppet Show of Memory* where he describes the vast funeral procession in Moscow of the veterinary surgeon Bauman who was a victim of shooting in the streets during political demonstrations. A hundred thousand men marched with the coffin, which was covered by a scarlet pall, and hushedly sang revolutionary songs, expressing 'the commonplaceness of all that is determined and unflinching, mingled with an accent of weary pathos'. He never forgot the impression of the moment, but in his play he caught little of its spirit.

In *His Majesty's Embassy* Baring used materials he knew well, com-bining the schoolboy antics of junior diplomatic clerks with a hopeless love-affair at ambassadorial level. The play conjures up, out of insistent trivia of the daily diplomatic round, but with the tyrannical and reckless power of all secrets, the central love story, an affair between the British ambassador to Rome and the wife of a sophisticated member of the Italian Diplomatic Corps. The story is made of heartbreak and helplessness, and convention protects itself, and the train-guard blows his whistle, and on goes the current, sweeping into separate channels the lives that long to come together, however disastrous the brink of the falls waiting ahead. Of this play *The Times* of London said that it was a 'fragment of English life as alive as it is unique'; and we have a hint that in any but a com-mercially controlled theatre Baring might eventually have achieved recognition as a playwright; for, again, Shaw wrote to Ethel Smyth that 'It was really a calamity that the theatre was incapable of him'. If this was an extravagant statement, it is of interest for the flat placement it makes of where the incapability lay. To Baring himself Shaw wrote, 'I do not see why the dickens you should not go regularly into the trade of playwriting', and after reading *His Majesty's Embassy* Shaw told him that the play was 'quite a miraculous success', and ended up saying that 'if it were attractively cast, anything might happen'. It is difficult not to be impressed by such a judgement from the supreme, and supremely sceptical, professional of the twentieth-century English-speaking theatre. Henry Bernstein (the French playwright who dominated the popular dramatic stage of Paris after Sardou), whatever his claim to literary sagacity, had a right to an opinion about box-office values, and he said to Baring after a production of Baring's second play, 'What will you do with all the money you'll make?' The play closed at once. But if he failed in the theatres of the West End of London, Baring left evidence in his published plays of how delicately he could lay back the layers of convention to reveal the passions that society both generated and concealed.

Perhaps it was Vernon Lee who gave the most meaningful clue to why Baring's writings for the stage never made their way. 'You have, dear Maurice,' she wrote, 'a quite peculiar, great and enchanting gift . . . how to define . . .? It is a gift of the love-duet; of giving in metaphors, and lyric flights and pathetic snatches, the equivalent of the deepest unspoken feeling.' And here it is: the theatre cannot very effectively deal with 'unspoken feeling'. Its best effects depend on feelings, and all the suggestions they contain, quite audibly spoken. It was to be the novel in which Baring's particular nuance could linger between the lines, where the real values always linger in significant fiction, which would release his whole talent and give it the long breath, the unconstricted range, which it required for full expression.

[ vii ]

And yet we must not omit reference to his verse. He wrote poetry from his boyhood onward. At Eton in 1891 he engaged a printer to produce a small volume called *Pastels and Other Rhymes*, containing verses seriously intended, which inevitably, in the tone of a responsive schoolboy, echoed the current styles of Wilde, Morris, and the pre-Raphaelite vision. A booklet of prose, *Damozel Blanche and Other Faery Tales*, printed for him in the same year, was also consciously literary, as its title suggests.

His poetry had only a few themes – the same ones which informed his novels. These were nostalgia, death, love recognized but unrealizable, honour, God's mysterious way and power. Over much of the verse lingers an air of weekendish polite accomplishment, conventional and pallidly felicitous. But the best of it holds true emotion, contained in formal rhymes, stanzas, and metres, yet with an effect of inner freedom which is particularly his own – possibly the metaphor for his life as well as for his art.

His best poetry is to be found in a handful of sonnets; in several long elegies for friends lost in war (written in a flowing form of ode with

15

irregular lines and deliberately simple rhymes which summon up feeling through the effects of simple literate speech); and in a small group of translations of Russian lyrics which survive as English poetry while scholars praise them as successful equivalents of Russian originals. Poetry was not Baring's major achievement – and yet his love of the act of poetry, his ingenuousness which was so intuitive as to lie far beyond sophistication, and his vulnerability to true feeling, all entitle him to inclusion among the lesser spirits who have so loved the English language and voice that their proper element can be said to be that of poetry, however small their contribution to the great stream of English verse may be. Valuable as he is as a poet in his best poems, it is in his best novels that his poetic gift most truly rests plain; for what his poems celebrate under strict metrical governance finds its most convincing presence as it hovers insubstantially behind the lines of his prose. He was one of those artists in literature whose quality comes into view not at once but only after a long time and many pages in its presence. The brief lyric and even the funerary panegyric of several pages do not allow this emergence its full opportunity.

His versatility expressed his many responses to the external terms of life, each demanding its characteristic style or medium. Delight in literature required him to compose essays and criticism, impressions and prose sketches, which he gathered in various volumes. His most notable work in literary study is his small book, *An Outline of Russian Literature*, written for the Home University Library series. Along with the thin volume by Lytton Strachey on French literature, done for the same series, Baring's book on the Russians is a model of its kind.

His own prose was never better than in this brief survey, and his most personal responses set off by his excellent knowledge of the literature he discusses, whose masterpieces he read in the original language, come through at their most felicitous and penetrating. He had a strong affinity for the Russian vision of the literary art, and time and again as he discusses Pushkin or Lermontov or Tolstoy he makes you think of aspects of his own imaginative works. We are assured that he knew the Russian language perfectly, with an intuitive power far beyond all the grammatical apparatus. By 1899, on the evidence of his Russian exercise notebook (now in the Beinecke Rare Book and Manuscript Library at Yale) he was already studying Russian. Sir Edward Marsh later said that 'Russians used to appeal to him on points of their own grammar'. He lived like a native of many literatures, and out of his love of these, and moved by the compunction for life from which he so often diverted notice by his cheerful idiocies of behaviour and his literary pranks, he moved in the final phase of his work toward the creation of his own unmistakable style.

[ viii ]

The last categories of his abundant production – he published almost fifty books – whose air and substance I shall try to suggest are two: the first, his literary jokes; the second, his major novels.

When I say literary jokes I do not mean to suggest offhand japes or mockeries. On the contrary, Baring's literary jokes are to be taken with respect for all the ingenuity, the extended and expert knowledge, and the special sense of fun, out of which they are made. Informally, in correspondence and in sustained exchanges with companion spirits, he always enjoyed literary games. One of these was a contest to remember the first lines of Shakespeare's plays. He played it with one of his dearest friends, Lady Diana Cooper. Both of them, noted Arnold Bennett, were 'very good at this'. Literature could have its meaning for him as a playful as well as a serious *genre*, and he kept alive into maturity the schoolboy's genius for historical travesty, sublimely wrongheaded construction, and inventive misunderstanding. Much British humour is built upon these foundations; and Baring refined the use of them in a delicious set of nonsense inventions published first in three separate volumes as *Diminutive Dramas*, *Dead Letters*, and *Lost Diaries*, which he later collected in one volume under the title *Unreliable History*.

Typically in these pieces – they run to perhaps six or eight pages each – he took a famous historical or literary situation or set of characters and treated them in the accents of the modern social condition. The colloquial is imposed on the classical, the suburban upon the historically august, the irreverent upon the sacrosanct; and the results, informed with all the range and penetration of Baring's knowledge, are hilarious to the degree in which the reader shares Baring's culture and its allusions. To amuse friends who would receive the joke, he wrote satires in French on eminent English social figures after the styles of Flaubert, Bourget, Maupassant. His lifelong delight in sportive distortion of great subjects of history and letters, playing with translations, committing impersonations of all styles and periods and characters, are not really just parody or pastiche, but something beyond these, for they all draw upon wide learning. His jokes are often profound jokes, and further, they reflect the general notion of life that runs through his work in whatever literary form. He gave himself in his humour as fully as he did in his more serious efforts.

His pleasure in trifling with literature, as opposed to making it, was illustrated by the play of variations throughout his life in collecting excerpts, *pensées*, felicitous scraps of writing brought together in a small harvest of intellectual pleasures referring to literary styles. The particular Baring aspect of the earliest of such little collections is that all the small literary pieces were written by him in the manner of other authors,

17

classical or modern, and presented with no clue to their actual origin. If they were imitations, they were also serious, and were meant to call up intimations of recognition in an experienced reader, yet without rewarding him with identifications. In 1916 a small book appeared under the title, *Translations (Found in a Commonplace Book), Edited by S.C.*, and published at Oxford by B. H. Blackwell. Translations? But no sources are given, and in a prefatory Note we read, 'The editor of these translations has not been able to trace the originals even in the rare cases where the author states the language from which the translations are made.' So the private joke solemnly extends to the posture of scholarship. In 1925 Heinemann published the same text, but now with significant additions – not only with nine more pieces, bringing the total to thirty-eight, but also, at last, with presumed original texts from which the 'translations' were made. Each English piece was faced by its supposed source in another language. And here the joke went into a further dimension, for in the small book now called *Translations Ancient and Modern (With Originals)* his 'fictitious translations of imaginary originals', as he said, 'from ancient or modern languages on any subjects', were supplied with their imaginary sources by various distinguished literary friends, including Monsignor Ronald Knox for the Latin and Greek, André Maurois for the French, Prince D. S. Mirsky for the Russian, Mario Praz for the Italian, and others for the Swedish and the Spanish.

This sipping of many literary flavours and vintages was a continuing delight to him, and it had other demonstrations, private and public. He took pleasure all his life in making for any particular friends – Lady Lovat, Sir Ronald Storrs – a unique scrapbook of literary fragments and excerpts. He called such a collection *Gepäch*. Several survive in private hands. They surely reflect his fancy and taste of the moment, and his sensitiveness to the interest of the recipient. The *Gepäch* was the ancestor of his published books of fragments taken from many literatures. In 1928 he published, through Heinemann, a small volume called *Algae, An Anthology of Phrases*, and in 1930, privately printed for him by the Cambridge University Press, another gathering of *Algae* with the designation *Second Series*. The little excerpts come from literatures in English, Greek, Italian, French, German, Spanish, Latin, and Russian and are printed in the original languages, with a few translations by himself or others, and all are real, as against the earlier impersonations. His fabrications and his selections from actual writings eventually led to a late work, the anthology *Have You Anything to Declare?* but with the addition of his own commentary and, in the cases of certain actual translations, with alternative versions. In most of these 'commonplace' books he gave a full page to each text, however small, so that it stood an island of printed letters in a sea of white space. If the process was extravagant, it was not wasteful, if the purpose of the selection was to be fulfilled –

the chance to reflect without distraction on each small passage until its particular evocations could sound in the inner ear for us, as it did for him.

Such undertakings bring Maurice Baring's highly sophisticated fancy close to us. Precious, learned, delicate, painstaking for the sake of keeping the fraud plausible, where fraud was intended, they were characteristic of his literary atmosphere and the friends who inhabited it with him. If this sort of thing had been all, there would have been no career to restore – only attractive and appreciative wisps of reference to him in other people's memoirs, in which he would be seen as a witty and expert amateur at the art of carving cameos. But along with the exercise of the informed amusements of his early life he was also becoming a professional journalist who dealt with the coarse world of war; and when he was ready to become a novelist, he was master of a greater reach than his early diversions suggested. In time he became far more concerned with grasping life itself in his writing than with pursuing scholarly and private references to its echoes. Of course his erudite gaiety persisted, and when he published his various sketches in 'unreliable history', he was confronting us with a straight face, while hoping to make us laugh.

A synopsis of one of the *Dead Letters* may suggest the style of his humour, and the cheekiness of its assumptions, out of which the whole joke arises. He calls the piece 'Lady Macbeth's Trouble' and it purports to be a letter from Lady Macbeth to Lady Macduff. It is superscribed 'most private', and is dated from 'the palace, Forres', and begins, in an air of simple social correspondence, 'My dearest Flora, I am sending this letter by Ross, who is starting for Fife tomorrow morning. I wonder if you could possibly come here for a few days', and goes on to the reasons why Lady Macduff is needed. There will be a few tiresome circumstances – the pipers begin their shrill tunes a little after sunrise and this is trying for Lady Macbeth who, as she reminds her friend, is 'a bad sleeper'. Indeed, she reports that she nearly fell out of her window a couple of nights ago walking in her sleep. The doctor, in fact, is giving her something to make her sleep. But she mustn't dwell on her own personal woes – the real difficulty is that 'Macbeth is not at all in good case'. He has never rallied from the tragedy of King Duncan's death, and Macbeth, known to be superstitious, has been upset, ever since, returning home, he met three witches who, Lady Macbeth reports, 'had apparently been uncivil to him'. She sensibly assumed they were gipsies – but her husband couldn't get them out of his mind, and when the frightful event followed, of the murder of the king, it had the most unlikely results, and Lady Macbeth, in strictest confidence, is obliged to report them to Lady Macduff. But they got through the terrible days, and the 'extra worry' of the coronation, and they left Inverness for Forres, and then the worst came to light, for, poor woman, she has to report that Macbeth is suffering

19

from hallucinations, for *he thinks he himself killed King Duncan.* 'You can imagine,' writes Lady Macbeth, 'what I am going through!' And then another calamity – Banquo was out riding and fell and was killed, and that very night, during a state dinner which they 'could not possibly put off' Macbeth had 'another attack', and Lady Macbeth 'had only just time to get every one to go away before he began to rave'. No wonder she needs her friend for a few days of comfort! 'I am in a terrible position. I never know,' she says, 'when these fits are coming on, and I am afraid of people talking, because if it once gets about, people are so spiteful that somebody is sure to start the rumour that it's true. Imagine our position, then! So I beg you, dear Flora, to keep all this to yourself, and if possible to come here as soon as possible', and she signs herself, Her affectionate, Harriet R., and adds a postscript: 'P.S. Don't forget to bring Jeamie. It will do Macbeth good to see a child in the house.'

The nonsense is enchanting because everything as Lady Macbeth gives it fits neatly with the Shakespearean sequence of the events – but everything in her account is explained altogether differently, in worried accents of family trouble. Not the least of our joys in reading this pseudo-historic letter is that of discovering the first name of Lady Macbeth. 'Harriet' is somehow idiotically right.

There is no point in being pedantic about all this aspect of Baring's multifarious talent, but it is of interest to note that his inspired triflings with solemn matters for the most part had the added interest of good scholarship. This scholarship was not an affectation – was not boned up for the occasion. It was simply his by nature, and when he wanted to be funny about heavy affairs, he had what he needed in his head. For what it may be worth as incidental satisfaction, let me quote what Ronald Knox wrote about Baring's classical learning as it bore upon his managed nonsense.

'More than half of the *Diminutive Dramas*, more than a third of the *Dead Letters*, and a quarter of the *Lost Diaries*, have a classical setting. Nor do I think he was ever better inspired than when he thus played on the eternal themes in Greek or Latin dress. . . . The utter simplicity of the décor suited his genius. And I never remember discovering', concludes the Monsignor, 'a single lapse of scholarship in the whole of the three volumes.'

We pause respectfully at this. But we have another word that lets us recover, for it makes just the right point, when Vernon Lee says of Baring's comic writing, 'What a wonderful and particular thing this kind of English funniness is.'

[ ix ]

After Maurice Baring's first appearance in print in 1891, thirty years elapsed before he published his first novel, *Passing By*, in 1921. In the

20

meantime he had worked in all the other forms of writing available to a man of letters, including the prose sketch and the short story; but it is for his best novels, and his autobiography – fiction and biography are related arts – that he will be remembered. Once opened up, this new run of novels poured forth in a steady stream until the mid-thirties. In all of them he seemed to find at last not only the satisfying form but also the proper spirit for his expression. His view of life had long since crystallized, but hitherto we had had only fragments and glimpses through his eyes, as his imaginative prose-writing had given us only a few pages at a time, and these mainly light in tone.

He published several books of tales or stories. *The Glass Mender* is a book of fourteen fairy tales which echoed his youthful study period of living in with a German professor's family at Hildesheim – but made non-Germanic and light to the point of triviality. Almost all of them begin with the words 'Once upon a time' and in their deliberately naïve presentation of little lyric loves in an atmosphere of sadness and perishable beauty they recall the rare and the precious after the manner of the *Yellow Book*. Another book of short inventions in the style of fairy tales was *Orpheus in Mayfair*. These are slender pieces, for the most part artificially symbolic, rather than rewarding for their inherent narrative value or charm of expression. One is a parody of history in the manner of Hilaire Belloc, but here it is only the terrible facts behind the burlesqued subject – the torture and death of Edward II at Berkeley Castle – which lend any meaning to it; and it is also a rare, possibly the only, example of a lapse of taste or sensibility in Baring's work, for the tragedy of Edward does not invite spoofing. He was more generally successful in the book which he called *Half a Minute's Silence and Other Stories*, though many of the stories were reprinted from *Orpheus in Mayfair*. He rescued the best stories from the earlier book, and added sketches drawn more from direct experience, such as his life in Russia and Manchuria, which had been printed earlier in his *Russian Essays and Studies*. Some new bravura pieces of gaiety and wit, first published in papers and magazines, completed the volume which, like all his others, had trouble in finding a publisher.

'For thirty years,' he wrote to Rupert Hart-Davis in 1925 in reply to a schoolboy letter of appreciation, 'I found it difficult to get a book published; I mean every fresh book, as I wrote on different subjects, was refused by the last publisher, every single book of mine (forgive all this egoism), until *Puppet Show of Memories* [sic] which went to at least five publishers, and *C* went to three, and then Cassell said he would publish it if I cut out the first six chapters. And I said, no, I wouldn't, but I would boil them down into one, but they were still adamant, and said, "Pas une virgule" must remain, and I was staying with an old lady whom I knew was very wise, who said to me, "Don't insist," and I refused

Cassell and sent it to Heinemann who took it; and that is the story of that . . . Oh dear.' (The letter was, characteristically, written on board H.M.S. *Barham*, where the author was presumably a wardroom guest.) It was not long, however, before Heinemann began to reward him with the publication of a collected, uniform edition which ran to more than twenty volumes.

## [ x ]

Turning now to Maurice Baring's novels, a few quotations from their pages are in order as we try to get at their general tone. He wanted them to sound like real life, and yet as an artist he must deal in arrangement and invention. But he took out a sort of double insurance as a novelist when he had someone say in one of his books, 'Such extraordinary things do happen. Nothing is too extraordinary to happen.' And again, when he said, 'Then one of those curious small coincidences happened which are so frequent in real life, of which writers of fiction fight shy, although they are not afraid of the grand ones'. And again, 'Things happen that no writer would dare to invent'. And finally, 'The French put things so well – so clearly. They are not afraid of platitudes.' Thus, anything, from the most amazing to the most familiar, is prepared for; and what sustains interest first of all is the simplicity, like the vision of a child, through which his stories take their course. The child's sense of first clear view was, of course, governed by the adult experience of consequences and values, but the uncomplicated vision which struck lightly and directly to the heart of whatever matter was consistently Baring's way.

He had a clear perception of the distance between the childhood and the grown-up view of life: speaking of a nursery calamity which produced storms of passion between small brothers and sisters, he wrote: 'It was a long time, a long time that is to say measured by the standards of childhood – in reality about a fortnight, and morally about an aeon – before' the effects of the calamity receded. The first makings of patterns to explain life came into play in much of his life and work, and we often overhear nannies or tutors or elder accomplices like uncles or godparents speaking through the dense traditions of Baring's characters. If much of his reference and tone recalls the eternal schoolboy, the British schoolboy, that is, it seems to do so in the tradition of the open secret that is the source of so much comedy in British life, even public life, the secret being that with enough cheek you can get away with pretty well anything. Winston Churchill had the touch for this. So did Kipling, various famous soldiers also, and Byron. In Baring it was never dishonourable, and in his novels honour binds men and women in all their final decisions if duty enters the design against desire.

The sacredness of a promise is implicit all through Baring's fiction, and often becomes the explicit point on which all turns. Once word is given in engagement to marry, however mistakenly, honour binds. True mutual love is sacrificed to duty or to precommitted pledges that have lost their emotional urgency. Divorce does not exist in the social world where he moves with his characters. Society had not yet broken in two on the issue, and history still had weight.

Indeed, historical tradition, the living breath of the great past, plays a part in his novels, sometimes through minor characters and allusions by the way; but they help to create a fabric of social and historical continuity which offers inestimable support in plausibility and richness of conviction. It substantiates the amplitude of the world in which one of Baring's leading characters lives when he meets in Versailles two old maiden ladies who 'seemed to be the living ghosts of pre-revolutionary Versailles', for 'the mother of one of them had been born seventeen years before the revolution, . . . and she herself remembered Napoleon at *Trianon* and the *Cent Jours* and the Battle of Waterloo with perfect distinctness. . . . The mother of the eldest [*sic*] remembered seeing the Dauphin playing in the gardens of Versailles.' Another of Baring's novels opens with the words, 'Henry Clifford was born in the year that Byron died'. *Cat's Cradle* begins two decades before the Franco-Prussian War – a whole generation before his own birth – and continues through full lifetimes until the outbreak of World War I. With the lightest use of the telling period reference, Baring keeps his long chronicle faithful to changing times. (Like Zola's *Nana*, with its final note of the popular 1870 war cry in the streets of Paris – '*à Berlin!*' – *Cat's Cradle* concludes with an echo of the patriotic song of the 1914 war, 'It's a Long, Long Way to Tipperary'.) The past is not lost, but lives in its transmitted reference and effect, and the people in Baring's novels bring it with them.

They bring, too, the world of cultivated taste. He is one of few novelists who can have his characters discuss ideas, art, literature, and music as vital matters, and keep these within the frame of the life of the book, and make them seem natural interests without which the book would lose dimension. To use himself completely as an artist he must use his culture. 'I think he was,' wrote Monsignor Knox, 'in the literary sense of the word, a humanist. He went largely, no doubt, to the romantics for his inspiration. But there was a restraint about everything he wrote which is utterly classical. I do not say he owed it to the reading of the classics; it may have been due to something in his own nature; but it made the classics congenial to him . . . with a sure instinct, he breathed the airs of them.'

So the romantic in him was drawn to dramatic patterns of emotional energy, and the classic in him strove to suppress or enclose these within the boundaries of pure simplicity. We might say of him what he said of Henry James, that he made a 'divination of what is going on under the mask of convention, prosperity, fashion, and extravagance'. One of

Baring's ruling interests and achievements was to illustrate the complex within the simple. In his essay on *Eugene Onegin* in *An Outline of Russian Literature* Baring gives us another quotation to turn upon himself. 'The scenes are as clear as the shapes in a crystal; nothing is blurred; there are no hesitating notes; nothing *à peu près*; every stroke comes off; the nail is hit on the head every time, only so easily that you don't notice the strokes, and all labour escapes notice. The poem arrests attention as a story, and it delights the intelligence with its wit, its digressions, its brilliance. . . . And when the occasion demands it, the style passes in easy transition to serious or tender tones.' If Baring did not reach Pushkin's degree of achievement, he clearly held as an ideal in kind the quality of the Russian poet. What is more, the very plot of Baring's novel *C*, which, along with *Cat's Cradle* and *The Coat Without Seam* is one of his three most considerable novels, could have been strongly influenced by *Eugene Onegin*.

Of all twentieth-century novelists in English, he is the most successful at giving us a sense of the power of society, of the worldly world – and that is a real world, no matter what various fashions may do to the novel as they come and go. Sometimes it seems to us that he wrote only one novel, and that all his separate ones are like great chapters. We continuously meet the same people from one novel to the next, though the central concerns are always newly accented and it is the new refractions from familiar surfaces which make the story. Life is played out all on the same stage (excepting, of course, his two historical novels of the Tudor epoch), and in the crowd, now in the foreground, now in the passing background, are familiar figures – Caryl Bramsley (C.), Blanche Roccapalumba, Walter Troumestre, Mrs Housman, Solway the virtuoso, Guy Cunninghame, George Ayton, the ambassadorial Hedworth Lawlesses, Leila Bucknell, and many others. Meeting these people so often we can imagine them writing letters to each other, so real do they seem. With few external strokes of portraiture or characterization, Baring brings these people into our awareness by two means. The first is his habit of telling us all about them in an accent of gossip, and the second is to let them talk to each other extensively once they are placed in their scenes.

If we sometimes wonder where all the pages and pages of flat-voiced trivia and gossip and social detail are taking us, we soon realize that we are witnessing the build-up of these lives in their world. The air of gossip in the general establishment constitutes the *donnée*. Once past it, the action can take over, and the general tone then arises from our feeling about what happens. We soon see how important are the fragments of information when we understand that they are needed in order to make the big changes and events, when they come in the novels, as powerful and meaningful as they would be in real life, which also mostly has its days and years of trifles. When Baring seems to be chattering rapidly and

24

carelessly, he is really making lives entire, including the trivial as well as the large.

So, knowing so well the styles and allusions of their common world, his people connect. There is no such thing as a meaningless meeting or relation. There is, even, moral danger in thinking about other people in a certain way, far this side of any outward enactment of the speculative thought. The point here is that Baring credits the human sensibility so seriously and importantly – the instrument of intuition itself – that he sees how the smallest hidden energy in any individual must have its effect on someone else; propose the possibility of resultant action; and thus, inevitably, become part of a moral equation to one or another degree. This ultimate awareness could, of course, belong only to highly civilized persons in that highly organized convention of human relationships called, in his time, society. All this acuity of feeling and effect is so subtle and delicate in Baring's novels that it takes much attention to catch it – but once caught, there is caught also a most remarkable and exquisitely attuned penetration into love, and sympathy, and regret, for the human condition. In *Darby and Joan*, through a scrap of dialogue, tossed away without direct admissions by anyone, a meaningful new relationship is revealed:

Alexander said he was willing to do anything she liked, but that he was not free Sunday afternoon. He had to go to say good-bye to an old gentleman who had been kind to him.

Lady Alice wanted to know, who, why, and what.

Alexander explained.

'I know,' said Lady Alice, 'there's a daughter, isn't there? What is she like?'

'Oh, very nice,' said Alexander dispassionately.

'Pretty?'

'Not exactly.'

Lady Alice understood that it was not to be civil to an old gentleman that Alexander was going to pay the visit.

When Alexander spoke 'dispassionately' about the girl, and said she was 'not exactly' pretty, he told Lady Alice everything. People know the more by trifles once they belong to the enclosing social premise.

An important part of this premise was the importance of limits upon behaviour and statement. Convention in any world has great power. When it becomes involved with emotion, either through frustrating it or by transgression of it causing someone to suffer, events may suddenly take a turn. In *Daphne Adeane*, an unmarried man, Michael, and a married woman, Hyacinth, have been lovers for some time. Suddenly Hyacinth tells him that her husband 'knows' at last, and is being considerate and decent in his suffering. She is driven by her own fine feeling to send Michael away because she cannot bear to see her husband in pain. Furthermore, Michael himself ought to marry, because society says so. In vain he rages and cites his own suffering. The affair must end. It does end. There are points beyond which not to go. The parable is twice-effective because of the way it is told. We know the two are lovers, but without being given a single scene in bed – it is simply assumed that anybody with a sense of things would know or take for granted that they made love, and how people do make love, and that was enough. The imagination is animated and then convinced more by the implicit sense of being and action than by a remorseless presentation in detail of matters that belong to private feeling. In *Daphne Adeane* Baring makes the point. 'There was another peculiarity about this picture.' – Daphne's portrait – 'It was *intimate*. You were not sure you ought to be looking at it. Just as someone[1] said that Eleanora Duse's acting made you feel like a cad, as if one were looking through a keyhole at what was too private for alien eyes, so this picture made you feel you had trespassed upon a privacy unawares, as Hamlet stumbled on his uncle at his orisons.' This suggests the seed of a whole aesthetic of fiction, poetry, drama, by which Baring worked.

His novels were generally built around the chronicle of a complete life. His typical ones carry the central character from infancy to death, and in doing so traverse both outer and inner worlds. *C*, a novel of some three hundred thousand words, takes Caryl Bramsley (the title is the initial of his first name, the nickname by which he was always known) through his discoveries in the act of maturing, enlightenment through literature, music and art, and love, sorrow, passion and futility, faith and death. All through this novel, as in many of his others, is woven the pathos of the absolutely certain, young, inexperienced people who are at the mercy of the absolutely forgetful, experienced elders. The strongest themes are those of love and of that inner need for a purpose or at least a grasp in life which answers more than simple material requirements. It is the total architecture of a life that interests him rather than its high-keyed details or moments. He is a novelist with a long view and an enclosing faith. *Cat's Cradle*, his other extremely long novel, is a detailed chronicle of the whole life of an Englishwoman who marries without love to please her father, betrays her husband in intention but remains with him through duty when he falls ill or pretends to, and finally, widowed, claims her love by stealing him from another, younger woman, and pays bitterly for it when she comes to see herself as she really is, suffering agonies of jealousy as she watches the slow failure of her act of emotional thievery. *The Coat Without Seam* is a lifelong narrative of a

---

[1] He himself said it, in his essay, 'Actors, Actresses, and Goldfish,' in *Lost Lectures*, 1932.

young man who, born to the upper classes, though in poverty, is obsessed with the idea that he is patronized and despised by others of his world, and who through his resentment loses chance upon chance for proper advancement and even fulfilment in love, and who dies in war knowing that his worldly existence is of little importance next to the immortal life of his soul.

The lesser novels play variations on such themes, and several of them suggest in their very titles – *Passing By, Overlooked, The Lonely Lady of Dulwich, Comfortless Memory* – the ingrained melancholy, the sense of detached loss, the hurt regard of life, which linger between the lines of all of Baring's fiction. He seemed often to be the victim of a pang of intuition which must always have implications beyond the moment. One day he watched the brilliant young officer son of Count Benckendorff set out for Manchuria and the war. Baring said, 'He looked so radiantly young and adventurous, when he started, that we were all of us afraid that he would never come back.' The artist, here, feels so keenly that he not only feels the first meaning of what he observes, but also its second, and quite opposite one – life makes him think of death, happiness of grief, goodness of evil.

If all his novels are love stories, they are all unhappy ones. All his lovers are star-crossed, and this arises, we feel, less out of a story-teller's dramatic necessity than out of an unshakable view of life. Love is the worst thing that can happen, and at the same time it is the only thing worth wanting. Its pursuit begins in tremulous, bated breathings of hope and intention:

'Goodbye,' said C. 'May I come again?'
'Yes,' said Beatrice, 'please come again.'
And that little minute seemed again to take them farther, to open the door a little wider, and like all partings, even the happiest, it had a slight shiver lent by the shadow of death, but it seemed so slight that it was almost like a blessing.

It is a tiny fragment, hardly a scene, and yet within it we seem to embrace the full cycle of creature life, which must start in hope and desire, and can only end in death and dissolution, and all is the more poignant because we know much about life that the young lovers do not yet know. He understands love like a Tolstoy: 'She had one or two things to say to him. It was absurd' – this from *Daphne Adeane* – 'as she had seen him no longer ago than tea-time yesterday and yet so it was.' Separated lovers are alive in each other's thought daylong.

And yet love in Maurice Baring's novels is more often a fatal accident than a blessing. In his anthology, *Have You Anything To Declare?* he quotes a passage from *Don Quixote* which could stand as an epigraph for many of his stories: 'Love is too strong to be overcome by anything except flight, nor ought mortal creature to be so presumptuous as to stand the encounter, since there is need of something more than human, and indeed heavenly, powers to vanquish human passion.'

For his lovers, literature is the igneous matter of love, who exchange discoveries of great writers as they explore and discover each other: Heine among many others plays a recurring role in the love affairs, and the aching simplicity of such a stanza as this suggests the style of emotion which Baring captures:

> Das Meer hat seine Perlen,
> Der Himmel seine Sterne,
> Aber mein Herz, mein Herz
> Mein Herz, hat seine Liebe.

In *C*, Baring's character Madeleine Lapara, who is clearly Sarah Bernhardt, reads aloud a love poem, 'Obsession', by Sully-Prudhomme, and

> 'Yes,' the accents said, 'I know how sweet it is, and I know, too, how very bitter is that sweetness,' and as she ended, her eyes were full of the sorrow of all the lovers in the world. It was as if she had laid bare a secret wound, a wound that everyone had suffered and everyone had concealed, and that she had touched it with a divinely magical, healing, finger.

The love affairs are anguished and deep, the sense of desire and its tyranny are conveyed almost to a painful point – and yet there is not one word or line devoted to physical sex, not one example of what has been called 'the obligatory scene' in more recent fiction. As in the love affairs in Tolstoy – Vronsky and Anna – the fact of communion in desire is recognized and is made experience for us far more powerfully by the description of its effect and its demands than through literary voyeurism.

In Baring's portrait of Leila Bucknell in *C* we see a light woman disguised as a lady. She is always presented decorously, but in an affair that runs through two-thirds of that long novel we come to know her well. It is a harrowing knowledge of a remorseless user of men, a female liar, who has all the airs and entrées and expertly managed discretions that will seem to forgive her her infidelities to her husband and all her many simultaneous lovers. She can play superbly the role of the hurt and the deceived and the betrayed when she herself is incapable of a sincere or lasting sensation for anyone else at all. It is *C*.'s torture that, having known her as a child, and having found her in her full-blown beauty years later, he has fallen into her appetite and her hands. His youth, good looks and charm please her and whatever pleases her she uses, without understanding its quality. 'Every now and then C. would send her poems that he wrote, and she ended by treating them like bills; they got lost almost before she had looked at them.'

Her own taste is execrable, except in matters of chic. She has a scrap-book with banalities of sentiment pasted in and she copies these out in the letters with which she reproves those whom she tortures with her deceits and her unaccountabilities. Even C.'s excellent taste does not protect him against her, for it is her beauty, her animality, which holds him. We see her as the really wordly woman of full-blown sensuality when she makes a rendezvous with C. at the British Museum, where, she says, she wishes 'to renew her acquaintance with the Elgin marbles'. What a wealth of allusion there is here, in the presence of all that celebration of nakedness, as she meets her lover, whom she dangles and tortures as often as she sweetens and satisfies him. When inevitably C. is made to know her for what she is, he gives her up; but in doing so he gives up life also, for it is not long until he sickens and has no will to live, and he dies, thinking now not of the body but of the soul.

The plots of Maurice Baring's novels, as postulates of life, turn on mistakes, chances of misunderstanding, wrong-headed decisions, which occur early in the narratives, then to be followed by the relentless factoring out of their long consequences. If mechanical misunderstandings and the repetition of patterns sometimes seem to play too great a part in his narratives, the implication is there that life is like that; and, in the end, life does seem to be present in his fiction, with his own particular melancholy note responding in resonance – melancholy, not pessimism, for a lyric endurance is not the same as a hopeless one. Hope is blind, but lives on: 'If we knew the future', says one of his people, 'we could not endure it.' It is often a concern for 'the right thing', 'the best thing to do', which impels the fateful decisions of his people – touching echoes of how human beings behave when they call intelligence into play in the face of strong feeling. The cycle seems to be like this: desires imperious, con-sequences plain, decorum or duty relentless, and heartbreak waiting. One of his familiar situations is that of a marriage between a young, often very beautiful woman of taste and sensibility, and an older, much older, rich, busy, perhaps gross, intelligent man. The match is puzzling to the observer within the story, as if all his life he had seen marriages made up from the outside, so to speak, and romance, love itself, refuted by the union of beauty and the beast.

In *Cat's Cradle*, Blanche hopes until the last minute to be able to go against her father's wishes and break her engagement to Prince Roccapalumba. Her father points out how 'difficult' it would be to break off the engagement at the eleventh hour. Blanche replies: 'But that is just the beauty of the eleventh hour. That's what it's there for, surely.'

Her father holds fast, her life is committed, and years and years later, having made the first wrong decision, others having followed in train, she says: 'You see, I have only brought misery to every one I have ever known all my life, and the sooner I die the better.'

It is true, and that she must realize it is part of her salvation. For there is salvation, both inside and outside of his books, and it is the same that he found in his own life. We shall briefly return to it after a few more comments about literary aspects of his novels.

## [ xi ]

It is the artist's endless problem to make the commonplace, the universal experience, seem significant and unique. All love stories have essentially the same thing to say, but, as all literature shows us, it has to be said endlessly. It takes the artist to say it enduringly. He must see it as if for the first time every time he tries to tell the story. Reading Goethe one day, Baring said he had 'startling illuminations' about Goethe's work, 'purely personal', he said, 'and possibly wrong, but as clear and vivid as when a copy-book platitude leaps into letters of fire'. (These 'startling illuminations', which surely suggest how his own intuitive intellect worked, have dozens of repetitions in the experiences of his characters in the novels, who suddenly realize crucial understanding or information in 'a flash' – a device which he over-used, yet one which seemed wholly natural to him.) As for copy-book platitudes, often so maddeningly true, one thinks he wanted to make them come alive in his novels.

It takes a very long and absorbing book to let this process feel natural. Of *Cat's Cradle* Charles du Bos said – and he could have said it of *C* as well – that it is '*un livre long, et c'est là son premier mérite; car . . . la longueur est la nécessité primordiale du roman qui se propose de nous mettre en possession d'un monde*', and he added that it is in '*ce lent et quasi-imperceptible effet cumulatif où réside le triomphe de l'ouvrage*'. Quoting Laforgue, du Bos caught the essential air of reality in Maurice Baring's work: '*Dieu! que la vie est quotidienne!*' Oddly, what was virtue to du Bos was failing to Arnold Bennett, who said of *Cat's Cradle* that 'Its curious fault is that it reads as if it really had happened.'

Baring's method brings up the 'creative writing' class argument about how to write fiction: whether to *tell it* or *show it*. One of the first things a fledgling critic or editor tells writers is that they must *show* everything happening rather than *tell about* what happened. The only thing to be said about this is that it doesn't matter in the least which method is followed – either can be appropriate. All that matters is whether or not the writer is gifted. If he is, he can spend pages and chapters, like Tolstoy, simply telling what happened.

Baring spends much of his space in telling us directly who his people are. Almost all his novels open with a number of catalogue pages, as if he were replying to our request, 'Tell me what you know about them before you tell me what they did.' So in the design of his *données* we have set forth for us those ancestries, those traits, those tastes; those town houses in great squares, those castles and abbeys in the country, those palaces in Rome; those intermarriages and relationships between grand families, and those scandals, and lost ambitions, and present despairing acceptances; those Catholic or Protestant allegiances, and the rest, as if we were listening to gossip that must lead to further news in terms of what happened next.

Bertrand, in *The Lonely Lady of Dulwich*, says, 'When you are reading a novel, a novel must not be too life-like, or else where does the artist come in?' It is an amusing question, and answering it would lead to a history of changes of fashion in ideas of the novel. For himself, Baring, according to Ronald Knox, 'had a real meticulousness about getting things right. . . . I remember his spending a whole morning poking about . . . to discover whether the railway got as far as Rome, or still stopped short of Turin, at the time when Blanche first visited Rome in *Cat's Cradle*. Not one reader in a thousand would have caught him out if he had got it wrong, but (if only because a story, for him, always took on the colours of real life) he could not bear to make Blanche achieve the impossible. He *wrote* easily (as all his readers rightly infer), but the detailed building-up of a story . . . cost him hours of conscientious application.'

Yes – but more: he intended us to believe all we read as we went, and the air of flat truth about his books required his own conviction to be supported by accuracy where external facts could be confirmed. The novelist's invention always flies farther on real wings.

But there was a sort of information which interested Baring hardly at all – or, rather, it was of small importance in the lives of his characters. In all the novels there is scarcely an explanation or a reference to anyone's daily work, except for painters or journalists. For the rest, whether financier, soldier, sailor, diplomat, merely an establishing word or two sufficed. He had no interest in 'shop' – the mechanics of how jobs get done and how trades or professions are followed. This view seems odd perhaps to modern readers when so much of recent fiction devotes itself to respectful accounts of trades and vocations, a sad, anxious attention to the material preoccupation, laced with erotic episodes out of sexual case histories. Baring's population consisted of the 'decently clothed' and 'the civilly mannered', who were the people he grew up knowing. This can be taken quite simply, for there was no snobbism about it, in contrast to the hilarious moment in Evelyn Waugh's *Sword of Honour* when one character tells another that a third won't do at all as a proper British officer: 'Haven't they seen the fellow's hair? I don't mean the way it's cut. The way it grows.'

Baring's fictional world was divided, like his Lady Hengrave's, between those 'you knew and those you didn't know', and he was called on it by his frank literary friend Vernon Lee. 'Of course,' she wrote him, 'I *dislike* your people, personally. I dislike their mixture of footling uselessness [Miss Paget was a suffragette] and devouring passion [Miss Paget was a maiden lady]. . . . They have *time* for it, as they never do anything but go to parties.'

But, replied Maurice Baring, '*It is surprising how much time* is taken up by parties in the lives of *busy men. Henry James* puts on record 244 dinner parties in one year! *Robert Browning*, between 1870 and 1880, would have beaten that, I think.' Furthermore, 'Nothing seems to stop parties; neither death, earthquake, war, air-raids, revolutions; nor the plague: cf. Decameron, London plague, French Revolution, the Russian Revolution, the war.' In any case, he says, bringing the issue down to a matter of snobbism pure and simple, reviewers of both high- and low-brow papers who said his people never did anything but go to parties, didn't mean 'parties *qua* party' . . . they mean 'parties in Mayfair and Belgravia', and not parties 'in Bloomsbury and Chelsea'. For himself, he preferred the parties he grew up seeing in his father's house where great music was performed by superb artists for mannerly people, as against the parties he had seen given by the intelligentsia in Bloomsbury and Chelsea where . . . well, the tone was 'different, and sometimes (to the unmarried) *à faire rougir les singes*'. In view of such, he found his objectors 'comic'. Long ago he had suggested that Vernon Lee should remember 'the frequent combination of the socialist and the snob'.

[ xii ]

Baring's sense of the reality of the upper classes did not blind him to their vulnerability as objects of comedy, and much of his social fabric is devoted to drawing-room comedy, managed with a virtuoso technique. In *C* the formidable Lady Hengrave, in a discussion, is making no headway as she tries to convince another lady of a lesser social position who does not agree with her. As she gives it up, Lady Hengrave's explanation to herself of her failure is masterly: 'It's no good talking to her,' she thought. 'Either she's not listening, or she's not quite right in the head.'

A certain Mrs Maitland, in *C*, is done in a line or two: ' "I flatter myself" was a phrase which often crossed her lips. She did . . . she asked a great many questions, but she paid small heed to the answers.'

We see a whole world of travellers who used to spend the winter in Rome when we see Mr Crowe, who was 'an invalid without an illness'. One of the richest characterizations in all the novels, that of Prince Guido Roccapalumba in *Cat's Cradle*, is essentially stated in this one of many details – he was 'mysterious about nothing'. Tuke, in *Passing By*, 'said he kept his diary without missing a day for the last five years, but he always burnt it every New Year's Day'. A novel in which this could happen seems to make everything else in it strange, real and amusing. In the same book 'Mrs Fairbairn . . . is an affected woman who dresses in what are meant to be ultra-French clothes, and she speaks broken English on purpose. She pretends to be silly, but is far from being anything of the kind.' In a few lines we have a leading character for any drawing-room comedy: 'The Prince of Saxe-Altenburg walked into the room as the clock struck a quarter past eight. He wore a star and a red ribbon, and he shook hands slowly with all the guests, and said a word to each. To C. he said nothing, but favoured him with an august twinkle.'

Here is a good example of a more extended scene: An obscure English singer has just finished an excruciating performance of three songs at an evening party in the British Embassy at Rome. Before she can announce her next song, Lady Lawless, the Ambassadress, is by her side, at the pianoforte, pouring out compliments and thanks to her.

'I like that one best of *all*,' she said, 'and *how* kind of you to have been able to spare us a moment tonight, and to have given us *all such* a treat, and to have sung *so* many songs. I do hope it hasn't *tired* you; you must take care of that precious throat. The Ambassador has so enjoyed it; we *all* have, and you must come to tea and sing another song very soon.' And as she talked she took Miss Sims's music from the pianoforte, and rolled it up neatly in a *rouleau*, and tied it with a little piece of pink ribbon, and presented it to her with a charming but completely final bow, and calling Herbert Napier she said to him, 'Mr Napier, will you take Miss Sims to have a cup of tea and some lemonade?' And so saying, she led the guests back to the drawing-room, and Napier conducted Miss Sims to a small buffet on the top of the staircase, where there were refreshments, whence she was ultimately 'shown out'.

'She may do for concerts in England,' said Lady Lawless. 'One never knows what English people will like.'

There is a multitude of points for social study in this little scene. But not all social artifice is comedy – far from it. In sustained flights Baring was capable also of deep explorations of the art of malice, as in his relentless presentation of the ill-doing of Princess Julia Roccapalumba or Bessie Lacy in *Cat's Cradle*.

[ xiii ]

It is a light touch, and it is not reserved only for moments of social comedy – it is the touch he generally uses upon everything. In the moments of big significance this produces an air of understatement which is often

33

more effective than an effort to achieve intensity by elaborate rhetoric. Here is an example of how Baring seems to throw away a matter of utmost consequence to the story he is telling in *Cat's Cradle*. Blanche, Princess Roccapalumba, has, quite unknown to her Roman husband and his family, become a convert to the Catholic Church: 'Blanche was dressed early and she waylaid Guido on their way down to dinner and told him that she had been received into the church that day. . . . Guido seemed to be thunderstruck but he had no time to express his surprise.' The dinner-party must proceed, as life at large always must proceed, and the intense, private concerns of individuals must give way, or be suppressed, or adapted – this is what Baring seems to be saying in his technique with such an episode.

Still, in a fabric of revelations and discoveries mostly muted, there is opportunity, too, for confrontations of high drama. One such is the sudden appearance of Guido Roccapalumba, the invalid husband who has supposedly been unable to walk for years, to detect, bearing a lamp, the long, sweet, quiet tête-à-tête of his wife and the man who loves her, as they sit hand in hand in late night darkness, far distant from the invalid's room in the vast Roman palace of the Roccapalumbas. It is a chilling *coup de théâtre*, all the more effective for Baring's spare use of such a device, and, further, it succeeds because, melodramatic as it may be, it is entirely appropriate to Guido's character as given to us earlier.

In the same novel, *Cat's Cradle*, which is in many ways Baring's most beautifully designed long story, we may note another of his technical successes. Blanche, by now widowed, is at last free to marry Bernard, who had loved her years ago. But meanwhile he has become fond of Blanche's ward, the lovely young Rose Mary. With Rose Mary in mind, one day he asks Blanche if she does not think he might marry at last. Blanche knows at once – an example of how Baring's characters are given to what he called in one instance a 'fit of lucidity' and in many others referred to as 'flashes' of understanding – she knows at once that Bernard is thinking of marrying Rose Mary; but longing for him herself she lets him know that she is still willing to marry him. For the sake of the past, he agrees and they are married. Their life goes on comfortably, she is wonderfully happy, and Bernard is content. But she must live in the knowledge of her crime, the theft she made, for Rose Mary adores Bernard also, and must do without him. Because Blanche appropriated him, *faute de mieux* Rose Mary marries Bernard's best friend, and the families live near to each other. Years later Blanche recognizes a truth which Bernard himself does not yet know – that his love for her has faded and that really it is Rose Mary whom he loves after all. In her self-torture at losing his love, and at growing old (she is older than he), and at admitting the justice of how she is made to suffer, Blanche herself reveals to Bernard what he has honourably refused to know. It is a powerful revelation after all that time, and all those pages. It occurs in a scene when Blanche and Bernard are discussing the possibility of a visit from Rose Mary and her husband.

'You would like her to come?' said Blanche in a toneless voice.

'Yes, I should.'

'How you do love her!' said Blanche, biting her lips, and her voice quivering.

'Love her? What do you mean?' Bernard looked round, startled.

'I mean you love her – love her; that you are in love with her; that you think of no one else – of nothing else; that the sight of any one else is like so much dust, especially the sight of me.'

Blanche talked in a quick, low voice. She was panting and she looked at the ground. She tore her little handkerchief.

'My dear Blanche, I think you are off your head.'

But we know she was not. She knew the truth and she told it, and it shattered everything. It was the immense result of an immense crime – she had stolen Bernard from the love he had managed to forget, and now she had revived it for him. 'Bernard was stunned' – but the truth was out and he had finally to admit it to himself. Still, civilized behaviour prevailed, and the scene, after growing into a storm, ended in a reconciliation. But it ended also Blanche's hope that her youth, her beauty, her appeal, for which alone she had lived, were not yet gone.

How wonderfully is managed the long process of Blanche's growing old! Nothing is marked by descriptive reflections along the way to let us be reminded of how she changes. Through all the stages of her life, from childhood to death, we know how beautiful she is, and as years pass, we hear others remark how her beauty is greater than ever, but now they mean, how remarkable at her age to be so beautiful, and this tells us more than any other detail that she *is* older, that her beauty is defensively remarked where formerly it was acknowledged and granted its supremacy. And so by little marvels of atmosphere arising from her emotional storms, her hungry jealousy and doubt, we feel age, we age with her, and recognize the irony of the decline of the institutional beauty of her set, and we know pity for all the expensive, lovely, ingenious, and in the end hollow devices that have been brought to bear for all her life on preserving the all-devouring appearance of things. Once again, one of Baring's recurring themes has sounded, as in *Comfortless Memory*, where he wrote: 'There could be nothing, except retribution and punishment and the inevitable result of one's own folly.'

'Folly' may be taken to relate chiefly to the passion of love, and of love thwarted through one luckless circumstance or another. As for the many-skeined entanglement of love beyond one's power to foresee, and its often ruinous effect in life, there seems to be only one thing to conclude. Blanche, in *Cat's Cradle*, states it. 'It's insoluble,' she said to herself, 'unless one cuts it. I haven't the courage to do that.' Again, she says, 'I'm human . . . not reasonable.' Further, there is no immunity for anyone. Leila Bucknell, the exquisite cheat who ruined C.'s life, is, at the end of *Cat's Cradle*, quite probably at the very beginning of a possibly ruinous effect upon Bernard Windlestone, who, lately widowed of Blanche, has in a conviction of final stability married the woman from whom Blanche took him, and whom he has loved in secret for years. All looks safe and dear – and then he meets Leila. The suggestion of his eventual capture by her is barely indicated – but below the offhand air of Baring's observations lies an inexorable sophistication based on a scepticism whose only countervailing force is a humble power of belief beyond oneself; in short, a religious certainty. Even that will not necessarily prevent folly; but it may provide salvation through admission of the sorry truth about oneself, which as a direct result requires repentance.

## [ xiv ]

In *Darby and Joan* occurs a passage of dialogue which in one or another form recurs throughout Maurice Baring's novels and plays with the frequency of obsession:

'I suppose you'll marry some day?'
'I don't think so. I haven't been lucky so far, and perhaps it's just as well.'

Just as well? We cannot help wondering why, thinking about Baring's own life. He never married, though he became an anatomist of marriage in his books, where he touched skilfully on its emotional and social patterns, if never the sexual. Probably this exhibited a propriety of the period, and yet one feels more than this about it. Was there also a personal restraint which led him to discuss the matter of love only in the histories of other people's loves, and to let his own speak only between the lines of theirs? His own loves – for he must have had them – never seemed to have flowered openly, except for gallantries of an ideal nature alluded to in his sonnets. There could have been any number of reasons why, but it would be presumptuous, lacking direct evidence confided by himself, to impose firm assumptions about the subject with only conjecture, which cannot serve as authority, to sustain conclusions.

A homeless childhood recurs as a condition of life in many of his books, for example, in *Comfortless Memory*, where Charles Donne, the artist, having lost his mother while he was at school, 'had been brought up by two hectoring aunts'. Baring's mother died while he was a schoolboy.

Explaining why he had never written about her, even his autobiography, he told Ethel Smyth, 'Even if I could have done it, I don't know that I should have. The reason is that my love for her was so great, so immense, so whole-hearted and fundamental that I couldn't make something out of it for the public eye. . . . I did not, could not see her from the outside. I think the reason must be that we were too close together – there was too much of the same past in our compositions.' Losing her so early, it might be that he never grew up to her, in order to outgrow her in another love, which society would bless through the institution of marriage.

Behind all the chivalric chastity of the bachelors in his stories who say 'I shall never marry', there is, through sheer weight of their number, a hint that they cherished their self-denial. If they must settle for a memory of love, a love denied by fateful circumstance, even of a love only imagined, it is clear that to the best of their knowledge his people projected an utterly lofty ideal of life. The novel *Daphne Adeane* is built round the theme of a dead lady so lovely and so much beloved that she remains greatly influential as a memory in many lives. Her power in memory is so great that it seems to be stated with the effect of a principle. The novel is a biography of a *ghost* of love, and of how the echo, its repeated manifestations in later lives, goes on, without change in essence or design for ever and ever. Embodied in others, love itself lives on memory. If it comes too near, all there is to do – Baring quoted the Cervantes passage several times in his works – is to flee it, for otherwise there was no denial possible.

Why to flee? Because for the most of human life, love is a misfortune. When Madame Lapara declaimed Sully Prudhomme, 'her eyes were full of the sorrows of all the lovers in the world'. And we ask why 'sorrows'? Are there no joys in love? But love is 'a secret wound, a wound that every one had suffered and every one had concealed'. And in *Daphne Adeane* 'They could see each other only rarely, and for a brief space of time when they did meet, but this made their love and their happiness more intense and acute. . . . Their feasts when they met surpassed all Fanny had ever dreamt of. She was so happy she felt something dreadful must happen.' Love's image is linked to fatality, and never seems safe, as real things seem safe. Nothing is certain, except that love is equally a gift of the gods and a curse.

He once asked Ethel Smyth what, if he were to execute her will, he should do with her love-letters, which freely referred to her long affair with Henry Brewster. She evidently had wondered whether she should show the letters to Baring. He replied:

'I don't know why you should have any *pudeur* with regard to showing me things? It is as you say probably my fault. I have no feelings of *pudeur* about it but sometimes Ethel I am *shy* about things, and this

37

raises a temporary barrier and prevents me from discussing things I want to discuss or prevents me from discussing the things they want to discuss with me. This only happens on rare occasions by chance – and can really always be got over.'

It is a statement that supports our sense that in his novels he is sometimes shy, also, quivering on the edge of the explicit, and yet unable to fall upon it. His hopeless gallantries about chivalrously endistanced ladies may have been a propriety folded about himself for reasons which he felt need not be discussed. The more credit to him as an artist, then, that within such limitations, imposed no matter by what qualms, he was able to summon so full a sense of life into his best writing.

## [ xv ]

To consider the matter of Maurice Baring's style, let us listen to what he said about it: 'In the art of writing, and in fact all the arts, the best style is that where there is no style, or rather where we no longer notice the style, so appropriate and inevitable, so easy the thing said, sung, or done is made to appear.'

It is one of the two official attitudes about the act of art, the other attitude being that which loves for its own sake the gestures of virtuosity. As an argument it can never be resolved, since great artists have worked under both attitudes. Who would sacrifice the rich textures of Shakespeare? And who would change the unadorned line of Racine? Style is, simply, the sympathetic response of temperament to intellectual or emotional stimulus.

It was Maurice Baring's whole temperament which led him to adopt the tone of a cultivated and sympathetically intelligent man talking gossip rapidly and evenly, in a level voice, with never a hesitation to choose between ways to say things, but simply running on to capture a sense of life because life – any life – is so important to catch before it is gone. Behind the offhand manner, of course, lies a fine sense of the organization of material, of design, but this must be concealed. As a youth he wrote in his private *Poems by M. B. Written 1891–92*:

> Does faultless shape force human hearts to feel?
> Perchance: But I do rather love a dash
> Of true soul-fire than all perfection's spheres,
> The untaught instinct bursting, drawing tears,
>                                        . . . the flash
> That lights to Heaven human hopes and fears!

Ultimately an ideal for his own work seemed to be drawn from La

38

Fontaine. In his essay on the *Fables*, commenting on a favourite passage, he exclaimed, 'What divine economy! What an illustration of La Fontaine's favourite maxim, *"Rien de trop!"* ' It is not ignoble to recognize one's own values in admired works of the past. He found qualities in the *Chanson de Roland* which he could properly claim if he was of a mind to do so: the 'true epic quality of pathos, simplicity, and restraint'. Speaking of Villehardouin, he said, 'He was a realist. He wrote *choses vues.*' Baring was the same sort of realist, and by his offhand manner, appeared to tell us that much of life is offhand, too. It is one thing to speak in an offhand way, quite another to get the same effect on the page. He was perfectly capable of rich densities if he chose to make effects intended to impress. But no, as the author-narrator of *Comfortless Memory* says, 'When I try, I *please*, but I don't convince.'

Using the artifice of the artless, then, he disposed of almost all his 'big' moments in a line or two, while all the smaller, supporting circumstantiations go on for pages, with the effect of creating the texture for the big moments when they come. If we believe all the little *tesserae* in the mosaic, then, however astonishing it may be when it is fully revealed, we will believe the total design they make. Baring states his principle when he has Christopher, in *The Coat Without Seam*, speak of 'that careless artlessness which can be achieved by only the most consummate art'. He uses words so common and yet precise that they seem almost not to be there. We are reminded of Blanche, again, when 'she heard the voice of truth speaking without the noise of words'. He seemed to attempt the impossible – to write without words.

Vernon Lee wrote to him to thank him for his 'bony, dry style', which she called 'a blessing after so much lusciousness (sleepy pears with wasps hidden in them)'. When his fiction was translated into French, it was remarked that 'his clear, unaccented style' seemed 'in some ways to read as well, if not better, than in the original', and Princesse Marthe Bibesco noted that the French writers whom he most admired were Racine, La Fontaine, and Stendhal. 'That dry little style,' said Vernon Lee of *C*, 'which looks as if it weren't one at all, is quite right.' And she said again that he had 'somehow, and perhaps by this very thinness of texture, contrived to give an extraordinary sense of passion, rather like what music gives'.

This does catch a sense of his ideal, which again we detect in his essay on Racine, when speaking of the tragic farewell of Bérénice, he says, 'the words are those of everyday conversation, the sentiments exactly what a woman in the situation of Bérénice would say at any time in any country, and the effect is that of great poetry'.

If Baring's whole aim was to give us life without getting in the way, he sometimes allowed himself carelessness perilously close to self-parody. In his very refusal to be literary, he sometimes strung out too many declarative sentences in his passages of establishment like this from *The Coat Without Seam*:

> Countess Linsky was an old lady with shrewd eyes and an infectious laugh. Her son Karl, who was sixteen years old, was delicate. He had short, rather curly hair, and a gentle expression like that of a spaniel. His sister, Alex, was seventeen, and just out. She was short, with light brown hair, clear, dark blue, laughing eyes, and a quiet smile that seemed to search the whole room like a sunbeam. . . . Elsa was the same age as Alex. She was fresh and pretty, with a snub nose and pale blue eyes, and fair hair. She was not a beauty, but she reminded you of a white rose. Christopher liked Countess Felsen at once. She was gentle and reflective and purred like a good-natured cat. She was a widow and had a married son. There was an English nurse in the house called Hanna.

It is all useful information, some of it is important, and presently, with what we know, we are entering into the action of the story, and if we are bothered by what seems carelessness, Baring says to us, as he wrote in a letter, 'I don't care twopence for chiselled masterpieces of form, for exquisite impeccability' – a clear statement about his intention in composing his three long novels. 'I don't mind the *longueurs* and the lapses, the twigs in the current as long as the river is there.'

And he was, whenever he chose, wonderfully suggestive through his very simplicities.

'Blanche's attention drifted away like a balloon, although she seemed to be listening intently,' and we know exactly how this was. There is a perfect use of expressive detail in *The Coat Without Seam*, where Baring gives a whole battle in a phrase or two, just as Velazquez, in the painting of 'The Surrender at Breda', made us see a vast army by the judicious placing of a dozen or so lances. The scene is the battlefront in World War One: 'The German attack had begun, and after a morning of shining peace, there was suddenly a tremendous fire; leaves and branches were falling in the wood.'

'Shining peace' – the falling leaves and branches – these details make you think of a literal translation from a classic – like something in Homer or Virgil, where even the simplest statement when it is perfect can summon up every reminder in one's own experience and achieve a completion.

Finally, in respect to the tone, the effect, of Maurice Baring's writing, we must apply to him another of his literary judgements made upon someone else. In *An Outline of Russian Literature* he says Krylov has 'the talisman which defies criticism, baffles analysis, and defeats time: namely, charm'.

One strand of the threads which made up his biography had recurrent power as an element in his novels. Ethel Smyth said to him one day in 1900 when they were out bicycling, that he would eventually become a Catholic. A long time afterwards he recalled that at that moment, though he would ask nothing better, 'Nothing was more impossible'.

But one of those tiny seeds had been planted without ulterior purpose which in time could grow to an overarching design, and after many years, and much soul-searching, as evidenced by the exposition of conversion in his novels, Baring was received into the Church and came into possession of the ultimate reality for which he had long been looking. It is Baring's triumph that, in a literary world generally oriented to scepticism, he is able to make religion a matter of reality and importance in his writing. It is for his characters and in the fabric of his world a reality in respect to social condition, a reality in culture, and a reality in what is most significant of all, private conviction. His manners as a Catholic apologist are better than those of other English literary men of his persuasion. He is never bantering or patronizing, like Chesterton, or rude, impatient and contemptuous like Evelyn Waugh, or glumly rebellious, like Graham Greene. He is always delicately respectful of explanations of life that differ from his own; and in fact he is scrupulous to echo the sceptical world's case against the Catholic Church.

Speaking of a lady who is to become a nun, someone says in his novel *Passing By*, 'I can't help thinking she has been the victim of an inexorable system and of a training which bends the human mind into a twisted shape that can never be altered or put straight.' In Rome C. goes to a memorial mass with his uncle the British Ambassador, who says later, 'Did you see the faces of the people, all of them either fools or fanatics?' A sceptical man of the world goes to light a candle to Saint Anthony in support of an intention, and explains as he does so that if it will do no good, neither will it do any harm.

Again, C. says impatiently to Beatrice, the lovely Catholic whose faith holds an irritating spiritual attraction for him:

'What can it matter what church one goes to? – if one thinks it necessary to go to church.'

'Catholics think it does matter,' said Beatrice.

'Yes, but Protestants don't,' said C. 'That's the beauty of being a Protestant.'

'Yes, but although they don't mind anything else, they do mind Catholics,' said Beatrice.

Much later C. agrees with this, for he has noticed that 'what's so odd is that those who mind most that anybody is converted to the Roman Catholic Church are just those who care least about religion – those who haven't really got any religion at all'.

Yet the subject of religion is one that spreads like a slow-moving stain in the concerns of the people in his novels. Once mentioned, it falls from sight, or is held suspended for chapters. And then it re-enters, and is seen or is referred to as a social triviality with convenient forms useful in a stabilized society. And then something occurs of religious significance, or a person of parts is suddenly discovered to be a Roman Catholic, and religion is seen as through a pane of glass, *there*, untouchable, not here, but clear, real. And then through an incident of importance, the faith suddenly becomes inescapable, and at once begins to determine all; and often it brings ruin, in worldly terms, and only in ultimate spiritual terms does it satisfy. Faith, belief in Christ, love above and beyond the world, are, really, a catastrophe – but a catastrophe through which alone can anyone gain the only possible entry into full life, meaningful death, and a livable eternity. It becomes, finally, the largest theme of all; and more significantly than other recent novelists in English Maurice Baring has made it the largest in a body of serious literature.

For as he never loses the view of man as fallible and life as confusing and inscrutable, he never fails either in charity and respect for the individual person. 'The point of this life is – I think,' says C., 'its imperfection. . . . I believe that nature never repeats herself; and that every note that is struck in the universe is struck once only, and for ever.' And Christopher, in *The Coat Without Seam*, says, 'Do you know, I think our lives, although they seem patchy, untidy and purposeless, are very likely, every one of them, coats without a seam, and have a perfect unity, so that they could not be cut up or divided without being spoilt.' Madame D'Alberg replies, 'But they appear to be cut up already', and Christopher says, 'Yes, that's just it – but supposing that is because we can't see them properly – supposing we are looking from the wrong angle and the wrong perspective?' In *Cat's Cradle* Blanche says to her confessor, 'I feel so utterly helpless.' Father Michael answers, 'We all feel that. We are of ourselves helpless.'

When Blanche completed her own conversion, and attended mass as a communicant, she 'realized how impossible it was to explain . . . to people on the other side of the door. If you spoke of the *beauty* of the mass they thought you meant architecture, stained glass, candles, incense, music, or flowers. It was not aesthetic beauty; it was the satisfaction of the soul in the presence of reality – the only reality; the eternal, the everlasting, the supernatural. . . .'

The experience of this led François Mauriac to say, 'What I most admire about Baring's work is the sense he gives you of the penetration of grace.' Of his own conversion to the Catholic Church, Maurice Baring said – and it was all he ever said about it – it was 'the only action of my life I am quite sure I have never regretted'.

If the statement has the air of a defence, it was perhaps called forth by the sort of remark Vernon Lee, in the fierce candour of her emancipation, made to him. She was bored, she said, by 'the everlasting theology' which got into his books. Had he made a vow? she wondered, and she thought so, a vow to provide 'so much theology for every glass of vodka!'

Truth to tell, her irritable wit had some justification, for there is at times a hint of tractarianism about his presentation of his religious case, through characters and situations in his novels. He was always gentler than such a modern English literary missionary as Evelyn Waugh, for he never seemed to snub through ridicule or bruise with rudeness those whom he may have wanted to enlighten. But we guiltily wonder whether he pressed his theology in an effort to keep the Faith as a convert by demonstrating it more often than necessary. Else why such frequent statement of the central premise of Roman Catholicism? Mere statement of the Catholic involvement could not always be sufficient to be convincing of its theological value. We can admire Renaissance madonnas without feeling pious. In this connection, it was more his artistry, even careless as it so often was, which carried us when, we suspect, he wanted his philosophy to do so instead.

The theme of the social difficulties attending Catholicism in upper-class life runs through many of his novels, determining private lives, and wreaking earthly unhappiness in the name of an unearthly happiness certain to come in eternity. But not until his last two novels did he dramatize with full zeal the passionate power of the Catholic cause as a course leading not to private misery and public inconvenience, but straight to martyrdom, executed on the public stage of history. *Robert Peckham* and *In My End Is My Beginning* are historical novels set in Tudor times. The central issue is that which divided England between the old religion and the reformed. Robert Peckham must remain true to Rome, and in the other novel Mary Queen of Scots – for it is her tragic history which is played out there – knows that she goes to her death for her Faith as much as for any other political reason. Here the theological argument is entwined with large issues in history – the arch of events, passions, and varying orthodoxies (political and theological) of the time, and it takes its place as proper to the material and holds us fascinated.

One of the strengths of *Robert Peckham* is that Robert and the others interest us for their own human sake, and as we go with their story we go with the ethical argument which lies at the root of their relationships. Baring makes, as always, a more than intelligent and fair case for the Reformer opposition. The novel follows his familiar diagonals of personal involvement, criss-crossings of love, suppressed, with all but hopeless inner commitments. Honour, retribution, a life-tissue of mistakes, God's law, appear again. In his style for the two novels, he has recourse to only a few repeated archaisms to suggest the period.

He can never be far from social comedy. Robert Peckham's father takes him on summons to Henry VIII at Windsor Castle. The Tudor king is very like a broadly done sketch of Edward VII – indeed, much of the book makes us think that it is a Tudor tale with Edwardian trappings. For example, Henry's first interest after a kingly greeting is to criticize the cut of the ruff worn by the elder Peckham, indicating an alertness to imperfections in military or ceremonial dress which we have often been assured is a characteristic of royalty responsive to the exhausting require-ments of exalted position. (Sir Herbert Read used to tell a story about Edward VII being received by the Kaiser in the Berlin railway station when the Kaiser was wearing the uniform of colonel-in-chief of 'his' British regiment. The English king surveyed him critically and said to him, with his echo of a Hanoverian guttural 'r', 'The str-r-ipes on your tr-r-ousers are too br-r-oad.')

The seed of this novel came to Baring when about 1900 his friend Reggie Balfour – a Catholic convert – sent to him from Rome an epitaph which he had found in the Church of St Gregory. Translated, presumably from Latin, it read:

> Here lies Robert Peckham, Englishman and Catholic, who, after England's break with the Church, left England because he could not live in his country without the Faith and, having come to Rome, died there because he could not live apart from his country.

It was thirty years before the book was published. Did he work on several books at a time, or, anyhow, cultivate several books in notes, allowing them to germinate, develop in their ideas, until ready at last to be taken in turn and composed? In any case *Robert Peckham* grew, faithful to the atmosphere of that melancholy and lyric epitaph, and before the lonely end in Rome, Robert Peckham had glimpses of the possibilities of happiness, and the loveliness of which the world was fleetingly capable. In his late maturity Robert seems about to be restored to his first true love: 'I lived in the present thinking of neither tomorrow nor of yesterday, content to float upon the stream, in the calm and sunshine that seemed too fair to last. It was as if the spring had been unburied and were enjoying a second life in the serenity of the reaped fields and the glory of the golden woods. I was afraid to disturb the silence lest I should break the spell.' And, 'Windsor Castle gleamed among the trees,' wrote Robert. 'The air was sultry and the sky covered with cloud. A few drops of rain would fall now and again on the grey water of the river and over the flat tower of the Castle, the end of a rainbow was near it, and its reflected phantom glimmered in the greyness.' It is a small landscape out of the notebooks of Constable or Turner. And who else but Baring, in an historical novel, would engage to do Ronsard's verse into English Alexandrines?

At the end of *Robert Peckham* we feel he rather throws away the structure – but we cannot be sure. The Roman passage sounds like a seventeenth-century travelogue, and Robert's misery in exile is given us only by indirect means, where hitherto we have heard his own narrative. But after his death we discover what his suffering in exile has meant to him when we read a separate short chapter devoted wholly to poems written by him, and his voice sounds more clearly and poignantly to us than ever. Finally the story is completed for us by a report of his last days composed by a person not previously in the story. We can only reflect that there is something rather grand in this indifference to the conventions of fiction and of the well-made story, and as we recognize that he has tried to break the novel into new form, we agree that any such attempt is welcome.

So, too, in his long novel about Mary of Scotland, he gives us an experiment in form – to have four young women of the queen's bed-chamber tell her story, covering much the same ground, with the first three coming to a halt just short of the queen's execution; then letting the fourth tell the same story and bring it all the way to its terrible end. The difficulty here is that there is small evidence of any difference in character or style between the four, and whatever variations there are in the narrative, these seldom seem significant. The effect of the book is that of a love song to Mary of Scotland, in four long prose stanzas, and perhaps it is fair to see the whole composition as a late and lavish gesture of that chivalry with which earlier novels celebrated ladies unattainable in life, as this one made love to one unattainable in history. Both in *Robert Peckham* and *In My End Is My Beginning* there are rhapsodic passages about the Queen – everyone had but to see her only once to be ready to die of love for her. Again Baring attempted to animate the historical novel with fresh ideas of form. It does not here succeed, and, though it is a wholly serious work, its 'scholarly' method makes us sigh for his much earlier triumphs in 'unreliable history' with their brief, hilarious impersonations of historical persons in their period trappings.

These were among Maurice Baring's last novels. The following one – *The Lonely Lady of Dulwich*, which many believe to be his most beautifully realized work of fiction, will speak for itself in full text later in this book. His other, lesser, novels – *Passing By*, *A Triangle*, *Darby and Joan*, *Comfortless Memory*, *Friday's Business*, *Tinker's Leave* – give us his familiar virtues and fleeting echoes of an appealing self but without the pressing energy of his fullest use of his material.

There remained with him something of the sublime amateur, which seems characteristic of much in the British genius. You think of Byron, and the Sitwells, and even supremely of Shakespeare, as against the less original, more formal, more surely professional, men of letters on the continent, and in other, more coherent careers in English. Sometimes he was little more than clever, as when someone in society or in a club is admired for saying a number of 'good things'. If he was at times careless, he was careless only with regard to mechanical detail and trivial repetition. Professionalism interested him less than life. His range was limited but what he saw he saw and felt deeply, and if he was not an original thinker, it was fortunate that he need not be such in order to write enduring novels, since distilled feeling is of more importance to the artist than intellectual acuity.

In *The Coat Without Seam* he gives us the character Altamura, of whom he says, 'His eyes seemed to see everything, and everything about him – especially his hands – gave one the impression of centuries and hidden stores of pent-up civilization.' 'Pent-up civilization' – it is a convenient epitome of Maurice Baring's climate of life and work, for he was concerned always with what lay at the heart of humanity's prime need, the need to compose the inner life. He was among those few writers who could convey in fiction the sense of a spiritual, or intellectual, or artistic experience. Since he was never concerned with the literary, psychological, or economic fashions of his time, he was never limited by them. His intuitiveness and his own observation were the mainsprings of his work, and since they were not lost with the passing of intellectual fads and social theory, good or bad, they have kept their effectiveness. It is satisfying to move with him through lives that relate to immutable human qualities set forth in a vision and an expression that are now free to come into their own appeal after a long period of eclipse by more insistent, though naturally inconstant, theories of society, literature, art, and the spiritual life.

We are in the end not deceived by his air of dealing matter-of-factly with the acts of life. We have his own clue to how we must see this in his description of his Madame Lapara-Bernhardt reciting the dream of Athalie from Racine's play.

'The words were hammered out in icy, low, metallic tones, in a matter-of-fact voice, but a matter of tremendous fact, as of someone who had been the eye-witness of a ghastly tragedy, and who had not yet recovered from the shock of the spectacle. The words had the ring of truth and the accent of calamity. She was telling the bare facts.' *A matter of tremendous fact* – the phrase contains the polarities of manner and substance we may find throughout his best work, by which alone it is meaningful to judge him. Like anyone else, he is now and then betrayed by his fidelity

46

to the surface style of his period. 'Christopher thought she looked like a priestess performing a holy sacrificial rite' – an image out of Alma Tadema or Leighton, a sort of watered-down Pre-Raphaelite ideal; and he wrote of a time when it was possible to speak of a woman's 'dazzling shoulders', and these images now make us smile; but it is the period that makes us smile, not his own reflection of it. He held to his own vision of the larger aspects of life, unswayed by the clamorous vogues of other views which pressed all about him. In his book about Sarah Bernhardt he suggested his view of values when he alluded to works which 'startle more by their modernity than by their truth to nature'.

Writers who are honest in their view of their materials even as they see these as no one else sees them, and who have the gift of expression to a high degree, will outlive fashion, and come to be recognized for values more enduring than those that prevailed socially and intellectually in their lifetimes. 'A book,' remarked Edmond de Goncourt in his journal, 'is never a masterpiece offhand. It becomes one. Genius is the talent of a dead man.'

## [ xviii ]

In a summary of his career in 1945 *The Times* of London was able to say, 'Time may perhaps confirm the judgement of those who see in him one of the subtlest, profoundest, and most original of recent English writers.'

It is not necessary to speak of him in superlatives, or to elevate him at the expense of anyone else. As he said himself of the great poets, nothing 'is so futile and so impertinent as giving marks' to them. In any epoch, there are few enough workers in writing of whom we can say that they are artists. Great or small, they are the ones who receive and understand a tradition, discover themselves in relation to it by extension of its energy, and leave behind them in felicitous form a vision of life which is true to the world because in it they are true to their own discoveries of the meeting of life and art.

Their own discoveries: this is the key statement, it seems to me, about artists; and the key word is *own*. It is this word which saves the genuine artist from possibly fatal identification with the modish habits of thought of his time. Commercial and critical, even intellectual, modishness is always in a state of change. The mode is often dictated by values other than those of art or literature. The higher slang of current thought in any period – for us it has been Freudian jargon, or Marxist, or existentialist, or pornographic – the higher slang gets into the air of the universities or the quarterlies or even the newspaper reviews, and life and letters are talked about in its terms, rather than in terms of what the literary artist is concerned with apart from the prevailing accents of his time. The writer who above other values concerns himself with the mode may reap

47

immediate and impressive returns – he will seem to state enduring truths in the currently accepted language of the intellectualist establishment. But as surely as the mode changes, he is lost with it.

The prevailing art-expressions of our period seem concerned more with illustrations of systems of social theory than with individual discoveries innately artistic, which is to say intuitive. Novels – and we will stay with them as we are dealing with Baring, who was primarily a novelist – many novels now seem obliged to 'make a statement'. What about? Political issues, the unconscious, 'the human dilemma' in its current configurations, the claim of uttermost freedom of expression about sexual experience, reflecting the bankruptcy of society's ideas for an endurable corporate convention. In relation to subject matter, none of these need be unavailable. But they tend now to be set forth fictionally more like case studies or self-indulgences rather than artistic creations. These catch on in intellectual circles if they use reassuringly familiar cant. Critics and professors nod fraternally to each other in their essays while uttering the cliché of the prevailing view. We may expect that reputations made by such utterances will recede with the vocabulary.

What survives in Baring's work to speak to others living after him? He grew up in a world bombarded by Marx and Shaw, Freud and Dada, but he felt no necessity to conform to their styles or commandments, which vastly affected so many others in literature, the arts, and social concern. The modes of Baring's late Victorian, Edwardian, and neo-Georgian lifetime are gone, and the world of letters and society is again, as always, influenced by the modes of innovators. But Baring's work needs none of these period atmospheres to sustain it. He was without the innocent – the naïve – view that the 'present' time has a closer touch upon truth than all earlier times. He seemed to suggest by his detachment that, even of his own time, which necessarily gave him his images of reality, the evanescent imperative, however profuse and powerful, would settle away, and the really meaningful would remain and, with it, literature. This – as his thought proposes – would be a regard for the wholeness of the human being. Rewarded as an artist by his own sense of life, which was essentially a tragic one, he saw and met the nature of its enduring wants, errors, and final resolution, as partaking of human meanings common to us all. The last thing that interested him was to turn inside out the obscurities of his own nature in terms meaningful only to himself. Neither was it his purpose to write social history, though his descriptions of his own natural worlds of privileged society and artistic circles are marvellous in their 'thrown-away' detail and atmosphere. Influential critics who have been trained to discern literary value only in neo-radical subject-matter and sympathy have possibly downgraded his work because of its predominantly upper-class material and tone. If judgement so naïvely derived is worth answering, the answer is simple:

Baring was merely faithful to life as he knew it, both in his aristocratic heritage and among all classes of the Russian people whom he loved at large. He sought through literary means to bring alive as clearly and simply as possible the eternal need, the desire for completion, of the whole being, and in doing so, to make language and design bestow a second life without end on the characters and places of his vision. He loved the idea of the individual instead of the mass of men, the conscious mind instead of the unconscious, others more than himself, a bare-boned style instead of one well fleshed out, and purity of communion resting on respect for the receptive intelligence which, he hoped, awaited his offer of shared experience.

The history of Maurice Baring's literary position is interesting, even if typical in many ways of the treatment of important writers in the period immediately following their death. Having achieved a uniform collected edition put out during the 'thirties by Heinemann he could not today see a volume of it remaining in print. Ten of his books were translated into French, and one – *Daphne Adeane* – went through twenty-three printings in the edition of the Librairie Stock. Others were translated into Italian, Dutch, Swedish, Hungarian, Czech, Spanish, and German, and several titles were included in the Tauchnitz editions. Serious studies of his work were made in England, France, Germany, and the Argentine. After reading *C*, André Maurois wrote that since reading Tolstoy, Proust and certain novels by E. M. Forster, he had not known such pleasure from a book. In 1950 Baring was given a stylish accolade by Max Beerbohm, who, calling him 'the brilliant, the greatly gifted Maurice Baring', added a deliciously pointed parody of his fictional manner to a new edition of *A Christmas Garland*. The memoirs of the time give us frequent references to him and his work, with delighted fondness for the one and critical respect for the other. And yet now [1970], only two of his books remain in print – the Home University Library edition of *An Outline of Russian Literature*, and a related treatise called *Landmarks of Russian Literature*, published in the University Paperbacks.

But there is a growing and active underground, so to speak, devoted to his work. Wherever in the world you find civilized company, you are certain to find people who collect his books, read them over many times, receive rewarding impressions of continuing life from his vision of humanity, and hand his pages on to others who have not yet discovered them. There are signs that a new generation has taken to reading and discussing him. The market for secondhand copies of his works continues, and of course the supply keeps dwindling. There are several people to whom I have long promised copies of *C* and for years I have not been able to find one. Those who borrow and read are always, I find, delighted by the experience of reading him, and are given appetite for more. A large collection of his letters is now being gathered and edited,

to be followed by a full biography. A general restoration of Maurice
Baring as a contributor to the continuing stream of literature in English
seems not far off.

### [ xix ]

So long as he was able, he lived in his small house at Rottingdean, by
the sea, facing across to France, surrounded by books and mementoes.
The house – like his small place in Chelsea – was, as Lady Diana Cooper
saw, 'arranged in the taste of his young days, with the same William
Morris wallpaper of spraying olive-branches, with water-colours of Italy
and Switzerland and a grand piano'. He loved to play and sing pieces
from the operas of Gilbert and Sullivan, though all by ear. He kept
in view 'faded photographs of Sarah Bernhardt, famous beauties,
Russians, Danes, literary Frenchmen and women'. In his house he had a
private chapel where Mass was frequently said. Friends were constantly
by him. Lady Diana came every week to see him – especially when during
the 1930s he began to suffer progressively from a malaise which had
occasioned many visits to doctors. Even before the 1914 war, when they
went out together and he was performing his fooleries to amuse her, Lady
Diana noticed that he did so with trembling hands – 'they always
trembled', she said. It must have been an ominous signal. For another
decade it did not seem to signify anything serious, but in the 1920s, as
he supped with her during the London season, when he 'never got any
older or laughed less or resisted the lighted candles at any grand London
ball', she noted that as 'we ate our quail and drank our champagne
together', his hands were still 'trembling', while 'he wrote verses on the
back of menu-cards'. They were verses to her – her beauty, grace, wit,
and beguiling presence.

In the mid-'thirties he was 'trembling more than he used to. He did not
speak of anxiety.' But one day as she was trying to help him into his
overcoat, he said to her, 'I'm becoming paralysed. I'm sure I am.' She
felt it to be true, she said later, and could not bring herself to exclaim,
'Nonsense!' He – everyone – knew the truth soon enough. He was
suffering from Parkinson's disease – *paralysis agitans*. At Rottingdean
with the help of a faithful nurse he spent his time in simple awareness of
each day. If he could no longer handle a pen, he could still dictate typed
notes, and if he could not easily move about, he had other ways of
knowing and continuing with life. 'Crocuses are out here in the garden,
so I'm told, and snowdrops, and the birds sing quite beautifully in the
early morning.' He could hear them, as he slept hardly at all during the
nights. 'Don't think I claim to have learnt anything at Eton,' he told
someone through a dictated note. 'I don't, except the art of enjoying life,
which is something.'

He enjoyed it most, perhaps, when Lady Diana was able to come to him at Rottingdean. She might find him sitting in the garden or, later, bedridden. 'He did not yearn for death,' she saw, 'though every day was racking and his nights were without rest. His valiance was never daunted.' One of his daily amusements was to listen to his budgerigar, whose name was Dempsey, as it sat on his head and chattered privately into his ear. Maurice Baring listened fixedly, and repeated to Lady Diana the 'perfect sense' which, he said, the unintelligible bird spoke. He translated for her from bird-talk 'whole lines in the Chinese tradition: "The pear-blossom floats on the sad waters where alone I sit. . . ."' It was an hilariously solemn extension of his earlier joy in parody, even, as she saw, how he 'was enduring with saintly fortitude a slow and merciless over-throw'.

During the month of July in what came to be called the 'invasion summer' of 1940, she saw him at Rottingdean and he was 'half the size he used to be'. Dempsey was still talking to him. Two weeks later she found him 'in high spirits today, owing, he said, to being in acute pain. . . . The visit passed in a flash. We both felt so gay, sipping sherry, and nibbling chocolates, and arguing about the Pope.' The bombing raids from Nazi Germany were now incessant. The home artillery on the high chalk cliffs near his house spoke night and day. In mid-August Lady Diana thought, in an exquisite and loving phrase, that 'he had best take his last patience' far removed from the explosions of war, and go to Scotland, to his kinswoman, Laura Lady Lovat, who was waiting to keep him at Beaufort Castle.

There went Lady Diana to see him for the last time, in the winter of 1942–43. It moved her dearly to see him in such 'patience' – a person 'so near to one's heart and still alive and alert'. She said he was 'playful all his life and to the end – playful as snow, weightless as it dances down. . . . Newman said there were angels in disguise; some get canonized, some, like Maurice, don't.' She saw that 'he was in the centre of the Faith he proclaimed'. So she left him, with what feeling we know through her words.

At Beaufort Castle, at Beauly, in Inverness-shire, he was cared for by the family of his cousin. It was well that he had moved, for his house at Rottingdean was later demolished by Nazi bombing.

Lady Lovat has left a memoir of that time. It is a further record of grace under difficulty. 'From all angles,' she wrote, 'life beat down on him and through him; he lived with a fierce intensity and a perfect resignation at one and the same time. . . . His thought at times seemed to travel as swiftly as light, nor could it always be expressed in speech. . . . Others have known Maurice's enormous erudition,' observed Lady Lovat, 'of the wit and brilliance of his conversation, but perhaps I knew him best in the last five and a half years of his life as a lover of small children, of unimportant and neglected people, of minor episodes in the potpourri of wartime life, of fantastic nonsense and laughter and gaiety, so far flung despite so much suffering that at times one followed him with difficulty. I also knew his stark understanding of sorrows great or small.' Another wrote of him as the 'incomparable friend' who had 'the grace of innocence', and another said 'In such fortitude as his there surely is something given that pays the ransom of the world.'

Once during his last vigil days, his cousin said to him:

'You are tired.'

He replied, 'I am never tired. Sit near me. It is so strange. I cannot say a prayer these days – not a single prayer.'

'So unnecessary,' replied Lady Lovat, '– so many are saying your name to God – night and day.'

'Tell them to *shout* it,' he exclaimed in the high comic style that did not desert him even in the hour.

In December 1945 he developed pneumonia. There were to be only a few more days. In his discomfort he took joy from listening to recordings of Beethoven's Seventh Symphony and a Schubert Quintet, and various poems of Heine, read out to him by his cousin. Though as always he remained reticent about great things those near him were moved by the sense of God's peace within him. A friend said to him, 'It is a miracle to us all that your inner peace is never disturbed'.

Having within him his knowledge of God's peace as 'a matter of tremendous fact', he answered, 'How could it be?'

He died an hour before midnight on 14 December 1945. The *Magnificat* was said over him immediately by his friend, an Air Force chaplain from a nearby RAF base.

His last book of favourite fragments was the anthology of literary extracts, with commentary, entitled *Have You Anything to Declare?* The last lines of that late book convey something of his sense of the life beyond his own mortal nature, and the expectation of his own humble and anonymous immortality. These are the lines:

*Et à l'heure de ma mort soyez le refuge de mon âme étonnée et recevez-la dans le sein de votre miséricorde.*

And in the hour of my death harbour my awestruck soul and receive me into the heart of Thy mercy.

PAUL HORGAN

Center for Advanced Studies
Wesleyan University, 1969.

# 1

## Childhood

(the first four chapters of *The Puppet Show of Memory*)

To bring us into the life of Maurice Baring, and let us watch the early development of the sensibility which was the main instrument of his later work, we can do no better than trace with him his earliest memories, from infancy and childhood. He was an intensely imaginative child – and he remained a responsively imaginative man and writer. Childhood for such an individual gave him his most memorable idea of happiness, and as he grew away from the occasions of this, he yet retained, as an artist, the child's acuity of feeling and observation – with the addition, not always happy, of mature meanings necessarily unknown to the child.

I have chosen the first four chapters of his autobiography with which to open this collection because it is both pleasurable and instructive to share in the dawning knowledge with which he would meet its later corollaries in life. Most of these, despite his gaiety and careless simplicity of expression, were only to be resolved in a melancholy view of human affairs – a view which would have been insupportable but for his ultimate spiritual resolution.

In a poem written in middle life he saw boyhood as a long dream of happiness, and leaving it he spoke of 'crossing the Stream'. We can only think of the Styx, and wonder why he equated the departure from boyhood with a crossing into the realm of the shades. But imaginative children live with burning intensity, as these chapters, and the early pages of C, show us; and if he was never so happy ever after, he brought with him into his works the primal sharpness of feeling and the immediacy of response to experience which gave him his power as an artist in maturity, who reaches us still with the sense of life complete.

# CHAPTER I

## *The Nursery*

WHEN PEOPLE SIT DOWN to write their recollections they exclaim with regret, 'If only I had kept a diary, what a rich store of material I should now have at my disposal!' I remember one of the masters at Eton telling me, when I was a boy, that if I wished to make a fortune when I was grown up, I had only to keep a detailed diary of every day of my life at Eton. He said the same thing to all the boys he knew, but I do not remember any boy of my generation taking his wise advice.

On the other hand, for the writer who wishes to recall past memories, the absence of diaries and notebooks has its compensations. Memory, as someone has said, is the greatest of artists. It eliminates the unessential, and chooses with careless skill the sights and the sounds and the episodes that are best worth remembering and recording. The first thing I can remember is a Christmas tree which I think celebrated the Christmas of 1876. It was at Shoreham in Kent, at a house belonging to Mr H. B. Mildmay, who married one of my mother's sisters. I was two years old, and I remember my Christmas present, a large bird with yellow and red plumage, which for a long time afterwards lived at the top of the nursery wardrobe. It was neither a bird of Paradise nor a pheasant; possibly only a somewhat flamboyant hen; but I loved it dearly, and it irradiated the nursery to me for at least two years.

The curtain then falls and rises again on the nursery of 37 Charles Street, Berkeley Square, London. The nursery epoch, which lasted till promotion to the schoolroom and lessons began, seems to children as long as a lifetime, just as houses and places seem to them infinitely large. The nursery was on the third floor of the house, and looked out on to the street. There was a small night-nursery next door to it, which had coloured pictures of St Petersburg on the wall.

I can remember the peculiar roar of London in those days; the four-wheelers and hansoms rattling on the macadam pavement through the fog, except when there was straw down in the street for some sick person;

and the various denizens of the streets, the lamplighter and the muffin-man; often a barrel-organ, constantly in summer a band, and sometimes a Punch and Judy. During the war, when the streets began to be darkened, but before the final complete darkness set in in 1917, London looked at night very much as it was in my childhood. But the strange rumbling noise had gone for ever. Sometimes on one of the houses opposite there used to be an heraldic hatchment. The nursery was inhabited by my brother Hugo and myself, our nurse, Hilly, and two nurserymaids, Grace Hetherington, and Annie. Grace was annexed by me; Annie by Hugo. Hilly had been nurse to my sisters and, I think, to my elder brothers too. She had the slightly weather-beaten but fresh agelessness of Nannies, and her most violent threat was: 'I'll bring my old shoe to you,' and one of her most frequent exclamations: 'Oh, you naughty boy, you very naughty boy!' The nursery had Landseer pictures in gilt frames, and on the chest of drawers between the two windows a mechanical toy of an entrancing description. It was a square box, one side of which was made of glass, and behind this glass curtain, on a small platform, a lady sat dressed in light blue silk at an open spinet; a dancing master, in a red silk doublet with a powdered wig and yellow satin knee-breeches, on one side of it, conducted, and in the foreground a little girl in short skirts of purple gauze covered with spangles stood ready to dance. When you wound up the toy, the lady played, the man conducted elegantly with an open score in one hand and a baton in the other, and the little girl pirouetted. It only played one short, melancholy, tinkling, but extremely refined dance-tune.

At one of the top windows of the house opposite, a little girl used to appear sometimes. Hugo and I used to exchange signals with her, and we called her Miss Rose. Our mute acquaintance went on for a long time, but we never saw her except across the street and at her window. We did not wish to see more of her. Nearer acquaintance would have marred the perfect romance of the relation.

There were two forms of light refreshment peculiar to the nursery, and probably to all nurseries: one was Albert biscuits, and the other toast-in-water. Children call for an Albert biscuit as men ask for a whisky-and-soda at a club, not from hunger, but as an adjunct to conversation and a break in monotony. At night, after we had gone to bed, we used often to ask monotonously and insistently for a drink of water. 'Hilly, I want a drink of water'; but this meant, not that one was thirsty, but that one was frightened and wanted to see a human being. All my brothers and sisters, I found out afterwards, had done the same thing in the same way, and for the same reason, but the tradition had been handed down quite unconsciously. I can't remember how the nursery epoch came to an end; it merges in my memory without any line of division, into the schoolroom period; but the first visits in the country certainly belonged to the nursery epoch.

## The Nursery

We used to go in the summer to Coombe Cottage, near Malden, an ivy-covered, red-brick house, with a tower at one end, a cool oak hall and staircase, a drawing-room full of water-colours, a room next to it full of books, with a drawing-table and painting materials ready, and a long dining-room, of which the narrow end was a sitting-room, and had a verandah looking out on to the garden. There was also a kitchen garden, lawns, a dairy, a gardener, Mr Baker, who made nosegays, a deaf-and-dumb under-gardener who spoke on his fingers, a farmyard, and a duck-pond into which I remember falling.

Coombe was an enchanted spot for us. My recollection of it is that of a place where it was always summer and where the smell of summer and the sounds of summer evening used to make the night-nursery a fairy place; and sometimes in the morning, red-coated soldiers used to march past playing 'The Girl I left behind me', with a band of drums and fifes. The uniforms of the soldiers were as bright as the poppies in the field, and that particular tune made a lasting impression on me. I never forgot it. I can remember losing my first front tooth at Coombe by tying it on to a thread and slamming the door, and I can remember my sisters singing, 'Where are you going to, my pretty Maid?' one of them acting the milkmaid, with a wastepaper basket under her arm for a pail. Best of all, I remember the garden, the roses, the fruit, trying to put salt on a bird's tail for the first time, and the wonderful games in the hayfields.

We are probably all of us privileged at least once or twice in our lives to experience the indescribable witchery of a perfect summer night, when time seems to stand still, the world becomes unsubstantial, and Nature is steeped in music and silver light, quivering shadows and mysterious sound, when such a pitch of beauty and glamour and mystery is achieved by the darkness, the landscape, the birds, the insects, the trees and the shadows, and perhaps the moon or even one star, that one would like to say to the fleeting moment what Faust challenged and defied the devil to compel him to cry out: 'Verweile doch, du bist so schön!'

It is the moment that the great poets have sometimes caught and made permanent for us by their prodigious conjury: Shakespeare, in the end of the *Merchant of Venice*, when Lorenzo and Jessica let the sounds of music creep into their ears, and wonder at patines of bright gold in the floor of heaven; Keats, when he wished to cease upon the midnight with no pain; Musset, in the 'Nuit de Mai'; Victor Hugo, when, on their lovely brief and fatal bridal night, Hernani and Doña Sol fancy in the moonlight that sleeping Nature is watching amorously over them; and the musicians speak this magic with an even greater certainty, without the need of words: Beethoven, in his Sonata; Chopin, again and again; Schumann, in his lyrics, especially 'Frühlingsnacht'; Schubert, in his 'Serenade'.

I have known many such nights: the dark nights of Central Russia

57

before the harvest ends, when the watchman's rattle punctuates and intensifies the huge silence, and a far-off stamping dance rhythm and a bleating accordion outdo Shakespeare and Schubert in magic; June nights in Florence, when you couldn't see the grass for fireflies, and the croaking of frogs made a divine orchestra; or in Venice, on the glassy lagoon, when streaks of red still hung in the west; May nights by the Neckar at Heidelberg, loud with the jubilee of nightingales and aromatic with lilac; a twilight in May at Arundel Park, when large trees, dim lawns, and antlered shapes seemed to be part of a fairy revel; and nights in South Devon, when the full September moon made the garden and the ilex tree as unreal as Prospero's island.

But I never in my whole life felt the spell so acutely as in the summer evenings in the night nursery at Coombe Cottage, when we went to bed by daylight and lay in our cots guessing at the pattern on the wall, to wake up later when it was dark, half conscious of the summer scents outside, and of a bird's song in the darkness. The intense magic of that moment I have never quite recaptured, except when reading Keats' 'Ode to the Nightingale' for the first time, when the door on to the past was opened wide once more and the old vision and the strange sense of awe, unreality, and enchantment returned.

But to go back to nursery life. Our London life followed the ritual, I suppose, of most nurseries. In the morning after our breakfast we went down, washed and scrubbed and starched, into the dining-room, where breakfast was at nine, and kissed our father before he drove to the city in a phaeton, and played at the end of the dining-room round a pedestalled bust of one of the Popes. Then a walk in the Park, and sometimes as a treat a walk in the streets, and possibly a visit to Cremer's, the toy-shop in Bond Street. Hugo and I detested the Park, and the only moment of real excitement I remember was when one day Hilly told me not to go near the flower-beds, and I climbed over the little railing and picked a towering hyacinth. Police intervention was immediately threatened, and I think a policeman actually did remonstrate; but although I felt for some hours a pariah and an outcast, there was none the less an after-taste of triumph in the tears; attrition, perhaps, but no contrition.

When we got to be a little older . . . older than what? I don't know . . . but there came our moment when we joined our sisters every morning to say our prayers in my mother's bedroom, every day before breakfast. They were short and simple prayers – the 'Our Father' and one other short prayer. Nevertheless, for years the 'Our Father' was to me a mysterious and unintelligible formula, all the more so, as I said it entirely by the sound, and not at all by the sense, thinking that 'Whichartinheaven' was one word and 'Thykingdomcome' another. I never asked what it meant. I think in some dim way I felt that, could I understand it, something of its value as an invocation would be lost or diminished. I also remember learning at a very early age the hymn, 'There is a green hill far away', and finding it puzzling. I took it for granted that most green hills had city walls round them, though this particular one hadn't. Besides going to Coombe we went at the end of the summer to Devonshire, to Membland, near the villages of Noss Mayo, and Newton, and not far from the river Yealm, an arm of the sea. It was when getting ready for the first of these journeys that I remember, while I was being dressed in the nursery, my father's servant, Mr Deacon, came up to the nursery and asked me whether I would like a ticket. He then gave me a beautiful green ticket with a round hole in it. I asked him what one could do with it, and he said, 'In return for that ticket you can get Bath buns, Banbury cakes, jam-rolls, crackers, and pork sausages.' In the bustle of departure I lost it. Paddington Station resounded with the desperate cries of the bereaved ticket-holder. In vain I was given half a white first-class ticket. In vain Mr Bullock, the guard, offered every other kind of ticket. It was not the same thing. That ticket, with the round hole, had conjured up visions of wonderful possibilities and fantastic exchanges. Sausages and Banbury cakes and Bath buns (all of them magic things), I knew, would be forthcoming to no other ticket. The loss was irreparable. I remember thinking the grown-up people so utterly wanting in understanding when they said: 'A ticket? Of course, he can have a ticket. Here's a ticket for the dear little boy.' As if that white ticket was anything like the unique passport to gifts new and unheard of, anything like that real green ticket with the round hole in it. At the end of one of these journeys, at Kingsbridge Road, the train ran off the line. We were in a saloon carriage, and I remember the accident being attributed to that fact by my mother's maid, who said saloon carriages were always unsafe. It turned out to be an enjoyable accident, and we all got out and I was given an orange.

Mr Bullock, the guard, was a great friend of all of us children; and our chief pleasure was to ask him a riddle: 'Why is it dangerous to go out in the spring?' I will leave it to the reader to guess the answer, with merely this as a guide, that the first part of the answer to the riddle is 'Because the hedges are shooting,' and the second part of the answer is peculiarly appropriate to Mr Bullock. I am afraid Mr Bullock never saw why, although no doubt he enjoyed the riddle.

I have already said that I cannot fix any line of division between the nursery and the schoolroom epochs, but before I get on to the subject of the schoolroom I will record a few things which must have belonged to the pre-schoolroom period.

One incident which stands out clearly in my mind is that of the fifty-shilling train. There were at that time in London two toy-shops called Cremer. One was in New Bond Street, No. 27, I think, near Tessier's, the jeweller; another in Regent Street, somewhere between Liberty's and Piccadilly Circus.

In the window of the Regent Street shop there was a long train with people in it, and it was labelled fifty shillings. In the year 1921 it is only a small mechanical train that can be bought for fifty shillings. I can't remember whether I had reached the schoolroom when this happened, but I know I still wore a frock and had not yet reached the dignity of trousers. I used constantly to ask to go and look at this shop window and gaze at the fifty-shilling train, which seemed first to be miraculous for its size, and, secondly, for its price. Who in the world could have fifty shillings all at once?

I never went so far as thinking it was possible to possess that train; but I used to wonder whether there were people in the world who could store up fifty shillings. We were each of us given sixpence every Saturday, but it was always spent at once, nor could I calculate or even conceive how long it would take to save enough sixpences to make fifty shillings.

One evening, when we were at Coombe, in the summer, I was sent for to the drawing-room and then told to go into the dining-room. I opened the door, and there, on the floor, was the fifty-shilling train. If a fairy had flown into the room and lifted me to the ceiling I could not have thought a fact more miraculous. From that moment I knew for certain that miracles could happen and do happen, and subsequent experience has confirmed the belief. Alas! the funnel of the engine was soon broken, and Mr Toombs, the carpenter, was said to be able to mend it, and I looked forward to another miracle. He did, but in a way which was hardly satisfactory considered as a miracle, although perfect for practical usage. He turned on a lathe a solid funnel made of black wood, but not hollow, and he stuck it in where the funnel ought to be. I pretended I was satisfied, but my private belief was that Mr Toombs didn't know how to make funnels.

Another thing which happened when I was six years old was a visit to the Drury Lane pantomime, which was *Mother Goose*. This, of course, with a transformation scene with a large fairy with moving emerald butterfly-like wings and Arthur Roberts who, when playing a trumpet, spat out all his teeth on to the floor as if they were an encumbrance, was an ecstasy beyond words.

Another event almost more exciting was the arrival of a doll's house. I played with dolls, but not as girls do, mothering them and dressing them. Mine were little tiny dolls, and could not be dressed or undressed, and they were used as puppets. I made them open Parliament, act plays and stories, and most frequently take the part of the French Merovingian kings. This was at the beginning of the schoolroom period, and the dolls were called Chilpéric, Ermengarde, Clotilde, Blanche de Castille, Frédégonde, Brunehaut, Galswinthe, and Pépin le Bref, and other names belonging to the same remote period of history. One day I was told that a doll's house was coming. I couldn't sleep for excitement, and Hilly,

Grace, and Annie gravely held a conclave one night when I was in bed and supposed to be asleep, over their supper, and said that so exciting a thing as a doll's house ought not to be allowed me. It would ruin my health. I feigned deep sleep, and the next day pretended to have lost all interest in dolls' houses, but when it came, all its furniture was taken out, put on the floor, and arranged in two long rows, with a throne at one end, to enable Chilpéric and Frédégonde to open Parliament.

One year in London I actually saw Queen Victoria drive to the opening of Parliament in a gilded coach with a little crown perched on her head and an ermine tippet. It was not quite a satisfactory crown, but still it was a crown, and the coach had the authentic Cinderella quality.

To go back to the dolls for a moment. I used to go to Membland sometimes for Easter with my father and mother when the rest of the family stayed in London, and Margaret used to write me letters from the dolls, beginning 'Cher Papa' and ending 'Ermengarde' or 'Chilpéric', as the case might be. These letters used to cover me with confusion and mortification before the grown-up people, as I kept it a secret that I ever played with dolls, knowing it to be thought rather eccentric, and liable to be misunderstood, especially when there were other boys about, which there were.

Of course, in the nursery, Hugo and I had endless games of pretending, especially during bath-time (baths were hip-baths), and I remember Hugo refusing to have his bath because when we were playing at fishes I seized the shark's part and wouldn't let him be a shark. 'Hilly,' he wailed, 'I *will* be a shark.' But no, I wouldn't hear of it, and he had to be a whale, which the shark, so I said, easily mastered.

Promotion to the schoolroom meant lessons and luncheon downstairs. The schoolroom was inhabited by my three sisters, Elizabeth, Margaret, and Susan, and ruled over by the French governess, Chérie. I thought Chérie the most beautiful, the cleverest, and altogether the most wonderful person in the world. My earliest recollection of her almost magical powers was when she took a lot of coloured silks and put them behind a piece of glass and said this was *une vision*. I believed there was nothing she didn't know and nothing she couldn't do. I was also convinced that one day I would marry her. This dream was sadly marred by the conduct of my sister Elizabeth. Elizabeth was the eldest, Margaret the second, and Susan the third, of my sisters. I firmly believed in fairies. Elizabeth and Margaret fostered the belief by talking a great deal about their powers as fairies, and Elizabeth said she was Queen of the fairies. One day she said: 'Just as you are going to be married to Chérie, and when you are in church, I will turn you into a frog'. This was said in the schoolroom in London. The schoolroom was on the floor over the nursery. No sooner had Elizabeth made this ominous remark when I ran to the door and howled in a manner which penetrated the whole house from the housemaids' rooms upstairs to the housekeeper's room in the basement. Screams and yells startled the whole house. Hilly came rushing from the nursery; Chérie came from her bedroom, where she had been doing some sewing; Dimmock, my mother's maid, whom we called D., came downstairs, saying: 'Well, I never'; Sheppy, the housekeeper, peered upwards from the subterranean housekeeper's room; and, lastly, my mother came from the drawing-room. The cause of the crisis was explained by me through sobs. 'She says' . . . sob, sob, yell . . . 'that she's a fairy' . . . sob, sob . . . 'and that she'll turn me into a frog' . . . sob, sob . . . 'when I marry Chérie. . . .' All attempts to calm me were in vain. Elizabeth was then appealed to, and the whole house in chorus said to her, 'Say you're not a fairy.' But Elizabeth became marble-constant. She said, 'How can I say I'm not a fairy when I am one?' A statement which I felt to be all too true and well founded. More sobs and yells. Universal indignation against Elizabeth. My paroxysm was merely increased by all the efforts everyone made to soothe me. Elizabeth was cajoled, persuaded, argued with, bribed, threatened, exhorted, blamed, anathematised, entreated, appealed to, implored, but all in vain. She would not budge from her position, which was that she *was* a fairy.

The drama proceeded. Nothing stopped the stream of convulsive sobs, the flood of anguish – not all Chérie's own assurances that the wedding would be allowed to take place.

Elizabeth was taken downstairs to be reasoned with, and after an hour and a half's argument, and not before she had been first heavily bribed with promises and then sent to bed, she finally consented to compromise. She said, as a final concession, 'I'll say I'm not a fairy, but I am'. When this concession was wrung from her the whole relieved household rushed up to tell me the good news that Elizabeth had said she was not a fairy. The moment I heard the news my tears ceased, and perfect serenity was restored. But although Elizabeth capitulated, Margaret was firmer, and she continued to mutter (like Galileo) for the rest of the afternoon, 'But *I* am a fairy all the same.'

Margaret was the exciting element in the schoolroom. She was often naughty, and I remember her looking through the schoolroom window at Coombe, while I was doing lessons with Chérie, and making faces. Chérie said to her one day: 'Vous feriez rougir un régiment'. Elizabeth was pleasantly frivolous, and Susan was motherly and sensible, and supposed to be the image of her father, but Margaret was dramatic and imaginative, and invincibly obstinate.

She knew that for Chérie's sake I didn't like admitting that the English had ever defeated the French in battle, so every now and then she would roll out lists of battles fought by the English against the French and won, beginning with Crécy, Poitiers, getting to Agincourt with a crescendo, and ending up in a tremendous climax with Waterloo. To which I used to retort with a battle called Bouvines, won by Philippe Auguste, in some most obscure period over one of the Plantagenet kings, and with Fontenoy. I felt them both to be poor retorts.

Another invention of Margaret's was a mysterious Princess called Louiseaunt, who often came to see her, but as it happened always when we were out. If we suddenly came into the room, Margaret would say, 'What a pity! Louiseaunt has just been here. She'll be so sorry to have missed you.' And try as we would, we always just missed Louiseaunt.

If we went out without Margaret, Louiseaunt was sure to come that day. We constantly just arrived as Louiseaunt had left, and the inability ever to hit off Louiseaunt's precise visiting hours was a lasting exasperation.

Another powerful weapon of Margaret's was recitation. She used to recite in English and in French, and in both languages the effect on me was a purge of pity and terror. I minded most 'Lord Ullin's Daughter', declaimed with melodramatic gesture, and nearly as much a passage from *Hernani*, beginning –

>'Monts d'Aragon! Galice! Estramadoure!
>Oh! Je porte malheur à tout ce qui m'entoure!'

which she recited, rolling her eyes in a menacing attitude.

'Lord Ullin's Daughter', said with the help of Susan, whose rendering had something reassuringly comfortable and homely about it – Susan couldn't say her 'r's', and pronounced them like 'w's' – in contradistinction to Margaret's sombre and vehement violence, did a little to mitigate the effect, but none the less it frightened me so much that it had to be stopped. Hugo was not yet in the schoolroom then.

Lessons in London began soon after breakfast. They were conducted by Chérie and by an English governess, Mrs Christie, who used to arrive in a four-wheeler, always the same one, from Kentish Town, and teach us English, Arithmetic, and Latin. Mrs Christie was like the pictures of Thackeray, with spectacles, white bandeaux, and a black gown. During lessons she used to knit. She was in permanent mourning, and we knew we must never ask to learn 'Casabianca', as her little boy who had died had learnt it. She used to arrive with a parcel of books from the London Library, done up in a leather strap. She was the first of a long line of teachers who failed to teach me Arithmetic. She used to stay the whole morning, or sometimes only part of it. During lessons she used to have a small collation, a glass of claret, and a water biscuit. She also taught other families.

At Coombe the schoolroom looked out on the lawn, a long, flat lawn which went down by steps on a lower lawn, at the bottom of which we had our own gardens and where there was a summer-house. I remember sitting in the schoolroom next to Chérie while, with a large knitting needle, she pointed out the words *pain* and *vin* written large in a copy-book, with a picture of a bottle of red wine and a picture of a piece of bread, to show what the words meant, while Margaret was copying out Clarence's dream in a copy-book and murmuring something about skulls, and all the time through the window framed with clematis came the sound, the magic sound of the mowing-machine, the noise of bees, and a smell of summer, tea-roses and of hayfields.

On certain days of the week Mademoiselle Ida Henry used to come and give us music lessons. Our house was saturated with an atmosphere of music. My mother played the violin and was a fine concertina player, and almost before I could walk I had violin lessons from no less a person than Mr Ries. Until I was three I was called *Strad*, and I think my mother cherished the dream that I would be a violinist, but I showed no aptitude.

My first music lesson I received from Mademoiselle Ida over Stanley Lucas' music shop in Bond Street. I was alone in London with my mother and father, one November, and I suppose about six. Mademoiselle Ida was very encouraging, and – unduly, as it turned out – optimistic, and said: 'Il a de mains faites pour jouer du piano,' and soon my *morceau* was Diabelli's duets. While I was learning Diabelli's duets, Susan was learning a Fantasia by Mozart, which I envied without malice. It had one particular little run in it which I learnt to play with one finger. One day I played this downstairs in the drawing-room. A few days later Mademoiselle Ida came to luncheon, and my mother said: 'Play that little bar out of the Mozart to Mademoiselle Ida.' I was aghast, feeling certain, and quite rightly, that Mademoiselle Ida would resent my having encroached on a more advanced *morceau*, and indeed, as it became clear to her what the bar in question was, she at once said: 'Je ne veux pas que tu te mêles des morceaux des autres.' That was what I had feared. My mother was quite unconscious of the solecism that she was committing, and pressed me to play it. Finally I hummed the tune, which satisfied both parties.

I never liked music lessons then or ever afterwards, but I enjoyed Mademoiselle Ida's conversation and company almost more than anything. Every word she ever said was treasured. One day she said to Mrs Christie: 'Bonjour, Madame Christé. J'ai bien mal à la tête.' 'Je suis très fâchée de le savoir, Mademoiselle Henri,' said Mrs Christie in icy tones, and this little dialogue was not destined ever to be forgotten by any of us. We used often afterwards to enact the scene.

Elizabeth and Susan learnt the piano, and Margaret was taught the violin by Herr Ludwig, a severe German master. John, my eldest brother, was an accomplished pianist and organist; Everard, my third brother, played the piccolo. Cecil sang, and my mother was always bewailing that he had not learnt music at Eton, because his house-master said it would be more useful for him to learn how to shoe a horse. This, alas! did not prove to be the case, as he has seldom since had the opportunity of making use of his skill as a blacksmith. The brothers were all at Eton when I first went into the schoolroom, but they often used to visit us in the evening at tea-time, and sometimes they used to listen when Chérie read aloud after tea.

Echoes of the popular songs of the day reached both the nursery and the schoolroom, and the first I can remember the tunes of are: 'Pop goes the Weasel', which used to be sung to me in the nursery; 'Tommy, make room for your Uncle'; 'My Grandfather's Clock'; 'Little Buttercup' from *Pinafore*, which used to be played on a musical box; 'Oh where and oh where is my little wee Dog?' with its haunting refrain.

Later we used to sing in chorus and dancing a *pas de trois*, a song from a Gaiety burlesque:

> 'We'll never come back any more, boys,
> We'll never come back any more.'

And, later still, someone brought back to London for Christmas the unforgettable tune of 'Two Lovely Black Eyes', which in after-life I heard all over the world – on the lagoon of Venice and in the villages of Mongolia.

One day after luncheon – on Sunday – John played the 'Two Grenadiers' at the pianoforte, and I remember the experience being thrilling, if a little alarming, but a revelation, and a first introduction into the world of music.

## CHAPTER II

# *The Nursery and the Schoolroom*

LIFE WAS DIVIDED between London from January to August, then Devonshire till after Christmas. In the nursery and the early part of the schoolroom period we used to go to Coombe in the summer. Coombe seemed to be inextricably interwoven with London and parallel to it; and I remember dinner-parties happening, and a Hungarian band playing on the lawn, unless I have dreamt that. But there came a time, I think I must have been six or seven, when Coombe was sold, and we went there no more, and life was confined to Membland and Charles Street. London in the winter, and summer in Devonshire, with sometimes brief visits to Devonshire at Easter and Whitsuntide, and brief visits to London in November, when my father and mother went up by themselves.

It is not any false illusion or the glamour of the past that makes the whole of that period of life until school-time was reached seem like fairyland. I thought so at the time, and grown-up people who came to Coombe and Membland felt, I think, that they had come to a place of rare and radiant happiness.

But I will begin with London first.

This was the routine of life. We all had breakfast at nine downstairs. I remember asking how old my father was, and the answer was fifty-three. As he was born in 1828 and I was born in 1874, I must have been seven years old at the time of this question. I always thought of my father as fifty-three years old. My brothers John, Cecil, and Everard were at Eton at Warre's House, and Hugo was five years old and still in the nursery.

After breakfast, at about a quarter to ten, my father drove to the City, and he never came home to luncheon except on Saturdays.

We went for a walk with Chérie, and after this lessons lasted from eleven, I think, till two, in the schoolroom.

The schoolroom was a long room with three windows looking out on to the street. There was a cottage pianoforte at an angle, and in the niche of one of the windows a small table, where Chérie used to sit and read the *Daily News* in the morning. We each of us had a cupboard for our toys, and there were some tall bookcases, containing all the schoolroom books, Noel and Chapsal's Grammar, and many comfortable, shabby books of fairy-tales. We each of us had a black writing-desk, with a wooden seat attached to it, in which we kept our copybooks, and at which we did our work. A long table ran right down the middle of our room, where we did our lessons, either when everyone did them together, collectively, with Chérie, who sat at the head of the table, or with Mrs Christie, who sat at one side of the table at the farther end.

At two o'clock we all came down to luncheon, and as my mother was at home to luncheon every day, stray people used to drop in, and that was a great excitement, as the guests used to be discussed for hours afterwards in the schoolroom.

Lady Dorothy Nevill, who lived in the same street, used often to come to luncheon and make paper boats for me. She used also to shock me by her frank expression of Tory principle, not to say prejudice, as we were staunch Liberals, and Lady Dorothy used to say that Mr Gladstone was a dreadful man.

Mr Alfred Montgomery was a luncheon visitor, and one day Bobby Spencer, who was afterwards to be Margaret's husband, was subjected to a rather sharp schoolroom criticism owing to the height of his collars. I sometimes used to embarrass Chérie by sudden interpellations. One day, when she had refused a dish, I said: 'Prends-en, Chérie, toi qui es si gourmande.' Another day at luncheon a visitor called Colonel Edgecombe bet my mother a pound there would be war with France within three years. I expect he forgot the bet, but I never did. Another time my mother asked Mademoiselle Ida what was the most difficult piece that existed for the pianoforte, and Mademoiselle Ida said Liszt's 'Spinnelied'. My mother bet her a pound she would learn it in a month's time (and she did).

There were two courses at luncheon, some meat and a sweet, and then cheese, and we were not allowed to have the sweet unless we had the meat first, but we could always have two helpings if we liked. After luncheon we went for another walk. At five there were more lessons, and then schoolroom tea, presided over by Chérie, and after that various games and occupations, and sometimes a visit to the drawing-room.

There were two drawing-rooms downstairs, a front drawing-room with three windows looking out on to the street, and a back drawing-room at right angles to it. The drawing-rooms had a faded green silk on the walls. Over the chimney-piece there was a fine picture by Cuyp, which years later I saw in a private house in the Bois de Boulogne. The room was full of flowers and green Sèvres china. In the back drawing-room there was a grand pianoforte and some bookcases, and beyond that a room called the gilding-room, a kind of workshop where my mother did gilding. I only once saw a part of the operation, which consisted of making size. Later on this room became the organ room and was enlarged. The drawing-room led to a small landing and a short staircase to the front hall. On the landing wall there was an enormous picture of Venice, by Birket Foster, and from this landing, when there was a dinner-party, we used to peer through the banisters and watch the guests arriving. We were especially forbidden to slide down the banisters, as my mother used to tell us that when she was a little girl she had slid down the banisters and had a terrible fall which had cut open her throat, so that when you put a spoon in her mouth it came out again through her throat. When Hugo, the last of the family to be told this story, heard it, he said, 'Did you die?' And my mother was obliged to say that she did not.

On the ground floor was a room looking out into the street, called the library, but it only possessed two bookcases let into Louis XV white walls, and this led into the dining-room, beyond which was my father's dressing-room, where, when we were quite small, we would watch him shave in the morning.

Dinner downstairs was at eight, and when we were small I was often allowed to go down to the beginning of dinner and draw at the dinner-table on a piece of paper, and the girls used to come down to dessert, bringing an occupation such as needlework. We were always supposed to have an occupation when we were downstairs, and I remember Susan, being asked by Chérie what needlework she was going to take to the dining-room, saying: 'Mon bas, ma chemise, et ma petite wobe, Chéwie.'

On Saturday afternoons we often had a treat, and went to the German Reed's entertainment and Corney Grain, or to Maskelyne and Cook, and Hengler's Circus, and on Sundays we often went to the Zoo, or drove down to Coombe when Coombe existed.

Lessons were in the hands of Chérie and Mrs Christie. Chérie taught me to read and write in French, French history out of Lamé Fleury, not without arguments on my part to learn it from the bigger grown-up book of Guizot, and French poetry. Every day began with a hideous ordeal called 'La Page d'Ecriture'. Chérie would write a phrase in enormous letters in a beautiful copy-book handwriting on the top line of the copy-book, and we had to copy the sentence on every other line, with a quill pen. Mrs Christie, besides struggling with my arithmetic, used to teach us English literature, and make us learn passages from Shakespeare by heart, which were quite unintelligible to me, and passages from Byron, Walter Scott, Campbell, and Southey, and various pieces from the *Children's Garland* and Macaulay's *Lays of Ancient Rome*. I enjoyed the latter whole-heartedly.

Sometimes Mrs Christie and Chérie used to have conversations across the children, as it were, during lessons. I remember Mrs Christie saying to Chérie while I was doing my lessons by Chérie's side one day: 'That child will give you more trouble than all the others.'

I liked history lessons, especially Lamé Fleury's French history and mythology; and in Lamé Fleury's French history the favourite chapter was that beginning: 'Jean II dit le bon commença son règne par un assassinat.' The first book I read with Mrs Christie was called *Little Willie*, and described the building of a house, an enchanting book. I did not like any of the English poetry we read, not understanding how by any stretch of the imagination it could be called poetry, as Shakespeare blank verse seemed to be a complicated form of prose full of uncouth words; what we learnt being Clarence's dream, King Henry IV's battle speeches, which made me most uncomfortable for Chérie's sake by their anti-French tone, and passages from *Childe Harold*, which I also found difficult to understand. The only poems I remember liking, which were revealed by Mrs Christie, were Milton's *L'Allegro* and *Penseroso*, which I copied out in a book as soon as I could write. One day she read me out Gray's *Elegy* and I was greatly impressed. 'That is,' she said, 'the most beautiful Elegy in the language.' 'Is it the most beautiful poem in the language?' I asked, rather disappointed at the qualification, and hankering for an absolute judgment. 'It's the most beautiful *Elegy* in the language,' she said, and I had to be content with that.

I don't want to give the impression that we, any of us, disliked Mrs Christie's lessons in English literature. On the contrary, we enjoyed them, and I am grateful for them till this day. She taught us nothing soppy nor second-rate. The piece of her repertoire I most enjoyed, almost best, was a fable by Gay called 'The Fox at the Point of Death'. She was always willing to explain things, and took for granted that when we didn't ask we knew. This was not always the case. One of the pieces I learnt by heart was Shelley's 'Arethusa', the sound of which fascinated me. But I had not the remotest idea that it was about a river. The poem begins, as it will be remembered:

> Arethusa arose
> From her couch of snows
> In the Acroceraunian mountains.

For years I thought 'Acroceraunian' was a kind of pin-cushion.

Mrs Christie had a passion for Sir Walter Scott and for the Waverley Novels. 'You can't help,' she said, 'liking any King of England that Sir Walter Scott has written about.' She instilled into us a longing to read Sir Walter Scott by promising that we should read them when we were older. One of the most interesting discussions to me was that between Chérie and Mrs Christie as to what English books the girls should be allowed to read in the country. Mrs Christie told, to illustrate a point, the following story. A French lady had once come across a French translation of an English novel, and seeing it was an English novel had at once given it to her daughter to read, as she said, of course, any English novel was fit for the *jeune personne*. The novel was called *Les Papillons de Nuit*. 'And what do you think that was?' said Mrs Christie. '*Moths*, by Ouida!'

The first poem that really moved me was not shown me by Mrs Christie, but by Mantle, the maid who looked after the girls. It was Mrs Hemans': 'Oh, call my Brother back to me, I cannot play alone'. This poem made me sob. I still think it is a beautiful and profoundly moving poem. Besides English, Mrs Christie used to teach us Latin. I had my first Latin lesson the day after my eighth birthday. This is how it began: 'Supposing,' said Mrs Christie, 'you knocked at the door and the person inside said, "Who's there?" What would you say?' I thought a little, and then half-unconsciously said, 'I.' 'Then,' said Mrs Christie, 'that shows you have a natural gift for grammar.' She explained that I ought reasonably to have said 'Me.' Why I said 'I,' I cannot think. I had no notion what her question was aiming at, and I feel certain I should have said 'Me' in real life. The good grammar was quite unintentional.

As for arithmetic, it was an unmixed pain, and there was an arithmetic book called *Ibbister* which represented to me the final expression of what was loathsome. One day in a passion with Chérie I searched my mind for the most scathing insult I could think of, and then cried out, 'Vieille Ibbister'.

I learnt to read very quickly, in French first. In the nursery Grace and Annie read me *Grimm's Fairy Tales* till they were hoarse, and as soon as I could read myself I devoured any book of fairy-tales within reach, and a great many other books; but I was not precocious in reading, and found grown-up books impossible to understand. One of my favourite books later was *The Crofton Boys*, which Mrs Christie gave me on 6th November 1883, as a 'prize for successful card-playing'. It is very difficult for me to understand now how a child could have enjoyed the intensely sermonizing tone of this book, but I certainly did enjoy it.

I remember another book called *Romance*, or *Chivalry and Romance*. In it there was a story of a damsel who was really a fairy, and a bad fairy at that, who went into a cathedral in the guise of a beautiful princess, and when the bell rang at the Elevation of the Host, changed into her true shape and vanished. I consulted Mrs Christie as to what the Elevation of the Host meant, and she gave me a clear account of what Transubstantiation meant, and she told me about Henry VIII, the Defender of the Faith, and the Reformation, and made no comment on the truth or untruth of the dogma. Transubstantiation seemed to me the most natural thing in the world, as it always does to children, and I privately made up my mind that on that point the Reformers must have been mistaken. One day Chérie said for every *devoir* I did, and for every time I wasn't naughty, I should be given a counter, and if I got twenty counters in three days I should get a prize. I got the twenty counters and sallied off to Hatchard's to get the prize. I chose a book called *The Prince of the Hundred Soups* because of its cover. It was by Vernon Lee, an Italian puppet-show in narrative, about a Doge who had to eat a particular kind of soup every day for a hundred days. It is a delightful story, and I revelled in it. On the title-page it was said that the book was by the author of *Belcaro*. I resolved to get *Belcaro* some day; *Belcaro* sounded a most promising name, rich in possible romance and adventure, and I saved up my money for the purpose. When, after weeks, I had amassed the necessary six shillings, I went back to Hatchard's and bought *Belcaro*. Alas, it was an aesthetic treatise of the stiffest and driest and most grown-up kind. Years afterwards I told Vernon Lee this story, and she promised to write me another story instead of *Belcaro*, like *The Prince of the Hundred Soups*. The first book I read to myself was *Alice in Wonderland*, which John gave to me. Another book I remember enjoying very much was *The King of the Golden River*, by Ruskin.

I enjoyed my French lessons infinitely more than my English ones. French poetry seemed to be the real thing, quite different from the prosaic English blank verse, except La Fontaine's *Fables*, which, although sometimes amusing, seemed to be almost as prosy as Shakespeare. They had to be learnt by heart, nevertheless. They seemed to be in the same relation to other poems, Victor Hugo's 'Napoléon II' and 'Dans L'Alcôve sombre', which I thought quite enchanting, as meat was to pudding at luncheon, and I was not allowed to indulge in poetry until I had done my fable, but not without much argument. I sometimes overbore Chérie's will, but she more often got her way by saying: 'Tu as toujours voulu écrire avec un stylo avant de savoir écrire avec une plume.' I learnt a great many French poems by heart, and made sometimes startling use of the vocabulary. One day at luncheon I said to Chérie before the assembled company: 'Chérie, comme ton front est nubile!' the word *nubile* having been applied by the poet, Delavigne, to Joan of Arc.

The first French poem which really fired my imagination was a passage from *Les Enfants d'Édouard*, a play by the same poet, in which one of the little princes tells a dream, which Margaret used to recite in blood-curdling tones, and his brother, the Duke of York, answers lyrically something about the sunset on the Thames.[1] Those lines fired my imagination as nothing else did. We once acted a scene from this play, Margaret and I playing the two brothers, and Susan the tearful and widowed queen and mother, and Hugo as a beefeater, who had to bawl at the top of his voice: 'Reine, retirez-vous!' when the queen's sobs became excessive,

---

[1] 'Libre, je rends visite à la terre, aux étoiles;
Sur la Tamise en feu je suis ces blanches voiles.'
*Les Enfants d'Édouard*, Act III. Sc. 1.
CASIMIR DELAVIGNE.    [M.B.]

and indeed in Susan's rendering there was nothing wanting in the way of sobs, as she was a facile weeper, and Margaret used to call her 'Madame la Pluie'. Indeed there was a legend in the schoolroom that the decline of Louis XIV, King of France, moved her to tears, and being asked why she was crying, she sobbed out the words: 'la vieillesse du grand Woi'.

As far back as I remember we used to act plays in French. The first one performed in the back drawing-room in Charles Street was called *Comme on fait son lit on se couche*, and I played some part in it which I afterwards almost regretted, as whenever a visitor came to luncheon I was asked to say a particular phrase out of it, and generally refused. This was not either from obstinacy or naughtiness; it was simply to spare my mother humiliation. I was sure grown-up people could not help thinking the performance inadequate and trifling. I was simply covered with prospective shame and wished to spare them the same feeling. One day, when a Frenchman, Monsieur de Jaucourt, came to luncheon, I refused to say the sentence in question, in spite of the most tempting bribes, simply for that reason. I was hot with shame at thinking what Monsieur de Jaucourt – he a Frenchman, too – would think of something so inadequate. And this shows how impossible it is for grown-up people to put themselves in children's shoes and to divine their motives. If only children knew, it didn't matter what they said!

Another dramatic performance was a scene from Victor Hugo's drama, *Angelo*, in which Margaret, dressed in a crimson velvet cloak bordered with gold braid, declaimed a speech of Angelo Podesta of Padua, about the Council of Ten at Venice, while Susan, dressed in pink satin and lace, sat silent and attentive, looking meek in the part of the Venetian courtesan.

All this happened during early years in London.

Mademoiselle Ida used to enliven lessons with news from the outside world, discussions of books and concerts, and especially of other artists. One day when I was sitting at my slate with Mrs Christie, she was discussing English spelling, and saying how difficult it was. Mrs Christie rashly said that I could spell very well, upon which Mademoiselle Ida said to me, 'You would spell "which" double u i c h, wouldn't you?' And I, anxious to oblige, said, 'Yes'. This was a bitter humiliation.

Besides music lessons we had drawing lessons, first from a Miss Van Sturmer. Later we had lessons from Mr Nathaniel Green, a water-colourist, who taught us perspective. One year I drew the schoolroom clock, which Mr Jump used to come to wind once a week, as a present for my mother on her birthday, the 18th of June.

Sometimes I shared my mother's lesson in water-colours. Mr Green used to say he liked my washes, as they were warm. He used to put his brush in his mouth, which I considered dangerous, and he sometimes used a colour called Antwerp blue, which I thought was a pity, as it was supposed to fade. I was passionately fond of drawing, and drew both indoors and out of doors on every possible opportunity, and constantly illustrated various episodes in our life, or books that were being read out at the time. I took an immense interest in my mother's painting, especially in the colours: Rubens madder, cyanine, aureoline, green oxide of chromium, transparent – all seemed to be magic names. The draughtsman of the family was Elizabeth. None of my brothers drew. Elizabeth used to paint a bust of Clytie in oils, and sometimes she went as far as life-size portraits. Besides this, she was an excellent caricaturist, and used to illustrate the main episodes of our family life in a little sketch-book.

Lessons, on the whole, used to pass off peacefully. I don't think we were ever naughty with Mrs Christie, although Elizabeth and Margaret used often to rock with laughter at some private joke of their own during their lessons, but with Chérie we were often naughty. The usual punishment was to be *privé de pudding*. When the currant and raspberry tart came round at luncheon we used to refuse it, and my mother used to press it on us, not knowing that we had been *privé*. Sometimes, too, we had to write out three tenses of the verb *aimer*, and on one occasion I refused to do it. It was a Saturday afternoon; there was a treat impending, and I was told I would not be allowed to go unless I copied out the tenses, but I remained firm throughout luncheon. Finally, at the end of luncheon I capitulated in a flood of tears and accepted the loan of my mother's gold pencil-case and scribbled *J'aime, tu aimes, il aime*, etc., on a piece of writing-paper.

In the drawing-room we were not often naughty, but we were sometimes, and tried the grown-ups at moments beyond endurance. My mother said that she had had to whip us all except Hugo. I was whipped three times. Before the operation my mother always took off her rings.

Upstairs, Margaret and Elizabeth used sometimes to fight, and Susan would join in the fray, inspired by the impulse of the moment. She was liable to these sudden impulses, and on one occasion – she was very small – when she was looking on at a review of volunteers, when the guns suddenly fired, she stood up in the carriage and boxed everyone's ears.

Not long ago we found an old mark-book which belonged to this epoch of schoolroom life, and in it was the following entry in Chérie's handwriting: 'Elizabeth et Marguerite se sont battues, Suzanne s'est jetée sur le pauvre petit Maurice.' Whenever Margaret saw that I was on the verge of tears she used to say that I made a special face, which meant I was getting ready to cry, and she called this *la première position*; when the corners of the mouth went down, and the first snuffle was heard, she called it *la deuxième position*; and when tears actually came, it was *la troisième position*. Nearly always the mention of *la première position* averted tears altogether.

On Monday evenings in London my mother used to go regularly to the Monday Pops at St James's Hall, and on Saturday afternoon also. Dinner was at seven on Mondays, and we used to go down to it, and watch my mother cut up a leg of chicken and fill it with mustard and pepper and cayenne pepper to make a devil for supper. Margaret was sometimes taken to the Monday Pop, as she was supposed to like it, but the others were seldom taken, in case, my mother used to say, 'You say when you are grown up that you were dragged to concerts, and get to dislike them'. The result was a feverish longing to go to the Monday Pop. I don't remember going to the Monday Pop until I was grown up, but I know that I always wanted to go. I was taken to the Saturday Pop sometimes, and the first one I went to was on 8th November 1879. I was five years old. This was the programme:

QUARTET, E FLAT . . . . . . . *Mendelssohn*
MME NORMAN NERUDA, RIES, ZERBINI, PIATTI.

SONG . . . 'O Swallow, Swallow' . . *Piatti*
MR SANTLEY.
Violoncello obbligato, SIGNOR PIATTI.

SONATA, C SHARP MINOR . 'Moonlight' . . . *Beethoven*
MLLE JANOTHA.

SONATA IN F MAJOR FOR PIANOFORTE AND VIOLIN, No. 9 *Mozart*
MLLE JANOTHA AND MME NORMAN NERUDA.

SONG . . . . 'The Erl King' . . . *Schubert*
MR SANTLEY.

TRIO IN C MAJOR . . . . . . . *Haydn*
MLLE JANOTHA, MME NORMAN NERUDA, SIGNOR PIATTI.

Every winter we were taken to the pantomime by Lord Antrim, and the pantomimes I remember seeing were *Mother Goose*, *Robinson Crusoe*, *Sinbad the Sailor*, *Aladdin*, and *Cinderella*, in which the funny parts were played by Herbert Campbell and Harry Nicholls, and the Princess sometimes by the incomparably graceful dancer, Kate Vaughan.

I also remember the first Gilbert and Sullivan operas. *Pinafore* I was too young for; but I saw the *Children's Pinafore*, which was played by children. *Patience* and *Iolanthe* and *Princess Ida* I saw when they were first produced at the Savoy.

Irving and Ellen Terry we never saw till I went to school, as Irving's acting in Shakespeare made my father angry. When he saw him play Romeo, he was heard to mutter the whole time: 'Remove that man from the stage.'

Then there were children's parties. Strangely enough, I only remember one of these, so I don't expect I enjoyed them. But I remember a children's garden party at Marlborough House, and the exquisite beauty, the grace, and the fairy-tale-like welcome of the Princess of Wales.

74

Two of the great days for the children in London were Valentine's Day, on the eve of which we each of us sent the whole of the rest of the family Valentines, cushioned and scented Valentines with silken fringes; and the 1st of April, when Susan was always made an April fool, the best one being one of Chérie's, who sent her to look in the schoolroom for *Les Mémoires de Jonas dans la baleine*. She searched conscientiously, but in vain, for this interesting book.

On one occasion, on the Prince of Wales' wedding-day, in March, the whole family were invited to a children's ball at Marlborough House. The girls' frocks were a subject of daily discussion for weeks beforehand, and other governesses used to come and discuss the matter. They were white frocks, and when they were ready they were found to be a failure, for some reason, and they had to be made all over again at another dressmaker's, called Mrs Mason. It was on this occasion that Chérie made a memorable utterance and said: 'Les pointes de Madame Mason sont incomparables,' as Elizabeth had for the first time risen to the dignity of a *pointe* (the end of the pointed 'bodies' of the fashions of that day). It was doubtful whether the new frocks would be ready in time. There was a momentous discussion as to whether they were to wear black stockings or not. Finally the frocks arrived, and we were dressed and were all marshalled downstairs ready to start. My father in knee-breeches and myself in a black velvet suit, black velvet breeches, and a white waistcoat. I was told to be careful to remember to kiss the Princess of Wales' hand.

I can just remember the ballroom, but none of the grown-up people – nothing, in fact, except a vague crowd of tulle skirts.

One night there was a ball, or rather a small dance, in Charles Street, and I was allowed to come down after going to bed all day. People shook their heads over this, and said I was being spoilt, to Chérie, but Chérie said: 'Cet enfant n'est pas gâté, mais il se fait gâter.'

The dance led off with a quadrille, in which I and my father both took part. After having carefully learnt the *pas chassé* at dancing lessons, I was rather shocked to find this elegant glide was not observed by the quadrille dancers.

All this was the delightful epoch of the 'eighties, when the shop windows were full of photographs of the professional beauties, and bands played tunes from the new Gilbert and Sullivan in the early morning in the streets, and people rode in Rotten Row in the evening, and Chérie used to rush us across the road to get a glimpse of Mrs Langtry or the Princess of Wales.

Dancing lessons played an important part in our lives. Our first dancing instructor was the famous ex-ballerina, Madame Taglioni, a graceful old lady with grey curls, who held a class at Lady Granville's house in Carlton House Terrace. It was there I had my first dancing lesson and learnt the

Tarantelle, a dance with a tambourine, which I have always found effective, if not useful, in later life. Then Madame Taglioni's class came to an end, and there was a class at Lady Ashburton's at Bath House, which was suddenly put a stop to owing to the rough and wild behaviour of the boys, myself among them. Finally we had a class in our own house, supervised by a strict lady in black silk, who taught us the *pas chassé*, the five positions, the valse, the polka, and the Lancers.

Another event was Mrs Christie's lottery, which was held once a year at her house at Kentish Town. All her pupils came, and everyone won a prize in the lottery. One year I won a stuffed duck. After tea we acted charades. On the way back we used to pass several railway bridges, and Chérie, producing a gold pencil, used to say: 'Par la vertu de ma petite baguette', she would make a train pass. It was perhaps a rash boast, but it was always successful.

We used to drive to Mrs Christie's in a coach, an enormous carriage driven by Maisy, the coachman, who wore a white wig. It was only used when the whole family had to be transported somewhere.

Another incident of London life was Mademoiselle Ida's pupils' concert, which happened in the summer. I performed twice at it, I think, but never a solo. A duet with Mademoiselle Ida playing the bass, and whispering: 'Gare au dièse, gare au bémol,' in my ear. What we enjoyed most about this was waiting in what was called the artists' room, and drinking raspberry vinegar.

But the crowning bliss of London life was Hamilton Gardens, where we used to meet other children and play flags in the summer evenings.

This was the scene of wild enjoyment, not untinged with romance, for there the future beauties of England were all at play in their lovely teens. We were given tickets for concerts at the Albert Hall and elsewhere in the afternoon, but I remember that often when Hugo and I were given the choice of going to a concert or playing in the nursery, we sometimes chose to play. But I do remember hearing Patti singing 'Coming thro' the Rye' at the Guildhall, and Albani and Santley on several occasions.

But what we enjoyed most of all was finding some broken and derelict toy, and inventing a special game for it. Once in a cupboard in the back drawing-room I came across some old toys which had belonged to John and Cecil, and must have been there for years. Among other things there was an engine in perfectly good repair, with a little cone like the end of a cigar which you put inside the engine under the funnel. You then lit it and smoke came out, and the engine moved automatically. This seemed too miraculous for inquiry, and I still wonder how and why it happened. Then the toy was unaccountably lost, and I never discovered the secret of this mysterious and wonderful engine.

During all this time there were two worlds of which one gradually became conscious: the inside world and the outside world. The centre of the inside world, like the sun to the solar system, was, of course, our father and mother (Papa and Mamma), the dispenser of everything, the source of all enjoyment, and the final court of appeal, recourse to which was often threatened in disputes.

Next came Chérie, then my mother's maid, Dimmock, then Sheppy, the housekeeper, who had white grapes, cake, and other treats in the housekeeper's room. She was a fervent Salvationist and wore a Salvationist bonnet, and when my father got violent and shouted out loud ejaculations, she used to coo softly in a deprecating tone.

Then there was Monsieur Butat, the cook, who used to appear in white after breakfast when my father ordered dinner; Deacon, his servant, was the source of all wordly wisdom and experience, and recommended brown billycock hats in preference to black ones, because they did not fade in the sea air; Harriet, the housemaid, who used to bring a cup of tea in the early morning to my mother's bedroom, and Frank the footman. I can't remember a butler in London, but I suppose there was one; but if it was the same one we had in the country, it was Mr Watson.

Dimmock, or D., as we used to call her, played a great part in my early life, because when I came up to London or went down to the country alone with my father and mother she used to have sole charge of me, and I slept in her room. One day, during one of these autumnal visits to London, I was given an umbrella with a skeleton's head on it. This came back in dreams to me with terrific effect, and for several nights running I ran down from the top to the bottom of the house in terror. The umbrella was taken away. I used to love these visits to London when half the house was shut up, and there was no one there except my father and mother and D., and we used to live in the library downstairs. There used to be long and almost daily expeditions to shops because Christmas was coming, as D. used to chant to me every morning, and the Christmas-tree shopping had to be done. D. and I used to buy all the materials for the Christmas-tree – the candles, the glass balls, and the fairy to stand at the top of it – in a shop in the Edgware Road called Eagle. I used to have dinner in the housekeeper's room with Sheppy, and spent most of my time in D.'s working-room. One day she gave me a large piece of red plush, and I had something sewn round it, and called it *Red Conscience*. Never did a present make me more happy; I treated it as something half sacred, like a Mussulman's mat.

On one occasion D. and I went to a matinée at St James's Theatre to see *A Scrap of Paper*, played by Mr and Mrs Kendal. This year I read the play (it was translated from Sardou's *Pattes de Mouche*) for the first time, and I found I could recollect every scene of the play, and Mrs Kendal's expression and intonation.

Another time Madame Neruda, who was a great friend of my mother's, whom we saw constantly, gave me two tickets for a ballad concert at which she was playing. The policeman was told to take me into the artists' room during the interval. D. was to take me, but for some reason she thought the concert was in the evening, and it turned out to be in the afternoon; so as a compensation my father sent us to an operetta called *Falka*, in which Miss Violet Cameron sang. I enjoyed it more than any concert. The next day Madame Neruda came to luncheon and heard all about the misadventure. 'And did you enjoy your operetta?' she asked. 'Yes,' I said, with enthusiasm. 'Say, not as much as you would have enjoyed the ballad concert,' said my mother. But I didn't feel so sure about that.

I used to do lessons with Mrs Christie, and have music lessons from Mademoiselle Ida, and in the afternoon I often used to go out shopping in the carriage with my mother, or for a walk with D. But I will tell more about her later when I describe Membland.

The girls had a maid who looked after them called Rawlinson, and she and the nursery made up the rest of the inside world in London.

In the outside world the first person of importance I remember was Grandmamma, my mother's mother, Lady Elizabeth Bulteel, who used to paint exquisite pictures for the children like the pictures on china, and play songs for us on the pianoforte. She often came to luncheon, and used to bring toys to be raffled for, and make us, at the end of luncheon, sing a song which ran:

'A pie sat on a pear tree,
And once so merrily hopped she,
And twice so merrily hopped she,
Three times so merrily hopped she,'

Each singer held a glass in his hand. When the song had got thus far, everyone drained their glass, and the person who finished first had to say the last line of the verse, which was:

'Ya-he, ya-ho, ya-ho'.

And the person who said it first, won.

Everything about Grandmamma was soft and exquisite: her touch on the piano and her delicate manipulation of the painting-brush. She lived in Green Street, a house I remember as the perfection of comfort and cultivated dignity. There were amusing drawing-tables with tiles, pencils, painting-brushes; chintz chairs and books and music; a smell of pot-pourri and lavender water; miniatures in glass tables, pretty china, and finished water-colours.

In November 1880 – this is one of the few dates I can place – we were in London, my father and mother and myself, and Grandmamma was not well. She must have been over eighty, I think. Every day I used to go to Green Street with my mother and spend the whole morning illuminating a text. I was told Grandmamma was very ill, and had to take the nastiest medicines, and was being so good about it. I was sometimes taken in to see her. One day I finished the text, and it was given to Grandmamma. That evening when I was having my tea, my father and mother came into the dining-room and told me Grandmamma was dead. The text I had finished was buried with her.

The next day at luncheon I asked my mother to sing 'A pie sat on a pear tree', as usual. It was the daily ritual of luncheon. She said she couldn't do 'Hopped she', as we called it, any longer now that Grandmamma was not there.

Another thing Grandmamma had always done at luncheon was to break a thin water biscuit into two halves, so that one half looked like a crescent moon; and I said to my mother, 'We shan't be able to break biscuits like that any more.'

# CHAPTER III

# *Membland*

───────

TO MENTION ANY of the other people of the outside world at once brings me to Membland, because the outside world was intimately connected with that place. Membland was a large, square, Jacobean house, white brick, green shutters and ivy, with some modern gabled rough-cast additions and a tower, about twelve miles from Plymouth and ten miles from the station Ivy Bridge.

On the north side of the house there was a gravel yard, on the south side a long, sweeping, sloping lawn, then a ha-ha, a field beyond this and rookery which was called the Grove.

When you went through the front hall you came into a large billiard-room in which there was a staircase leading to a gallery going round the room and to the bedrooms. The billiard-room was high and there were no rooms over the billiard-room proper – but beyond the billiard-table the room extended into a lower section, culminating in a semicircle of windows in which there was a large double writing-table.

Later, under the staircase, there was an organ, and the pipes of the great organ were on the wall.

There was a drawing-room full of chintz chairs, books, pot-pourri, a grand pianoforte, and two writing-tables; a dining-room looking south; a floor of guests' rooms; a bachelors' passage in the wing; a schoolroom on the ground floor looking north, with a little dark room full of rubbish next to it, which was called the *Cabinet Noir*, and where we were sent when we were naughty; and a nursery floor over the guests' rooms.

From the northern side of the house you could see the hills of Dartmoor. In the west there was a mass of tall trees, Scotch firs, stone-pines, and ashes.

There was a large kitchen garden at some distance from the house on a hill and enclosed by walls.

Our routine of life was much the same as it was in London, except that the children had breakfast in the schoolroom at nine, as the grown-ups did not have breakfast till later.

Then came lessons, a walk, or play in the garden, further lessons, luncheon at two, a walk or an expedition, lessons from five till six, and then tea and games or reading aloud afterwards. One of the chief items of lessons was the *Dictée*, in which we all took part, and even Everard from Eton used to come and join in this sometimes.

Elizabeth won a kind of inglorious glory one day by making thirteen mistakes in her *dictée*, which was the record – a record never beaten by any one of us before or since; and the words *treize fautes* used often to be hurled at her head in moments of stress.

After tea Chérie used to read out books to the girls, and I was allowed to listen, although I was supposed to be too young to understand, and indeed I was. Nevertheless, I found the experience thrilling; and there are many book incidents which have remained for ever in my mind, absorbed during these readings, although I cannot always place them. I recollect a wonderful book called *L'Homme de Neige*, and many passages from Alexandre Dumas.

Sometimes Chérie would read out to me, especially stories from the *Cabinet des Fées*, or better still, tell stories of her own invention. There was one story in which many animals took part, and one of the characters was a partridge who used to go out just before the shooting season with a telescope under his wing to see whether things were safe. Chérie always used to say this was the creation she was proudest of. Another story was called *Le Prince Muguet et Princesse Myosotis*, which my mother had printed. I wrote a different story on the same theme and inspired by Chérie's story when I grew up. But I enjoyed Chérie's recollections of her childhood as much as her stories, and I could listen for ever to the tales of her *grand'mère sévère* who made her pick thorny juniper to make gin, or the story of a lady who had only one gown, a yellow one, and who every day used to ask her maid what the weather was like, and if the maid said it was fine, she would say, 'Eh bien, je mettrai ma robe jaune,' and if it was rainy she would likewise say, 'Je mettrai ma robe jaune.' Poor Chérie used to be made to repeat this story and others like it in season and out of season.

She would describe Paris until I felt I knew every street, and landscapes in Normandy and other parts of France. The dream of my life was to go to Paris and see the Boulevards and the Invalides and the Arc de Triomphe, and above all, the Champs Elysées.

Chérie had also a repertory of French songs which she used to teach us. One was the melancholy story of a little cabin-boy:

> 'Je ne suis qu'un petit mousse
> A bord d'un vaisseau royal,

Je vais partout où le vent me pousse,
  Nord ou midi cela m'est égal.
Car d'une mère et d'un père
  Je n'ai jamais connu l'amour.'

Another one, less pathetic but more sentimental, was:

'Pourquoi tous les jours, Madeleine,
  Vas-tu au bord du ruisseau?
Ce n'est pas, car je l'espère,
  Pour te regarder dans l'eau,
"Mais si," répond Madeleine,
  Baissant ses beaux yeux d'ébène.
Je n'y vais pour autre raison.'

I forget the rest, but it said that she looked into the stream to see whether it was true, as people said, that she was beautiful – 'pour voir si gent ne ment pas' – and came back satisfied that it was true.

But best of all I liked the ballad:

En revenant des noces j'étais si fatiguée
  Au bord d'un ruisseau je me suis reposée,
L'eau était si claire que je me suis baignée,
  Avec une feuille de chêne je me suis essuyée,
Sur la plus haute branche un rossignol chantait,
  Chante, beau rossignol, si tu as le coeur gai,
Pour un bouton de rose mon ami s'est fâché,
  Je voudrais que la rose fût encore au rosier.'

or words to that effect.

Besides these she taught us all the French singing games: 'Savez-vous planter les choux?' 'Sur le pont d'Avignon', and 'Qui est-ce qui passe ici si tard, Compagnons de la Marjolaine?' We used to sing and dance these up and down the passage outside the schoolroom after tea.

Round about Membland were several nests of relations. Six miles off was my mother's old home Flete, where the Mildmays lived. Uncle Bingham Mildmay married my mother's sister, Aunt Georgie, and bought Flete; the house, which was old, was said to be falling to pieces, so it was rebuilt, more or less on the old lines, with some of the old structure left intact.

At Pamflete, three miles off, lived my mother's brother, Uncle Johnny Bulteel, with his wife, Aunt Effie, and thirteen children.

And in the village of Yealmpton, three miles off, also lived my great-aunt Jane who had a sister called Aunt Sister, who, whenever she heard carriage wheels in the drive, used to get under the bed, such was her disinclination to receive guests. I cannot remember Aunt Sister, but I remember Aunt Jane and Uncle Willie Harris, who was either her brother or her husband. He had been present at the battle of Waterloo as a drummer-boy at the age of fifteen. But Aunt Sister's characteristics had descended to other members of the family, and my mother used to say that when she and her sister were girls my Aunt Georgie had offered her a pound if she would receive some guests instead of herself.

On Sundays we used to go to church at a little church in Noss Mayo until my father built a new church, which is there now.

The service was long, beginning at eleven and lasting till almost one. There was morning prayer, the Litany, the Ante-Communion service, and a long sermon preached by the rector, a charming old man called Mr Roe, who was not, I fear, a compelling preacher.

When we went to church I was given a picture-book when I was small to read during the sermon, a book with sacred pictures in colours. I was terribly ashamed of this. I would sooner have died than be seen in the pew with this book. It was a large picture-book. So I used every Sunday to lose or hide it just before the service, and find it again afterwards. On Sunday evenings we used sometimes to sing hymns in the schoolroom. The words of the hymns were a great puzzle. For instance, in the hymn, 'Thy will be done', the following verse occurs – I punctuate it as I understood it, reading it, that is to say, according to the tune –

> Renew my will from day to day,
> Blend it with Thine, and take away.
> All *that* now makes it hard to say
> Thy will be done.'

I thought the blending and the subsequent taking away of what was blent was a kind of trial of faith.

After tea, instead of being read to, we used sometimes to play a delightful round game with counters, called *Le Nain Jaune*.

Any number of people could play at it, and I especially remember Susan triumphantly playing the winning card and saying:

'Le bon Valet, la bonne Dame, le bon Woi. Je wecommence.'

In September or October, Chérie would go for her holidays. I cannot remember if she went every year, but we had no one instead of her, and she left behind her a series of holiday tasks.

During one of her absences my Aunt M'aimée, another sister of my mother's, came to stay with us. Aunt M'aimée was married to Uncle Henry Ponsonby, the Queen's Private Secretary. He came, too, and with them their daughter Betty. Betty had a craze at that time for Sarah Bernhardt, and gave a fine imitation of her as Doña Sol in the last act of *Hernani*. It was decided we should act this whole scene, with Margaret as Hernani and Aunt M'aimée reading the part of Ruy Gomez, who appears in a domino and mask.

Never had I experienced anything more thrilling. I used to lie on the floor during the rehearsals, and soon I knew the whole act by heart. I thought Betty the greatest genius that ever lived.

When Chérie came back she was rather surprised and not altogether pleased to find I knew the whole of the last act of *Hernani* by heart. She thought this a little too exciting and grown-up for me, and even for Margaret, but none the less she let me perform the part of Doña Sol one evening after tea in my mother's bedroom, dressed in a white frock, with Susan in a riding-habit playing the sinister figure of Ruy Gomez. I can see Chérie now, sitting behind a screen, book in hand to prompt me, and shaking with laughter as I piped out in a tremulous and lisping treble the passionate words:

'Il vaudrait pour vous mieuxzaller (which I made all one word) au tigre même
Arracher ses petits qu'à moi celui que j'aime.'

Chérie's return from her holidays was one of the most exciting of events, for she would bring back with her a mass of toys from Giroux and the *Paradis des Enfants*, and a flood of stories about the people and places and plays she had seen, and the food she had eaten.

One year she brought me back a theatre of puppets. It was called Théâtre français. It had a white proscenium, three scenes and an interior, a Moorish garden by moonlight, and a forest, and a quantity of small puppets suspended by stiff wires and dressed in silk and satin. There was a harlequin, a columbine, a king, a queen, many princesses, a villain scowling beneath black eyebrows, an executioner with a mask, peasants, pastry-cooks, and soldiers with halberds, who would have done honour to the Papal Guard at the Vatican, and some heavily moustached gendarmes. This theatre was a source of ecstasy, and innumerable dramas used to be performed in it. Chérie used also to bring back some delicious cakes called *nonnettes*, a kind of gingerbread with icing on the top, rolled up in a long paper cylinder.

She also brought baskets of bonbons from Boissier, the kind of basket which had several floors of different kinds of bonbons, fondants on the top in their white frills, then caramels, then chocolates, then fruits confits. All these things confirmed one's idea that there could be no place like Paris.

In 1878, when I was four years old, another brother was born, Rupert, in August, but he died in October of the same year. He was buried in Revelstoke Church, a church not used any more, and then in ruins except for one aisle, which was roofed in, and provided with pews. It nestled by the seashore, right down on the rocks, grey and covered with ivy, and surrounded by quaint tombstones that seemed to have been scattered haphazard in the thick grass and the nettles.

I think it was about the same time that one evening I was playing in my godmother's room, that I fell into the fire, and my little white frock was ablaze and my back badly burnt. I remember being taken up to the nursery and having my back rubbed with potatoes, and thinking that part, and the excitement and sympathy shown, and the interest created, great fun.

All this was before Hugo was in the schoolroom, but in all my sharper memories of Membland days he plays a prominent part. We, of course, shared the night nursery, and we soon invented games together, some of which were distracting, not to say maddening, to grown-up people. One was an imaginary language in which even the word 'Yes' was a trisyllable, namely: 'Sheepartee', and the word for 'No' was even longer and more complicated, namely: 'Quiliquinino'. We used to talk this language, which was called 'Sheepartee', and which consisted of unmitigated gibberish, for hours in the nursery, till Hilly, Grace, and Annie could bear it no longer, and Everard came up one evening and told us the language must stop or we should be whipped.

The language stopped, but a game grew out of it, which was most complicated, and lasted for years even after we went to school. The game was called 'Spankaboo'. It consisted of telling and acting the story of an imaginary continent in which we knew the countries, the towns, the government, and the leading people. These countries were generally at war with one another. Lady Spankaboo was a prominent lady at the Court of Doodahn. She was a charming character, not beautiful nor clever, and sometimes a little bit foolish, but most good-natured and easily taken in. Her husband, Lord Spankaboo, was a country gentleman, and they had no children. She wore red velvet in the evening, and she was *bien vue* at Court.

There were hundreds of characters in the game. They increased as the story grew. It could be played out of doors, where all the larger trees in the garden were forts belonging to the various countries, or indoors, but it was chiefly played in the garden, or after we went to bed. Then Hugo would say: 'Let's play Spankaboo', and I would go straight on with the latest events, interrupting the narrative every now and then by saying: 'Now, you be Lady Spankaboo', or whoever the character on the stage might be for the moment, 'and I'll be So-and-so'. Everything that happened to us and everything we read was brought into the game – history, geography, the ancient Romans, the Greeks, the French; but it was a realistic game, and there were no fairies in it and nothing in the least frightening. As it was a night game, this was just as well.

Hugo was big for his age, with powerful lungs, and after luncheon he used to sing a song called 'Apples no more', with immense effect. Hugo was once told the following riddle: 'Why can't an engine-driver sit down ?' – to which the answer is, 'Because he has a tender behind'. He asked this to my mother at luncheon the next day, and when nobody could guess it, he said: 'Because he has a soft behind'. There was a groom in the stables who had rather a Japanese cast of face, and we used to call him *le Japonais*. One day Hugo went and stood in front of him and said to him: 'You're the Japonais'. On another occasion when Hugo was learning to conjugate the auxiliary verb *être*, Chérie urged him to add a substantive after 'Je suis', to show he knew what he was doing. 'Je suis une plume,' said Hugo.

We were constantly in D.'s room and used to play sad tricks on her. She rashly told us one day that her brother Jim had once taken her to a fair at Wallington and had there shown her a Punch's face, in gutta-percha, on the wall. 'Go and touch his nose,' had said Jim. She did so, and the face being charged with electricity gave her a shock.

This story fired our imagination and we resolved to follow Jim's example. We got a galvanic battery, how and where, I forget, the kind which consists of a small box with a large magnet in it, and a handle which you turn, the patient holding two small cylinders. We persuaded D. to hold the cylinders, and then we made the current as strong as possible and turned the handle with all our might. Poor D. screamed and tears poured down her cheeks, but we did not stop, and she could not leave go because the current contracts the fingers; we went on and on till she was rescued by someone else.

Another person we used to play tricks on was M. Butat, the cook, and one day Hugo and I, to his great indignation, threw a dirty mop into his stock-pot.

A great ally in the house was the housekeeper, Mrs Tudgay. Every day at eleven she would have two little baskets ready for us, which contained biscuits, raisins and almonds, two little cakes, and perhaps a tangerine orange.

To the outside world Mrs Tudgay was rather alarming. She had a calm, crystal, cold manner; she was thin, reserved, rather sallow, and had a clear, quiet, precise way of saying scathing and deadly things to those whom she disliked. Once when Elizabeth was grown up and married and happened to be staying with us, Mrs Tudgay said to her: 'You're an expense to his Lordship.' Once when she engaged an under-housemaid she said: 'She shall be called – nothing – and get £15 a year.' But for children she had no terrors. She was devoted to us, bore anything, did anything, and guarded our effects and belongings with the vigilance of a sleepless hound. She had formerly been maid to the Duchess of San Marino in Italy, and she had a fund of stories about Italy, a scrap-book full of Italian pictures and photographs, and a silver cross containing a relic of the True Cross given her by Pope Pius IX. We very often spent the evening in the housekeeper's room, and played Long Whist with Mrs Tudgay, D., Mr Deacon, and John's servant, Mr Thompson.

When, in the morning, we were exhausted from playing forts and Spankaboo in the garden, we used to leap through Mrs Tudgay's window into the housekeeper's room, which was on the ground floor and looked out on to the garden, and demand refreshment, and Mrs Tudgay used to bring two wine glasses of ginger wine and some biscuits.

Sometimes we used to go for picnics with Mrs Tudgay, D., Hilly, and the other servants. We started out in the morning and took luncheon with us, which was eaten at one of the many keepers' houses on the coast, some of which had a room kept for expeditions, and then spent the afternoon paddling on the rocks and picking shells and anemones. We never bathed, as there was not a single beach on my father's estate where it was possible. It was far too rocky. Mrs Tudgay had a small and ineffectual Pomeranian black dog called Albo, who used to be taken on these expeditions. Looking back on these, I wonder at the quantity of food D. and Mrs Tudgay used to allow us to eat. Hugo and I thought nothing of eating a whole lobster apiece, besides cold beef and apple tart.

Sometimes we all went expeditions with my mother. Then there used to be sketching, and certainly more moderation in the way of food.

Membland was close to the sea. My father made a ten-mile drive along the cliffs so that you could drive from the house one way, make a complete circle, and come back following the seacoast all the way to the river Yealm, on one side of which was the village of Newton Ferrers and on the other the village of Noss Mayo. Both villages straggled down the slopes of a steep hill. Noss Mayo had many white-washed and straw-thatched cottages and some new cottages of Devonshire stone built by my father, with slate roofs, but not ugly or aggressive. Down the slopes of Noss there were fields and orchards, and here and there a straw-thatched cottage. They were both fishing villages, the Yealm lying beneath them, a muddy stretch at low tide and a brimming river at high tide. Newton had an old grey Devonshire church with a tower at the west end. At Noss my father built a church exactly the same in pattern of Devonshire stone. You could not have wished for a prettier village than Noss, and it had, as my mother used to say: 'a little foreign look about it'.

At different points of this long road round the cliffs, which in the summer were a blaze of yellow gorse, there were various keepers' cottages, as I have said. From one you looked straight on to the sea from the top of the cliff. Another was hidden low down among orchards and not far from the old ruined church of Revelstoke. A third, called Battery Cottage, was built near the emplacement of an old battery and looked out on to the Mewstone towards Plymouth Sound and Ram Head. The making of this road and the building of the church were two great events. Pieces of the cliff had to be blasted with dynamite, which was under the direction of a cheery workman called Mr Yapsley, during the road-making, and the building of the church which was in the hands of Mr Crosbie, the Clerk of the Works, whom we were devoted to, entailed a host of interesting side-issues. One of these was the carving which was done by Mr Harry Hems of Exeter. He carved the bench-ends, and on one of them was a sea battle in which a member of the Bulteel family, whom we took to be Uncle Johnny, was seen hurling a stone from a mast's crows' nest in a sailing ship, on to a serpent which writhed in the waves. Hugo and I both sat for cherubs' heads, which were carved in stone on the reredos. There were some stained-glass windows and a hand-blown organ on which John used to play on Sundays when it was ready.

The church was consecrated by the Bishop of Exeter, Bishop Temple.

Hugo and I learned to ride first on a docile beast called Emma, who, when she became too lethargic, was relegated to a little cart which used to be driven by all of us, and then on a Dartmoor pony called the Giant, and finally on a pony called Emma Jane.

The coachman's name was Bilky. He was a perfect Devonshire character. His admiration for my brothers was unbounded. He used to talk of them one after the other, afraid if he had praised one, he had not praised the others enough. My brother Everard, whom we always called the 'Imp', he said was as strong as a lion and as nimble as a bee. 'They have rightly, sir, named you the Himp,' one of the servants said to him one day.

During all these years we had extraordinarily few illnesses. Hugo once had whooping-cough at London, and I was put in the same room so as to have it at the same time, and although I was longing to catch it, as Hugo was rioting in presents and delicacies as well as whoops, my constitution was obstinately impervious to infection.

We often had colds, entailing doses of spirits of nitre, linseed poultices, and sometimes even a mustard poultice, but I never remember anything more serious. Every now and then Hilly thought it necessary to dose us with castor-oil, and the struggles that took place when Hilly used to arrive with a large spoon, saying, as every Nanny I have ever known says: 'Now, take it!' were indescribable. I recollect five people being necessary one day to hold me down before the castor-oil could be got down my throat. We had a charming comfortable country doctor called Doctor Atkins, who used to drive over in a dog-cart, muffled in wraps, and produce a stethoscope out of his hat. He was so genial and comfortable that one began to feel better directly he felt one's pulse.

When we first went to Membland the post used to be brought by a postman who walked every day on foot from Ivy Bridge, ten miles off.

He had a watch the size of a turnip, and the stamps at that time were the dark red ones with the Queen's head on them. Later the post came in a cart from Plympton, and finally from Plymouth.

In the autumn, visitors used to begin to arrive for the covert shooting, which was good and picturesque, the pheasants flying high in the steep woods on the banks of the Yealm, and during the autumn months the nearing approach of Christmas cast an aura of excitement over life. The first question was: Would there be a Christmas tree? During all the early years there was one regularly.

After the November interval in London, which I have already described, the serious business of getting the tree ready began. It was a large tree, and stood in a square green box.

The first I remember was placed in the drawing-room, the next in the dining-room, the next in the billiard-room, and after that they were always in the covered-in tennis court, which had been built in the meanwhile. The decoration of the tree was under the management of D. The excitement when the tree was brought into the house or the tennis court for the first time was terrific, and Mr Ellis, the house-carpenter, who always wore carpet shoes, climbed up a ladder and affixed the silver fairy to the top of the tree. Then reels of wire were brought out, scissors, boxes of crackers, boxes of coloured candles, glass-balls, clips for candles, and a quantity of little toys.

Hugo and I were not allowed to do much. Nearly everything we did was said to be wrong. The presents were, of course, kept a secret and were done up in parcels, and not brought into the room until the afternoon of Christmas Eve.

The Christmas tree was lit on Christmas Eve after tea. The ritual was always the same. Hugo and I ran backwards and forwards with the servants' presents. The maids were given theirs first – they consisted of stuff for a gown done up in a parcel – then Mrs Tudgay, D., and the upper servants. One year Mrs Tudgay had a work-basket.

Then the guests were given their presents, and we gave our presents and received our own. The presents we gave were things we had made ourselves: kettle-holders, leather slippers worked in silk for my father, and the girls sometimes made a woollen waistcoat or a comforter. Chérie always had a nice present for my mother, which we were allowed to see beforehand, and she always used to say: 'N'y touchez pas, la fraîcheur en fait la beauté.'

Our presents were what we had put down beforehand in a list of 'Christmas Wants' – a horse and cart, a painting-box, or a stylograph pen.

The house used to be full at Christmas. My father's brothers, Uncle Tom and Uncle Bob, used to be there. Madame Neruda I remember as a Christmas visitor. Godfrey Webb wrote the following lines about Christmas at Membland:

## CHRISTMAS AT MEMBLAND

Who says that happiness is far to seek?
Here have I passed a happy Christmas week.
Christmas at Membland – all was bright and gay,
Without one shadow till this final day,
When Mrs Baring said, 'Before you go
You must write something in the book, you know.'
I must write something – that's all very well,
But what to write about I cannot tell.
Where shall I look for help? – it must be found,
If I survey this Christmas party round.
There's Ned himself, our most delightful host,
Or Mrs Baring, she could help me most,
The Uncles too, if I their time might rob.
Shall I ask Tom? or try my luck with Bob?
Madame Neruda, ah, would she begin,
We'd write the story of a violin,
And tell how first the inspiration came
Which took the world by storm and gave her fame.
There's Harry Bourke, with him I can't go wrong,
Could I but write the words he'd sing the song.
So sung, my verse would haply win a smile
From his bright beauty of the sister Isle,
Who comes prepared her country's pride to save,
For every Saxon is at once her slave;
But no, I must not for assistance look,
So, Mrs Baring, you must keep your book
For cleverer pens and I no more will trouble you,
But just remain your baffled bard.          G. W. (1879).

Mr Webb was a great feature in the children's life of many families.
With his beady, bird-like eye and his impassive face he made jokes so
quietly that you overheard them rather than heard them. One day out
shooting on a steep hill in Newton Wood, in which there were woodcock
and dangerous shots, my father said to him, 'You take the middle drive,
Godfrey; it's safer, *medio tutissimus*'. 'Is there any chance of an *Ibis*?'
Mr Webb asked quietly. Another time, he went out duck-shooting. He
was asked afterwards whether he had shot many. 'Not even a *Mallard
imaginaire*,' was his answer.

Another Christmas event was the French play we used to act under
the stage management of Chérie.

When I was six I played the part of an old man with a bald forehead
and white tufts of hair in a play called *Le Maître d'École*, and I remember

playing the part of Nicole in scenes from the *Bourgeois Gentilhomme* at Christmas in 1883, and an old witch called Mathurine in a play called *Le Talisman* in January 1884.

One of our most ambitious efforts was a play called *La Grammaire*, by Labiche: it proved too ambitious, and never got further than a dress rehearsal in the schoolroom. In this play, Elizabeth had the part of the heroine, and had to be elegantly dressed; she borrowed a grown-up gown, and had her hair done up, but she took such a long time preening herself that she missed her cue, which was: 'L'ange, la voici!' It was spoken by Margaret, who had a man's part.

'L'ange, la voici!' said Margaret in ringing tones, but no *ange* appeared. 'L'ange, la voici!' repeated Margaret, with still greater emphasis, but still no *ange*; finally, not without malice, Margaret almost shouted, 'L'ange, la voici!' and at last Elizabeth tripped blushing on to the stage with the final touches of her toilette still a little uncertain. In the same play, Susan played the part of a red-nosed horse-coper, dressed in a grey-tailed coat, called *Machut*.

Another source of joy in Membland life was the yacht, the *Waterwitch*, which in the summer months used to sail as soon as the Cowes Regatta was over, down to the Yealm River. The *Waterwitch* was a schooner of 150 tons; it had one large cabin where one had one's meals, my mother's cabin aft, a cabin for my father, and three spare cabins. The name of the first captain was Goomes, but he was afterwards replaced by Bletchington. Goomes was employed later by the German Emperor. He had a knack of always getting into rows during races, and even on other occasions.

One day there was a regatta going on on the Yealm River; the gig of the *Waterwitch* was to race the gig of another yacht. They had to go round a buoy. For some reason, I was in the *Waterwitch's* gig when the race started, sitting in the stern next to Goomes, who was steering. All went well at first, but when the boats were going round the buoy they fouled, and Goomes and the skipper of the rival gig were soon engaged in a hand-to-hand combat, and beating each other hard with the steering-lines. My father and the rest of the family were watching the race on board the yacht. I think I was about six or seven. My father shouted at the top of his voice, 'Come back, come back,' but to no avail, as Goomes and the other skipper were fighting like two dogs, and the boats were almost capsizing. I think Goomes won the fight and the race. I remember enjoying it all heartily, but not so my father on board the yacht.

Bletchington was a much milder person and, besides being a beautiful sailor, one of the gentlest and most beautiful-mannered mariners I have ever met. He was invariably optimistic, and always said there was a nice breeze. This sometimes tempted the girls, who were bad sailors, to go out sailing, but they always regretted it and used to come back saying, 'How foolish we were to be taken in!' Hugo and I were good sailors and enjoyed the yacht more than anything. John was an expert in the handling of a yacht, but the 'Imp' nearly died of sea-sickness if ever he ventured on board.

Captain Bletchington taught Hugo and myself a song in Fiji language. It ran like this:

'Tang a rang a chicky nee, picky-nicky wooa,
Tarra iddy ucky chucky chingo.'

Which meant:

'All up and down the river they did go;
The King and Queen of Otahiti.'

I think what we enjoyed most of all were games of Hide-and-seek on board. One day one of the sailors hid us by reefing us up in a sail in the sail-room, a hiding-place which baffled everyone. The *Waterwitch* was a fast vessel, and won the schooners' race round the Isle of Wight one year and only narrowly missed winning the Queen's Cup. The story of this race used to be told us over and over again by D., and used to be enacted by Hugo and me on our toy yachts or with pieces of cork in the sink. This is what happened. Another schooner, the *Cetonia*, had to allow the *Waterwitch* five minutes, but the *Waterwitch* had to allow the *Sleuthhound*, a cutter, twenty-five minutes. D. was watching from the shore, and my mother was watching from the R.Y.S. Club. The *Cetonia* came in first, but a minute or two later the *Waterwitch* sailed in before the five minutes' allowance was up. Then twenty minutes of dreadful suspense rolled by, twenty-three minutes, and during the last two minutes, as D. dramatically said, 'That 'orrid *Sleuthhound* sailed round the corner and won the race.' Hugo and I felt we could never forgive the owner of the *Sleuthhound*.

Besides the *Waterwitch* there was a little steam launch called the *Wasp* which used to take us in to Plymouth, and John had a sailing-boat of his own.

## CHAPTER IV

# *Membland*

---

IN THE SUMMER HOLIDAYS of 1883 Mr Warre came to stay with us. John, Cecil, and Everard were at his house at Eton. Cecil was to read with him during the holidays. Cecil was far the cleverest one of the family and a classical scholar.

Mr Warre was pleased to find I was interested in the stories of the Greek heroes, but pained because I only knew their names in French, speaking of Thésée, Médée, and Égée. The truth being that I did not know how to pronounce their names in English, as I had learnt all about them from Chérie. Chérie said that Mr Warre had 'une tête bien équilibrée'. We performed *Les Enfants d'Édouard* before him.

The following Christmas, Mr Warre sent Hugo a magnificent book illustrating the song 'Apples no more', with water-colour drawings done by his daughter; and he sent me Church's *Stories from Homer*, with this Latin inscription at the beginning of it:

MAURICIO BARING
JAM AB INEUNTE AETATE
VETERUM FAUTORI
ANTIQUITATIS STUDIOSO
MAEONII CARMINIS ARGUMENTA
ANGLICE ENUCLEATA
STRENIÂ PROPITIÂ
MITTIT
EDMUNDUS WARRE
KAL. JAN.
MDCCCLXXXIII.

Nobody in the house knew what the Latin word *streniâ* meant, not even Walter Durnford, who was then an Eton master and destined to be the house tutor of Hugo and myself later. But Chérie at once said it

93

meant the feast of the New Year. The scholars were puzzled and could not conceive how she had known this. The French word *étrennes* had given her the clue.

The whole of my childhood was a succession of crazes for one thing after another: the first one, before I was three, was a craze for swans, then came trains, then chess, then carpentry, then organs and organ-building. My mother played chess, and directly I learnt the game I used to make all the visitors play with me. My mother used to say that she had once bet my Aunt Effie she would beat her twenty-one games running, giving her a pawn every time. She won twenty games and was winning the twenty-first, late one night after dinner, when my father said they had played long enough, and must go to bed, which of course they refused to do. He then upset the board, and my mother said she had never been so angry in her life; she had bent back his little finger and had, she hoped, really hurt him.

I can remember playing chess and beating Admiral Glyn, who came over from Plymouth. His ship was the *Agincourt*, a large four-funnelled ironclad. One day we had luncheon on board, and my father was chaffed for an unforgettable solecism, namely, for having smoked on the quarter-deck.

Another craze was history. Chérie gave the girls a most interesting historical task, which was called doing *Le Siècle de Périclès* and *Le Siècle de Louis XIV*, or whose-ever the century might be.

You wrote on one side of a copy-book the chief events and dates of the century in question, and on the other side short biographies of the famous men who adorned it, with comments on their deeds or works. I implored to be allowed to do this, and in a large sprawling handwriting I struggled with *Le Siècle de Périclès*, making up for my want of penmanship by the passionate admiration I felt for the great men of the past. My *History of the World* was the opposite to that of Mr H. G. Wells!

Somebody gave me an American *History of the World*, a large flat book which told the histories of all the countries of the world in the form of a pictured chart, the countries being represented by long, narrow belts or strips, so that you could follow the destinies of the various Empires running parallel to each other and see the smaller countries being absorbed by the greater. The whole book was printed on a long, large, glazed linen sheet, which you could pull out all at one time if you had a room long enough and an unencumbered door. You could also turn over the doubly folded leaves. That was the more convenient way, although you did not get the full effect. This book was a mine of interest. It had pictures of every kind of side-issue and by-event, such as the Seven Wonders of the World, the Coliseum, pictures of crusaders, and portraits of famous men.

About the same time a friend of Cecil's, Claud Lambton, gave me an historical atlas which was also a great treat. Lessons continued with Chérie, and I used to learn passages of Racine ('Le Récit de Théramène') and of Boileau ('La Mollesse', from the *Lutrin*) by heart, and 'Les Imprécations de Camille'. I also read a good deal by myself, but mostly fairy-tales, although there were one or two grown-up books I read and liked. The book I remember liking best of all was a novel called *Too Strange not to be True*, by Lady Georgiana Fullerton, which my mother read out to my cousin, Bessie Bulteel. I thought this a wonderful book; I painted illustrations for it, making a picture of every character.

There was another book which I read to myself and liked, if anything, still better. I found it in Everard's bedroom. It was a yellow-backed novel, and it had on the cover the picture of a dwarf letting off a pistol. It was called the *Siege of Castle Something* and it was by – that is the question, who was it by? I would give anything to know. The name of the author seemed to me at the time quite familiar, that is to say, a name one had heard people talk about, like Trollope or Whyte-Melville. The story was that of an impecunious family who led a gay life in London at a suburban house called the Robber's Cave, at the beginning of the nineteenth century. They were always in debt, and finally, to escape bailiffs, they shut themselves up in a castle on the seacoast, where they were safe unless a bailiff should succeed in entering the house, and present the writ to one of the debtors in person. The bailiffs tried every expedient to force a way into the castle, one of them dressing up as an old dowager who was a friend of the family, and driving up to the castle in a custard-coloured carriage. But the inmates of the house were wily, and they had a mechanical device by which coloured billiard balls appeared on the frieze of the drawing-room and warned them when a bailiff was in the offing.

One day when they had a visitor to tea, a billiard ball suddenly made a clicking noise round the frieze. 'What is that for?' asked the interested guest. 'That,' said the host, with great presence of mind, 'is a signal that a ship is in sight.' As tea went on, a perfect plethora of billiard balls of different colours appeared in the frieze. 'There must be a great many ships in sight today,' said the guest. 'A great many,' answered the host.

Whether a bailiff ever got into the house I don't know. The picture on the cover seems to indicate that he did. The book was in Everard's cupboard for years, and then, 'suddenly, as rare things will, it vanished'. I never have been able to find it again, although I have never stopped looking for it. Once I thought I had run it to earth. I once met at the Vice-Provost's house at Eton a man who was an expert lion-hunter and who seemed to have read every English novel that had ever been published. I described him the book. He had read it. He remembered the picture on the cover and the story, but, alas! he could recall neither its name nor that of the author.

In French *Les Malheurs de Sophie*, *Les Mémoires d'un Âne*, *Sans Famille*, were the first early favourites, and then the numerous illustrated works of Jules Verne.

Walter Scott's novels used to be held before us like an alluring bait. 'When you are nine years old you shall read *The Talisman*.' Even the order in which Scott was to be read was discussed. *The Talisman* first, and then *Ivanhoe*, and then *Quentin Durward*, *Woodstock* and *Kenilworth*, *Rob Roy* and *Guy Mannering*.

The reading of the Waverley Novels was a divine, far-off event, to which all one's life seemed to be slowly moving, and as soon as I was nine my mother read out *The Talisman* to me. The girls had read all Walter Scott except, of course, *The Heart of Midlothian*, which was not, as they said, for the J.P. (*jeune personne*) and (but why not, I don't know) *Peveril of the Peak*. They also read Miss Yonge's domestic epics. There I never followed them, except for reading *The Little Duke*, *The Lances of Lynwood*, and the historical romance of *The Chaplet of Pearls*, which seemed to me thrilling.

I believe children absorb more *Kultur* from the stray grown-up conversation they hear than they learn from books. At luncheon one heard the grown-up people discussing books and Chérie talking of new French novels. Not a word of all this escaped my notice. I remember the excitement when *John Inglesant* was published and Marion Crawford's *Mr Isaacs* and, just before I went to school, *Treasure Island*.

But besides the books of the day, one absorbed a mass of tradition. My father had an inexhaustible memory, and he would quote to himself when he was in the train, and at any moment of stress and emotion a muttered quotation would rise to his lips, often of the most incongruous kind. Sometimes it was a snatch of a hymn of Heber's, sometimes a lyric of Byron's, sometimes an epitaph of Pope's, some lines of Dryden or Churchill, or a bit of Shakespeare.

One little poem he was fond of quoting was:

> 'Mrs Gill is very ill
> And nothing can improve her,
> Unless she sees the Tuileries
> And waddles round the Louvre.'

I believe it is by Hook.[1] I remember one twilight at the end of a long train journey, when Papa, muffled in a large ulster, kept on saying:

> 'False, fleeting, perjured Clarence,
> That stabbed me in the field by Tewkesbury,'

[1] It is by Thackeray. [M. B.]

and then Byron's 'I saw thee weep', and when it came to

'It could not match the living rays that filled that glance of thine,'

there were tears in his eyes. Then after a pause he broke into Cowper's hymn, 'Hark my soul', and I heard him whispering:

'Can a woman's tender care
Cease towards the child she bare?
Yes, she may forgetful be,
Yet will I remember thee.'

But besides quotations from the poets he knew innumerable tags, epitaphs, epigrams, which used to come out on occasions: Sidney Smith's receipt for a salad; Miss Fanshawe's riddle, ''Twas whispered in heaven, 'twas muttered in hell'; and many other poems of this nature.

My father spoke French and German and Spanish. He knew many of Schiller's poems by heart. Soon after he was married, he bet my mother a hundred pounds that she would not learn Schiller's poem 'Die Glocke' by heart. My mother did not know German. The feat was accomplished, but the question was how was he to be got to hear her repeat the poem, for, whenever she began he merely groaned and said, 'Don't, don't.' One day they were in Paris and had to drive somewhere, a long drive into the suburbs, which was to take an hour or more, and my mother began, 'Fest gemauert in der Erde', and nothing would stop her till she came to the end. She won her hundred pounds. And when my father's silver wedding came about, in 1886, he was given a silver bell with some lines of the 'Glocke' inscribed on it.

Mrs Christie was decidedly of the opinion that we ought to learn German, and so were my father and mother, but German so soon after the Franco-Prussian War was a sore subject in the house owing to Chérie, who cried when the idea of learning German was broached, and I remember one day hearing my mother tell Mrs Christie that she simply couldn't do it. So much did I sympathize with Chérie that I tore out a picture of Bismarck from a handsome illustrated volume dealing with the Franco-Prussian War – an act of sympathy that Chérie never forgot. So my father and mother sadly resigned themselves, and it was settled we were not to learn German. I heard a great deal about German poetry all the same, and one of the outstanding points in the treasury of traditions that I amassed from listening to what my father and mother said was that Goethe was a great poet. I knew the story of *Faust* from a large illustrated edition of that work which used to lie about at Coombe.

But perhaps the most clearly defined of all the traditions that we absorbed were those relating to the actors and the singers of the past, especially to the singers. My father was no great idolator of the past in the matter of acting, and he told me once that he imagined Macready and the actors of his time to have been ranters.

It was French acting he preferred – the art of Got, Delaunay, and Coquelin – although Fechter was spoken of with enthusiasm, and many of the English comedians, the Wigans, Mrs Keeley, Sam Sothern, Buckstone. The Bancrofts and Hare and Mrs Kendal he admired enormously, and Toole made him shake with laughter.

At a play he either groaned if he disliked the acting or shook with laughter if amused, or cried if he was moved. Irving made him groan as Romeo or Benedick, but he admired him in melodrama and character parts, and as Shylock, while Ellen Terry melted him, and when he saw her play *Macbeth*, he kept on murmuring, 'The dear little child.' But it was the musical traditions which were the more important – the old days of Italian Opera, the last days of the *bel canto* – Mario and Grisi and, before them, Ronconi and Rubini and Tamburini.

My mother was never tired of telling of Grisi flinging herself across the door in the *Lucrezia Borgia*, dressed in a parure of turquoises, and Mario singing with her the duet in the *Huguenots*. Mario, they used to say, was a *real* tenor, and had the right *méthode*. None of the singers who came afterwards was allowed to be a real tenor. Jean de Reszke was emphatically not a real tenor. None of the German school had any *méthode*. I suppose Caruso would have been thought a real tenor, but I doubt if his *méthode* would have passed muster. There was one singer who had no voice at all, but who was immensely admired and venerated because of his *méthode*. I think his name was Signor Brizzi. He was a singing-master, and I remember saying that I preferred a singer who had just a little voice.

My father loathed modern German Opera. Mozart, Donizetti, Rossini, and Verdi enchanted him, and my mother, steeped in classical music as she was, preferred Italian operas to all others. Patti was given full marks both for voice and *méthode*, and Trebelli, Albani, and Nilsson were greatly admired. But Wagner was thought noisy, and *Faust* and *Carmen* alone of more modern operas really tolerated.

Sometimes my mother would teach me the accompaniments of the airs in Donizetti's *Lucrezia Borgia*, while she played on the concertina, and she used always to say: 'Do try and get the bass right.' The principle was, and I believe it to be a sound one, that if the bass is right, the treble will take care of itself. What she and my Aunt M'aimée called playing with a *foolish* bass was as bad as driving a pony with a loose rein, which was for them another unpardonable sin.

On the French stage, tradition went back as far as Rachel, although my mother never saw her, and I don't think my father did; but Desclée was said to be an incomparable artist, of the high-strung, nervous, delicate type. The accounts of her remind one of Eleonora Duse, whose acting delighted my father when he saw her. 'Est-elle jolie?' someone said of Desclée. 'Non, elle est pire.'

Another name which meant something definite to me was that of Fargeuil, who I imagine was an intensely emotional actress with a wonderful charm of expression and utterance. My father was never surprised at people preferring the new to the old. He seemed to expect it, and when I once told him later that I preferred Stevenson to Scott, a judgment I have since revised and reversed, he was not in the least surprised, and said: 'Of course, it must be so; it is more modern.' But he was glad to find I enjoyed Dickens, laughed at *Pickwick*, and thought *Vanity Fair* an interesting book, when I read these books later at school.

We were taken to see some good acting before I went to school. We saw the last performances of *School* and *Ours* at the Haymarket with the Bancrofts. My mother always spoke of Mrs Bancroft as Marie Wilton: we saw Hare in *The Colonel* and the *Quiet Rubber*; Mrs Kendal in the *Ironmaster*, and Sarah Bernhardt in *Hernani*. She had left the Théâtre français then, and was acting with her husband, M. Damala. This, of course, was the greatest excitement of all, as I knew many passages of the play, and the whole of the last act by heart. I can remember now Sarah's exquisite modulation of voice when she said:

> 'Tout s'est éteint, flambeaux et musique de fête,
> Rien que la nuit et nous, félicité parfaite.'

The greatest theatrical treat of all was to go to the St James's Theatre, because Mr Hare was a great friend of the family and used to come and stay at Membland, so that when we went to his theatre we used to go behind the scenes. I saw several of his plays: Pinero's *Hobby Horse*, *Lady Clancarty*, and the first night of *As You Like It*. This was on Saturday, 24th January 1885.

One night we were given the Queen's box at Covent Garden by Aunt M'aimée, and we went to the opera. It was *Aïda*.

We also saw Pasca in *La joie fait peur*, so that the tradition that my sisters could hand on to their children was linked with a distant past.

When Mary Anderson first came to London we went to see her in the *Lady of Lyons*, and never shall I forget her first entrance on the stage. This was rendered the more impressive by an old lady with white hair making an entrance just before Mary Anderson, and Cecil, who was with us, pretending to think she was Mary Anderson, and saying with polite resignation that she was a little less young than he had expected. When Mary Anderson did appear, her beauty took our breath away; she was dressed in an Empire gown with her hair done in a pinnacle, and she looked like a picture of the Empress Josephine: radiant with youth, and the kind of beauty that is beyond and above discussion; eyes like stars, classic arms, a nobly modelled face, and matchless grace of carriage. Next year we all went in a box to see her in *Pygmalion and Galatea*, a play that I was never tired of reproducing afterwards on my toy theatre.

As I grew older, I remember going to one or two grown-up parties in London. One was at Grosvenor House, a garden party, with, I think, a bazaar going on. There was a red-coated band playing in the garden, and my cousin, Betty Ponsonby, who was there, asked me to go and ask the band to play a valse called 'Jeunesse Dorée'. I did so, spoke to the bandmaster, and walked to the other end of the lawn. To my surprise I saw the whole band following me right across the lawn, and taking up a new position at the place I had gone to. Whether they thought I had meant they could not be heard where they were, I don't know, but I was considerably embarrassed; so, I think, was my cousin, Betty.

Another party I remember was at Stafford House. My mother was playing the violin in an amateur ladies' string-band, conducted by Lady Folkestone. My cousin, Bessie Bulteel, had to accompany Madame Neruda in a violin solo and pianoforte duet. The Princess of Wales and the three little princesses were sitting in the front row on red velvet chairs. The Princess of Wales in her orders and jewels seemed to me, and I am sure to all the grown-up people as well, like the queen of a fairy-tale who had strayed by chance into the world of mortals; she was different and more graceful than anyone else there.

There is one kind of beauty which sends grown-up people into raptures, but which children are quite blind to; but there is another and rarer order of beauty which, while it amazes the grown-up and makes the old cry, binds children with a spell. It is an order of beauty in which the grace of every movement, the radiance of the smile, and the sure promise of lasting youth in the cut of the face make you forget all other attributes, however perfect.

Of such a kind was the grace and beauty of the Princess of Wales. She was as lovely then as Queen Alexandra.

I was taken by my father in my black velvet suit. I was sitting on a chair somewhere at the end of a row, and couldn't see very well. One of the little princesses smiled at me and beckoned to me, so I boldly walked up and sat next to them, and the Princess of Wales then took me on her knee, greatly to the surprise of my mother when she walked on to the platform with the band. The audience was splendid and crowded with jewelled beauties, and I remember one of the grown-ups asking another: 'Which do you admire most, Lady Clarendon or Lady Dudley?'

Another party I remember was an afternoon party at Sir Frederic Leighton's house, with music. Every year he gave this party, and every year the same people were invited. The music was performed by the greatest artists: Joachim, Madame Neruda, Piatti the violoncellist, and the best pianists of the day, in a large Moorish room full of flowers. It was the most intimate of concerts. The audience, which was quite small, used to sit in groups round the pianoforte, and only in the more leisurely London of the 'eighties could you have had such an exquisite performance and so naturally cultivated, so unaffectedly musical an audience. The Leighton party looked like a Du Maurier illustration.

When we were in London my father would sometimes come back on Saturday afternoons with a present for one of us, not a toy, but something much more rare and fascinating – a snuff-box that opened with a trick, or a bit of china. These were kept for us by Chérie in a cupboard till we should be older. One day he took out of a vitrine a tiny doll's cup of dark blue Sèvres which belonged to a large service and gave it me, and I have got it now. But the present I enjoyed more than any I have ever received in my life, except, perhaps, the fifty-shilling train, was one day when we were walking down a path at Membland, he said: 'This is your path; I give it to you and the gate at the end.' It was the inclusion of the little iron gate at the end which made that present poignantly perfect.

There was no end to my father's generosity. His gifts were on a large scale and reached far and wide. He used to collect Breguet watches; but he did not keep them; he gave them away to people who he thought would like one. He had a contempt for half measures, and liked people to do the big thing on a large scale. 'So-and-so,' he used to say, 'has behaved well.' That meant had been big and free-handed, and above small and mean considerations. He liked the *best*: the old masters, a Turner landscape, a Velasquez, a Watteau; good furniture, good china, good verse, and good acting; Shakespeare, which he knew by heart, so if you went with him to a play such as *Hamlet*, he could have prompted the players; Schiller, Juvenal, Pope, and Dryden and Byron; the acting of the Comédie française, and Ellen Terry's diction and pathos. Tennyson was spoilt for him by the mere existence of the 'May Queen'; but when he saw a good modern thing, he admired it. He said that Mrs Patrick Campbell in her performance of Mrs Ebbsmith, which we went to the first night of, was a real *Erscheinung*, and when all the pictures of Watts were exhibited together at Burlington House he thought that massed performance was that of a great man. He was no admirer of Burne-Jones, but the four pictures of the 'Briar Rose' struck him as great pictures.

He was quite uninsular, and understood the minds and the ways of foreigners. He talked foreign languages not only easily, but naturally, without effort or affectation, and native turns of expression delighted him, such as a German saying, 'Lieber Herr Oberkellner', or, as I remember, a Frenchman saying after a performance of a melodrama at a Casino where the climax was rather tamely executed, 'Ce coup de pistolet était un peu mince.' And once I won his unqualified praise by putting at the end of a letter, which I had written to my Italian master at Florence, and which I had had to send *via* the city in order to have a money order enclosed with it, 'Abbi la gentilezza di mandarmi un biglettino.' This use of a diminutive went straight to my father's heart. Nothing amused him more than instances of John Bullishness; for instance, a young man who once said to him at Contrexéville: 'I hate abroad.'

He conformed naturally to the customs of other countries, and as he had travelled all over the world, he was familiar with the mind and habit of every part of Europe. He was completely unselfconscious, and was known once when there was a ball going on in his own house at Charles Street to have disappeared into his dressing-room, undressed, and walked in his dressing-gown through the dining-room, where people were having supper, with a bedroom candle in his hand to the back staircase to go up to his bedroom. His warmth of heart was like a large generous fire, and the people who warmed their hands at it were without number.

With all his comprehension of foreigners and their ways, he was intensely English; and he was at home in every phase of English life, and nowhere more so than pottering about farms and fields on his grey cob, saying: 'The whole of that fence must come down – every bit of it,' or playing whist and saying about his partner, one of my aunts: 'Good God, what a fool the woman is!'

Whist reminds me of a painful episode. I have already said that I learnt to play long whist in the housekeeper's room. I was proud of my knowledge, and asked to play one night after dinner at Membland with the grown-ups. They played short whist. I got on all right at first, and then out of anxiety I revoked. Presently my father and mother looked at each other, and a mute dialogue took place between them, which said clearly: 'Has he revoked?' 'Yes, he has.' They said nothing about it, and when the rubber was over my father said: 'The dear little boy played very nicely.' But I minded their not knowing that I knew that they knew, almost as much as having revoked. It was a bitter mortification – a real humiliation. Later on when I was bigger and at school, the girls and I used to play every night with my father, and our bad play, which never improved, made him so impatient that we invented a code of signals saying, 'Bêchez' when we wanted spades to lead, and other words for the other suits.

A person whom we were always delighted to see come into the house was our Uncle Johnny. When we were at school he always tipped us. If we were in London he always suggested going to a play and taking all the stalls.

When we went out hunting with the Dartmoor foxhounds he always knew exactly what the fox was going to do, and where it was going. And he never bothered one at the Meet. I always thought the Meet spoilt the fun of hunting. Every person one knew used to come up, say that either one's girths were too tight or one's stirrups too long or too short, and set about making some alteration. I was always a bad horseman, although far better as a child than as a grown-up person. And I knew for certain that if there was an open gate with a crowd going through it, my pony would certainly make a dart through that crowd, the gate would be slammed, and I should not be able to prevent this happening, and there would be a chorus of curses. But under the guidance of Uncle Johnny everything always went well.

Whenever he came to Membland, the first thing he would do would be to sit down and write a letter. He must have had a vast correspondence. Then he would tell stories in Devonshire dialect which were inimitable.

There are some people who, directly they come into the room, not by anything they say or do, not by any display of high spirits or effort to amuse, make everything brighter and more lively and more gay, especially for children, and Uncle Johnny was one of those. As the Bulteel family lived close to us, we saw them very often. They all excelled at games and at every kind of outdoor sport. The girls were fearless riders and drivers and excellent cricketers. Cricket matches at Membland were frequent in the summer. Many people used to drive from Plymouth to play lawn-tennis at Pamflete, the Bulteels' house.

We saw most of Bessie Bulteel, who was the eldest girl. She was a brilliant pianist, with a fairylike touch and electric execution, and her advent was the greatest treat of my childhood. She told thrilling ghost stories, which were a fearful joy, but which made it impossible for me to pass a certain piece of Italian furniture on the landing which had a painted Triton on it. It looks a very harmless piece of furniture now. I saw it not long ago in my brother Cecil's house. It is a gilt writing-table painted with varnished figures, nymphs and fauns, in the Italian manner. The Triton sprawls on one side of it recumbent beside a cool source. Nothing could be more peaceful or idyllic, but I remember the time when I used to rush past it on the passage in blind terror.

A picturesque figure, as of another age, was my great-aunt, Lady Georgiana Grey, who came to Membland once in my childhood. She was old enough to have played the harp to Byron. She lived at Hampton Court and played whist every night of her life, and sometimes went up to London to the play when she was between eighty and ninety. She was not deaf, her sight was undimmed, and she had a great contempt for people who were afraid of draughts. She had a fine aptitude for flat contradiction, and she was a verbal conservative, that is to say, she had a horror of modern locutions and abbreviations, piano for pianoforte, balcōny for balcŏni, cucumber for cowcumber, Montagu for Mountagu, soot for sut, yellow for yallow.

She wore on her little finger an antique onyx ring with a pig engraved on it, and I asked her to give it me. She said: 'You shall have it when you are older.' An hour later I went up to her room and said: 'I am older now.

Can I have the ring?' She gave it me. Nobody ever sat at a table so bolt upright as she did, and she lived to be ninety-nine. She came back once to Membland after my sisters were married.

Perhaps the greatest excitement of all our Membland life was when the whole of the Harbord family, our cousins, used to arrive for Christmas. Our excitement knew no bounds when we knew they were coming, and Chérie used to get so tired of hearing the Harbords quoted that I remember her one day in the schoolroom in London opening the window, taking the lamp to it and saying: 'J'ouvre cette fenêtre pour éclairer la famille Harbord.'

On rainy days at Membland there were two rare treats: one was to play hide-and-seek all over the house; the other was to make toffee and perhaps a gingerbread cake in the stillroom. The toffee was the ultra-sticky treacle kind, and the cake when finished and baked always had a wet hole in the middle of it. Hugo and I used to spend a great deal of time in Mr Ellis' carpenter's shop. We had tool-boxes of our own, and we sometimes made Christmas presents for our father and mother; but our carpentry was a little too imaginative and rather faulty in execution.

Not far from Membland and about a mile from Pamflete there was a small grey Queen Anne house called 'Mothecombe'. It nestled on the coast among orchards and quite close to the sandy beach of Mothecombe Bay, the only sandy beach on our part of the South Devon coast. This house belonged to the Mildmays, and we often met the Mildmay family when we went over there for picnics.

Aunt Georgie Mildmay was not only an expert photographer, but she was one of the first of those rare people who have had a real talent for photography and achieved beautiful and artistic results with it, both in portraits and landscapes.

Whenever Hugo and I used to go and see her in London at 46 Berkeley Square, where she lived, she always gave us a pound, and never a holiday passed without visiting Aunt Georgie.

Mothecombe was often let or lent to friends in summer. One summer Lady de Grey took it, and she came over to luncheon at Membland, a vision of dazzling beauty, so that, as someone said, you saw green after looking at her. It was like looking at the sun. The house was often taken by a great friend of our family, Colonel Ellis, who used to spend the summer there with his family, and he frequently stayed at Membland with us. I used to look forward to going down to dinner when he was there, and listening to his conversation. He was the most perfect of talkers, because he knew what to say to people of all ages, besides having an unending flow of amusing things to tell, for he made everything he told amusing, and he would sometimes take the menu and draw me a picture illustrating the games and topics that interested us at the moment. We had a game at one time which was to give someone three people they liked equally, and to say those three people were on the top of a tower; one you could lead down gently by the hand, one you must kick down, and the third must be left to be picked by the crows.

We played this one evening, and the next day Colonel Ellis appeared with a charming pen-and-ink drawing of a Louis-Quinze Marquis leading a *poudrée* gently by the hand. If he gave one a present it would be something quite unique – unlike what anyone else could think of; once it was, for me, a silver mug with a twisted handle and my name engraved on it in italics, '*Maurice Baring's Mug*, 1885'. His second son, Gerald, was a little bit older than I was, and we were great friends. Gerald had a delightfully grown-up and blasé manner as a child, and one day, with the perfect manner of a man of the world, he said to me, talking of Queen Victoria, 'The fact is, the woman's raving mad'.

We used to call Colonel Ellis 'the gay Colonel' to carefully distinguish him from Colonel Edgcumbe, whom we considered a more serious Colonel. The Mount Edgcumbes were neighbours, and lived just over the Cornish border at Mount Edgcumbe. Colonel Edgcumbe was Lord Mount Edgcumbe's brother, and often stayed with us. He used to be mercilessly teased, especially by the girls of the Bulteel family. One year he was shooting with us and the Bulteels got hold of his cartridges and took out the shot, leaving a few good cartridges.

He was put at the hot corner. Rocketing pheasants in avalanches soared over his head, and he, of course, missed them nearly all, shooting but one or two. He explained for the rest of the day that it was a curious thing, and that something must be wrong, either with his eyes or with the climate. Some new way of tormenting was always found, and, although he was not the kind of man who naturally enjoys a practical joke, he bore it angelically.

His sister, Lady Ernestine, was rather touchy in the matter of Devonshire clotted cream. As Mount Edgcumbe was just over the border in Cornwall, and as clotted cream was made in Cornwall as well as in Devonshire, she resented its being called Devonshire cream and used to call it Cornish cream; but when she stayed with us, not wishing to concede the point and yet unwilling to hurt our feelings, she used to call it West-country cream.

Another delightful guest was Miss Pinkie Browne, who was Irish, gay, argumentative, and contradictious, with smiling eyes, her hair in a net, and an infectious laugh. As a girl she had broken innumerable hearts, but had always refused to marry, as she never could make up her mind. She was extremely musical, and used to sing English and French songs, accompanying herself, with an intoxicating lilt and a languishing expression. As Dr Smyth says about Tosti's singing, it was small art, but it was real art. And her voice must have had a rare quality, as she was about fifty when I heard her. Such singing is far more enjoyable than that of professional singers, and makes one think of Tosti's saying: 'Le chant est un truc.' She would make a commonplace song poignantly moving. She used to sing a song called 'The Conscript's Farewell':

'You are going far away, far away, from poor Jeanette,
There's no one left to love me now, and you will soon forget;'

of which the refrain was:

'Oh, if I were Queen of France,
Or still better Pope of Rome,
I would have no fighting men abroad,
No weeping maids at home.'

Membland was always full of visitors. There were visitors at Easter, visitors at Whitsuntide, in the autumn for the shooting, and a houseful at Christmas: an uncle, General Baring, who used to shoot with one arm because he had lost the other in the Crimea; my father's cousin, Lord Ashburton, who was particular about his food, and who used to say: 'That's a very good dish, but it's not *veau à la bourgeoise*'; Godfrey Webb, who always wrote a little poem in the visitors' book when he went away; Lord Granville, who knew French so alarmingly well, and used to ask one the French for words like a big stone upright on the edge of a road and a ship tacking, till one longed to say, like the Red Queen in *Alice in Wonderland*: 'What's the French for fiddle de dee?'; Lord and Lady Lansdowne, Mr and Mrs Percy Wyndham – Mr Wyndham used to take me out riding; he was deliciously inquisitive, so that if one was laughing at one side of the table he would come to one quietly afterwards and ask what the joke had been about; Harry Cust, radiant with youth and spirits and early success; Lady de Clifford and her two daughters (Katie and Maud Russell), she carrying an enormous silk bag with her work in it – she was a kind critic of our French plays; Lady Airlie, and her sister, Miss Maude Stanley, who started being a vegetarian in the house, and told me that Henry VIII was a much misunderstood monarch; Madame Neruda, and once, long before she married him, Sir Charles Hallé. Sir Charles Hallé used to sit down at the pianoforte after dinner, and nothing could dislodge him. Variation followed variation, and repeat followed repeat of the stiffest and driest classical sonatas. And one night when this had been going on past midnight, my father, desperate with impatience and sleep, put out the electric light. I am not making an anachronism in talking of electric light, as it had just been put in the house, and was thought to be a most daring innovation.

We had a telegraph office in the house, which was worked by Mrs Tudgay. It was a fascinating instrument, rather like a typewriter with two dials and little steel keys round one of them, and the alphabet was the real alphabet and not the Morse Code. It was convenient having this in the house, but one of the results was that so many jokes were made with it, and so many bogus telegrams arrived, that nobody knew whether a telegram was a real one or not.

Mr Walter Durnford, then an Eton House master, and afterwards Provost of King's, in a poem he wrote in the visitors' book, speaks of Membland as a place where everything reminded you of the presence of fairy folk, 'Where telegrams come by the dozen, concocted behind the door'.

Certainly people enjoyed themselves at Membland, and the Christmas parties were one long riot of dance, song, and laughter. Welcome ever smiled at Membland, and farewell went out sighing.

As I got nearer and nearer to the age of ten, when it was settled that I should go to school, life seemed to become more and more wonderful every day. Both at Membland and in Charles Street the days went by in a crescendo of happiness. Walks with Chérie in London were a daily joy, especially when we went to Covent Garden and bought chestnuts to roast for tea. The greatest tea treat was to get Chérie, who was an inspired cook, to make something she called *la petite sauce*. You boiled eggs hard in the kettle; and then, in a little china frying-pan over a spirit lamp, the sauce was made, of butter, cream, vinegar, pepper, and the eggs were cut up and floated in the delicious hot mixture. A place of great treats where we sometimes went on Saturday afternoons was the Aquarium, where acrobats did wonderful things, and you had your bumps told and your portrait cut out in black-and-white silhouette. The phrenologist was not happy in his predictions of my future, as he said I had a professional and mathematical head, and would make a good civil engineer in after-life.

Going to the play was the greatest treat of all, and if I heard there was any question of their going to the play downstairs, and Mr Deacon, my father's servant, always used to tell me when tickets were being ordered, I used to go on my knees in the night nursery and pray that I might be taken too. Sometimes the answer was direct.

One night my mother and Lord Mount Edgcumbe were going to a pantomime together by themselves. Mr Deacon told me, and asked me if I was going too, but nothing had been said about it. I prayed hard, and I went down to my mother's bedroom as she was dressing for dinner. No word of the pantomime was mentioned on either side. She then, while her hair was being done by D., asked for a piece of paper and scribbled a note and told me to take it down to my father.

I did so, and my father said: 'Would you like to go to the pantomime, too?' The answer was in the affirmative.

What a fever one would be in to start in time and to be there at the beginning on nights when we went to the play! how terribly anxious not to miss one moment! How wonderful the moment was before the curtain went up! The delicious suspense, the orchestra playing, and then the curtain rising on a scene that sometimes took one's breath away, and how calm the grown-up people were. They would not look at the red light in the background, the pink sky which looked like a real pink sky, or perhaps some moving water. People say sometimes it is bad for children to go to the theatre, but do they ever enjoy anything in after life as much? Is there any such magic as the curtain going up on the Demon's cave in the pantomime, or the sight in the Transformation scene of two silvery fairies rising from the ground on a gigantic wedding cake, and the clown suddenly breaking on the scene, shouting, 'Here we are again!' through a shower of gold rain and a cloud of different-coloured Bengal lights? Is there any such pleasure as in suddenly seeing and recognizing things in the flesh one had been familiar with for long from books and stories, such as Cinderella's coach, the roc's egg in Sinbad the Sailor, or Aladdin's cave, or the historical processions of the kings of England, some of whom you clapped and some of whom you hissed? Oh! the charm of changing scenery! a ship moving or still better sinking, a sunset growing red, a forest growing dark; and then the fun! The indescribable fun, of seeing Cinderella's sisters being knocked about in the kitchen, or the Babes in the Wood being put to bed, and kicking all their bedclothes off directly they had settled down; or best of all, the clown striking the pantaloon with the red-hot poker and the harlequin getting the better of the policeman! Harry Paine was the clown in those days, and he used, in a hoarse voice, to say to the pantaloon: 'I say, Joey.' 'Yes, master,' answered the pantaloon in a feeble falsetto.

Childhood bereft of such treats I cannot help thinking must be a sad affair; and it generally happens that if children are not allowed to go to the play, so that they shall enjoy it more when they are grown-up, they end by never being able to enjoy it at all.

One great event of the summer was the Eton and Harrow match, when Cecil and Everard used to come up from Eton with little pieces of light blue silk in their black coats. John had gone to Cambridge, and I hardly remember him as an Eton boy. We used to go on a coach belonging to some friends, and one year one of the Parkers bowled three of the Harrow boys running.

As Chérie had been with Lord Macclesfield in the Parker family before she came to us, and as this boy, Alex Parker, had either been or nearly been one of her pupils, she had a kind of reflected glory from the event.

Eton was always surrounded with a glamour of romance. John had rowed stroke in the Eton eight, and when Cecil rose to the dignity of being Captain of the Oppidans we were proud indeed. One summer we all went down to Eton for the 4th of June.

We went to speeches and had tea in Cecil's room, and strawberry messes, and walked about in the playing-fields and saw the procession of boats and the fireworks.

From that day I was filled with a longing to go to Eton, and resented bitterly having to go to a private school first.

Another exciting event I remember was a visit to Windsor, to the Norman Tower in Windsor Castle, where my uncle, Henry Ponsonby, and my Aunt M'aimée lived. This happened one year in the autumn. We stayed a Sunday there. The house was, for a child, fraught with romance and interest. First of all there were the prisons. My aunt had discovered and laid bare the stone walls of two octagonal rooms in the tower which had been prisons in the olden times for State prisoners, and she had left the walls bare. There were on them inscriptions carved by the prisoners. She had made these two rooms her sitting-rooms, and they were full of books, and there was a carpenter's bench in one of these rooms, with a glass of water on it ready for painting.

Windsor was itself exciting enough, but I think what struck me most then was the toy cupboard of the boys, Fritz, Johnny, and Arthur. All their toys were arranged in tiers in a little windowless room, a tier belonging to each separate boy, and in the middle of each beautiful and symmetrical arrangement there were toys representing a little room with a table and lamp on it. As if all this was not exciting enough, my Cousin Betty told me the story of the Corsican Brothers.

Before I went to school my father had to go to Contrexéville to take the waters. My father and mother took me with them. I faintly regretted not playing a solo at Mademoiselle Ida's pupils' concert, which was to have been part of the programme, but otherwise the pleasure and excitement at going were unmitigated. We started for Paris in July. Bessie Bulteel came with us, and we stopped a night in Paris, at the Hôtel Bristol. My father took me for a walk in the Rue de la Paix, and the next day we went to Contrexéville. I never enjoyed anything more in my life than those three weeks at Contrexéville. There were shops in the hotel gardens called *les Galeries*, where a charming old lady, called Madame Paillard, with her daughter, Thérèse, sold the delicious sweets of Nancy, and spoilt me beyond words. The grown-up people played at *petits chevaux* in the evening, and as I was not allowed to join in that game, the lady of the *petits chevaux*, Mademoiselle Rose, had a kind of rehearsal of the game in the afternoon at half-price, in which only I and the actresses of the Casino, whom I made great friends with, took part. My special friend was Mademoiselle Tusini of the Eldorado Paris Music Hall. She was a songstress.

One day she asked me to beg Madame Aurèle, the *directrice* of the Theatre, to let her sing a song at the Casino which she had not been allowed to sing, and which was called 'Les allumettes du Général'.

Mademoiselle Tusini said it was her greatest success, and that when she had sung it at Nancy, nobody knew where to look. I pleaded her cause; but Madame Aurèle said, 'Un jour quand il n'y aura que des Messieurs,' so I am afraid the song can hardly have been quite nice. When we went away, Mademoiselle Tusini gave me a large photograph of herself in the rôle of a *commère*, carrying a wand. Chérie was slightly astonished when she saw it, and when I described the great beauty and the wonderful goodness of Mademoiselle Tusini, she was not as enthusiastically sympathetic as I could have wished.

There were a great many French children at Contrexéville, and I was allowed to join in their games. There was a charming old curé who I made friends with in the village, and his church was the first Catholic church I ever entered.

My mother and father used to go to the Casino play every night. I was allowed to go once or twice, as Mademoiselle Tusini had threatened to strike if I left Contrexéville without seeing her act, so I was taken to *Monsieur Choufleury restera chez lui*, a harmless farce, which is, I believe, often acted by amateurs.

We stayed there three weeks, and I left in sorrow and tears. We went on for a *Nachkur* to a place in the Vosges called Géradmer, which is near a lake. One day we drove to a place called the *Schlucht*, and saw the stone marking the frontier into Alsace, which was, of course, Germany. It was suggested that we should cross over, but I, mindful of Chérie, refused to set foot on the stolen and violated territory.

On the way back we stayed a day and night in Paris, and bought presents for all those at home. In the evening we went to the Théâtre français and saw no less an actor than Delaunay in Musset's play, *On ne badine pas avec l'Amour*. Delaunay had a voice like silver, and his diction on the stage was incomparable. I remember Count Benckendorff once saying about him that whereas one often bewailed the failure of an actor to look the part of a *grand seigneur*, when one saw Delaunay one wished anyone off the stage could be half as distinguished as he was on the stage.

My father took me to the Louvre and showed me the *Mona Lisa* and Watteau's large picture of a Pierrot: 'Gilles' and the *Galerie d'Apollon,* and late in the afternoon we drove to the Bois de Boulogne.

Chérie had always told us of the *Magasins du Louvre*, where as children went out they were given, as George, in the poem, when he had been as good as gold, an immense balloon. This balloon had always been one of my dreams, and we went there, and the reality was fully up to all expectations.

We bought some *nonnettes* in the Rue St Honoré and a great many toys at the *Paradis des Enfants*.

The next time I went to Contrexéville I was at school. I wore an Eton jacket and a top hat in Paris; this created a sensation. A man said to me in the Rue de Rivoli, 'Monsieur a son Gibus.' I also remember receiving a wonderful welcome in the *Galeries*.

With the end of the first visit to Contrexéville I will end this chapter, for it was the end of a chapter of life, the happiest and most wonderful chapter of all. New gates were opened; but the gate on the fairyland of childhood was shut, and for ever afterwards one could only look through the bars, but never more be a free and lawful citizen of that enchanted country, where life was like a fairy-tale that seemed almost too good to be true, and yet so endlessly long and so infinitely happy that it seemed as if it must last for ever.

# 2

*Common Sense and Culture*

For Maurice Baring all the arts, and their point in society and the individual's fulfilment through them, were as real as the material daily facts of living. He was marvellously the enactor as well as the creator of an artistic body of life. He took from his cultural inheritance his daily bread, even as he gave this back to the posterity which he was too modest to expect, and which we now draw upon. In his letters, essays, novels, anecdotes, parodies, and comedies of all sorts, he relied on a common assumption of educated understanding and addressed it with the easiest possible conversational air.

When he ventured into the otherwise esoteric realms of criticism, he behaved with the same delicious innocence with which he made sport of history – but never in ignorance. He disdained the pressure of intellectualistic fads and by-passed them with politeness, trusting his own taste, which was founded on rooted knowledge and wide experience, to lead him to his critical opinions, even if these were out of tune with prevailing and restless modes of literary, psychological, and artistic judgement.

To represent Maurice Baring's abiding delight in the art of theatre – actors, events, literature – we must always begin with his love for Sarah Bernhardt. In any aspect of life that interested him he always looked for certain qualities – bravery, originality, style, and above all, artistry. In Bernhardt he found them all, and over and over he paid her tribute for these, and for her incandescent personality. Apart from his biography of her, and an essay, and various reviews, he wrote of her in his novels. She is alive in his pages. 'She was not tall, but slim, supple, and slight; she had the body of a waif. She was not pretty, but much more – her face was infinitely intelligent and could express anything. She could act beauty. Great beauty.' (Daphne Adeane.) A once fashionable portrait painter – W. Graham Robertson in Life Was Worth Living – said the same thing of her: 'Beauty with her was a garment which she could put on or off as she pleased.'

# High-Brows and Low-Brows

(from *Lost Lectures*)

IT HAS BEEN my misfortune to have been considered a high-brow among low-brows and a low-brow among high-brows: and while such a position has many disadvantages it has one advantage: it enables one to discuss the relative merits of the two categories with a certain impartiality. Let us take the case of the high-brow first. And first of all let us define our terms.

The question has often been debated before. It is constantly being discussed, and you will notice that whenever it is mentioned by the intellectual the first thing he makes clear is that he, although he may be passionately interested in the things of the mind, is not a high-brow: other people are high-brows, not he himself.

If a high-brow means a scholar – but what do we mean by a scholar? Someone once defined a businessman as one who can read a balance sheet as easily as a musician can read the page of a full score, and a scholar as a man who could read Greek with his feet on the fender. If a high-brow means a scholar, or if a high-brow means a lower genus to which I claim to belong, people who are not and never will be scholars, who cannot read the Classics comfortably without a crib, and who have read very few serious books, and have not remembered what they have read, who have no sense of quantity, make false concords as easily as some people fall off a log, and are lax in grammar, but who, nevertheless, like reading books; if a high-brow means the first of these two categories, and to be pro-high-brow implies admiration for it, then I am on the side of the high-brows; and if it means belonging to the second category, then I am a high-brow myself: very high-brow of very high-brow.

At the same time there are bad high-brows as well as good high-brows: let us face the fact.

And even among high-brows, Class A, the scholars, there are some who are sometimes very severe on Class B, the non-scholars, who like reading: they treat these more severely than they treat the quite ignorant. I know this because I have suffered from them.

But let us first consider the case of the good high-brow: the real high-brow. I have known a great many. It is these people I mean to defend and to praise. I admire them immensely. I mean the people who read Greek for fun, and who can write Latin verse as easily as some people can guess crossword puzzles, who remember the history they have read and who can quote Thucydides and Lucretius, and can do a quadratic equation, and addition and subtraction in their head, and can count their change at a booking-office. When people say of such people 'high-brows', and sniff, I am annoyed; when the high-brows themselves are ashamed of their knowledge and of their culture, I am angry.

When people hide or deny their culture – and I mean *deny* it, not modestly conceal it – and laugh at the cultured when they are still more cultured themselves, I see red; because I regard this culture as the bulwark of our civilization, rapidly, alas! being undermined by the relentless tide of education, and our most precious heritage, which we are fast losing.

Things were very different in the eighteenth century. In the eighteenth century Dr Johnson said that any man who wore a sword and a wig was ashamed of being illiterate, and that Greek was like lace: a man had as much of it as he could. Dr Johnson was talking of ordinary men of the world; the men who went to clubs and drank three bottles of claret. They were small bottles, what we call pints. The same cannot be said of men who wear plus-fours or polo boots. If they have Latin and Greek they hide it, and if taxed with it they would probably deny it.

When people quote Latin in the House of Commons, the quotation is now greeted with cries of 'Translate': in the eighteenth century there would have been no need of translation, and those who did not know what the quotation meant would have concealed their ignorance decently. This is due to the spread of what is called Education. More people are taught things, but they are taught less. In fact, they are taught hardly anything; in former times they were taught little, but that little they learnt. It was beaten into them.

I am speaking of England.

In Scotland everything is different. The Scotch people are highly educated. You will notice I say Scotch, and not Scottish. If I were writing for one of the daily morning or evening newspapers the sub-editor would automatically cut out the word Scotch and substitute the word Scottish, and yet if you look out the word Scottish in the dictionary you will see that the word Scottish was originally used only technically for matters of law, or institutions, such as the Scottish Archers, but the ordinary English adjective, meaning native of Scotland, was Scotch, and the word Scotch was used by Shakespeare, Dr Johnson, Sir Walter Scott and Stevenson,[1] and we still say, 'I would like some Scotch whisky to drink', or

[1] See *Kidnapped*, chapter xvii – 'which we have no name for either in Scotch or English'. [M. B.]

'A Scotch and splash, miss', and we do not say, 'A Scottish and splash, miss'. This use of the word 'Scottish' is a piece of pedantry first started by some Dons, by the kind of high-brows who are going to be attacked later on in this lecture, and then popularized by the Press when the standard style of writing Pitman's instead of Cranmer's English was adopted by the Board Schools.

They adopted many other things of the same kind. Pedants of this kind and their disciples in the Press swoon when a split infinitive is used, and make a sentence perform acrobatic feats so as to avoid the use of one. But why in Heaven's name should one not use the split infinitive if the emphasis of the sentence demands it? Why should you not say, I wish to emphatically deny, if you want to emphatically deny, when to say I wish to deny emphatically breaks the torrent of your wrath? Good writers can be quoted as using a split infinitive, and in Milton's lines:

> Alas! what boots it with incessant care
> To tend the homely slighted shepherd's trade
> And strictly meditate the thankless Muse.

'Strictly meditate' is a moral split infinitive, because the word 'to' is understood, and 'meditate' is governed by 'to'.[1]

Dr Swift is said to have used a split infinitive, but I can't find it. As the poet says:

> What are you doing? As I live!
> You're splitting an infinitive!
> Go, get your little pot of glue,
> And mend the wretched creature, do!

All this is a digression suggested by the word Scotch or Scottish. And I was saying that the Scotch were well educated: their education has done them no harm in the practical affairs of life, and our best doctors, our best engineers, our best gardeners, and our best mechanics are Scotch.[2]

I remember a year or two after the Great War a firm in the north of England advertised for a young man who had taken Honours in Classics: they were tired of the products of the modern side.

All this may annoy my friend Mr Wells. Mr Wells thinks that not only the Latin and Greek languages, but Latin and Greek history and architecture ought to be eliminated; that they are so much antiquated ivy, choking and rotting the vital growths and strong shoots of the young idea; that the classical ideal is all wrong; what is wanted is modern stuff and modern art. I have nothing against modern art, but I want to know

---

[1] This statement is controversial. [M. B.]
[2] I know there is another side to this question. [M. B.]

exactly what people mean when they talk of modern art. If they mean the products due to the fresh impressions and to the ardent vision of the young, I am with them; but if they mean that modern art must have no roots in the past, and no connection with anything that has gone before, I think they are talking nonsense.

The laws of strategy, someone said in the war, are subject to the laws of common sense, and so are the laws of art.

When people make a thing, it is made with a special purpose and for special use, whether it is a house, a boat, a house-boat, a spoon, or a ship. A house is made to live in, a house-boat to catch cold in, a spoon to feed with, a ship to sail or to row in, a church to pray in, a theatre to hear plays in, a railway station is a place for people to get into a train from or for people to get out of a train into. (My prepositions are at the end of my sentence: and I mean them to be.) Given that fact, these things are subject to certain laws. A spoon that is flat cannot hold foodstuffs; it may be beautiful as a work of art, but it is not a spoon. A ship which has masts on its keel and a spherical rudder at the end of the bowsprit may be interesting, but cannot be serviceable. A theatre in which there is no room for the audience is not a theatre, and so on. Now the people who understood the laws of supply and demand with regard to concrete objects of use, and who made these things for use, most economically and most practically, so that while they were as closely appropriate to their functions they were also as pleasing to the eye as possible – the people who accomplished this feat as well as possible were the Greeks; so that when we admire a modern work of art because it is appropriate and fulfils its object, we are admiring the spirit and the example of the Greeks, whether we know it or not. The Transylvania Railway Station, the Pierpont [Morgan] Library, and any skyscraper in New York are Greek in that they fulfil their purpose as economically and as beautifully as possible: and to admire American architecture and deny that Greek architecture is beautiful, is a contradiction, a nonsense.

'But,' someone will say, 'I don't care a button for the Parthenon; but I do admire Epstein's Underground Station.' The answer is that if Epstein's Underground Station fulfils its purpose as a station for underground trains, it fulfils one of the aims of Greek architecture; if the ornament on it strikes you as beautiful, it fulfils the other: that is all it aims at, for it is not trying to be useless or ugly. It is striving to be useful and beautiful: if it strikes some people as ugly, that is either their fault for not being able to understand Epstein's meaning, or Epstein's fault for not making his meaning clear or impressive; but the aim in both is the same.

In the case of a new work of art, the expression of a new-fashioned way of looking at things (which may turn out to be an old-fashioned but forgotten way), you need time before you can tell whether the artist has

118

had enough skill to make his meaning plain to a sufficient number of people: if so, his work of art will live . . . for a time, perhaps a long time, perhaps for centuries. Or whether he has not: if so, it will be forgotten in a comparatively short time.

Nobody writes masterpieces, said Anatole France, but some people write what may become masterpieces with the aid of Time,

*'Qui est un galant homme'*.

Mozart aimed at writing tuneful music, and when his first works were produced they were thought harsh. Wagner aimed at weaving webs of beautiful sound, and for a long time these webs were thought to be hideous, until they reached the great public, which never had the slightest difficulty in detecting and enjoying the intricate conglomeration of his recurring snatches of tune.

Whistler's nocturnes were abused by Ruskin and hissed at Christie's when they were put up for auction; but Whistler, as is plain to small children now, was not trying to destroy the art of the old masters; he was trying to do what they had done before him: to depict nature as well as he could as he saw her.

So the theory that because modern art is good ancient art must be destroyed is based on nothing at all. And when people, as I have heard them do, in one breath praise masterpieces of Russian fiction and deplore time spent on the Classics, they are in one breath commending and abusing works that have been produced according to precisely the same standard, and which follow the same laws, and which are good or bad for the same reasons.

I now perceive that I have not yet defined the good high-brow. I will do so at once. I mean by the good high-brow the man who is well educated and glad of the fact without thrusting it down other people's throats, who, without being ashamed of his knowledge, his intellectual or artistic superiority, or his gifts and aptitudes, does not use them as a rod to beat others with, and does not think that because he is the fortunate possessor of certain rare gifts or talents, he is therefore a better or a more useful man: such is the good high-brow. I have known many. The late Vice-Provost of Eton was a good high-brow; the late Lord Balfour was a good high-brow; and there are hosts of others who are dead, and there are some still alive. My point is that the more of these there are the better for the nation, the better for all of us. When there shall be no more of them, it will mean the extinction of our civilization. My point is also that to abuse these people, to despise them, to laugh at them, to be ashamed of them, and, worse still, to be ashamed of being one of them if you happen to be one of them, is to sin against Light, to deny your birthright, and to be false to yourself and to everything else.

It is an unforgivable sin, and the worst form of snobbishness, that is to say, of cowardice.

Now we come to the bad high-brow, which no high-brow will admit that he can be; but, as a Master of Trinity once said, we are none of us infallible, not even the youngest of us. And the moment we fall into the temptation of despising the interests and the recreations of others, however futile they may seem to us, we become bad high-brows.

The worst kind of high-brow is he who calls other people high-brows. It is bad when high-brows despise people for going racing; but it is worse when they despise them for not going racing, for one suspects insincerity at once.

The worst faults of the bad high-brow are not (putting aside his knowledge, learning, scholarship or culture, which are not faults at all, but the gifts of Heaven, if they are genuine, and the curse of the devil if they are false) his pride, arrogance and narrow-mindedness; but his envy of others who are either high-brows like himself and possibly better ones, or, worse still, his envy of others who are not high-brows at all, but people who are amusing themselves in their own way. If you want to know what envy is, said Lord Beaconsfield, you should live among artists; but were he alive now he would have said you must live among high-brows. But the bad high-brow is not a new thing: he is as old as the hills. Aristophanes knew him and satirized him; Molière knew him, male and female, and shot some of his most pointed arrows at the species, fixing them to remain for ever before our delighted gaze.

In fact, the bad high-brow has had his full meed of satire and censure, and we may be sure that as long as satirists exist, and as long as he exists, he will always get it.

The bad low-brow gets his share too. Tony Lumpkin was essentially a low-brow, and so was Mr G. P. Huntley's Algy, who was awfully good at algebra, and all the well-dressed swells satirized by different generations of comedy artists (musical or not), from Sothern's Lord Dundreary, and Nelly Farren, to the days of Vesta Tilley or Nelson Keys; by writers such as Mr Anstey, Mr Belloc, Mr P. G. Wodehouse and Mr A. P. Herbert.

Mr Wodehouse excels at drawing the contrast and the conflict between the high-brow and the low-brow, between the male low-brow and the female high-brow, and especially between the male English high-brow and the American female high-brow.

For in America most high-brows are female and most low-brows are male. In fact, they are just Brows. Of course when American high-brows are male, they excel all other Brows in the height of their brows, just as American skyscrapers are the highest in the world: that is because America is such a big country; and also because Americans generally export that kind.

I was once travelling from St Petersburg to Moscow, and in the same carriage with me there happened to be two high-brows – a Russian student and a Japanese student. The Russian student was expansive and talkative, and the Japanese was civil but reserved. The Russian could not talk Japanese, and the Japanese could, besides Japanese, only talk English. When the Russian talked to the Japanese the Japanese made a noise like a syphon; but the Russian, not contented with that, insisted on my interpreting his questions to the Japanese:

'Ask him if he knows English,' said the Russian.

I did. The Japanese made a hissing noise. I thought that meant 'yes'.

'Ask him,' continued the Russian, 'if he has read any English books.'

The Japanese said he had read the English lyric, but not the English epic.

'Ask him if he has read the great English modern authors,' said the Russian.

'Which?' I asked.

'Lord Byron, Oscar Wilde, Jerome K. Jerome, Mrs Humphry Ward, Herbert Spencer, and Jack London,' said the Russian, all in one breath.

I put the question. The Japanese smiled, and said he had read the English novel.

'Which one?' asked the Russian (through me).

'All of it,' answered the Japanese (through me).

'All of which one?'

'All the English novel.'

'Dickens?'

A negative hiss.

'Thackeray?'

Another negative hiss.

'George Eliot?'

A double hiss.

'George Meredith?'

A vacant look.

'Marie Corelli?'

A raised eyebrow.

'Conan Doyle?'

Silence, which implied definite disapproval.

'Thomas Hardy?'

Complete silence.

I began to give it up.

The Japanese then opened a bag and produced a book printed in Japanese.

He pointed to it and said:

'The English novel.'

But as it was printed in Japanese and began at the end, we were not much wiser.

He then produced another book, and, pointing to it, said:
'The English lyric.'
It seemed to be rather a long lyric.

We then gave it up, and the Russian explained to me what was worth reading in English literature. He said that the greatest English writer after Lord Byron was Oscar Wilde. That Jerome K. Jerome's *Three Men in a Boat* was a very funny book, but that Jerome K. Jerome's masterpiece was *Mark Clever*. (I had not read it, to his immense surprise. I have read it since, and I do think it is a very good book.) But the greatest English story-teller was Mrs Humphry Ward. Her greatest book was *Marcella*, but *Sir George Tressady* was very good, too. There was no English drama. It was a pity.

'Shakespeare?' I said. And then I thought we might try the Japanese with Shakespeare, but he only hissed.

'Shakespeare,' said the Russian, 'never existed. There was no such man.'

'But his plays exist,' I said.

'They are reactionary,' said the Russian. 'We are past all that. We no longer understand it. They are no longer acted.'

I begged his pardon, there was one of them being acted in Moscow at the present moment – *Julius Caesar* – I had seen it.

'All that,' said the Russian, 'is nothing. Shakespeare is nothing; besides which he never existed.'

'Have you ever read *Hamlet*?' I asked.

'*Gamlet*,' he corrected me. Yes, he had read *Gamlet* at school. 'We read that at school,' he explained, 'and then we forget it; it does not interest us – it is outside of our movement.'

I asked what his movement was. He said that in politics he was an amorphist, but that his movement was towards the left phase of the middle right in literature, but towards the left phase of the left in music, and towards the left phase of the right in painting. He thought there should be no words in the drama: only gymnastics and facial expression. Then he corrected himself and said:

'No,' with great vehemence. 'No facial expression. Masks, like the Greeks.'

I asked him if he liked Greek plays. He said No, the Greeks were anti-social, except the *Antigone* of Sophocles, which was good left. I asked him whether he had heard of Bernard Shaw. At first he did not understand. Then he said Sheu? pronounced like the French *le*. He understood. Yes, he had seen a play of his in St Petersburg. It is what they called left-centre. Very old-fashioned. The play was called *Mistress Ooaren*.

All this time the Japanese looked on and smiled and said nothing. Then we neared a station, and the Japanese took a French book from his bag and pointed to it, saying: 'The French novel.'

It was called *Le Roman Russe*, by the Count Melchior de Vogüé.

Over and over again it has been my fortune to be told about English literature by foreign high-brows in trains, and to be initiated in the secrets of the literature of my country. I once met a Serbian professor who told me that he had written a book about Shakespeare. He spoke French (not Shakespeare – the Serb). Shakespeare was a well-known case, he said, of self-hallucination. He knew, because he was a mind-doctor. *Hamlet* was a well-known case of a man who thinks he sees ghosts.

'But,' I said, 'the other people in the play saw the ghost.'

'They caught his infection,' he said.

'But they saw it first,' I objected.

'It was Suggestion,' he said; 'it often happens. The infection comes from the brain of the man who thinks he sees a ghost *before* he has seen the ghost, and his coming hallucination infects other brains. Shakespeare was hallucinated, or he could not have described the case so accurately. All his characters are hallucinated – Macbeth, King Lear, Brutus (he saw a ghost).'

I said enough things had happened to King Lear to make him go mad.

'Not in that way,' he said. 'Ophelia is mad; Lady Macbeth is mad; Othello is mad; Shylock is mad; Timon of Athens is very mad; Antonio is mad; Romeo is mad. The cases are all accurately described by one who has the illness himself.'

'Was Falstaff mad?' I asked.

'Falstaff,' said the doctor, 'is a case of what we call metaphenomania. He was a metaphenomaniac; he could not help altering facts and changing the facets of appearances.'

'What we call a liar?' I suggested.

The doctor said that was an unscientific way of putting it, but it was true. Then he got out.

Of foreign high-brows, Germans are the most learned, but the most comfortable; perhaps because they drink beer. Russians are the most uncompromising, because their opinions upon matters of literature and art, music and games depend upon their politics. The French are the most lucid, the English the most arrogant. There is a story about an English high-brow who was a great mathematician and philosopher when he grew up; but he was, to start with, a little boy, and, like other little boys, he went to school. The first night he went to bed in his dormitory he noticed that all the other boys knelt down to say their prayers; but he, having been brought up among the ruthless, thought that to say one's prayers was a piece of old-fashioned and pernicious superstition, and he went to bed without saying his prayers; and all the other boys threw boots at his head and called him a heathen and other rude names; but at the end of the term none of the boys said their prayers.

I now perceive that I have nearly finished this lecture, and I have not defined either the good or the bad low-brow, which I ought to have done at the very beginning. I will now do so at the end, because it is never too late to end.

A good low-brow is a man who, although he enjoys outdoor sports and games, and likes racing, gambling, eating, drinking, smoking, telling lies, the society and affection of the female beautiful, the female vivacious and the male vivacious and hospitable, the sporting newspapers, coloured pictures, moving pictures, musical comedy, music-halls, frivolous conversation, new stories and old stories, does not want to shoot pianists, painters, writers, poets, men of science, philosophers, inventors, mathematicians, thinkers and professional chess-players. He is just as nice to them as he is to the beautiful and to the vivacious and to bookmakers. He lives and lets live, and he endures high-brows, if not gladly, with patience; whereas a bad low-brow is one who would like all books and plays to be potted and translated into American; who can only tell anecdotes that you have heard before, and which are unrefined without being witty, and repeat limericks that were made up long ago at the Shanghai Bar, and these he quotes wrongly, spoiling the rhythm.

It is a mistake to think that all high-brows belong to the learned professions: soldiers, sailors and tinkers are often high-brows; poets and painters are often the lowest of low-brows.

All Dons are high-brows. Some high-brows are sailors. Therefore some sailors are Dons.

That I believe to be a good example of false logic.

124

# The Nineties

(from *Lost Lectures*)

IT WAS IN THE NINETIES – about which books are written now, in which the period is represented as being something peculiar, exciting and exotic.

To those who lived in London during this period there seemed to be nothing at all unusual about the place. London seemed to be just what it had always been, and the process of change which is never ending was, as it always is, imperceptible to those who were partaking of it and living in it.

We had no idea we belonged to an epoch, or that one day people would talk of the 'naughty' nineties. Perhaps they will talk of the nineteen hundred and thirties in the same way, and call them 'goody-goody' nineteen hundred and thirties; and we may now be living through what will seem to coming generations a period fantastically puritanical and incredibly demure.

Some day somebody, pointing at an old man, will perhaps say: 'He knew Beverley Nichols', just as today someone might say, 'He knew the Prince Consort'.

But we who were young in the nineties were unconscious of any romance, nor did the times seem very gay, and if we were being crammed, as I was, we did not find the process very inspiriting.

We wore top hats every day in London, and on occasions of gloom, such as weddings, garden parties, and funerals, we wore frock coats. Nobody under the age of forty wore a white hat at a race meeting; nobody wore a short coat and a black tie in the evening. Our collars were straight and ties could be sailor's knots, bows or four-in-hand with frock coats, silk with a cut-away coat or cotton with the lounge suit; and in the country we wore straw hats.

Telephoning was done by sending messages in four-wheelers, until the messenger-boy service was introduced: it was sometimes quicker than the telephone, certainly less nerve-racking, and you seldom got on to the wrong number, and nobody overheard your notes.

I was crammed at Mr Scoones's establishment in Garrick Chambers,

125

Garrick Street. The purpose of this establishment was to prepare young men for the examination they had to pass to get into the Foreign Office or the Diplomatic Service, and there were sometimes candidates for the Civil Service.

We attended lectures on the various subjects which we had to master, and these lectures began at ten in the morning and lasted until one, and then began in the afternoon and lasted until four or five.

Mr Scoones presided over the establishment with tact, discretion and insight.

He was short, electric, vivacious, beautifully dressed in a frock coat, and he wore a black satin tie tied in a sailor's knot, and with it a pearl pin. He was light in hand, and tedium vanished in his presence as quickly as a minor devil escapes from the proximity of holy water.

He was a fascinating talker: he made his experiences and the most ordinary occurrences, an adventure at a Customs House, the production of a new dull play, entrancing.

He lectured on French and on History, and he gave his pupils a compendium of all the out-of-the-way words in the French language: the word for caulking a ship; the words for a finial and a rochet and a crotchet, for the connecting-rod of an engine, and the space between the star actors and the lesser actors on the poster announcing the cast of a new play.

This word[1] is very important in the French theatrical world, because star actors are annoyed if the space between their name and the rest of the cast has not a certain number of millimetres, and M. Flers, the part author of so many witty plays, was seen one day measuring a poster with his umbrella, and on being asked what he was doing, he said he was measuring Mademoiselle X's, which she had complained to him was less wide than that between the name of Mademoiselle Y and the rest of the cast.

The work was leisurely, except when the news came of an Ambassador's death. Then Mr Scoones used to arrive at his chambers with an extra-carefully tied black satin tie, and an expression of moment, and break the news with restrained dramatic power; because the death of an Ambassador meant a vacancy in the Service, and a vacancy meant an examination.

Mr Scoones used to have luncheon at the Garrick Club every day, and sometimes he would bring us back the latest anecdotes current in the theatrical world, and what 'Bogey' Bancroft had said, and sometimes he would ask two of his pupils to luncheon.

He was a first-nighter and an acute critic of acting. He knew the form of his pupils as well as a good trainer knows that of his horses, and the pupils' possible chances. He seldom made a mistake, and he had the gift

_____
[1] *Fromage.* [M. B.]

of subtle encouragement; passing one on the stairs he would say, in a confidential whisper: 'How's the German?' or 'How's the arithmetic?' At the end of the term he wrote a report to one's parents, which was short, to the point and generally an excellent diagnosis: he would touch lightly on the weak point and commend what there was to be commended. When the examination was in sight and the pupils had received their nomination, work increased to fever pitch, and the lectures were supplemented by private lessons at home in shorthand, arithmetic or whatever might be necessary.

Another mainstay of the establishment was the Reverend Dawson Clarke, who taught geography, arithmetic and précis-writing.

He was a Yorkshireman, bearded, and broad in body and in talk, and a monument of sense and shrewdness. He described most countries in units of Yorkshire, such and such a country being four times as large as Yorkshire, with asides, such as, 'Florence, a one-eyed place', or such and such a place 'famous for its woodcock – an overrated bird', or such a wine (Californian, for choice) being 'a three-man wine, taking two to hold you down, and a third man to pour it down your throat'.

Then there was Mr Allen, who gave brilliant lectures on Modern History; and M. Esclangon, who taught French. He was like a character from one of Anatole France's novels come to life – gentle as a mouse, as sensitive as a microphone and as acute as a needle. He left technical terms and what the examiners might ask to others: he concentrated on style and elegance, and I remember one of his subjects for an essay began like this. It was a quotation, he said, from some book, which I was never able to obtain:

> 'Aimez-vous les uns les autres: c'est beaucoup dire. Supportez-vous les uns les autres: c'est déjà assez difficile.'

In gentle accents he would describe the Provençal sun, the white roads, the dust, the sun-baked houses and the small crackling wood fires on the hearth, the lure and the charm of the South, as he regretfully, on a foggy afternoon, asked you, with exquisite courtesy, to light the gas.

Then there was Signor di Azarta, who we believed, I don't know whether rightly, had fought with Garibaldi, and who taught us Italian; he was a man of great distinction, but he had forgotten Italian long ago. And there were others who taught subjects which were outside my range.

We used to have luncheon at the various restaurants in the neighbourhood: at 'The Cavour' in Leicester Square, sometimes at 'Scott's', and much rarer, as a great treat, at the 'Café Royal'. When there was no examination in the immediate future, the life was easy-going and varied with stays abroad to study foreign languages; and in summer amusement got the upper hand altogether.

There was a ball somewhere every night in the summer, except during

Ascot and Newmarket weeks, and even during those there were sometimes dances. There were balls in the large houses: Stafford House, Grosvenor House, Montagu House, Dorchester House, Devonshire House, Bridgewater House, and in small houses as well – here the rooms and staircase and balconies were packed with people.

Nothing was danced but valses, except sometimes the lancers.

People danced very fast *trois temps*, the men's arms being carried stiff and straight out, and their partners being whirled round the room. Only foreigners knew how to reverse. The men always wore white gloves, and when you went into the cloakroom there was a smell of peaches from the supper-tables. There were some men whom you saw only at balls and who disappeared with the link-man, and were rolled up with the red carpet and the awning during the winter. The women wore satin, or at least it looked like satin: white, pink, yellow, light blue, and the older women and sometimes the hostess wore tiaras. Bouquets were over. *Cotillons* were over except as exceptions, when they happened all by themselves, and you were asked to a *cotillon* and nothing else. I cannot recall what were the popular dance tunes of that time. I remember those before and after: there is only one which floats up to the surface of my memory from that epoch, a Viennese valse called 'Sei nicht böse', that has an entrancing lilt.

The tunes of the 'Geisha', which was produced in 1896, were being played in the streets then and afterwards, and before this a song called 'Linger longer Lucy' was whistled and Miss May Yohe had taken the town with a negro song in 'Little Christopher Columbus', 'Oh! come my love, Oh! come my love to me!'

Yvette Guilbert in long black gloves was singing in French and in English at the Empire, a song called 'I want you my honey, yes I do'. Mrs Patrick Campbell had made a sensation by her 'Mrs Tanqueray', in the summer of 1893. Sarah Bernhardt and Duse had seasons in London; and then there was the opera, which was very much like what it is now, except that in those days the young high-brows were indifferent to Mozart, and could not abide anything but Wagner, and snorted when Verdi or any Italian opera was mentioned.

Jean de Reszke, past his prime, was singing in Wagner, a little old to play a blacksmith just out of his teens, but a magnificent Tristan, with Albani singing 'Isolde' in her best Balmoral manner. Beerbohm Tree was at the Haymarket playing *Svengali*, Irving and Ellen Terry were at the Lyceum acting *Cymbeline*, *King Arthur*, and other plays by Messrs. Shakespeare, Bacon and Co. We did not make much of our opportunities of seeing these remarkable artists, because one felt they were always with us.

I remember a Cambridge friend telling me he had seen a very funny play at the Avenue Theatre called *Arms and the Man*, by a man called

Shaw. Mr Shaw was then writing the dramatic criticism in the *Saturday Review*, while Walkley wrote in the *Speaker*, and William Archer in the *World*. The high-brows liked William Archer's criticisms best. They said Walkley was amusing; Shaw, of course, preposterous, if funny; but Archer was *sound*.

And it is true that Archer devoted pages and pages of closely-reasoned analysis in the *World* to plays that are now as forgotten as Nineveh, and could not even be revived as a joke.

What did the people admire, what did the young admire and read in those days?

In discussing the question of what the young read, the interesting point is not what new books they read, for young and old from necessity generally read the same *new* books – the new books that are available at the book-clubs and the libraries, in the shops and on the bookstalls, the books people are talking about; but to gauge the taste of the young it is necessary to find out not what new books they are reading but what older books they admire.

When I was at Cambridge the young high-brows had discovered Verlaine. They may possibly have admired Henry James, but I do not remember his being talked about by the young: I remember his being discussed by the older generation; and this was true of George Meredith.

When I left school in 1891 Meredith was still only accepted by a few eclectic high-brows; and I remember the consternation caused by Mrs Strong (then Miss Sellers), when she declared at a luncheon that for her part she preferred George Meredith to George Eliot. I also remember the wife of one of the Eton masters present saying that she regarded Meredith[1] as a test of stupidity. 'A kind of foolometer,' someone suggested. 'Yes,' she said, 'a foolometer.' I discovered his novels for myself a year after this, and dubbed myself a fool,[2] as we were constantly recommended to do by one of our division masters at Eton if we did not appreciate *Lycidas* and Horace's odes.

But by the time I reached Cambridge, two years later, all this was changed. Meredith was accepted by all the high-brows: his boom was to come later (he had been writing for years and years before all this happened – his *Modern Love* came out in 1862) – his boom, his apotheosis, and then his deposal and banishment to Limbo, whence presumably he will be rescued and discovered by a generation as yet unborn, who will think he has never been discovered before. The French are already busy doing this now.

Byron was completely neglected, except by Henley, who, with a staff of brilliant young men, edited the *National Observer*, and hit right and left with a flashing rapier. Charles Whibley was one of his most downright

---

[1] She meant a liking for Meredith was the mark of the fool. [M. B.]
[2] For liking him. [M. B.]

henchmen. Dickens was little read, except by the public. George Eliot had not begun to be forgotten, but she was just beginning to be cavilled at; she was still respected. Nobody dared say she was not an authoress. If you quoted Mrs Poyser, people knew whom you meant. Hardy was passionately admired by a few; Stevenson was probably the favourite author of the literary majority; worshipped by some and tolerated by the extreme high-brows; Kipling was a real excitement.

The little grey books: *Soldiers Three, Under the Deodars, The Story of the Gadsbys,* had come out while I was still at school. I remember seeing them snatched from the counter of the bookseller by a greedy master, and wondering what they were about. Now (1894) some of the Jungle Stories were coming out in the *Pall Mall Gazette*: Kipling was a constant topic of discussion and argument, and sometimes a cause of quarrel and beer-throwing.

Someone said to me at a dinner in 1892 – this was in the autumn after the publication of *Barrack Room Ballads* – there was actually talk of making Rudyard Kipling Poet Laureate! I remember thinking it would be an admirable choice and saying so, and being suspected of paradox. As it was, the laurels were given to Mr Alfred Austin, a good Conservative prose-writer, and a supporter of the Conservative Party, whose cause he had upheld for many years in leading articles in the *Standard*. So he was just the man to write poems about the Jameson Raid, beginning 'Wrong, is it wrong?' (The answer was in the affirmative.)

John Oliver Hobbes was attracting a great deal of attention by her wisdom and her wit; she gives in her books an admirable picture of social life, especially of county life during that period. Rhoda Broughton is perhaps the best historian of English well-to-do county life from the seventies to the nineties, and her books at the time I am speaking of were still sent from the circulating libraries to country houses.

Swinburne was enjoyed, except by the very highest young brows. Tennyson was not despised; Rossetti was greatly admired, and Browning had to be admired. It was as indecent for a high-brow not to admire Browning, as it was for a low-brow to smoke a Virginia cigarette.

The eighteenth century had been forgotten: but Wordsworth and the Lake School were talked about: it was all right to admire them. Shelley and Keats were beyond discussion.

Wilde's brief theatrical career was passing like a flash, and his latest *mots* were in constant circulation. He was despised by the high-brows as a writer, but acknowledged as a wit. Here is one *mot* which was repeated to me at the time by John Lane, and which I have never seen in print.

His publisher, Osgood, had just died, and his new publisher (John Lane) asked Wilde whether he was going to the funeral.

'I don't know where to go,' said Wilde.

'What do you mean?' asked Lane.

'Well,' said Wilde, 'he is going to be buried simultaneously in London and New York.'

People said he prepared his good sayings beforehand. It always struck me this mattered little, for some people might sit up all night preparing good sayings and bring nothing to birth except a platitude.

The best sellers of that day were Marie Corelli and Hall Caine, whose names were frequently bracketed together in conversation, although they had nothing in common save popularity. Sarah Grand, whose book *The Heavenly Twins* was much discussed, was the first writer to be what is called 'frank' about certain indispositions: and no book was ever more talked about than Mr E. F. Benson's *Dodo* when it first came out. A little time later he wrote a book called *The Babe B.A.*, which gives an admirable picture of Cambridge life at that date.

The young high-brows were very serious; far more serious than the young high-brows are today. There was no such things as cocktails, and nobody sat on the floor.

There was a mass of young poets, despised by the high-brows. Poetry, it was said, had been made to pay: England was, as usual, a nest of singing birds: the first editions of these poets commanded prices. Some of these poets were very good: Francis Thompson, Mr Yeats, Sir William Watson, and John Davidson: one of the most highly-praised poets was Mr Richard le Gallienne, who some of the critics said had done for Tennyson; others were Mr Arthur Symons, Ernest Dowson and Lionel Johnson.

Russian literature was little known. Turgenev had been heard of. Mr Bertrand Russell had read Dostoyevsky, but no one else had; and some years after this I remember seeing Dostoyevsky mentioned in a serious article in a serious review, as being a kind of Russian writer of shockers, a sort of Eugene Sue or Xavier de Montépin.

But there was Ibsen. Ibsen dominated the high-brow world. His plays were read and his plays were acted at *matinées*, and were feverishly discussed and violently abused in some of the organs of the daily Press by critics of the old school. Ibsen was being preached by the middle-aged, and he was the excitement of the young.

If you wish for a picture of the literary and intellectual taste of that day, the best way to get it is to read Mr Bernard Shaw's collected dramatic criticisms, one of the most entertaining books ever written, published in two volumes, called *Dramatic Opinions and Essays*.

One thing will strike you, which I remember noticing at the time – people spoke then as if the educated world had entered into a new era, and as if nothing could ever be old-fashioned again. There was talk of the New Woman: Ibsen seemed to have revolutionized the stage once and for all, and Wagner was thought to have revolutionized music and opera once and for all. It was thought impossible that there could ever be a new serious drama except on Ibsenite lines, or a new opera except on Wagnerian lines. Nobody foresaw a possible reaction. If you had told people then that in 1931 Verdi would be more popular than Wagner among the young, that Pope and Cowper would be more popular than Swinburne or Rossetti, they would not have believed you: 'believed' is a mild word; they would have thought you stark staring mad.

I have forgotten to mention the *Yellow Book*. That I should have forgotten it shows the part it really played in the epoch: a quite insignificant part, although later historians and students of the period have taken it as a symbol representing the whole epoch. Apart from Aubrey Beardsley's drawings which came out in the earlier numbers, it was exactly like any literary review which has appeared in England before or since, in that it mustered all the best-known authors of the day and the best illustrators available: in the very first number there were drawings by Sir Frederick Leighton as well as by Aubrey Beardsley; a poem by Arthur Benson as well as by Arthur Symons; a story by Henry James, a poem by Edmund Gosse, and contributions by Dr Garnett and Mr Saintsbury. It lasted for several years, and once the novelty of its colour was forgotten it went along the humdrum lines of all English reviews, which begin as a rule with a galaxy of stars and end by being largely written by the editor, and then die.

There was also Mr Hichens' book, *The Green Carnation*, which reflects one phase of the talk of the period; but the talk of a very small circle. Epigram was not the universal jargon of the intelligentsia, still less that of the general public.

What did the low-brows read?

They had forgotten Marion Crawford; they ignored Ibsen and all that; they were happy with a nice new Marie Corelli; or, if he was a very low-brow and had very good taste, with the tales of 'Pitcher'. Or, if they read French, a Georges Ohnet; Kipling was read by high and low; there was no great rage for detective stories. Stanley Weyman and Merriman provided sufficient excitement, and Jerome K. Jerome was enormously popular as a comic. He was not, as in Russia, preferred as a serious author. Sherlock Holmes was just beginning to glimmer in the sky in the *Strand Magazine*, which was by far the most popular reading among the low-brows, and *Trilby* took the town by storm. There was plenty of musical comedy for the low-brows; Arthur Roberts was at his zenith, and the music halls, the Tivoli and the Pavilion, were bright with the genius of Dan Leno and Marie Lloyd, two of the greatest artists England has ever known, besides a host of minor constellations. The Empire and the Alhambra had promenades, in which ladies of the town were allowed to circulate freely and to join in the conversation, and partake of light refreshment; and at the Continental Hotel there was supper after the play, which lasted till the lights were put out; people were ejected by force into the street at half-past twelve, with a skirmish and noise and language.

There was a small Music Hall near Charing Cross frequented by the young and cheerfully inebriate, whence they were instantly thrown out as soon as they gave tongue. I suppose there were some people who stayed till the end of the performance; I never saw anyone last more than one song.

It was an epoch of catchwords.

Somebody, Dan Leno maybe, Arthur Roberts, or a member of the staff of the *Sporting Times* or of the Stock Exchange, started a catchword, which went round England like a prairie fire: such as 'There's air' ('air' being short for 'hair'), started by Dan Leno, or 'What ho! she bumps!' or 'Let's all go down the Strand!' 'I don't think' was much later.

Then there were pictures, stationary pictures.

Whistler, after having been derided and hissed at Christie's, was now universally accepted; Watts was greatly admired; Burne-Jones was still admired; Rossetti was not talked of; Leighton was still thought to be a painter. Sargent attracted attention; he was neither greatly praised by the high-brows nor liked by the multitude; but he was noticed. George Moore said his pictures were like a first night in Paris with Sarah Bernhardt playing in a new part.

Concerts were very much like what they are now: the Monday and Saturday Popular Concerts of classical music were still going on, on Monday evenings and Saturday afternoons; they consisted of Chamber music and *Lieder*: and Patti gave a farewell concert twice a year at the Albert Hall.

Melba was suffering from the Wagner regime, and nearly spoilt her voice in America trying to sing the part of Brunnhilde.

One of the greatest social changes in the nineties was the sudden use of the bicycle among the leisured. The bicycle had been there for a long time, first as the velocipede, an enormous high contraption, one huge wheel and a little wheel; then as the bone-shaker, without tyres; then as the 'safety bicycle', with india-rubber tyres. But nobody dared ride it; not from physical fear, but because it was not the thing. When I was at Cambridge it was as little the thing as anything could be. It was as bad as wearing a billycock hat and a frock coat. Then suddenly, in the summer of 1894, I think, it began to be the thing, and people bicycled just for the fun of bicycling anywhere, even indoors if they could not bicycle out of doors, and there were bicycling breakfast-parties in Battersea Park; and people went to France to bicycle, and discussed the makes of their bicycles; somebody once had a bicycle that could go uphill. It was called *le rêve*, and it was but a dream, and it was broken.

There was also a minor craze, which has recurred once or twice since, for ice-skating indoors at a place called 'Niagara'; and as for outdoor games, tennis had been eclipsed, and croquet had come back, a difficult kind of croquet that took hours and hours and tried the patience; golf existed, but hadn't become a religion.

In London, after dinner there were no cards. Bridge had not been invented, and whist was only played at clubs. It was certainly played at the Queen's Guard, because I remember dining there and having to play (not having played since nursery days), and not knowing exactly (like the man in *Happy Thoughts*) how to score. My partner was another guest, a red-faced white-moustached *viveur* – an authority on food; and suddenly, after one game had been played, he glared at me and said: 'You called for trumps, sir'.

As we won seventeen shillings and sixpence, I didn't care . . . not afterwards, that is to say.

Instead of playing bridge after dinner the guests sat in twos in different parts of the room; two here, two there and two somewhere else. It did not last as long as bridge; it was nearly always over at eleven: but while it lasted it was more exhausting.

I remember going to a dinner party given by rather a severe lady. I had been crammed all day and I had sat up till five the night before. I was very sleepy. It fell to my lot to talk to my hostess after dinner. I suddenly felt that sleep was mastering me. I made a great effort. It was of no avail. I fell asleep, and, what is more, I woke, because I suddenly heard myself saying to my hostess: 'And now that we've got it, we had better enjoy it'. (What Pope Leo X said about the Papacy.) This had been a part of my dream.

While one was being crammed social life was supposed to play no part in one's life, and it is true that during the winter months, and just before an examination, it played no part.

In the summer it did, unless one went abroad. I went abroad generally, except during the summer of 1897, and Mr Scoones said that my work had suffered from the distractions of that summer.

I went to Bayreuth twice, and once I bought a ticket for a performance of *Parsifal* at the station when I arrived, and drove straight to the theatre, and was just in time for the performance. On this occasion I was sleepy too. I had travelled all night and uncomfortably, and I fell sound asleep and slept during the whole of the first act of *Parsifal*: and after the agony of resisting and fighting sleep (and even that is delicious), I never enjoyed a sleep so much. I had to be awakened by force.

Social life for a young man meant balls, sometimes invitations to Saturday to Monday parties, and rarely dinner parties except among intimate friends.

Then there was Bohemian life and literary life. I had a glimpse of what was called Bohemian life. I was taken by a barrister to an artist's studio, and the barrister and his friends told me they were out-and-out Bohemians, but the barrister wore a frock coat, and the friends seemed to me very much like other people, so it was a disappointment.

But among the literary world I made friends, largely owing to the friendship of Edmund Gosse, whom I first met in the summer of 1893 at Arthur Benson's house at Eton, at the end of summer half. I was then just about to go to a crammer's in order to try and get into Cambridge. Edmund Gosse was very kind to me, and when I came to cram in London he used to ask me to his house on Sundays, and I used to go in the afternoon and stay for supper.

This was not my positively first introduction into the world of letters. I had before that made the acquaintance of Mrs Humphry Ward through her son, who was at Eton with me, and she had asked me to luncheon. It was just after her book, *The History of David Grieve*, had been published, and the reviews were pouring in. They were very favourable. She was very kind to me, but there were no authors at luncheon, so it was a slight disappointment; and immediately after that I went to Germany. When I came back to Cambridge, and was being crammed at Scoones's, I used to go almost every Sunday to the Gosses.

But I am going to keep Edmund Gosse for another story. Before actually passing my examination, I went to another crammer's at Bournemouth to be taught arithmetic. But without success. This establishment was kept by a very nice clergyman, who had sons and daughters. One of his sons was a clergyman, and one, by living in the West of America, had turned into an American. That is to say his talk was indistinguishable from that of an American. You are bound to talk like that if you live long enough in America, in order to make yourself understood. Personally, I think it is a nice clear way of talking, and not untuneful.

When I went up for my last examination, although I knew I had failed in arithmetic, I thought I had done well in my English essay, because when I had finished it I copied it out in shorthand and sent it to the *Saturday Review*, and they printed it. It was about 'Taste'.

There were also public events during this period.

Most of the more important public events during this period, from 1891 until the Boer War, took place in private. That is to say, we were within an ace of going to war with France three times – once about Siam, once about Nigeria, and once about Fashoda: only the last crisis reached the public. That was at the end of the nineties, just before the Boer War.

Public events which were noticed were the Queen's Diamond Jubilee in 1897; the Devonshire House Fancy Dress Ball; the Prince of Wales winning the Derby with Persimmon on June 3, 1896; and Mrs Patrick Campbell failing in *Magda* at the Lyceum that same night after having the year before won such a tremendous success in *The Notorious Mrs Ebbsmith*, that it seemed as if her career could not fail to be one long triumph. Then there was the Battle of Omdurman in the Soudan, which Mr Winston Churchill attended.

And the result of this battle was that Lord Kitchener was ultimately put in charge of the Commissariat in the South African War, and some experts say he disorganized the supply of mules.

There were also other events, but they can be found in Whitaker's Almanack.

# Voltaire (1694–1778)

(from *French Literature*)

THE SECOND HALF of the eighteenth century is dominated by Voltaire. Voltaire, indeed, dominated the whole century. He was first talked of in 1714, and he died in 1778; but during the first half of the century his influence was purely literary; until 1755 he was famous as a poet and a dramatist. After 1755 until his death he became world famous as a philosopher, a pamphleteer, and the foremost adversary of religion and the old régime.

Voltaire, whose real name was François Arouet, was the son of a notary; he was educated by the Jesuits, who taught him how to think, and instilled into him the principles of taste, which he never forgot. As Anatole France says somewhere, the only weapons which the Church finds dangerous are those which she has forged herself. He was twice imprisoned in the Bastille, and at least twice beaten by personal enemies. He went to England as an exile, returned to France (to Cirey, on the frontier), made friends with the King of Prussia, lived at Berlin, quarrelled with him, and finally settled down in Switzerland at Les Délices and Ferney. He returned to Paris in his old age, and died a year after in and *of* a blaze and apotheosis of popularity.

As this is a review of the literature and not of the history of France, the far-reaching influence of Voltaire on French history is beyond its scope; but even if we judge him from the point of view of literature alone, the importance of Voltaire remains enormous. It is easy to detail his limitations. He had all the vanities and all the faults that come from irritable and irritated nerves; he summed up in himself all the possible weaknesses of the *genus irritabile vatum*. He was as savage and unreliable as Pope, and almost as great an invalid; capable at the same time of servility and insolence. But . . . he was a good friend, a friend of the poor, and, what is still rarer, of the needy, a defender of the innocent and of the oppressed. He had the real sense of justice; he was charitable and generous. His purse was open, but he could only give physical, and never moral, medicine; he had no balm for the suffering soul, because he did not understand its malady. He was never a comforter of the sorrowful. And yet it was not only his reason and his logic that were shocked by injustice; it was his spirit. He had a passionate sense of injustice, which burnt in his frail being like a flame. He rehabilitated the calumnied dead, as in the *Affaire Calas*, and he protected the persecuted living (*Affaire Sirven*). The limitations of his character are reflected in his work and in his art. The greatest things escape his notice: he has no sense of mystery, no historic vision, although he is an admirable writer of history; that is to say, he had an unrivalled capacity for collecting, sorting, and presenting historical facts. He ignored religion, he had no sense of poetry, and no appreciation for what was greatest in art. He worshipped the goddess of reason, but he created her in his own image; nor did he believe she could be manifested otherwise.

What, then, is the secret of Voltaire's greatness? In the first place, his supremely acute and active intelligence, his insatiable curiosity. In the second place, his energy, his activity. He had the courage and the restlessness of a fly, and the sting of a wasp. His style reflects all his faults and all his qualities. It is neither eloquent nor poetical nor coloured; he has not the imagination which transmutes sensations and impressions by the alchemy of art into a mysterious metal. He sees everything from the point of view of reason, in black and white; there exist for him certain things which are true, and certain things which are false and therefore foolish, folly. Follies must be remedied, or killed by ridicule; that is to say, by reason. In this he is 'French of the French' and lord of human sneers. He was, and always remained, more than a spoilt child, a naughty boy. He was a disintegrator. He nibbled like a tireless mouse with formidable corrosive teeth at the pillars of Society and the old régime, and left them, shaking and rotten, for the Revolution to pull down.

If it is true, as a Frenchman once said, that 'la France n'est pas gouvernable', Voltaire is in part to blame. Nobody ever more successfully undermined the prestige of all possible government. He undermined the faith of the *bourgeoisie* in two things – government and religion. His philosophy was entirely practical. He was temperamentally irreligious and disrespectful; he preached disbelief, not only by precept, but by example; he made disrespect easy and popular; he taught the *bourgeoisie* and the half-educated not only how to do without religion, but how to laugh at it, how to treat it as something absurd. His god was a philosophical axiom acceptable to the reason; far more than Peter the Great, he was the first Bolshevist. His fundamental ideas and his philosophy are based on the all-importance of material welfare and progress. According to Mermilod, the cry of the masses is: 'Vous m'avez ôté l'espérance du ciel, et la crainte de l'enfer; il ne me reste que la terre: Je l'aurai.'

The cry might have been addressed to Voltaire.

## Voltaire (1694–1778)

The last word about Voltaire must be about his literary gifts. He was the greatest journalist who ever lived, and one of the greatest letter writers. His literary output was inexhaustible, and he never wrote a bad sentence. He corresponded with men all over Europe, and ten thousand of his letters are still in existence. In history he wrote *Le Siècle de Louis Quatorze*, tragedies which, though devoid of beauty, can still be acted (*Zaire, Mérope, Alzire, Rome Sauvée, Tancrède*), comedies (*La Prude*), philosophy (*Le Dictionnaire philosophique*), light verse, innumerable articles, pamphlets, and broadsheets, and, finally, stories (*Zadig, Candide*).

If all Voltaire's work were to perish except his *Candide*, it would still put him in the first rank of all French writers. It was written as an answer to a letter of Rousseau's, in which Rousseau upbraided him for his atheism. In it he sums up all the evils to which the flesh is heir, and the disasters that can happen to man, laughs at them, and makes us share his laughter; but in the bitter after-taste that his laughter leaves there is something tonic, a cleansing common sense, 'il faut cultiver notre jardin'.

It is noteworthy that in French histories of literature little is said about Voltaire's style except that it is easy and *coulant*. Possibly most French writers write so well that they do not notice it. They notice bad writing, but they are like the man in Heine's story, who, on arriving in El Dorado, was surprised at picking up a piece of gold in the street, until he found that all the stones were made of gold. Heine said this was true of ideas in Germany. It is possibly true of good writing in France. It needed a stranger to notice the streets in El Dorado were full of gold; but even in the El Dorado of French literature there are no golden pebbles more scintillating, more seemingly casual and common in their occurrence, nor more rare in their alloy, and precious in their artistic value, than the prose of Voltaire.

# A Dialogue on Artists

## (from *Daphne Adeane*)

'ARTISTS ARE THE MOST ruthless egotists in the world. They only think of
the thing they are doing for themselves, and in relation to themselves.
They may be passionately devoted to it – to their work – and if they are
artists, they *are* devoted to it. But woe betide the poor human people who
come in their way! They use them like so much cannon fodder; so many
meat bones to make stock with!'

'Is it true?'

'Of course it is. Look at Goethe. Have you read his life?'

'Yes, I have.'

'Well, look at all those poor people – Lili, Lotte, Frau von Stein,
whatever their names are. Why, he used human beings for copy for his
poems till he was eighty. He was right. We are the gainers, but they, poor
people, were sacrificed, and all other great artists did the same – Shelley,
Victor Hugo; and, I dare say, if you knew the truth, Shakespeare and
Homer. We haven't got Shakespeare's autobiography, but we have got
his sonnets, which are more intimate than any autobiography. I read a
thing in a poem the other day which said:

> Even to one I dare not tell
> Where lies my Heaven, where lies my Hell,
> But to the world I can confide
> What's hid from all the world beside.

That is the motto, the creed, the confession, the *sine qua non* of *all* real
artists. That is the secret of art. That, I think, was Shakespeare's case,
Homer's, if we only knew, any artist's case, what all artists do – every
one of them – unconsciously no doubt. But Francis Greene is not an
artist, and he would never dream of doing such a thing. He would think
it *abominable*. Not that he doesn't take as much interest in his work as we
artists do in ours. He does. He takes more interest in it, because we don't

140

– or I don't, at any rate – like talking of our work out of hours, but he is never happy unless he is talking of his work, in season and out of season, every day and all day to every one or any one. But he would never dream of making copy out of any one or anything that had touched him personally. He is like a priest in these ways.'

'But no more would you, would you?'

'Oh yes, I would – unconsciously, perhaps, but I would do it.'

'Do you mean to say that you would use things that you had seen, which had affected you personally, for your books as copy?'

'Well, it depends what you mean by "copy". I don't mean copy in the same way as news. I don't mean that I would say, "That's a good thing; I will put it in my next book", making a note of it for the purpose. But I do mean that everything I see and do, every emotion I feel, every impression I receive, every relation I have to any one else, every experience I go through, every pain I suffer, every joy I share in, every enthusiasm that catches me, every affection, every passion which falls to my lot, are ultimately destined to be transmuted and made use of, directly or indirectly; they are turned into something else. All the experiences of any artist – however sordid, however sublime, however holy, however passionate or intimate – go through, you can call it the crucible, or the furnace, if you like, as in Huntley & Palmer's biscuit factory, and ultimately come out at the other end as diamonds (or as biscuits) – works of art good or bad, as good as Shakespeare, or as bad as – well, as any of mine, if you like. But this is the process; so it is, and so it has always been, and so it will always be. The moral is, don't love an artist.'

# A Composite Portrait of Sarah Bernhardt

## (i) Sarah Bernhardt

### (from *Punch and Judy and Other Essays*)

#### [i]

'*Sans doute il est trop tard pour parler encor d'elle.*' So Alfred de Musset began his beautiful poem to La Malibran, in which he said almost all there is to be said about the death of one of the queens of the stage. Only, in the case of La Malibran, the world's regret, which found so lovely an echo in the song of the poet, was all the more poignant because La Malibran died in the flower of her youth.

Sarah Bernhardt, according to standards which we should apply to any one else, was an old woman when she died; old, and full of glory, 'having seen, borne, and achieved more than most men on record,' and yet when the news of her death flashed through the world it seemed an incredible thing, and the blackness and the void that the disappearance of her presence left behind were felt by the whole world. The world seemed a duller and a greyer place without her:

> 'She, she is dead; she's dead: when thou knowst this,
> Thou knowst how wan a ghost this our world is.'

That was the feeling we had when the news of her death came. It came with the shock, as of something living, vital, and actual leaving us, and not as the final vibration of an echo of the past. For Sarah Bernhardt never grew old. She remained young because her spirit was able to serve the novitiate which, La Rochefoucauld tells us, awaits the human being at every stage of his life, and she was ready at each revolution to face the possibilities of the new phase. So that death caught her acting for the cinematograph.

Many years ago, in 1882, after her first performance of Sardou's

142

*Fédora*, Jules Lemaître, bidding her farewell as she was starting for America, in one of the most graceful tributes to her genius ever written, advised her, when she was weary of travel, adventure, and struggle, to come back and find a final home at the Théâtre français and to rest in the admiration and sympathy of 'ce bon peuple Parisien', who, he said, would forgive her anything, as it owed her some of its greatest pleasures. And then, he added: 'Un beau soir, mourez sur la scène subitement, dans un grand cri tragique, car la vieillesse serait trop dure pour vous.' No doubt he was right, if he thought of Sarah retiring, as others have done, to some quiet suburb, living in the company of a parrot and an old servant, and weeping over old Press cuttings, a living ghost, and only a name to the present generation. Only that was just what did not and what could not happen. Although she had lost a leg, and though she was over seventy, she was still finding new things to do, and things which she, and she only, could do, and till the hour of her death she continued to adjust new means to a fresh end, and never gave the world the chance of saying 'What a pity!'

Indeed, one of the triumphs of her career was the twelve performances she gave of *Athalie* after the war, for one of which all the theatres of Paris closed to give the whole theatrical profession the chance of witnessing this example of her incomparable art.

[ ii ]

What remains of it all? What idea will future generations have of the art and the power of Sarah Bernhardt? What will they believe? Will they just think of her as an old-fashioned catchword brandished to check the enthusiasm of the young as they swing their censers to a new idol? No, she will be more than that: the very photographs that exist of her, from her early days at the Comédie française, when she was as slender as a sylph, and a puff of wind seemed sufficient to blow her away, until the other day, when she embodied the sumptuous malignity of Athalie, bear witness to the feline grace, the exotic poetry, the electric power, the enigmatic expression, the strange splendour, as baffling to analysis as the scent of an aromatic herb, that emanated from her personality.

I believe there are cinematograph films which reveal at least some of the most telling of her gestures, some of the most poignant of her silences, and I used myself to have a gramophone record which held a poor ghost of her voice; but all that is nothing, for Sarah Bernhardt's art was a complex whole, a combination of rhythmical movement, gesture, look, speech, hands, hair, body, and spirit; and those who never saw her will only be able to guess at it, but it will be one of the beautiful and permanent guesses of mankind; one of the lasting dreams of poets, one of the most magical speculations of artists and of all smokers of 'enchanted cigarettes', like the charm of Cleopatra, the voice of the masters of the *bel canto*, the colours of Greek paintings and the melodies of Greek music. The record of her struggles, her efforts, her achievements, and her triumphs, exists in full and analytical detail. We can find it in the collected writings of Sarcey, Jules Lemaître, T. T. Weiss, and in the articles of Jacques de Tillet, Faguet, and others. I have lately been reading a number of the articles that Sarcey wrote on the various plays in which Sarah Bernhardt appeared, from the outset of her career, and I feel as if I had been watching the long and crowded panorama of her artistic destiny.

It was a difficult career from the start. She did not want to be an actress. She once told me herself, that her ambition had been to be a painter, but since she was forced to go on the stage she decided that if she had to be an actress, she would be the first. *Aut Caesar, aut nullus.* There should be no question about it. I enjoyed her friendship for many years, and that was one of the few remarks I ever heard her make on the subject of acting or the stage. She never theorised about her parts, or the plays she acted in. They were to her, I think, so much plastic material that she kneaded and moulded and shaped with all the skill and force at her command. In kneading them she was guided by instinct, and she made herself perfect in execution by unremitting, relentless practice.

When, as a little girl, she was taken by her mother to face the entrance examination for the Conservatoire before a jury headed by Auber, she recited, instead of a tirade from Corneille or Racine, La Fontaine's Fable, 'Les Deux Pigeons' (just as Trilby sang, 'Au clair de la Lune').

Scarcely had the lines, so says a contemporary record,

> 'Deux pigeons s'aimaient d'amour tendre,
> L'un d'eux s'ennuyant au logis,'

passed her lips, when Auber interrupted her, spoke to her and told her she was admitted. The story has often been told, but it has always struck me that the recitation of those two lines probably contained, as in a microcosm, the whole of Sarah Bernhardt's genius, just as in some early lines of a poet written in the April of his genius you sometimes find the blossom that foretells the whole majesty and all the golden fruits of the tree. Such a poem is the short sigh written by the boy D'Annunzio and beginning:

> 'O falce di luna calante,'

or Keats's sonnet on Chapman's Homer.

When Sarah Bernhardt played Adrienne Lecouvreur she used to recite the opening of that fable, and one felt as one heard it that for the perfect utterance of beautiful words this was the Pillars of Hercules of mortal achievement, that it was impossible to speak verse more beautifully.

144

[ iii ]

The sighing of La Fontaine's Fable by this little girl at the Conservatoire was the prelude, the prophecy, and in one sense the epitome of all her long and glorious career; but the career was far from being one of roses, roses all the way. The whole of Sarah Bernhardt's artistic life was a fight against apparently insurmountable difficulties – obstacles from the moment when she was handicapped by her frailty, the delicacy of her constitution, the weakness of her lungs and her vocal organs, until the moment she had to face, first the inability to move, owing to invading rheumatism, and then the loss of a leg. She prolonged the wrestle until she was on her death-bed. It was a long time before she won the suffrages of the critical. She made her début at the Théâtre français in 1862, but all that Sarcey, who as a conscientious and hard-working critic expressed for so many years the opinion of the play-going world of Paris, said of her on this occasion was that she held herself well and spoke her lines distinctly.

It is interesting in following her career as it is revealed in his articles to note the gradual crescendo of his appreciation. When she played *Le Passant*, by Coppée, at the Odéon in 1869, he noted the delicate charm with which she spoke the verse. The performance made her famous. In 1872 she left the Odéon, returned to the Théâtre français and played in *Mademoiselle de Belle-Isle*. Sarcey notes her delicious diction, but doubts whether she will ever find those strong and vibrating accents that carry an audience away. Nature had, he said, denied her that, otherwise she would be a complete artist, and such a thing, he added, did not exist on the stage. She followed this up by playing the part of Junie in Racine's *Britannicus*. Sarcey notes that she has 'Je ne sais quel charme poétique, elle dit le vers avec une grâce et une pureté raciniennes'. In 1873 she plays the small part of Aricie in *Phèdre*, and Sarcey says of her voice that it is music itself and of an unimaginable purity and transparency. In 1876 she had belied Sarcey's prophecy that she would never have the strength to move an audience, by her performance of the Roman Vestal's mother in Parodi's tragedy, *Rome Vaincue*. In this tragedy she played an old woman, Posthumia, who is blind, and who, at the end of the tragedy, stabs her daughter to save her from being buried alive; the daughter is bound and cannot stab herself, and the mother, being blind, has to fumble for the place of her heart.

'Elle était admirablement costumée et grimée,' wrote Sarcey, 'un visage amaigri, ridé, et d'une majesté extraordinaire; des yeux vagues et ternes, un manteau qui, tombant des deux côtés quand les bras se soulevaient, semblait figurer les ailes immenses de quelque gigantesque et sinistre chauve-souris. Rien de plus terrible et de plus poétique ensemble . . . ce n'était plus là une comédienne; c'était la nature même, servie par une intelligence merveilleuse, par une âme de feu, par la voix la plus juste, la plus mélodieuse, qui jamais ait enchanté les oreilles humaines. Cette femme joue avec son coeur et ses entrailles. Elle hasarde des gestes qui seraient ridicules chez tout autre et qui emportent une salle. . . .'

No completer criticism of the art of Sarah Bernhardt is to be found than in these lines. Many have thought her rendering of this old woman, Posthumia, one of the two greatest triumphs of her career, and it is doubtful whether she ever excelled it; she chose an act of this play together with an act of *Phèdre* for the celebration of her jubilee in Paris.

It must have been about this time that she first appeared in *Phèdre*, for in 1877 Sarcey talks of her success in *Andromaque* as exceeding that of her *Phèdre*, and he notes the number of shades she can indicate by the simple modulation of her voice in three lines of verse, without any seeming search after effect or time-taking effort, and also the continuous tremor that thrilled the audience as she spoke her lines; she was interrupted by unstiflable bravos, as happens sometimes to great singers.

In the same year, she played Doña Sol in *Hernani*, and from that time forth she was recognized not only as an actress of genius, but as a personality that counted not only in the life of the world of art, but in life in general. She became henceforth to France something as well known as the Arc de Triomphe, and more than that, an object of unceasing interest and curiosity, the theme of poets, the godsend of gossips and paragraph makers, the centre of a legend.

In 1879 she went to London with the Comédie française, and she appeared in *Phèdre*, *Hernani*, *Andromaque*, *L'Etrangère*, *Le Sphinx*, and *Zaïre*. The London public went mad about her, and Sarah Bernhardt having tasted blood, in the shape of the conquest of London, determined on the conquest of the world. She abandoned the Théâtre français after a quarrel, and went to America.

That was the first great break in her career.

## [ iv ]

All this time, her travels, her adventures, her extravagances, her tantrums, her quarrels, her facile successes, her cheap victories, never prevented her from continuing, at the same time, as if on a parallel line, her personal battle and wrestle with the angel of art, and from every now and then discovering and achieving a new victory, conquering a fresh province.

In 1880, she plays Adrienne Lecouvreur for the first time, and in London, and reveals to Sarcey, who goes to London to hear her, what were to him unsuspected stops of pathos and passion. In the same year she plays *Froufrou* in London, and she has to compete with memories of

Aimée Desclée. She must succeed or die. 'Eh, bien!' says Sarcey, comparing them in the scene which was Desclée's greatest triumph, 'elle en est venue à bout. C'est tout autre chose et c'est aussi puissant. . . . Au quatrième acte, il n'y a pas de discussion possible, Mad<sup>elle</sup> Sarah Bernhardt s'est montrée supérieure à sa devancière.'

Then came more journeys and more world-tours, and, in 1882, the beginning of her association with Sardou, her production of *Fédora*, the first of those ingenious and powerful melodramas which were cunningly constructed in order to bring out her especial qualities, garments which were cut tightly to her measure, and which no one else has been able to wear since. *Théodora, La Tosca, Gismonda, La Sorcière* – she toured the world with these, and no plays brought her louder applause, and in no plays could she produce a more certain and sometimes a more stunning effect. But although her performance in them was certainly a unique phenomenon, which nobody since has been able to imitate or to emulate, they were for her easy triumphs, and it was not in them that she reached anywhere near the high-water mark of her art. She could sometimes content herself by merely imitating herself in them, and by letting the strong situations do the business, with the minimum effort on her part, although I can bear witness that there was often a vast difference between Sarah Bernhardt playing listlessly in a part of Sardou's, and any one else playing the same part with all their might.

The wrestle with art went on in spite of Sardou. Again she moved Sarcey to an ecstasy of surprise when she first plays in *La Dame aux Camélias* in Paris in 1883: 'I have seen something perfect!' he exclaims. She continues to experiment. She plays Lady Macbeth. At one time she has the idea of playing it in English, and takes lessons from Madame de Guythères, an inhabitant of Versailles, who told me of the first lesson. When she arrived for the second lesson, Sarah Bernhardt was selling her furniture and starting for America. The facts of life had intervened. She plays in Richepin's *Nana Sahib*; she plays Cleopatra in an adaptation of Shakespeare by Sardou; she plays Joan of Arc. She visits London every year. She still tours the world. Then there comes to her a moment when she instinctively feels that the public is tired of her repertory and irritated by her producing stuff that is inferior to her, so on her return from a prolonged tour in South America she turns over quite a new leaf. She takes the Renaissance Theatre in Paris, either in 1892 or 1893, and produces a delicate play by Jules Lemaître, *Les Rois*. 'The Sarah of the seventies has come back to us,' said the critics. In 1893 she plays Phèdre, and Sarcey says that in the part she is younger and more beautiful than she was at the Théâtre français in the 'seventies, when her powers were not quite ripe enough for the part.

'Chose étrange, inouïe, inexplicable, mais qui est vraie cependant, Mme Sarah Bernhardt est plus jeune, plus éclatante et, tranchons le mot, plus belle qu'elle n'a jamais été, d'une beauté artistique qui fait passer dans tout le corps un frisson d'admiration comme à l'aspect d'une belle statue.' Lemaître speaks in the same note. With one voice the French critics agreed that never was anything finer seen. It was here she reached the high-water mark of her genius. She does not stop; she brings into prominence Rostand, and produces *La Princesse Lointaine*, *La Samaritaine*, D'Annunzio's *Ville Morte*, and Sudermann's *Magda*. She takes a theatre of her own. She plays in *Hamlet* and *L'Aiglon*, and from this moment till the day of her death her artistic career alternates between hazardous experiments likely to be caviare to the general, such as Tristan Bernard's *Jeanne Doré*, and revivals of popular plays such as *La Dame aux Camélias*, or new productions calculated to please the crowd. She injures her leg, and her leg has to be amputated. No matter, she will appear in plays where it is not necessary for her to walk. The European war breaks out, she plays to the *poilus* in the trenches. And still the experiments continued; still the wrestle with great art continued, and culminated in her production of *Athalie* in 1920. Finally, while she was rehearsing a new play by Sacha Guitry, she fell ill from the malady from which she was destined never to recover. But she spent her last illness in rehearsing for the films, until, after the long contention, the moment for the final *recueillement* came and she received the last Sacraments.

## [ v ]

She spent her life in making discoveries and in surprising the public and her critics by finding out what she could not do, and in immediately doing it. She began by surprising herself in 1873 when playing in *Zaïre*; she thought she was dying, and she determined to die in real earnest, to spite the manager, with whom she had quarrelled. She gave a cry of real pain when the stage dagger struck her, and she thought she could never recover; but to her astonishment she found herself, after the tremendous effort, exertion, and nervous expenditure, as fresh as a daisy. After this experience she knew she could draw when she liked on her physical resources. Her energy, the amount of hard work she accomplished, were frightening to think of. Her recreation was change of work. She could command sleep when she wished, but she never rested. Yet she was fundamentally sensible. She made the best of the inevitable, and from the beginning to the end of her career she turned her limitations into virtues.

She had a weak voice by nature and a delicate constitution, yet she succeeded by self-training, practice, management, and tact, in achieving so great a mastery of modulation, pitch, and tone that she could express anything from the fury of the whirlwind to the sigh of a sleepy stream.

[ vi ]

What was the secret of her art, and what were the main characteristics of her genius?

I believe that the secret of her art was that of all great art: that she was guided by an infallible instinct, and that whatever she did she could not go wrong. When what she did was done, it seemed simple, inevitable, and easy; and so swiftly accomplished, that you had no time to think of the *how*; nor was your sense sharp enough, however carefully you watched, to detect the divine conjury. It was the same whether she spoke lines of La Fontaine and Racine, or whether she asked, as she poured out a cup of coffee, as she did in one play: 'Du sucre, deux morceaux?' She was artistically inerrant. It is this gift which was probably the secret of the great actors of the past: Garrick, Siddons, Talma, and Salvini. It is certainly to be seen in the work of the great singer of the present, Chaliapine, whether he is portraying Satan holding his court on the Brocken, or a foolish, good-natured Chinovnik, half-fuddled with drink after a night out. When such a gift is at work, the greater the material it is interpreting, the greater, of course, the effect.

The greater the play Sarah Bernhardt appeared in, the greater the demand on her instinct, which *was* her genius; the swifter and the fuller the response. As the occasion expanded, so did her genius rise to it.

Her Hamlet was and is still hotly discussed, and quite lately several eminent English writers have expressed opinions that are completely at variance with one another on the subject. But every critic when he reads *Hamlet* creates a Hamlet in his own image, and when he sees it acted, the more vivid the impersonation, the more likely it is to be at variance with his own conception. One critic finds her Hamlet an unpardonable Gallic liberty to take with Shakespeare; another, that she electrified Hamlet with the vigour of her personality. I remember a cultivated philosopher, who was a citizen of the world, telling me that he thought her Hamlet the only intelligible rendering he had seen of the part, just because it rendered the youthful inconsequence of the moods of the moody Dane. But whether you thought it justifiable or unjustifiable, true or untrue to Shakespeare, in witnessing it you were aware of the genius of the interpreter answering the genius of the dramatic poet. Deep was calling to deep.

When Hamlet looked into the guilty King's face at the end of the play within the play, or thought for one second that the King and not Polonius had blundered into death behind the arras; when Hamlet concealed his forebodings from Horatio, and when Hamlet looked at Laertes during the duel and let him know that he knew the swords had been exchanged and that one of them had been poisoned, all thought of

149

the part – the rendering, tradition, the language, the authorship – went to the winds: you knew only that something which had been invented by one great genius was being interpreted by another great genius, and that the situation had found an expression which was on its own level. That, at least, was the impression of many.

A brilliant Irish essayist (whose essays appeared during the war) arrived at just such a conception of Hamlet as Sarah Bernhardt did, and it should always be remembered that she was the first to give to the French stage a plain and accurate translation of *Hamlet* in which the play was allowed to speak for itself, and was neither 'adapted' nor dislocated by being put into romantic French verse.

A French friend of mine, an English scholar, who was a friend of M. Marcel Schwob, the translator of this version of *Hamlet*, assisted at some of the rehearsals, and once or twice, he told me, Sarah Bernhardt consulted him as to the meaning of a passage. He said what he thought, and she answered in a way which showed she had completely misunderstood him, had perhaps not even listened. Then, he said, she went on to the stage and played the passage in question, not only as if she understood the words that he had explained, but as if she had had access to the inner secrets of the poet's mind. This, again, was an instance of her instinct at work. If you pressed her for a theory about any part or passage she might invent something ready-made to please you, but it would have been an afterthought and not a preconceived plan. She acted by instinct and left the theory to others.

Her performance in Musset's *Lorenzaccio* was thought by some to be the most subtly interesting of all her achievements – nothing she ever did received greater praise from the critical in Paris (it received but little in London). M. Camille Mauclair speaks of 'ce magnifique "Lorenzaccio" dont elle faisait une des merveilles de sa carrière'. It is true that Musset's work was mangled to make an acting play, but as it was written it would probably be unactable, and given the nature of Sarah Bernhardt's performance it was worth it. But there was one part which, great as it was, needed no readjustment or alteration when she assumed it, and that was the part of Phèdre.

Of all the parts she played it demanded the greatest effort and exertion, and that is why, during her long career, she played it comparatively seldom. Here, at any rate, she was beyond discussion. When she played it for the first time in London in 1879 she was so overcome with nervousness that she had to be pushed on to the stage, and as she began to speak she pitched her voice too high. Whenever she played it afterwards, she told me herself that she went through an agonizing period of anguish, wondering whether she could bear the heavy load, and I remember seeing her between the acts of one performance in London, reading over her part, which was copied out in a large copy-book, murmuring the lines and saying to herself, with tears in her eyes: 'Quel rôle, quel rôle,' fearful even then of succumbing!

§

If *Phèdre* is not Racine's masterpiece (French critics generally concede that honour to *Athalie*), it is undoubtedly his most important play from a theatrical point of view: the *Hamlet* of the French stage. It moreover contains what is perhaps the most powerful and exacting woman's part in the whole range of dramatic literature. Two salient facts strike one in this play, and they have sometimes been noted as objections. The first is, that whereas the framework and machinery of the play and the central idea which informs it are Greek, its spirit is Christian. Phèdre herself is no Pagan. She is a victim of involuntary and irresistible passion; but she is full of remorse and reveals the consciousness of her guilt in her fear of Heaven, as manifested in the Sun-god and Minos, the judge of the dead. But this apparent discord in reality increases the poignancy of the drama, for in rendering Phèdre morally innocent the tragedy of her plight is heightened. The second fact, which is sometimes brought forward as an objection not only to *Phèdre* but to all Racine's plays, is akin to the first, namely, that the personages talk the language and express the sentiments of the epoch and surroundings of Louis XIV, whether the action takes place in Rome, Turkey, Greece, or Jerusalem. But it is really only the superficial and external forms of manner and speech which belong to the seventeenth century in these plays: the passions which these forms clothe are eternal and for all time, because they are human. And just as in *Bérénice*, Racine gives us the unchanging drama of the unwilling separation of willing lovers, so in *Phèdre* he presents us with the eternal drama of the woman who is the involuntary prey of an insuperable passion for a man whom she is debarred by circumstances from loving unless she would be criminal. And nowhere has this passion been more powerfully delineated, nor the gradations and phases of the martyrdom more subtly traced. Every touch tells; nothing is omitted; so that no modern psychologist could possibly add anything to the delicacy and reality of the study. For instance, Phèdre is haunted by the image of her stepson in her husband's features:

'Je l'évitais partout. O comble de misère!
Mes yeux le retrouvaient dans les traits de son père.'

In addition to the interest which the play derives from this masterful and moving analysis of passion, there is also the charm and the divine beauty of the diction in which the passion is clothed. It contains not only Racine's

§ The passage marked off by §–§ is interpolated from *Punch and Judy and Other Essays* where it appears as a separate study of Bernhardt as Phèdre.

most majestic and noble utterance, but also lines which have never been surpassed by any French poet for haunting melody of cadence. These qualities can only be realized to the full by those who have seen Madame Bernhardt in this part. Here she moves in the dominion which she has made her own: that of poetry and imaginative creation. She is equal to the part, and on the same scale. She seems to create it: to find always the unexpected, and yet the absolutely right intonation and rendering. There are two separate excellences in her interpretation of Phèdre; the first is its plastic beauty, and the second is its spiritual significance. The plastic beauty is a miracle in itself. Even if she acted the play in dumb show, it would still be a marvel of expressiveness. Her gestures are like phrases of silent music, and obey an invisible rhythm to which even her most violent outbursts of passion and anger are subordinate. Again, so varied and so artfully controlled, so ravishingly melodious are the modulations of her diction, that were she to read the play in an armchair, the evocation of passionate action would still be magically present. Just as Emerson says that Napoleon enlarged our conception of the capacity of man for business, so does Madame Bernhardt in this part enlarge our conception of the possibilities of the human being in dramatic art.

There is the mark of men and the mark of gods. Madame Bernhardt in *Phèdre* is superhuman: a superwoman. And had Racine seen her in this part he would have been compelled to adhere to the stage, and had Shakespeare seen her after writing *The Tempest* he would have spent the years of his retirement at Stratford in writing a woman's part for her, for, like Dante's Siren, she, and only she, could say:

> ' "Io son," cantava, "io son dolce sirena
> Che i marinari in mezzo il mar dismago." '

§

In reading the play again and conjuring up the visions, the sounds, of the harmonious, rhythmical, architectural symphony which was her Phèdre, the moments I remember most vividly were firstly her look, as of a frightened hunted animal suddenly caught in a trap, when in the first act Oenone first mentions the name of Hippolyte and Phèdre cries out, as if stabbed by a poisoned arrow, or feeling the fangs of a steel trap close:

> 'C'est toi qui l'as nommé!'

Then I see her sitting rigid with horror on her golden throne as she reflects that her Father is Judge in Hell and there is no refuge for her, the guilty, either on the earth, in the sky, or under the earth:

> 'Minos juge aux enfers tous les pâles Humains.'

As she said the line her eyes reflected the visions of Virgil and Dante:

'Terribiles visu formae! Letumque, Labosque!'

There was a line she charged with so great a sorrow and so grave a load of beauty that one thought Racine must have stirred in his tomb as she said it:

'On ne voit pas deux fois le rivage des morts.'

And the note of pathos was almost unbearable when she said:

'Est-ce un malheur si grand que de cesser de vivre?'

But perhaps most beautiful of all, and as striking in its restraint as the explosions of the preceding acts were formidable by their fury, was her utterance of Phèdre's final speech.

'J'ai voulu, devant vous exposant mes remords,
Par un chemin plus lent descendre chez les morts.
J'ai pris, j'ai fait couler dans mes brûlantes veines
Un poison que Médée apporta dans Athènes.
Déjà jusqu'à mon cœur le venin parvenu
Dans ce cœur expirant jette un froid inconnu.
Déjà je ne vois plus qu'à travers un nuage,
Et le ciel, et l'époux que ma présence outrage.
Et la mort à mes yeux dérobant la clarté
Rend au jour qu'ils souillaient toute sa pureté.'

After all the passion and the paroxysms, the storm and stress, the exultations and the agonies, she breathed out her final confession with that calm and harmonious unity of tone and absence of gesture and of facial expression which the quiet close of a great tragedy demands. She spoke as if she were already dead, with the impersonality and aloofness of what was no longer mortal. Her voice seemed to come from a distance, from the sunless regions; the chill of Cocytus was upon it, and as her head fell on the shoulder of the attendant slave, visions of the masterpieces of Greek sculpture were evoked, and all that the poets have said so briefly and so sweetly about the mowing down of beautiful flowers, and broken blossoms and ruined rhymes.

It was in moments such as these that Sarah Bernhardt enlarged rather than interpreted the masterpieces of the world. But praise of her now is no longer a living thing that might prove an incentive to others to go and see and hear for themselves. It is only a dirge of regret and a procession of melancholy shadows. Nevertheless, it is fitting to weave a few words, however idle and inadequate, and to honour her imperishable name with a perishable wreath.

## [ vii ]

When in the future people will say, 'But you should have heard Sarah Bernhardt in the part!' the newcomers will probably shrug their shoulders and say, 'Oh, we know all about that!'

But they will not know, nor will anybody be able to tell them or explain to them what Sarah Bernhardt could do with a modulated inflexion, a *trait de voix*, a look, a gesture, a cry, a smile, a sigh, nor what majesty, poetry and music she could suggest by the rhythm of her movements and her attitudes, what it was like to hear her speak verse, to say words such as:

'Songe, songe, Céphise, à cette nuit cruelle,'
or,
'Si tu veux faisons un rêve'.

Nobody will be able to tell them, because, in spite of the gramophone and the cinematograph, the actor's art dies almost wholly with the actor. It is shortlived, but only relatively shortlived; and nobody understood that better than Sarah Bernhardt, one of whose mottoes was 'Tout passe, tout casse, tout lasse.'

(It was tempered by another: 'Quand même'.)

On the loom of things the poems of Homer are only a little less ephemeral than a leading article, and the art of a Phidias is, after all, as perishable as the sketches of a 'lightning' music-hall artist.

'Le temps passe. Tout meurt. Le marbre même s'use.
Agrigente n'est plus qu'une ombre, et Syracuse
Dort sous le bleu linceul de son ciel indulgent.'

The most enduring monuments, the most astounding miracles of beauty achieved by the art and craft of man, are but as flotsam, drifting for a little while upon the stream of Time; and with it now there is a strange russet leaf, the name of Sarah Bernhardt.

## (ii) *Madame Lapara Recites*
### (from *C*)

THERE WAS SUDDENLY a breathless hush, then a great storm of applause, and Madame Madeleine Lapara was led on to the stage. She was not tall; she wore a large black hat, which seemed to be in the way, and a long, loose, dark brown cloak, plentifully trimmed with fur, and a fur boa round her neck. She carried a large bunch of violets. She put the flowers on the grand pianoforte, and then, taking a little piece of paper in her hand, she walked to the edge of the platform. C. was disappointed in her appearance. He had expected a romantic princess, instead of which, on the platform, there stood a lady who might have stepped out of an artistic fashion plate. She seemed to be intensely Parisian, ultra-modern, an *article de Paris*.

She paused a moment, looking down at the piece of paper in her hand. And then she said, '*Obsession de* Sully Prudhomme'. And as she spoke the title C. already seemed to feel a change in the moral temperature of the air.

> Un mot me hante, un mot me tue.
> Je l'écoute contre mon gré:
> A le bannir je m'évertue,
> Il me suit, toujours murmuré.
>
> A l'ancien chant de ma nourrice
> Je le mêle pour l'assoupir,
> Mais, redoutable adulatrice,
> La musique en fait un soupir.

She sighed the words, speech seemed too coarse and music too definite a word for the soft, rippling cascade of syllables which filled the large hall.

> Je gravis alors la montagne
> Pour l'étouffer dans le grand vent.
> Jusqu'au sommet il m'accompagne:
> Il y devient gémissement.

She raised her voice, her arms and her eyes; she lifted the soft pedal. The mystery took wings; her voice sounded clear and silvery, and the audience scaled that mountain with her, and felt the buffet of the great clean wind, and all at once the undying sadness following her even to the mountain top – it dimmed the glory and darkened the sun.

> Je demande à la mer sonore
> De le changer en bruit de flot.
> Plus plaintif et plus tendre encore,
> Hélas! il y devient sanglot. . . .

In the first two lines an abrupt modulation enlarged the sighing utterance; it became grave and deep, and then she pressed an ethereal pedal on her voice; it was once more unimaginably soft and caressing, and something more than soft: there was something subtle about it which defied analysis, like the scent of a flower at night. As she spoke the word *sanglot* there was a break in her voice, and it was her piteous eyes that seemed to be speaking. A murmured acclamation escaped from the audience, and here and there whispered *bravos* were heard. A well-known critic, commenting on the recitation in his *feuilleton* the following Monday, said there was no search after effect in it and nothing time-taking, '*point d'effets cherchés ni de temps pris; cependant que de nuances indiquées, d'un simple trait de voix courant!*' and he spoke of the tremor of applause. '*C'etait un frémissement continu dans la salle; . . . un murmure d'admiration et de plaisir qui coupait le vers.*'

> Je tente, comme un dernier charme,
> Le silence enchanté des bois;

You could have heard a pin drop.

> Mais je le sens qui devient larme
> Dès qu'il a cessé d'être voix.

The accent on the word *larme* trembled a little and stabbed the listeners, who had been taken to secret woodways and to lofty aisles of green trees.

> Ce qui pleure ou ne peut se taire,
> Est-ce en moi le remords? oh! non:
> C'est un souvenir solitaire
> Au plus lointain de l'âme . . . un nom.

The last stanza seemed to float by as swiftly as a puff of smoke. They were said almost before C. was aware she had begun; and far away, infinitely far away, from the starless end of the soul, the last word was sent to sound and softly die, leaving something behind that lingered after its death. And through all the plaintive sighing music there was something else, something which made itself felt, a poignant note, a stab, an immense sadness.

'Yes,' the accents said: 'I know how sweet it is, and I know, too, how very bitter is that sweetness,' and as she ended, her eyes were full of the sorrow of all the lovers in the world. It was as if she had laid bare a secret wound, a wound that every one had suffered and every one had concealed, and that she had touched it with a divinely magical, healing finger.

There were a few seconds of silence and then the audience burst into a great roar. C. didn't any longer know where he was nor what he was doing.

156

In the meantime Madeleine Lapara had bowled her way from the stage, but the audience stood up and shouted till she came back. She bowed from the corner of the platform and pressed her face against her bouquet of violets, but the enthusiasm of the audience when they saw her, rose into a frenzy, and there was one loud roar of *bis*.

She left the platform, but she was recalled again and yet again, but she showed no sign of being willing to repeat the performance. The roar of the audience became more insistent and more imperative, and all at once she apparently either changed her mind or made it up. The expression in her eyes seemed to say: 'Well, if you want it, you shall have it.'

She walked up to the pianoforte and she took off her hat, which was transfixed and held in place by a long dagger-like pin. This freed a great mane of picturesque rebellious hair. She put the hat down and the flowers as well, on the pianoforte, and she took a cane chair and dragged it right to the extreme front edge of the stage. Then she sat down, and said in ordinary commonplace tones, as of a schoolgirl saying a lesson: '*Le Songe d'Athalie.*' There came a gasp, partly of surprise, partly of expectation, from the audience, and C. felt that he was back in the schoolroom at Hengrave House. He saw Mademoiselle Walter, her determined jaw and the square, black ruler on the long polished table.

'*Caryl, tu perds ton temps,*' he heard the sharp reminder again.

Madeleine Lapara clasped her hands and bent her head. Then she raised her head again and looked straight in front of her and murmured to herself:

> Un songe (me devrai-je inquiéter d'un songe?)
> Entretient dans mon cœur un chagrin qui le ronge,
> Je l'évite partout, partout il me poursuit.

Ominous apprehension and the shadow of a coming nightmare descended upon the audience.

> C'était pendant l'horreur d'une profonde nuit.

As she spoke the line she opened her eyes wide, and they were full of fire and dread, like those of a frightened wild beast.

In the row in front opposite there was a little boy about nine years old sitting next to his mother, a large prosperous middle-class lady dressed in bright magenta.

'*Maman, j'ai peur,*' he whispered.

She took him on her knee, kissed him and quieted and soothed him. He buried his face on her shoulder and remained quite still till the end of the performance.

As Lapara spoke this first line her voice had the depth and sonority of a great bell, and C. suddenly felt how infinite in suggestion were these bare, bald words. He understood what Monsieur Jollivet, what Burstall, what the whole French nation meant when they said Racine was a great poet.

> Ma mère Jézabel devant moi s'est montrée,
> Comme au jour de sa mort pompeusement parée.
> Ses malheurs n'avaient point abattu sa fierté.
> Même elle avait encor cet éclat emprunté,
> Dont elle eut soin de peindre et d'orner son visage,
> Pour réparer des ans l'irréparable outrage.

The words were hammered out in icy, low, metallic tones, in a matter-of-fact voice, but a matter of tremendous fact, as of some one who had been the eye-witness of a ghastly tragedy, and who had not yet recovered from the shock of the spectacle. The words had the ring of truth and the accent of calamity. She was telling the bare facts, and as she did so the fallen Queen appeared to that vast audience in all her undiminished pride. The image evoked was horrible, and great, and piteous, as well as horrible; for she had come back with a painted face from the dead, and taken pains to make up even in the region of Tophet. And her arts had proved ineffectual, her pretence of youth a mockery. The reciter seemed to grow a hundred years older as she said the lines, and C. thought of Froude's description of the executioner holding up Mary Stuart's severed head, grown grey and suddenly that of an old woman, at Fotheringay. (He had read this at Eton in the Boys' Library.)

> 'Tremble,' m'a-t-elle dit, 'fille digne de moi,
> Le cruel Dieu des Juifs l'emporte aussi sur toi.
> Je te plains de tomber dans ses mains redoutables,
> Ma fille.'

A soul in hell seemed to be shrieking a warning with all its feeble might. There came a change of key.

> En achevant ces mots épouvantables
> Son ombre vers mon lit a paru se baisser,
> Et moi, je lui tendais mes mains pour l'embrasser.
> Mais je n'ai plus trouvé qu'un horrible mélange
> D'os et de chair meurtris, et trainés dans la fange,
> Des lambeaux pleins de sang, et des membres affreux,
> Que des chiens dévorants se disputaient entre eux.

There was a decrescendo in tone, but the horror it expressed went on increasing in pitch. She suited the gesture to the words, and she stretched out her hands. She stood up as she spoke, and became a classic figure. C. beheld the ghosts in Virgil, on the banks of the Styx, stretching their arms towards the forbidden shore. In the last four lines of the speech the voice rose to a high pitch of horror, and ended with a cry and a gesture – as though she were warding off the vision with her hands – of terror, pity, disgust – unendurable pain. The audience felt they were in the presence of a brutal catastrophe. C. remembered the first time he had been in at the death out fox hunting, and as he looked at the actress he saw reflected in her eyes the horror at an unbearable sight; and then she seemed to change and to become herself the fallen Queen at bay, Queen Jezebel, in all her borrowed youth, her malignant majesty and evil glamour, turning and snarling defiance at the murderous pack, and finally defeated, pulled down, chawed and mangled, and he seemed to hear a human cry drowned and stifled by a merciless baying and yelping. The audience, he felt, were all of them in at the death, and they knew it. It was a hideous *hallali*, and the quarry was an old painted queen. The audience swayed towards the platform; and C. noticed, in one brief second, that right up at the right-hand corner of the top gallery, two members of the *Garde Républicaine* were straining over the heads of the people in the back row, immobile, fascinated, spellbound, as every one else. The audience were shouting now, not with a clamorous enthusiasm as after the first piece, but with determination and in a rhythmical disciplined chorus, '*Bis, bis, bis*', that would take no denial. She said it all over again, beginning this time at

C'était pendant l'horreur d'une profonde nuit,

and C. was hardly conscious when it was over that she had begun, or that it had all happened twice; he was still in the vision; still on the spot of the tragedy; still in the presence of the murdered and mangled queen; still under the pressure of the prodigious nightmare. She was silent; and once more the audience, like one man, insisted on hearing it all over again. It seemed as if both they and the actress had been caught as workmen are caught by the flying wheel of a machine. Genius had escaped and got beyond control, and had maddened the audience beyond frenzy to a cold, relentless fury. They were determined to have their way. It was as though the actress had become the hunted quarry, and they the remorseless pack of hounds – or were they the quarry and she the inspired huntsman? A vicious circle of inspiration and enthusiasm had been forged from which there was no escape, and to which there could be no end.

C. had no idea how many times Madeleine Lapara repeated the passage, but, at last, he was conscious that the audience had risen to its feet, and that every one was leaving the hall in silence. The dream was over. She had, so Pelly said, repeated the sixteen lines five times running. It was, they said afterwards, unheard-of in the annals of the stage.

# 3

*History . . . As If*

*In his hilariously 'unreliable histories', Maurice Baring raised to a wild philosophy of historical comedy the notion of 'What if'. 'What if' all had come out quite differently, given the same persons and initial situations, say, in the case of Napoleon I, or Macbeth of Scotland, or Nero, or Shakespeare and Bacon, or whatever? The initial scraps of a situation might in any known life have been factored out in any number of ways, given one or another nudge in any number of other directions. If you take the received information of an illustrious life and play with it logically but with a wildly comic wrong-headedness, who knows where you might end up with a new interpretation? This is how Maurice Baring went at his parodies and his mischievous historical reconstructions.*

*The key to his method may be found in 'The Alternative', which opens this section of our book. With an hilarious knowledgeability, he gives us Napoleon, Byron, Shelley, and others, as they might have been had their lives taken one important turn aside from the known facts; and under the eternal impudence of the far-too-well-informed schoolboy, lies a reckless willingness to speculate with mock seriousness on what might have been.*

*Monsignor Knox said Maurice Baring's jokes rested on genuine learning. Even as we revere these credentials, we must remember that Baring himself said, 'The word research is not even remotely applicable here, for in my case it means the hazy memories of a distant education indolently received'.*

# The Alternative

(from *Half a Minute's Silence & Other Stories*)

I WAS READING HISTORY, and not for fun. I was reading for my schools. My third year at Balliol was drawing to an end, and I was expected to do well, and at the back of my dreams there was the hope of a fellowship and a quiet life in the security of Oxford.

I had been reading until late in the night. I was tired. I had been reading about Napoleon and the Russian Campaign of 1812. And now I had stopped reading and had fallen into an abstraction. I noticed that the time by the clock was 1.15. I was thinking of great men and the part they played in history, and to what extent events were modified by phenomena, such as Caesar or Napoleon; as to whether they made a difference, or whether writers such as Tolstoy were right, who maintained that they made no difference. I thought of many things: of William James' *Essay on Great Men*, of Carlyle's *Heroes*, of Ferrero, of Mr Wells' *Outline of History*. What would have happened, I said to myself, if Napoleon's father had sent his son into the British Navy, as he wanted to do at one moment, instead of into the French Army? Would everything have been different, or would everything have been exactly the same?

'Everything would have been different, but the result would have been just the same,' said a voice at my elbow.

I looked up and saw sitting in the arm-chair which stood on the left of my writing-table a little old man. He was old and yet he did not look old. He was ageless. He had a thick head of hair, and you could not tell whether it was white or grey. His eyes were clear and luminous. There were no lines on his face. There were none of the usual signs of old age about him, and yet he gave the impression of immense old age, and of an almost infinite experience.

I did not feel in the least surprised at this sudden apparition. It seemed to me quite natural that this strange unaged old man should be sitting in my arm-chair. I did not even interrupt; I merely waited for the old man to go on.

'Everything would have been different, but the result would have been the same,' the stranger repeated. 'You know how to play chess?' he asked. I said I was an enthusiastic but an unskilful chess player.

'Very well,' said the stranger. 'Supposing you play a game with a professional, you make certain mistakes, and you lose the game. Let us assume you keep a record of the moves, and that when the game is over your adversary allows you to play it over again. Say you rectify an initial blunder; you use different openings, different gambits; you have a new scheme, an improved strategical plan. Every move you make in this second game is different from those you made in the first game. But do you win? No. Because your adversary, the professional, changes his game in such a manner as to meet and answer the changed nature of your game. He replies to your new strategy with a new counter-strategy; his counter-moves lead you to move as he wishes, and in the end he checkmates you.

'So it is with men in history. Supposing you were to eliminate the great men of history, and substitute for them men of a different nature; or supposing you left them as they were, but changed the quality of the moves and shortened or lengthened their careers inversely to what happened in history, as you know it; then every move in the game would be different; but, in spite of that, the march of history and the fate of mankind would be the same.'

'I understand that's quite possible,' I said, 'but forgive the question, how do you know?'

'Because,' said the stranger, 'I am the historiographer of the Kingdom of Limbo. I teach the ghosts history – *alternative history*, in case they should be conceited.'

'Yes,' I said, 'but how I don't quite see. Films? A cinematograph?'

'Oh no,' said the stranger. 'We do better than that; we plunge the student into the life of an alternative world; alternative to the period in which he lived on earth; and we let him learn from experience, as an eyewitness, what that epoch would have been like had his part been either non-existent or different.'

'Very interesting,' I said. 'I should like a glimpse of an alternative world of that kind.'

'Nothing is easier,' said the stranger. 'Choose any epoch you like and I will take you there.'

'Well,' I said, 'I should like to see what would have happened in the period I am reading about, supposing Napoleon had entered the British Navy instead of the French Army.'

'Nothing is easier,' said the stranger. 'You shall have two peeps into that world between 1800 and 1850. Come along.'

I felt dazed for a moment, but only for a moment, and when I recovered from this fleeting flash of unconsciousness I found myself wide awake. I was sitting on a verandah; in front of me was a seacoast, against which large grey breakers were rolling; behind me sashed windows which reached to the ground opened on to a parlour; and something touched a cell or struck a note in my memory which made me think of Miss Austen's novels, of *Cranford*, and of the breakfast-room in a country house where I had once stayed in my childhood. Was it a faint smell of lavender that came from indoors, or the taste of the saffron bun I had just eaten, for I had just taken a bite from a saffron bun, or the elder-flower wine that I was sipping, or the picture of King George on the wall I could see over the chimney-piece of the room beyond the verandah? I don't know.

That parlour was bare, and might have belonged to almost any epoch. It was slightly damp. I knew that I was not in Europe, although there was nothing extra-European either behind or before me. I was talking to a man, who, although he was dressed in nankin, had something indefinably maritime about him. He was middle-aged, with a tawny beard streaked with grey hairs, and his face was tanned and worn by exposure; there was nothing rough, bluff, or hearty about him, but, on the contrary, an air of gentle and slightly melancholy refinement. He was smoking a pipe, and after taking a puff or two in silence, he took up the thread of his discourse again. I was certain that the conversation was being continued and not being begun, and I felt quite satisfied when my quiet interlocutor said:

'Yes, that was her first cruise.' It seemed the natural inevitable thing for him to say.

At that moment, a fat, sallow, dark-haired man dressed in nankin and wearing a broad panama hat strolled along the beach in front of us, whistling to himself a tune which I seemed to have heard before.

'Who's that?' I asked.

'That's the Captain,' said my host. 'He's——' He touched his forehead meaningly.

'Mad?' asked I.

'No, not mad, but queer,' said my host. 'Has illusions – thinks he's King of England one day, and Emperor of India the next. A curious career his as ever man had. His real name is Bonnypart, though he now goes by the name of Jackson, and his father, so they say, was an Italian skipper in one of the French colonial islands. He was anxious for his son to have a good education, so he sent him to England to be naturalized as an Englishman and to serve King George in the British Navy. The lad was partial to learning and took to the sea, like a duck takes to water, and all went well till the French Jacobites declared war on us a second time in 1805. He was already a Captain then, promotion in those times being speedy. He disobeyed orders, when the fleet was pursuing Admiral Villeneuve, and some say it was thanks to his breach of discipline that the fleet was not destroyed at Trafalgar. Be that as it may, the Admiralty had a black mark against his name from that moment, and he was warned that he had got off lightly the first time, owing to the victory and to Admiral Nelson's intercession; Admiral Nelson saying that he had no use for the man who did not know how to disobey orders at the right moment (that did not please their Lordships). But shortly after the battle he was accused of cheating at cards, whether rightly or wrongly I don't know, but I have seen men who have been shipmates with him, who said that never had they seen a man with a quicker brain for business and a slower head for cards; that there was no game he could master, and he cheated for very weariness, and neither for love of gain nor gambling. This time he was court-martialled, found guilty and dismissed from the service. Admiral Nelson could no longer intercede for him, for the Admiral himself had been superseded owing to the newspaper clamour which arose over his handling of the fleet at Trafalgar. Bonnypart changed his name to Jackson, and enlisted as a soldier in Wellesley's Army. He fought against the French Republic in Germany, and on the Eastern frontier against the Russians, and after a year or two he was given a commission. After the French Jacobites were defeated by the Germans and the Russians in 1814, he was once more promoted to the rank of Captain. This time he came into collision with Wellesley, now Lord Wellington. When the Allies occupied Paris, Lord W. declared he would go out fox-hunting in the Forest of Fontainebleau, and Captain Jackson, being a poor rider, and having foreign blood in him, and consequently no feeling for the sport, jeered openly at Wellington's intention. News of this got round to the General, who ordered Jackson to go out hunting with him the next day. Jackson did; but he shot the fox dead in the middle of a spanking run, and all but hit the General into the bargain. When he was had up before his Commanding Officer he answered with great insolence, and he was cashiered for insubordination. Being a restless fellow, he thought he would take service with the French or the Italians, and went to his old home, Sardinia or Elba. In 1815, when General Murat turned out the French King, Jackson enlisted in the French Navy, and the vessel he was in was captured not far from this island of St Helena by a British frigate just before peace was made in 1815. He was imprisoned here as a deserter, and would have been tried for his life, but by this time, the illusions which some say had been simmering in him for a long time, aggravated bv a blow on the head which he had received in the scrap at sea, got the better of him, and the doctors said he was not responsible for his actions. They kept him shut up in the hospital here at Longwood, but after a while the doctor, finding he was harmless, let him have the run of the island. Harmless he is, too, although there is a warder called Hudson who has an eye on him. You can see him now, behind that tree, some thirty yards behind the Captain. The Captain often stops to spin a yarn with me, and he is pleasant spoken and knowledgeable too about seamanship and the weather, and he has only one or two delusions. One is that he is King of

England, and the other that he can play cribbage, which he cannot do without cheating, but we keep cards out of his way lest they should upset him.

'Would you like to speak with him?' said my host. 'He is coming this way.'

I said I would be delighted to, and, as Captain Jackson walked towards the house where we were sitting, my host rose and beckoned to him.

Captain Jackson had a remarkable face, remarkable for its extreme pallor and for the brilliance of his penetrating eyes. He looked me up and down, and then asked in an abrupt way:

'Oxford or Cambridge?'

I felt embarrassed by his abruptness, but managed to get the word Oxford across my lips.

'What College?' he asked. 'Balliol, I suppose,' and without waiting for an answer he said, 'What are you studying?'

I said, 'History.'

'Bah,' he said, 'they can't teach history at Oxford. There are only two places where you can learn history. One is the Navy and the other the Army, and then only in times of war.'

Upon which, he took a pinch of snuff, turned his back, and walked quickly away.

Up to that moment, the conversation had seemed to me quite natural, as if I had belonged to the circumstances in which I suddenly found myself, as if I was a contemporary, taking part in the events of the day, but from the moment that Captain Jackson left us I seemed to be two people: the man who was on the island and who belonged to this remoter epoch, and my real twentieth-century self.

'Did Captain Jackson fight for Napoleon?' I asked.

'Napoleon?' said my host. 'I never heard of him.'

'The Emperor of the French,' I said.

'There never was no Emperor as I ever heard of,' said my host. 'There was a King and they cut his head off. And then there was a Jacobite republic which overran half Europe, spreading revolution wherever it went, in Italy, Spain, Germany, and even in Russia. They won victories, then they were beat. As soon as all the world made peace, they made war again and won victories again, and at last they were beat altogether, and the King came into his own.'

'Then who,' I asked, 'is King of France now?'

'Why, Louis the Eighteenth, of course. And, thanks to those Jacobites, of a much smaller France than belonged to his ancestors. He had to give up Alsace and half Lorraine to the Germans.'

His voice seemed to grow faint as he said this, and the scene melted. I rubbed my eyes and found that I was walking down a street, arm in arm with a stranger. I soon recognized the street. It was Whitehall.

'That,' said the man who was walking with me, 'is the Horse Guards.'

I realized that I was being shown over London. I was possibly a stranger of distinction. My guide was floridly dressed. He wore a crimson necktie and a carbuncle pin, a yellow satin waistcoat, a large choker, a little imperial; his eyes were bright and penetrating, his manner vivacious. There was something slightly histrionic about him.

I recognized certain familiar landmarks. The traffic, the hansom carriages, and the four-wheelers made a clatter in the street; elegant barouches passed us. The ladies wore crinolines; the men, Dundreary whiskers. I felt I had been landed into the world of Thackeray. We passed an unfamiliar statue which stood where the war memorial now stands.

'Who is that?' I asked.

'That,' said my guide, 'is the statue erected in memory of a poet who died fighting for the cause of royalty, order, and the Fleur-de-lys against the hosts of anarchy and murder in France during the great Jacobin War. He was killed fighting on the barricades in Paris. He showed great promise as a writer. His name was William Wordsworth.'

Just then we passed a dignified-looking old gentleman with white hair dressed in the fashion of an earlier period. He wore a blue swallow-tailed coat, a buff nankin waistcoat, and a fob with many seals hanging from it. He was a dignified and picturesque figure. He stooped slightly. His eyes were those of a mathematician or an inventor. There was an air of great distinction about him, not unmingled with a whiff of scholarship. I asked my guide who he was.

'That,' he answered, 'is the Conservative Member for Horsham, Sir Percy Shelley.'

'The son of the poet?' I asked.

'Oh dear, no,' said my guide. 'His father was not a poet. His father was a Squire, Sir Timothy Shelley. It is true that Sir Percy did write some verse as a youth, but we never refer to that now. I assure you nobody ever refers to it. Boyish peccadilloes. Very regrettable, as they were atheistic, often heathen in tone, and sometimes even licentious in character. But boys will be boys, and the young must sow their wild oats. He has amply atoned for all that. Fortunately few of those early effusions were printed, and Sir Percy was able to withdraw from circulation and to destroy every single copy of that most deplorable doggerel. Sir Percy is one of the pillars of the Conservative Party, and the speech he made against Reform, and the Extension of Suffrage Bill, is a classic. He is a great patriot, is Sir Percy, and he wrote some stirring words about the war which were published in *The Times* newspaper, and then set to music and enjoyed a wide popularity.

'The refrain ran:

> "We don't want to fight,
> But Zeus help them if we do."

You see, Sir Percy is a classical scholar and can never resist a Greek word. He never quotes Greek in the House, but Horace is always upon his lips. Horace, as he rightly says, is so quotable.'

'Then he never writes now?' I asked.

'He occasionally writes to *The Times* newspaper,' said my guide. 'You see,' he went on, 'he is a very busy man, Chairman of many Committees, and one of the most prominent Members of the Conservative Club, and on the Boards of I don't know how many hospitals and charitable institutions. He plays a fair hand at whist, and always rides to the meet of the foxhounds if it is not too far off, and he is a sound and earnest Churchman——'

'Not a ritualist, I suppose?'

'Oh no, not a ritualist, far from it. A sound, broad Churchman; not too high, and not too low. He reads the lessons on Sunday at Horsham, with much expression and fervour, although his voice is a little shrill.'

'Does he ever refer to his friendship with Lord Byron?' I asked.

'They meet sometimes on State occasions.'

'But isn't Lord Byron dead?'

'Dead? Dear me, no, unless he died last night. I haven't heard His Eminence was ill.'

'I thought he died at Missolonghi in 1824.'

'Oh no; he returned from that Grecian expedition much shattered in health, and after a period of solitary reflection, which he spent in the Channel Islands, he joined the Church of Rome. He is now, of course, a Cardinal and lives at Birmingham.'

'But his works?' I asked. 'Did he suppress them?'

'Oh dear, no, sir. He wrote a great deal, and the last cantos of *Don Juan*, which tell of the Don's conversion and *bona mors*, are reckoned to be among the most pious and edifying books of the century, by men of all religious denominations. He wrote, too, a fine sequel to *Cain*, called *The Death of Cain*, which is even more edifying, and even now he still writes hymns, some of which are popular both in the Roman, Anglican, and Evangelical Churches. Notably one which begins:

"The Assyrian came down like a wolf on the fold".

But Cardinal Byron is better known now for his sermons than for his lyrics. He preaches most eloquently, and it is worth a journey to Birmingham to hear him.'

'But who,' I asked, 'are the greatest contemporary poets?'

'Well,' said my guide, 'undoubtedly the greatest living poet is a woman: a portentous star of the first magnitude; I am talking of the fiery, volcanic, incandescent genius of Felicia Hemans, the author of that burning rhapsody *Casa Bianca*. She is undoubtedly the greatest woman poet since the days of Sappho, and perhaps even more passionate. We have just lost one great poet, James Montgomery. He was the greatest, in fact the only, epic poet since the days of Gray. Then there is Benjamin Disraeli, author of so many beautiful poetical dramas. Then you have the sombre and tortured broodings of Adelaide Proctor, and the fierce, bitter, biting etchings of Jean Ingelow; in fact, it is an age of poetesses more than of poets.'

'And what about Alfred Tennyson?' I asked.

'The brother of the poet, Frederick?' said my guide. 'Poor fellow, he was killed in the war a few months ago at Balaclava; a very gallant soldier.'

'And the poet Keats?' I said. 'Have you heard of him?'

'Of course,' was the answer. 'Who has not heard of him? It is impossible not to. He publishes a fresh volume of verse every year; but ever since he has lived at Torquay, where he originally settled down some thirty years ago, he has written practically nothing except about agriculture and crops and live stock. The hero of his last verse-narrative was a Shorthorn. He writes too much. All very instructive, of course, and parts of it are descriptive, but he writes a great deal too much. That's just what ruined Coleridge.'

'But Coleridge is surely not alive?' I said.

'He died,' I was informed, 'two or three years ago. He was eighty years old. He died of overwork. He had just finished the last book of his epic: *Kubla Khan*. It has fifteen books, you will remember, and it is the longest epic in the English language. His one fear was that he should die before he should complete it. As it was, he finished it just six months before his death, and he had the joy of seeing the massive work in print. It is longer than the *Iliad* and the *Odyssey* put together, and the building of it occupied the whole of the poet's life.'

'And did it meet with a satisfactory reception?' I asked.

'Most satisfactory. One critic in the *Quarterly Review* even went so far, it was perhaps a little extravagant on his part, as to put it in the same rank as Southey's immortal epics.'

'Did Coleridge finish all his poems?' I asked.

My guide seemed quite offended by this question – offended for Coleridge and shocked at my ignorance.

'Of course he did,' he said. 'Coleridge was the most hard-working and conscientious of writers, and, as I have already told you, he died of overwork.'

'But,' I persisted, 'did he ever finish *Christabel*?'

My guide smiled a superior tolerant smile.

'*Christabel*,' he said, 'is not by Coleridge at all. It is by De Quincey.'

I gasped with astonishment.

'De Quincey, the opium eater?'

170

'He wrote several things of the same kind. *The Albatross* and *The Dark Lady*, all most fantastic stuff. Poor man, he was light-headed at the last. It came from taking drugs.'

This account of the world of poetry so bewildered me that I thought I should feel on firmer ground if we passed to the domain of prose, and I asked who were considered the best novelists of the day.

'Well,' said my guide, 'there has been nothing very interesting in that way just lately. Mr Thackeray has written a most insignificant story called *Vanity Fair*; all about those trumpery Jacobin Wars, which interest nobody now. Mr Carlyle wrote a spirited romance some years ago which suffered from the same fault, namely, that of dealing with a hackneyed commonplace and dreary epoch: the Jacobin revolt. Indeed, Mr Carlyle's work is the more tedious as it deals solely with France and with the French, and nobody now takes any interest in that country. There are, of course, a fine series of romances by Froude, and the powerful but rather morbid studies of real life by Miss Charlotte Yonge; the monumental history of Harrison Ainsworth; the fantastic short stories of Ruskin, and the almost too sprightly, too flippant satire and Puck-like wit of Herbert Spencer.'

I asked whether the influence of the French was felt in recent literature. My guide said that the influence of French literature had been negligible. Ever since the restoration of the French monarchy, French literature had been pursuing an even but uninteresting course. During the prosperous and calm reign of Charles X, the most notable names in the literature of France were, as in England, nearly all those of women. There was Madame Desbordes Valmore, Mademoiselle Victor Hugo, Mademoiselle Lamartine, all of whom had written agreeable lyrics and some tuneful and melodious narrative poems. Among the male poets the most remarkable was Georges Sand. During the reign of Henry V the same pure and refined standards had been upheld, but it could not be denied that this literature, although admirable in tone, sane in its outlook, and exemplary in the lessons which it taught, did not go down across the Channel. The England of Miss Yonge and Mrs Gaskell – those unflinching realists, those intrepid divers into the unplumbed depths and mysteries of the human soul; those undaunted and ruthless surgeons of all the secret sores of the spirit and of the flesh – was used to stronger meat, and insisted on getting it.

'But,' I said, 'what about Musset and Baudelaire?'

My guide seemed astonished. 'Musset?' he said. 'I have never heard of a writer called Musset.'

'Alfred de Musset,' I suggested.

'There is a Secretary at the French Embassy here by that name, but as far as we know he has never written anything. As for Baudelaire, his hymns, psalms, and meditations are fervent and pious, and deserve respect, but they are so ultra-devotional and so full of technical theology and the jargon of the sacristy, that they would certainly find no public here. Cardinal Byron, it is true, admires them greatly, and has even published a translation of some of the hymns. No, we have little use for the goody-goody milk-and-water idealism here. All that would never go down in the country of Miss Austen.'

'But,' I objected, 'surely Miss Austen was a great artist.'

'Great, certainly, as great as the Pyramids, but *artist* is hardly the word. It is true she created a whole world, but she looked at the universe through the distorted lens of her lurid and monstrous imagination. She dipped her pen into the waters of Tartarus, so that she invests a page boy with the personality of a Hannibal, and lends Satanic proportions to the meanest of her rogues. Yet what she saw she described with such minute accuracy and with such wealth of detail, and abundance and even redundance of description, that the critics have almost universally acclaimed her as the founder of the great realistic-naturalistic English novel, whereas if they would only think more carefully they would see that Miss Austen is the last of the great romantic poets, the lineal descendant of Pope and Cowper, and the kindred spirit and rival of that most flamboyant of all the romantics, Crabbe.'

'And Russian literature?' I asked. 'Has that had any influence here?'

'Ever since the Russian Republic and the United States of Russia were called into being by the Emperor Alexander I in 1819, Russian art and literature practically came to an end. Politics and business engrossed the minds of the rising generation there, and, as General John Bright, that dashing cavalry soldier, so well put it: "The Russians are completely inartistic. They are a nation of shopkeepers." '

'But are not we fighting the Russians in the Crimea now?' I asked.

'We are fighting in the Crimea, but not against the Russians. They are our Allies and we are fighting the Turks. The Emperor Constantine has arranged with our Foreign Secretary, Feargus O'Connor, that Russia is to have Constantinople, we are to take Egypt, and the French are to have Syria. As for Palestine, it is possible that the Jews may be allowed to go there. Ever since their expulsion from England twenty years ago, they have greatly complained of having nowhere to live.'

Just at that moment an open carriage drove by drawn by four white horses with postilions and outriders. Inside the carriage a magnificent Englishman with a long black beard bowed to the populace, who cheered. I asked who it was.

'That is the King of Greece, once better known as Lord Elcho. He is here on a visit. The Greeks just now are very popular, as we are fighting the Turks.'

We had passed the Houses of Parliament and had reached the doors of what I took to be a large theatre.

'Here,' said my guide, 'I must leave you. I must go to rehearsal.'

'One moment,' I said. 'There is one name we have not mentioned connected with the world of literature: that of Charles Dickens. Are his works popular?'

My guide was convulsed with laughter.

'That,' he said, 'is a really good joke. Charles Dickens a writer!'

'But——' I said.

'My dear sir,' he answered, 'you surely are not going to argue the point with me. I am Charles Dickens, and your humble servant, an actor by profession, and if you would like to see me play Paul Pry tonight I can give you an order for a box and supper and some grilled bones afterwards.'

I was about to answer something when I once again felt dizzy, and when I recovered consciousness again I was sitting in my rooms. I was alone this time, and the time by the clock was 1.16. I had been asleep for a minute.

# Lady Macbeth's Trouble

---

(from *Dead Letters*)

## Letter from Lady Macbeth to Lady Macduff

*Most Private.*                              THE PALACE, FORRES,
                                                *October* 10.

My dearest Flora,

I am sending this letter by Ross, who is starting for Fife tomorrow
morning. I wonder if you could possibly come here for a few days. You
would bring Jeamie of course. Macbeth is devoted to children. I think
we could make you quite comfortable, although of course palaces are
never very comfortable, and it's all so different from dear Inverness. And
there is the tiresome Court etiquette and the people, especially the Heads
of the Clans, who are so touchy, and insist on one's observing every
tradition. For instance, the bagpipes begin in the early morning; the
pipers walk round the castle a little after sunrise, and this I find very
trying, as you know what a bad sleeper I am. Only two nights ago I
nearly fell out of the window walking in my sleep. The doctor, who I
must say is a charming man (he was the late King's doctor and King
Duncan always used to say he was the only man who really understood
his constitution), is giving me mandragora mixed with poppy and syrup;
but so far it has not done me any good; but then I always was a wretched
sleeper and now I am worse, because – well, I am coming at last to what
I really want to say.

I am in very great trouble and I beg you to come here if you can,
because you would be the greatest help. You shall have a bedroom facing
south, and Jeamie shall be next to you, and my maid can look after you
both, and as Macduff is going to England I think it would really be wiser
and *safer* for you to come here than to stay all alone in that lonely castle
of yours in these troublesome times, when there are so many robbers
about and one never knows what may not happen.

I confess I have been very much put about lately. (You quite under-

174

stand if you come we shall have plenty of opportunities of seeing each other alone in spite of all the tiresome etiquette and ceremonies, and of course you must treat me just the same as before; only in *public* you must just throw in a 'Majesty' now and then and curtchey and call me 'Ma'am' so as not to shock the people.) I am sorry to say Macbeth is not at all in good case. He is really not at all well, and the fact is he has never got over the terrible tragedy that happened at Inverness. At first I thought it was quite natural he should be upset. Of course very few people know how fond he was of his cousin. King Duncan was his favourite cousin. They had travelled together in England, and they were much more like brothers than cousins, although the King was so much older than he is. I shall never forget the evening when the King arrived after the battle against those horrid Norwegians. I was very nervous as it was, after having gone through all the anxiety of knowing that Macbeth was in danger. Then on the top of that, just after I heard that he was alive and well, the messenger arrived telling me that the King was on his way to Inverness. Of course I had got nothing ready, and Elspeth our housekeeper put on a face as much as to say that we could not possibly manage in the time. However, I said she *must* manage. I knew our cousin wouldn't expect too much, and I spent the whole day making those flat scones he used to be so fond of.

I was already worried then because Macbeth, who is superstitious, said he had met three witches on the way (he said something about it in his letter) and they had apparently been uncivil to him. I thought they were gipsies and that he had not crossed their palm with silver, but when he arrived he was still brooding over this, and was quite *odd* in his way of speaking about it. I didn't think much of this at the time, as I put it down to the strain of what he had gone through, and the reaction which must always be great after such a time; but now it all comes back to me, and now that I think over it in view of what has happened since, I cannot help owning to myself that he was not himself, and if I had not known what a sober man he was, I should almost have thought the 1030 (Hildebrand) whisky had gone to his head – because when he talked of the old women he was quite incoherent: just like a man who has had an hallucination. But I did not think of all this till afterwards, as I put it down to the strain, as I have just told you.

But now! Well, I must go back a little way so as to make everything clear to you. Duncan arrived, and nothing could be more civil than he was. He went out of his way to be nice to everybody and praised the castle, the situation, the view, and even the birds' nests on the walls! (All this, of course, went straight to my heart.) Donalbain and Malcolm were with him. They, I thought at the time, were not at all well brought up. They had not got their father's manners, and they talked in a loud voice and gave themselves airs.

Duncan had supper by himself, and before he went to bed he sent me a most beautiful diamond ring, which I shall always wear. Then we all went to bed. Macbeth was not himself that evening, and he frightened me out of my wits by talking of ghosts and witches and daggers. I did not, however, think anything serious was the matter and I still put it down to the strain and the excitement. However, I took the precaution of pouring a drop or two of my sleeping draught into the glass of water which he always drinks before going to bed, so that at least he might have a good night's rest. I suppose I did not give him a strong enough dose. (But one cannot be too careful with drugs, especially mandragora, which is bad for the heart.) At any rate, whether it was that or the awful weather we had that night (nearly all the trees in the park were blown down, and it will never be quite the same again) or whether it was that the hall porter got tipsy (why they choose the one day in the year to drink when one has guests, and it really matters, I never could understand!) and made the most dreadful noise and used really disgraceful language at the front door about five o'clock in the morning, I don't know. At any rate, we were all disturbed long before I had meant that we should be called (breakfast wasn't nearly ready and Elspeth was only just raking out the fires). But, as I say, we were all woken up, and Macduff went to call the King, and came back with the terrible news.

Macbeth turned quite white, and at first my only thought was for him. I thought he was going to have a stroke or a fit. You know he has a very nervous, high-strung constitution, and nothing could be worse for him than a shock like this. I confess that I myself felt as though I wished the earth would open and swallow me up. To think of such a thing happening in our house!

Banquo, too, was as white as a sheet; but the only people who behaved badly (of course this is strictly between ourselves, and I do implore you not to repeat it, as it would really do harm if it got about that I had said this, but you are safe, aren't you, Flora?) were Donalbain and Malcolm. Donalbain said nothing at all, and all Malcolm said when he was told that his father had been murdered was: 'Oh! by whom?' I could not understand how he could behave in such a heartless way before so many people; but I must say in fairness that all the Duncans have a very odd way of showing grief.

Of course the first thing I thought was 'Who can have done it?' and I suppose in a way it will always remain a mystery. There is no doubt that the chamber grooms actually did the deed; but whether they had any accomplices, whether it was just the act of drunkards (it turned out that the whole household had been drinking that night and not only the hall porter) or whether they were *instigated* by any one else (of course don't quote me as having suggested such a thing) we shall never know. Much as I dislike Malcolm and Donalbain, and shocking as I think their behaviour has been, and not only shocking but *suspicious*, I should not like any one to think that I suspected them of so awful a crime. It is one thing to be bad-mannered, it is another to be a parricide. However, there is no getting over the fact that by their conduct, by their extraordinary behaviour and flight to England, they made people suspect them.

I have only just now come to the real subject of my letter. At first Macbeth bore up pretty well in spite of the blow, the shock, and the extra worry of the coronation following immediately on all this; but no sooner had we settled down at Forres than I soon saw he was far from being himself.

His appetite was bad; he slept badly, and was cross to the servants, making scenes about nothing. When I tried to ask him about his health he lost his temper. At last one day it all came out and I realized that another tragedy was in store for us. Macbeth is suffering from hallucinations; this whole terrible business has unhinged his mind. The doctor always said he was highly strung, and the fact is he has had another attack, or whatever it is, the same as he had after the battle, when he thought he had seen three witches. (I afterwards found out from Banquo, who was with him at the time, that the matter was even worse than I suspected.) He is suffering from a terrible delusion. He thinks (of course you will never breathe this to a soul) that he killed Duncan! You can imagine what I am going through. Fortunately, nobody has noticed it.

Only last night another calamity happened. Banquo had a fall out riding and was killed. That night we had a banquet we could not possibly put off. On purpose I gave strict orders that Macbeth was not to be told of the accident until the banquet was over, but Lennox (who has no more discretion than a parrot) told him, and in the middle of dinner he had another attack, and I had only just time to get every one to go away before he began to rave. As it was, it must have been noticed that he wasn't himself.

I am in a terrible position. I never know when these fits are coming on, and I am afraid of people talking, because if it once gets about, people are so spiteful that somebody is sure to start the rumour that it's true. Imagine our position, then! So I beg you, dear Flora, to keep all this to yourself, and if possible to come here as soon as possible.

I am, your affectionate,

HARRIET R.

*P.S.* – Don't forget to bring Jeamie. It will do Macbeth good to see a child in the house.

# The Poet, the Player, and the Literary Agent

(from *Dead Letters*)

## Letter from Mr Nichols, Literary Agent, to Lord Bacon

My Lord,

I have now submitted the plays which your lordship forwarded to me to seven publishers: Messrs Butter, Mr Blount, Mr Thorpe, Mr Waterson, Mr Andrew Wise, Mr Steevens, and Mr G. Eld; and I very much regret to inform your lordship that I have not been able to persuade any of these publishers to make an offer for the publication of any of the plays, although Mr Thorpe would be willing to print them at your lordship's expense, provided that they appeared under your lordship's name. The cost, however, would be very great. No one of these publishers is willing to publish the plays anonymously, and they agree in saying that while the plays contain passages of exceptional merit, there is, unfortunately, at the present moment no demand in the market for the literary play. This form of literature is in fact at present a drug on the market; and they suggest that your lordship, whose anonymity I have of course respected, should convert these plays into essays, epics, masques, or any other form which is at present popular with the reading public. There is certainly very little chance at present of my being able to find a publisher for work of this description. Therefore I await your lordship's instructions before sending them to any other publishers.

At the same time I would suggest, should your lordship not consider such a course to be derogatory, that I should submit the plays in question to one or two of the best known theatrical managers with a view to performance. I would of course keep the authorship of the plays a secret.

Awaiting your lordship's commands in this matter,

I am,

Your lordship's most humble and obedient servant,

J. J. NICHOLS.

## *Letter from Mr Nichols to Lord Bacon*

My Lord,

I am in receipt of a communication from Mr Fletcher, the chief of the Lord Chamberlain's servants, now playing at the Globe Theatre. Mr Fletcher informs me that he has read the plays with considerable interest. He considers that they are not only promising but contain passages of positive merit.

Mr Fletcher, however, adds that your lordship is no doubt fully aware that such plays are totally unsuited to the stage; indeed it would be impossible to produce them for many reasons. With regard to the first batch, namely, the Biblical series, the David and Saul trilogy, Joseph and Potiphar, and King Nebuchadnezzar, there could of course be no question of their production, however much they might be altered or adapted for the stage; for it would be impossible to obtain a licence, not only on account of the religious subject matter, which of necessity must prove shocking to the greater part of the audience, but also owing to the boldness of the treatment. Mr Fletcher begs me to tell your lordship that he is far from suggesting that your lordship has handled these solemn themes in any but the most reverent manner; but at the same time he is anxious to point out that the public, being but insufficiently educated, is likely to misunderstand your lordship's intentions, and to regard your lordship's imaginative realization of these sacred figures as sacrilegious.

With regard to the second series, the tragedies, Mr Fletcher states that the play entitled 'Hamlet' might, if about three-quarters of the whole play were omitted, be made fit for stage presentation, but even then the matter would be extremely hazardous. Even if enough of the play were left in order to render the story coherent, the performance would still last several hours and be likely to try the patience of any but a special audience. Such a play would doubtless appeal to a limited and cultivated public, but as your lordship is aware, the public which frequents the Globe Theatre is neither chosen nor cultivated, and it is doubtful whether a public of this kind would sit through a play many of the speeches in which are over a hundred lines long. Mr Fletcher adds that a play of this kind is far more suited for the closet than for the stage, and suggests that your lordship should publish it as a historical chronicle. With regard to these tragedies Mr Fletcher further points out that there are already in existence several plays on the themes which your lordship has treated, which have not only been produced but enjoyed considerable success.

With regard to the third series, the comedies, Mr Fletcher states that these plays, although not without considerable charm and while containing many passages of graceful and melodious writing, are far more in the

179

nature of lyrical poems than of plays. Mr Fletcher adds that if these were also considerably reduced in length and rendered even still more lyrical and accompanied by music, they might be performed as masques or else in dumb show.

Finally, Mr Fletcher suggests, if the author of these plays is anxious that they should be performed, that your lordship should send the plays to an experienced actor who should alter and arrange them for stage presentation. Mr Fletcher suggests that should your lordship see your way to agree to this, he has in his company a player named William Shakespeare who is admirably fitted for the undertaking, and who has already had much experience in adapting and altering plays for the stage.

I am,

Your lordship's most obedient and humble servant,

J. J. NICHOLS.

## Letter from Mr Nichols to Lord Bacon

My Lord,

In accordance with your lordship's instructions I submitted the plays to Mr William Shakespeare. I am now in recept of Mr Shakespeare's full report on the plays.

Mr Shakespeare confirms Mr Fletcher's opinion that the plays in their present state are far too long for production. The religious series he does not discuss, as being by their nature precluded from performance. With regard to the historical tragedies, 'Edward III', 'Mary Tudor', 'Lady Jane Grey', and 'Katherine Parr' Mr Shakespeare points out that none of these plays would be passed by the Censor because they contain many allusions which would be considered to touch too nearly, and give possible offence to, certain exalted personages.

With regard to the tragedies, Mr Shakespeare is quite willing to arrange 'Hamlet, Prince of Denmark' for the stage. More than half of the play will have to be omitted: the whole of the first act, dealing with Hamlet's student days at Wittenburg, Mr Shakespeare considers to be totally irrelevant to the subsequent action of the play, although the long scene between the young prince and Dr Faustus contains many passages which are not only poetical but dramatic. Mr Shakespeare regrets to have to sacrifice these passages, but maintains that if this act be allowed to stand as it is at present, the play would be condemned to failure. Mr Shakespeare is also anxious to cut out the whole of the penultimate act, which deals entirely with Ophelia's love affair with Horatio. This act, though containing much that is subtle and original, would be likely, Mr Shakespeare says, to confuse, and possibly to shock, the audience. As to the soliloquies, Mr Shakespeare says that it is impossible to get an audience at the present day to listen to a soliloquy of one hundred lines. Mr Shakespeare suggests that if possible they should all be cut down to a quarter of their present length.

Out of the remaining plays, Mr Shakespeare selects the following as being fit for the stage: 'Macbeth', 'Romeo and Juliet', 'Mephistopheles', 'Paris and Helen', 'Alexander the Great', and 'Titus Andronicus'. Of all these Mr Shakespeare says that by far the finest from a stage point of view is the last. It is true that the action of this play is at present a little slow and lacking in incident, but Mr Shakespeare says that he sees a way, by a few trifling additions, of increasing its vitality; and he is certain that, should this play be well produced and competently played, it would prove successful. The tragedy of 'Macbeth' might also be adapted to the popular taste, but here again Mr Shakespeare says the play is at least four times too long.

I would be glad if your lordship would inform me what reply I am to make to Mr Shakespeare.

I am,

Your lordship's obedient and humble servant,

J. J. NICHOLS.

## *Letter from Lord Bacon to Mr Nichols*

Sir,

I am quite willing that Mr Shakespeare should try his hand on 'Hamlet', 'Macbeth', 'Romeo and Juliet', and 'Titus Andronicus', but I cannot consent to let him shorten my 'Mephistopheles', my 'Alexander the Great', or my 'Paris and Helen'. I should of course wish to see a printed copy of the play as arranged by Mr Shakespeare before it is produced.

I am,

Your obedient servant,

BACON.

## *Letter from Lord Bacon to Mr Nichols*

Sir,

I received the printed copies of my four plays as arranged by Mr Shakespeare. I would be much obliged if you would communicate to him the following instructions: (1) 'Hamlet' may stand as it is. The whole nature of the play is altered, and the chief character is at present quite unintelligible, but if Mr Shakespeare thinks that in its present form it will please an audience, he is at liberty to produce it, as it is not a piece of work for which I have any special regard, and it was written more as an exercise

181

than anything else. (2) I cannot allow 'Romeo and Juliet' to appear with the changed ending made by Mr Shakespeare. Mr Shakespeare is perhaps right in thinking that his version of the play, ending as it does with the marriage of Juliet and Paris and the reconciliation of Romeo and Rosaline, is more subtle and true to life, but in this matter I regard my knowledge of the public as being more sound than that of Mr Shakespeare. As a member of the public myself, I am convinced that the public is sentimental, and would be better pleased by the more tragic and romantic ending which I originally wrote. (3) With regard to Mr Shakespeare's suggestion that in 'Macbeth' the sleep-walking scene should fall to Macbeth, instead of to Lady Macbeth, I will not hear of any such change. (Confidential: The reason of my refusal is that this change seems to me merely dictated by the vanity of the actor, and his desire that the man's part may predominate over the woman's.) (4) 'Titus Andronicus.' I have no objection to Mr Shakespeare's alterations.

Your obedient servant,<br>BACON.

## Letter from Lord Bacon to Mr Nichols

Sir,

I was present last night at the Globe Theatre Theatre at the performance of my play 'Macbeth', as produced by Mr Shakespeare. I confess that I was much disgusted by the liberties which Mr Shakespeare has taken with my work, which I am certain far exceed the changes and alterations which were originally presented to me, and which I myself revised and approved. For instance, Mr Shakespeare has made a great many more omissions than he originally suggested. And at the end of many of the scenes he has introduced many totally unwarranted tags, such as, for instance:

> I'll see it done.
> What he hath lost noble Macbeth hath won.

And, worst of all:

> It is concluded: Banquo, thy soul's flight,
> If it find Heaven, must find it out tonight.

The whole play is riddled with such additions, not to speak of several incidents of an altogether barbarous and outrageous character, and of certain other interpolations of coarse buffoonery, inserted in the most serious parts of the play to raise a laugh among the more ignorant portions of the rabble. Of course I cannot now withdraw them from the stage without risking the discovery of their authorship. Mr Shakespeare is at liberty to produce and perform in any of the plays written by me which are now in his possession, provided that they appear under his name, and that the authorship is attributed to him.

Your obedient servant,

BACON.

# Nero Interviewed

Rome, A.D. 64

------

(from *Dead Letters*)

## *Letter from a Greek Traveller to his friend in Athens*

IT IS FIFTEEN YEARS since I was last at Rome, and although I was prepared
to find a change in everything, I had not expected this complete transformation. The Rome I knew, the Rome of the straggly narrow streets
and rotting wooden houses, has disappeared, and in its place there is a
kind of Corinth on a huge scale, marred of course by the usual want of
taste of the Romans, but imposing nevertheless and extraordinarily gay
and brilliant. The fault of the whole thing is that it is too big: the houses
are too high, the streets too broad, everything is planned on too large a
scale. From the artist's point of view the effect is deplorable; from the
point of view of the casual observer it is amusing in the highest degree.
The broad streets – a blaze of coloured marble and fresh paint – are now
crowded with brilliant shops where you see all that is new from Greece
and the East, together with curiosities from the North and the barbarian
countries. Everybody seems to be spending money. The shops are crowded
from morning till night. The display of gold trinkets, glass vases, carpets,
rugs, silks, gold and silver tissues, embroideries, all glittering in the
sunlight, dazzles the eye and imposes by the mass and glare of colour and
gaudiness.

There is no doubt that the Emperor is extraordinarily popular, and
whenever he shows himself in public he is greeted with frantic enthusiasm.
Of course there are some mal-contents among the old-fashioned Liberals,
but they have no influence whatever and count practically for nothing,
for what are their grumblings and their eternal lamentations about the
good old times and the Empire going to the dogs, in the scale with the
hard solid fact that ever since Nero came to the throne the prosperity of
the Empire has increased in every possible respect? For the first time for
years the individual has been able to breathe freely, and owing to the

splendid reforms which he has carried through in the matter of taxation, an intolerable load of oppression has been lifted from the shoulders of the poor, and I can assure you they are grateful.

A few nights ago I had dinner with Seneca, to meet some of the leading literary lights. He is somewhat aged. Discussing various differences between our people and his, Senecca said that it is all very well for us to talk of our intellectual superiority, our artistic taste, our wit, our sense of proportion, but we had no idea either of liberty of trade on the one side, or liberty of thought on the other. 'That kind of liberty,' said Seneca, 'always fares better under a King or a Prince of some kind than under jealous democrats. We should never tolerate the religious tyranny of Athens.' I could not help pointing out that what struck me at Rome today was that whereas almost everybody had 'literary' pretensions, and discussed nothing but eloquence, form, style, and 'artistry', nearly everybody wrote badly with the exception of Petronius Arbiter, whom the literary world does not recognize. The Romans talk a great deal of 'art for art's sake', and language, instead of being the simple and perfect vesture of thought, is cultivated for its own sake. 'This seems to us Greeks,' I said, 'the cardinal principle of decadence, and the contrary of our ideal which is that every-thing should serve to adorn, but all that is dragged in merely for the sake of ornament is bad.' I think Seneca agreed, but the younger literary men present smiled with pitying condescension on me and said patronizingly: 'We've got beyond all that.'

After that dinner I made up my mind that I had seen enough of the literary set. Seneca was kind enough to get me an audience with the Emperor. I was received yesterday afternoon in the new gold palace which Nero has built for himself. It is a sumptuous building, to our taste vulgar, but not unimposing, and suits its purpose very well, though all his *suite* complain of the insufficient accommodation and the discomfort of the arrangements. I was taken into a kind of ante-room where a number of Court officials, both civil and military, were waiting, and I was told that the Emperor would probably see me in about a quarter of an hour. They all talked for some time in subdued tones as if they were in a temple; as far as I could see there was no reason for this as the Emperor's room was at the other end of a long passage, and the doors were shut. At the end of a quarter of an hour a young officer fetched me and ushered me into the Emperor's presence.

He was seated at a large table covered with documents and parchments of every description, and had evidently been dictating to his secretary, who left the room on the other side as I entered. He is very like his pictures, which, however, do not give one any idea of his short-sighted, dreamy eyes, nor of his intensely good-humoured and humorous ex-pression. He has a kind of way of looking up at one in a half-appealing fashion, as much as to say 'For Heaven's sake don't think that I take all this business seriously.' His movements are quick but not jerky. He held in his hand a chain of amber beads which he kept on absent-mindedly fingering during the whole interview. His fingers are short, square, and rather fat. He spoke Greek, which he speaks very purely indeed and without any Latin accent. Indeed, he speaks it too well. He asked me whether I was enjoying my visit to Rome, how long it was since I had been here, what I thought of the improvements, and if I had been to the new theatre. I said I had not been to the theatre, but that I was told the games in the Circus were extremely well worth seeing. The Emperor laughed and shrugged his shoulders, and said that it was very civil of me to say so, since I knew quite well that those spectacles, although hugely enjoyed by the ignorant rabble, were singularly tedious to people of taste and education like myself. I bowed as he made this compliment. As for himself, he continued, the games frankly bored him to death, but, of course, it was a State duty for him to attend them. 'It is part of my profession,' he said, 'but if I had my own way I should witness nothing but Greek plays acted by my own company in my own house.' He asked after several of my relatives whom he had met in Greece, remembering their exact names and occupations. He asked me if I had been writing anything lately, and when I said that I was sick of books and intended henceforth to devote all my leisure to seeing people and studying them, he laughed. 'Nothing is so discouraging,' he said, 'as trying to improve the literary taste in this city. We are an admirable people; we do a great many things much better than other people – I do not mean only our colonization' – he said smiling – 'and our foreign trade, but our portrait painting and our popular farce. But as a general rule directly we touch Art we seem to go altogether wrong, and the result is nauseous. Therefore, if you want to find a Roman who will be thoroughly sympathetic, capable, and intelligent, and decent, choose one who knows nothing about Art and does not want to. With you it is different,' he added. 'Athens is a city of artists.' He then changed the subject and referred to the rather bitter criticisms published at Athens about his policy with regard to the Jews, especially that new sect among them who called themselves Christians.

'Of course,' he said, 'your sense of proportion is shocked when any extreme measures are adopted, but, believe me, in this case it is necessary. The Jews are everywhere, and everywhere they claim the rights of citizenship. But they do not live as citizens: they retain their peculiar status; they claim the rights of the citizen and exceptional privileges of their own – in fact, their own laws. They wish to have the advantages of nationality without being a nation, without taking part in the functions of the State. We cannot tolerate this. The whole matter has been brought to the fore by the attitude of these so-called Christians, who are, I am obliged to say, extremely difficult to deal with: In the first place because they adopt the policy of passive resistance, against which it is so difficult to act, and in the second place because they are getting the women on their side – and you know what that means. I have no personal objection either to Jews or Christians. What one can't tolerate is a secret society within the State which advocates and preaches neglect of the citizen's duty to the State, the worthlessness of patriotism, and the utter non-existence of citizenship.'

I said I quite understood this, but did not his Majesty agree with me in thinking that penal oppressions were rarely successful, and frequently defeated their own object.

The Emperor replied that there was a great deal in what I said, but that he did not consider he was dealing with a national or universal movement, which had any element of duration in it, but with a particular fad which would soon pass out of fashion, as the majority of all sensible people were opposed to it.

'The unfortunate part is,' he said, 'the women have got it into their heads that it is a fine thing, and of course the more they see it is opposed to the wishes of all sensible men the more obstinate they will be in sticking to it. The whole matter has been grossly exaggerated both as regards the nature of the movement and the nature of the measures taken against it; but that one cannot help. They have represented me as gloating over the sufferings of innocent victims. That is all stuff and nonsense. Great care has been taken to investigate all the cases which have arisen, so that the innocent should not suffer with the guilty. Besides which, any Jew or Christian who is willing to make a purely formal acknowledgement of the state authorities is entirely exempt from any possibility of persecution. But this is precisely what they often obstinately refuse to do – why, I cannot conceive. There is also a great deal of hysteria in the matter, and a large amount of self-advertisement, but one cannot get over the fact that the movement is a revolutionary one in itself, and can only be dealt with as such. I doubt whether in any country a revolutionary movement which has taken so uncompromising an attitude has ever been dealt with in so merciful a manner. So you see,' the Emperor concluded, 'how grossly unfair is the manner in which I have been treated in this matter. However, I suppose I can't complain: whatever one does it is sure to be wrong.'

He then rose from his table and said that the Empress wished to see me before I went away, and he led me into her apartment, which was next door.

The Empress Sabina Poppaea is the perfection of grace; she is more like a Greek than a Roman, and speaks Greek better than the Emperor, using the language not only with purity but with elegance. All the stories we were told of her extravagance in dress and of how she powdered her head with gold, are of course absurd. She was dressed with the utmost simplicity and did not wear a single ornament. She was absolutely natural, put one at one's ease, talking continuously herself on various topics without ever dwelling long on one, till she had said all she had got to say, and then by a gesture delicately shadowed, she gave me the sign that it was time for me to go.

The Emperor said that the Empress Mother would have seen me only she was suffering from one of her bad attacks of indigestion. He told me to be sure to let him know should I visit Rome again, that he hoped himself to be able to spend some months in Greece next year, but he did not think the pressure of affairs would allow him to. Farewell.

*P.S.* – Later. The gossips say that the Empress Mother is being poisoned.

# From the Diary of William the Conqueror

## (from *Lost Diaries*)

*Rouen*, 1066 – Disquieting news from London. My friend, benefactor and relation, my brother Sovereign, Edward of England, has again had one of his attacks. It comes, I am sure, from not eating meat. Were anything to happen to him, I should be obliged to go over to London at once and settle as to the carrying on of the Government with Harold. Nothing could be more inconvenient at the present moment. Have the utmost confidence in Harold; but I fear the influence of the English nobility. I like the English; but they are not to be trusted in foreign politics. They are naturally perfidious, and they don't know it. They think they are more virtuous than other people; or rather that they are exempted from the faults and the vices which are common to us all. The European situation seems unsatisfactory.

Among other things Father Anselm writes that a certain party among the Englishwomen want to be admitted to the Witenagemot. The majority of the women are against it. The agitators sent a deputation to Westminster, but the King said it would not be according to the precedents to receive them. They were so annoyed at this that they made a dastardly attack on the beautiful old Druid Temple of Stonehenge, almost completely destroying it. F. Anselm says only a few blocks of stone are left, and that the place is unrecognizable.

The ringleaders were taken and claimed the ordeal by fire and the matter was referred to the Archbishop of Canterbury, who said that it was not a matter to be dealt with by ordeal. (Quite right!) He put the case into the hands of a select body of matrons, chosen from all classes. These decided that the offenders should be publicly whipped by women, and sent home. This was done, much to the satisfaction of everybody.

*Rouen.* – Heard Mass and went out hunting. Excellent sport. Shot a fox and six thrushes. Had thrush-pie for dinner. Find it difficult to get on horseback without aid.

*Rouen.* – Received a letter from the Pope. He says that should anything happen to King Edward – he is, of course, far from suggesting such a thing, but one must take everything into consideration – I must be very firm about claiming the succession. H.H. says that although, of course, it would be indelicate for him to raise the question *just now*, he knows it is the King's wish that I should succeed him. He seems to think Harold may give trouble. But Harold is bound to me by oath. Also I saved his life.

*Rouen.* – Took William out hunting. His red hair frightens the ducks. Have told him over and over again to get a close-fitting green cap. The boys are always quarrelling. I don't know what is to be done with them. Robert broke his new battle-axe yesterday in a fit of passion.

My only consolation is that Henry is really making some progress with his tutor. He last learnt the alphabet as far as the letter F.

*Rouen.* – A fisherman arrived last night from Southampton with the news that King Edward is dead. The news, he said, was confirmed by the appearance of a strange star with a tail to it in the sky. I have questioned the courier and gathered he had only got the news at second-hand. The rumour is probably baseless.

*Rouen.* – The regular courier did not arrive this evening. The bag was brought by an Englishman. The official bulletin states that the King is slightly indisposed owing to a feverish cold, which he caught while inspecting the newly-raised body of archers, in the New Forest. A private letter from the archbishop tells me, in strict confidence, that the King's illness is more dangerous than people think. The children again quarrelled today. Matilda, as usual, took Henry's part, and said I was to blame. These domestic worries are very trying at such a critical moment. As a matter of fact, Henry teases his elder brothers, and boasts to them of his superior scholarship; they retaliate, naturally enough, by cuffing the boy, who complains at once to his mother. Since Henry has mastered the rudiments of the alphabet, his conceit has been quite beyond bounds. Of course, I admit it is clever of him. He is a clever boy. There is no doubt about that, but he shouldn't take advantage of it.

*Rouen.* – Again the regular courier has not arrived. The bag again brought by an Englishman. According to a bulletin the King is going on well. Received a very friendly note from Harold, putting Pevensey Castle at my disposal, should I visit England in the autumn – and suggesting sport in the New Forest.

*Rouen.* – Messenger arrived direct from London, *via* Newhaven. He says the King died last week, and that Harold has proclaimed himself King. Matilda said this would happen from the first. I think there can be no doubt that the news is authentic. The messenger, who is an old servant of mine, is thoroughly to be trusted. He saw the King's body lying in state. This explains why the regular messengers have not arrived. Harold had them stopped at the coast. This, in itself, is an unfriendly act. Matilda says I must invade England at once. Think she is right. But wish war could be avoided. Have written to the Pope asking for his moral support. Invasion a risky thing. Discussed the matter with General Bertram, who is an excellent strategist. He says he can devise fifty ways of landing troops in England, but not one way of getting them out again. That is just it. Supposing we are cut off? The English army is said to be very good indeed.

*Rouen.* – Invasion of England settled. Must say have great misgivings on the subject. If we fail, the King of France is certain to attack us here. Matilda, however, won't hear of any other course being taken. Have privately sent a message to Harold proposing that we should settle the matter in a friendly fashion – I offer him nearly all Wessex, Wales and Scotland and the North – I taking the rest of the Kingdom, including London and Winchester. His situation is by no means entirely enviable. His brothers are certain to fight him in the North, and the King of Norway may also give trouble.

*Rouen.* – Received letter from the Pope entirely approving of invasion. Sends me back banner, blessed. Received a letter from Harold also. Very insulting. Answers vaguely and commits himself to nothing. Ignores the past. Seems to forget I saved him from shipwreck and that he solemnly swore to support my claims. Seems also to forget that I am the lawful heir to the English throne. The crowning insult is that he addressed the letter to Duke William the Bastard.

Have ordered mobilization to take place at once. The war is popular. Matilda and I were loudly cheered when we drove through the market place this afternoon. War will be a good occupation for the boys. Robert wants to stop here as Regent. Do not think this wise.

*Hastings.* – Very disagreeable crossing. Took medicine recommended by Matilda (nettle leaves and milk and cinnamon), but did no good. Harold apparently defeated his brother in the North. Expect to fight tomorrow. Temper of the troops good. Terrain favourable, but cannot help feeling anxious.

*London.* – Everything sadly in need of thorough reorganization. Have resolved to carry out following initial reforms at once:

1. Everybody to put out their lights by 8. Bell to ring for the purpose. The people here sit up too late, drinking. Most dangerous.

2. Enroll everybody in a book. Make it compulsory for the leeches to attend the poor, and dock serfs of a part of their wage, in order to create a fund for paying the leeches. (Think this rather neat.)

Shall tolerate no nonsense from the women. Matilda agrees that their complaints are ridiculous.

News from Normandy disquieting. Robert seems to be taking too much upon himself. Something must be done.

Going next week to New Forest to hunt. Very fine wild pony hunting there.

# From the Diary of Mark Antony

(from *Lost Diaries*)

*Alexandria* (*undated*) – The reception went off very well. The Queen came to meet me by water in her State barge. She is different from what I remember her long ago, when I caught a glimpse of her in Rome. Then she was rather a colourless young girl, who had the reputation of being very well read, and rather affected. But now . . . when you look at her face and you look away, you see green from the flash, as though you had been staring at the sun. She dazzles and blinds you. I received her in the market place. Her curtsey was a miracle of grace. She was very civil and dignified. After I had received her in the market place, I went to her palace. Such is the etiquette. I invited her to supper; but she insisted on my being her guest. I accepted. Supper in her palace. Semi-state, as the court is in mourning for Archilaus, the King of Cappadocia's eldest son, the Queen's first cousin. The ladies in waiting wore gold ornaments only. One of them, Charmian, pretty. The Queen, dropping all formality, was very lively and excellent company. The supper was good (the boars *well* roasted) and not so stiff as those kind of entertainments are as a rule.

After supper we had music and some dancing. Egyptian Bacchanals, who did a modern thing called *Ariadne in Naxos*. Very noisy and not much tune in it; but the dancing good, although hardly up to the Scythian standard.

Mardian, who has a fine contralto voice (he has been admirably trained), sang a piece from a ballet on the siege of Troy arranged by Æschylus. Very good. I like those old-fashioned things much better. They say it's conventional and out of date; but I don't care. The Queen told me in confidence that she quite agreed with me, but that even classical music bored her, so after we had listened to one or two odes, she asked Mardian to sing something light, some songs in dialect, which he did. Very funny, especially the one which begins:

'As I was going to Brindisi, upon a summer's day'.

We made him sing that one twice. The Greeks know how to be witty without even being in the least vulgar.

*Alexandria, three weeks later.* – Time has passed very quickly. Everybody is being so kind, and the Queen has taken immense pains to make everything a success. Most amusing improvised banquet in fancy dress last night. The Queen disguised as a fish-wife. She made me dress up, too. I put on a Persian private soldier's uniform. After supper we went into the town, in our disguises. Nobody recognized us, and we had the greatest fun. I threw pieces of orange-peel on the pavement. It was too comic to see the old men trip up over them. Then we went into a tavern on the first floor, and ate oysters. The Queen heated some coppers at the fire, and, after putting them on a plate with a pair of pincers, threw them out of the window. It was quite extraordinarily funny to see the beggars pick them up and then drop them with a howl! I don't think I ever laughed so much! The Queen has a royal sense of humour. And I who thought beforehand she was a blue-stocking! It shows how mistaken one can be.

*Alexandria.* – Time seems to fly. No news from Rome. Wish the Queen would not be quite so ostentatiously lavish on my account. Eight wild boars for breakfast is too much. And the other night at supper she wasted an immense pearl in drinking my health in vinegar. This kind of thing makes people talk. She is wonderfully witty. She can mimic exactly the noises of a farmyard. Nothing seems to tire her, either. She will sit up all night and be ready early the next morning to go out fishing, sailing, or anything else. She must have a constitution of steel. Wonderful woman!

*Alexandria, later.* – News from Rome. Fulvia is dead: must go at once.

*Rome, a month later.* – Engaged to be married to Octavia, Caesar's sister, a widow. Purely a political alliance. Cleopatra is sure to understand the necessity of this. It is a great comfort to think that she is reasonable and has a real grip of the political situation.

*Athens, a month later.* – Political situation grows more and more complicated. Octavia is very dutiful and most anxious to please. Do not think the climate here agreeable. The wind is very sharp and the nights are bitterly cold. Never did care for Athens.

Think that if I went to Egypt for a few days I could (*a*) benefit by change of air, (*b*) arrange matters with the Eastern Kings. Caesar and Lepidus are trying to do me in the eye.

*Athens, a day later.* – Octavia has very kindly offered to go to Rome, so as to act as a go-between between myself and Caesar. She says she is quite certain it is all only a misunderstanding and that she can arrange matters. Thought it best not to mention possibility of Egyptian trip, as I may not go, after all.

*Alexandria.* – Back here once more after all. Doctors all said change of air was essential, and that the climate of Athens was the very worst possible for me, just at this time. They said I should certainly have a nervous breakdown if I stayed on much longer. Besides which, it was absolutely necessary for me to be on the spot, to settle the Eastern Question. It is now fortunately settled. Cleopatra delighted to see me; but most reasonable. Quite understood everything. She did not say a word about Octavia. Reception in Alexandria magnificent. Ovation terrific. Shows how right I was to come back. Settled to proclaim Cleopatra Queen of Egypt, Lower Syria, Cyprus and Lydia. Everybody agrees that this is only fair.

*Alexandria.* – Public proclamation in the market place. Settled to keep Media, Parthia and Armenia in the family, so divided them among the children. Ceremony went off splendidly. Cleopatra appeared as the Goddess Isis. This was much appreciated, as it showed the people she really is *national*. The cheering was terrific.

Staying with us at present are the King of Libya, the King of Cappadocia, the King of Paphlagonia, the King of Thrace, the King of Arabia, the King of Pont, the King of Jewry, the King of Comagena, the King of Mede, and the King of Lycaonia. Question of precedence a little awkward. Herod, the King of Jewry, claimed precedence over all the other Kings on the grounds of antiquity and lineage. The King of Mede contested the claim, and the King of Arabia said that he was the oldest in years. There is no doubt about this, as he is 99. It was obvious the first place belonged to him. Question very neatly settled by Cleopatra. That they should rank according to the number of years they have reigned. She said this was the immemorial Egyptian custom, established by the Pharaohs and written out very carefully on a step of the great Pyramid. Everybody satisfied. King of Arabia takes precedence, but *not* on account of his age. Herod still a little touchy, but had to give in.

Played billiards with Cleopatra. Gave her 20. Won with difficulty. Caesar is certain to make war on us. Have written to Octavia explaining everything fully.

*In Camp near Actium.* – Nothing doing. One wonders whether Caesar means to fight after all. The mosquitoes are very annoying. Impossible to get any milk.

*In Camp near Actium, later.* – Cleopatra has arrived. She is used to camp life and does not mind roughing it. Everybody advises me to fight on land and not by sea, but Cleopatra and myself think we ought to fight by sea. Caesar has taken Toryne. We have sixty sail. The thing is obvious; but soldiers are always prejudiced. Enobarbus worrying me to death to fight on land.

Cleopatra won't hear of it, and I am quite certain she is right. A woman's instinct in matters of strategy and tactics are infallible; and then – what a woman!

*Alexandria, later.* – Very glad to be home again. Cleopatra was perfectly right to retreat. Played billiards. Gave Cleopatra 25. She beat me.

She will soon be able to give me something. She is a surprising woman. Last night the Greek envoy dined. Too clever for me, but Cleopatra floored him over Anaxagoras. Wonderful woman! She sang, or rather hummed, in the evening a little Greek song, the burden of which is

$$\text{'}E\gamma\grave{\omega} \ \delta\grave{\epsilon} \ \mu\acute{o}\nu\alpha \ \kappa\alpha\theta\epsilon\acute{v}\delta\omega.\text{[1]}$$

I cannot get the tune out of my head.

[1] 'I sleep alone.'

# From the Mycenae Papers

(from *Dead Letters*)

### Clytaemnestra to Aegisthus

MYCENAE.

Honoured Sir,

I am sorry I was out when you came yesterday. I never thought that you seriously meant to come. I shall be very busy all next week, as Helen and Menelaus are arriving and I must get everything ready. Orestes was quite delighted with the cup and ball. You spoil him.

Yours sincerely,
CLYTAEMNESTRA.

### Clytaemnestra to Aegisthus

Most honoured Aegisthus,

One line to say that I have received your letter and *loved* it all except the last sentence. Please do not say that kind of thing again as it will quite ruin our friendship, which I thought was going to be so *real*.

Yours very sincerely,
CLYTAEMNESTRA.

### Clytaemnestra to Aegisthus

Most honoured Aegisthus,

The flowers are beautiful, and it was kind of you to remember my birthday. But your letter is really too naughty. . . .

(The rest of this letter is missing)

196

## *Clytaemnestra to Aegisthus*

MYCENAE.

Most honoured Sir,

This is to say that since you persist in misunderstanding me and refuse to listen to what I say, our correspondence must end. It is extraordinary to me that you should wish to debase what might have been so great and so wonderful.

Yours truly,<br>CLYTAEMNESTRA.

## *Clytaemnestra to Aegisthus*

MYCENAE.

Most honoured Aegisthus,

I was much touched by your letter and I will give you the one more trial you ask for so humbly and so touchingly.

Paris has arrived. I don't know if you know him. He is the second son of the King of Troy. He made an unfortunate marriage with a girl called Œnone, the daughter of a rather disreputable river-person. They were miserable about it. He is very good-looking – if one admires those kind of looks, which I don't. He dresses in an absurd way and he looks theatrical. Besides, I hate men with curly hair. He has a few accomplishments. He shoots well and plays on the double flute quite remarkably well for a man who is not a professional; but he is totally uninteresting, and, what is more, impossible. But Helen likes him. Isn't it extraordinary that she always has liked impossible men? They sit for hours together saying nothing at all. I don't in the least mind his paying no attention to me – in fact, I am too thankful not to have to talk to him; but I do think it's bad manners, as I am his hostess.

Helen is certainly looking better this year than she has ever looked; but she still dresses in that affectedly over-simple way, which is a pity. I don't know how long he is going to stay. I don't mind his being here, but Helen and he are really most inconsiderate. They use my sitting-room as though it were theirs, and they never seem to think that I may have things to do of my own, and they expect me to go out with them, which ends in their walking on ahead and my being left with Menelaus, whom I am very fond of indeed, but who bores me. He talks of nothing but horses and quoits. It is a great lesson to Queen Hecuba for having brought up her son so badly. Paris was educated entirely by a shepherd, you know, on Mount Ida. The result is his manners are shocking. Helen doesn't see it. Isn't it odd? I must say he's nice with children, and Orestes likes him.

I am your sincere friend,<br>CLYTAEMNESTRA.

197

## *Clytaemnestra to Aegisthus*

MYCENAE.

Most honoured Aegisthus,

We are in great trouble. I told you Helen was attracted by Paris. We of course thought nothing of it, because Helen always has flirted with rather vulgar men, and her flirtations were, we thought, the harmless distractions of a woman who has remained, and always will remain, a sentimental girl.

Imagine our surprise and dismay! Paris and Helen have run away together, and they have gone to Troy! Helen left a note behind for Menelaus saying she realized that she had made a mistake, that she hated hypocrisy, and thought it more honest to leave him. She said she would always think of him with affection. Poor Menelaus is distracted, but he is behaving beautifully.

Agamemnon is furious. He is overcome by the disgrace to his family, and he is so cross. We are all very miserable. Agamemnon says that the family honour must be redeemed at all costs, and that they will have to make an expedition against Troy to fetch Helen back. I think this is quite ridiculous. No amount of expeditions and wars can undo what has been done. I am sure you will sympathize with us in our trouble. I must say it is most unfair on my children. I shouldn't have minded so much if Iphigenia wasn't grown up.

Electra has got whooping-cough, but she is going on as well as can be expected. I have no patience with Helen. She always was utterly thoughtless.

Your sincere friend,
CLYTAEMNESTRA.

## *Clytaemnestra to Aegisthus*

MYCENAE.

Most honoured Aegisthus,

There is no end of worry and fuss going on. Odysseus, the King of Ithaca, has arrived here with his wife, Penelope. They discuss the prospects of the expedition from morning till night, and I am left alone with Penelope. She has borrowed my only embroidery frame, and is working some slippers for her husband. They are at least two sizes too small. She talks of nothing but her boy, her dog, her diary, and her garden, and I can't tell you how weary I am of it. She made me very angry yesterday by saying that I spoilt Orestes, and that I should be sorry for it some day. She is always throwing up her boy Telemachus to me. Whenever Helen is mentioned she puts on a face as much as to say: 'Do not defile me.'

Your sincere friend,
CLYTAEMNESTRA.

## Clytaemnestra to Aegisthus

MYCENAE.

Most honoured Aegisthus,

My worst fears have been realized. They are going to make an expedition against Troy on a large scale. Odysseus is at the bottom of it. I cannot say how much I dislike him. All the Kings have volunteered to go, but the Fleet will not be ready for two years, so I am in hopes that something may happen in the meantime to prevent it.

Iphigenia is learning to make bandages, and says she will go to the front to look after the wounded. I am, of course, against this, and think it's absurd, but unfortunately she can make her father do what she likes. My only consolation is that the war cannot possibly last more than a week. The Trojans have no regular army, They are a handful of untrained farmers, and the town cannot stand a siege. It is all too silly. It is too bad of Helen to have caused all this fuss.

Your sincere friend,<br>CLYTAEMNESTRA.

*P.S.* – No, of course I haven't written to Helen. She is as good as dead to me.

## Clytaemnestra to Aegisthus

(*Two years later*)

MYCENAE.

My dear Aegisthus,

We have at last got some news. The Fleet has arrived at Aulis, and they are waiting for a favourable wind to be able to go on. At present they are becalmed. They are all well. Iphigenia writes that she is enjoying herself immensely. She has the decency to add that she misses me. I have not had a good night's rest since they have started.

Your most sincere friend,<br>CLYTAEMNESTRA.

## Clytaemnestra to Aegisthus

My dear friend,

Please come here at once. I am in dreadful trouble. From the last letter I received from Agamemnon I understood there was something wrong and that he was hiding something. Today I got a letter from Calchas, breaking to me in the most brutal manner an appalling tragedy and a savage, horrible, and impious crime! They have sacrificed my darling

Iphigenia – to Artemis, of all goddesses! to get a propitious wind for their horrible Fleet! I am heartbroken. I cannot write another word. Please come directly.

Your friend,
CLYTAEMNESTRA.

## Clytaemnestra to Aegisthus

### (*Two months later*)

I see no reason why you should not come back; I have a right to ask whom I like to stay here. Do come as soon as possible; I am very lonely without you. Now that I no longer communicate with Agamemnon in order to get news I have written to Helen and sent the letter by a very clever silk merchant, who is certain to be able to worm his way into Troy. Come as soon as you get this.

C.

*P.S.* – Agamemnon still writes, but I do not take the slightest notice of his letters. I trust the Trojans will be victorious. They have at any rate determined to make a fight for it. Our generals are certain to quarrel, Achilles and Agamemnon never get on well. And Achilles' temper is dreadful.

## Clytaemnestra to Aegisthus

### (*Three months later*)

I can no longer bear these short visits and these long absences. I have arranged for you to stay here permanently.

I wrote to Agamemnon last month a cold and dignified business letter, in which I pointed out that unless some man came here to look after things, everything would go to pieces. I suggested you. I have now got his answer. He agrees, and thinks it an excellent plan.

Odysseus wrote me, I must say, a most amusing letter. He says everything is at sixes and sevens, and that Priam's eldest son is far the most capable soldier on either side. He expects to win, but says it will be a far longer business than they thought it would be at first. Come as quickly as you can. Best and most beloved.

Your C.

# Helen to Clytaemnestra

*(Ten years later)*

TROY.

Dearest Clytaemnestra,

Your letters are a great comfort to me when I get them, which is very seldom. Everything is going on just the same. It is now the tenth year of the siege, and I see no reason why it should ever end. I am dreadfully afraid the Greeks will never take Troy.

I can give you no idea of how dull everything is here. We do the same thing and see the same people every day. We know exactly what is going on in the Greek camp, and most of the time is spent in discussing the gossip, which bores me to death. You are quite right in what you say about Paris. I made a fatal mistake. It is all Aphrodite's fault. He has become too dreadful now. He is still very good-looking, but even compared with Menelaus he is pitiable in every way and every bit as cross. Hector is very nice, but painfully dull. The King and the Queen are both very kind, but as for Cassandra, she is intolerable. She is always prophesying dreadful calamities which never come off. She said, for instance, that I would lose my looks and make a long journey in Egypt. As if I would go to Egypt from here! As to my looks, you know, darling, I never was vain, was I? But I can honestly tell you that, if anything, I have rather *improved* than otherwise, and among the Trojans' women, who are absolute frights and have no more idea of dressing than sheep, I look magnificent. Andromache has got quite a nice face, and I really like her; but you should see her figure – it's like an elephant's, and her feet are enormous, and her hands red and sore from needlework. She won't even use a thimble! Cassandra always dresses in deep mourning. Why, we cannot conceive, because none of her relatives have been killed.

There is really only one person in the palace I can talk to – and that is Aeneas, who is one of the commanders. He is quite nice. What I specially like about him is the nice way in which he talks about his parents.

The Greeks are quarrelling more than ever. Achilles won't fight at all because Agamemnon insisted on taking away Briseis (who is lovely) from him. Wasn't that exactly like Agamemnon? I hope this won't make you jealous, darling, but I don't expect it will, because you have never forgiven Agamemnon, have you?

Everybody tries to be kind to me, and I have nothing to complain of. They all mean well, and in a way this makes it worse. For instance, every morning, when we meet for the midday meal, Priam comes into the room saying to me: 'Well, how's the little runaway today?' He has made this joke every day for the last ten years. And then they always talk about the cowardice and incompetence of the Greeks, taking for granted that as I have married into a Trojan family I must have become a Trojan myself.

201

It is most tactless of them not to understand what I must be feeling.

I suppose I am inconsistent, but the pro-Greek party irritate me still more. They are headed by Pandarus, and are simply longing for their own side to be beaten, because they say that I ought to have been given up directly, and that the war was brought about entirely owing to Priam having got into the hands of the Egyptian merchants.

I manage to get some Greek stuffs smuggled into the town, and the merchants tell me vaguely what people are wearing at Mycenae; but one can't get anything properly made here. Andromache has all her clothes made at home by her women – to save expense. She says that in times of war one ought to sacrifice oneself. Of course, I can't do this, however much I should like to, as the Trojans expect me to look nice, and would be very angry if I wasn't properly dressed.

I feel if I could only meet Odysseus we might arrange some plan for getting the Greeks into the town.

How is everything going on at home? There is a very strict censorship about letters, and we are all supposed to show our letters to Antenor before they go. I don't, of course. I daresay, however, many of your letters have been intercepted, because I have only heard from you five times since the siege began, and not once this year. Kiss the dear children from me.

Shall I ever see you again? I shall try my best to come home.

Your loving sister,
HELEN.

## Clytaemnestra to Helen

MYCENAE.

Dearest Helen,

Your last letter has reached me. I must implore you to be very careful about what you do. I hope with all my heart that the siege will be over soon; but if it is I don't think it would be quite wise for you to come back directly. You see everybody here is extremely unreasonable. Instead of understanding that Agamemnon and Odysseus were entirely responsible for this absurd war, Agamemnon has got his friends to put the blame entirely on you, and they have excited the people against you. It's so like a man, that, isn't it? I have been very lonely, because all our friends are away. Aegisthus is staying here just to look after the household and the affairs of the city. But he hardly counts, and he is so busy that I hardly ever see him now. There is a strong pro-Trojan party here, too. They say we had absolutely no right to go to war, and that it was simply an expedition of pirates and freebooters, and I must say it is very difficult to disprove it. If there is any talk of the siege ending, please let me know *at once.* Electra has grown into a fine girl; but she is not as lovely as poor darling Iphigenia.

Your loving sister,
CLYTAEMNESTRA.

## Penelope to Odysseus

ITHACA.

My darling Husband,

I wish you would write a little more distinctly; we have the greatest difficulty in reading your letters.

When will this horrid siege be over? I think it is disgraceful of you all to be so long about it. To think that when you started you only said that it would last a month! Mind you come back the moment it is over, and come back *straight*, by Aulis.

The country is looking lovely. I have built a new house for the swine-herd, as he complained about the roof letting the rain in. Next year, we must really have a new paling round the garden, as the children get in and steal the apples. We can't afford it *this* year. The people have no sense of honesty; they steal everything. Telemachus is very well. He can read and write nicely, but is most backward about his sums. He takes a great interest in the war, and has made up a map on which he marks the position of the troops with little flags.

I am surprised to hear of Achilles' *disgraceful* conduct. If I were there I would give him a piece of my mind. I hope Ajax has not had any more of his attacks. Has he tried cinnamon with fomented myrtle leaves? It ought to be taken three times a day *after* meals. The news from Mycenae is deplorable. Clytaemnestra appears to be quite shameless and callous. Aegisthus is now openly living in the house. All decent people have ceased to go near them. I have had a few visitors, but nobody of any importance.

I am working you a piece of tapestry for your bedroom. I hope to get it finished by the time you come back. I hope that when the city is taken Helen will be severely punished.

We have taught Argus to growl whenever Hector is mentioned. I don't, of course, allow any one to mention Helen in this house. Telemachus sends you his loving duty. He is writing to you himself, but the letter isn't finished.

Your devoted wife,
PENELOPE.

## Helen to Clytaemnestra

SUNIUM.

Dearest Clytaemnestra,

Since I last wrote to you several important things have happened.

203

Hector was killed yesterday by Achilles. I am, of course, very sorry for them all. All Cassandra said was, 'I told you so!' She is so heartless. I have at last managed to communicate with Odysseus; we have thought of a very good plan for letting the Greeks into the city. Please do not repeat this. I shall come home at once with Menelaus. He is my husband, after all. I shall come straight to Mycenae. I doubt if I shall have time to write again. I am sending this through Aenida, who is most useful in getting letters brought and sent.

Please have some patterns for me to choose from. I hope to be back in a month.

Your loving sister,<br>HELEN.

## Agamemnon to Clytaemnestra

SUNIUM.

Dear Clytaemnestra,

We have had a very good journey, and I shall reach Mycenae the day after tomorrow in the morning. Please have a hot bath ready for me. I am bringing Cassandra with me. She had better have the room looking north, as she hates the sun. She is very nervous and upset, and you must be kind to her.

Your loving husband,<br>AGAMEMNON.

## Odysseus to Penelope

THE ISLAND OF OGYGIA.

Dearest Penelope,

We arrived here after a very tiresome voyage. I will not tire you with the details, which are numerous and technical. The net result is that the local physician says I cannot proceed with my journey until I am thoroughly rested. This spot is pleasant, but the only society I have is that of poor dear Calypso. She means well and is most hospitable, but you can imagine how vexed I am by this delay and the intolerable tedium of this enforced repose. Kiss Telemachus from me.

Your loving husband,<br>ODYSSEUS.

## Clytaemnestra to Aegisthus

I am sending this by runner. Come back directly. I expect Agamemnon any moment. The bonfires are already visible. Please bring a good strong net and a sharp axe with you. I will explain when you arrive. I have quite decided that half measures are out of the question.

C.

# The Stoic's Daughter

## (from *Diminutive Dramas*)

SCENE. – *A room in the house of* BURRUS, *Prefect of the Praetorian Guards of Nero.* BURRUS *is discovered in an attitude of despondency.*
    *Enter a* SLAVE.
BURRUS: Well?
SLAVE: Caius Petronius would like to speak to you.
BURRUS: I will see him.
    *Enter* C. PETRONIUS – PETRONIUS ARBITER, *middle-aged, but very elegant.*
PETRONIUS: Good morning. I've come about that dinner. The Emperor quite approves of the list of guests . . .
BURRUS: I don't suppose you wish me to come now.
PETRONIUS: Why not?
BURRUS: Well, after Lucius's – er – unfortunate escapade——
PETRONIUS: My dear fellow, I assure you that's not of the slightest consequence. If we had to be responsible for our sons' misdeeds life would become impossible. As it is, the Emperor, while sympathizing with your feelings——
BURRUS: Please don't talk about it. You can understand how inexpressibly painful it is to me.
PETRONIUS: It might have been worse. He might have gone on the stage.
BURRUS: The gods spared us that. That would have killed Aemilia.
PETRONIUS: I suppose she feels it dreadfully.
BURRUS: It's not so much the thing she minds, but the family name being dragged into publicity – people making bets——
PETRONIUS: Yes, yes – but there's nothing to be done. After all, when all's said and done it is much less degrading to be a gladiator than an actor – or a charioteer. Piso's nephew is a charioteer, and Tigellinus's brother appeared on the stage for some charity.
BURRUS: I don't know what the world is coming to.
PETRONIUS: I suppose he'll drop it immediately. Then I should send him abroad for a little, and the world will forget all about it. These things

are forgotten so quickly. After all, boys will be boys. Believe me, young men must sow their wild oats, and the sooner they get it over the better. Well, please give my respects to Aemilia, and I can count on you for certain for the fifteenth?

BURRUS: I shall come without fail.              [*Exit* PETRONIUS.

    *Enter* AEMILIA – BURRUS'S *wife.*

AEMILIA: Well? What did he say?

BURRUS: Nothing, practically. The Emperor doesn't seem to have said anything.

AEMILIA: But do you mean to say you haven't arranged anything?

BURRUS: What about? The dinner-party?

AEMILIA: Dinner-party, indeed! I mean about Lucius not appearing at the Games again.

BURRUS: No, I haven't. What is there to arrange?

AEMILIA: You really are too helpless. You must get him banished, of course – just for a short time.

BURRUS: I didn't like to – but I'll write to Seneca.

AEMILIA: Seneca's no use. Write to Petronius. He'll arrange it without any fuss.

BURRUS: I hardly like——

AEMILIA: If Lucius appears once more in the circus as a gladiator I shall open my veins in my bath.

BURRUS: Oh, well, of course, if you insist——

AEMILIA: Yes, I do insist.

    *Enter a* SLAVE.

SLAVE: Lucius, Annaeus Seneca, and Annaeus Serenus wish to see you.

BURRUS: Show them in.

    *Enter* LUCIUS, A. SENECA, *and* A. SERENUS.     [*Exit* SLAVE.

SENECA: I've only just heard the news, or else I would have come sooner.

SERENUS: And I had no idea until Seneca told me.

BURRUS: I suppose it's all over Rome by now.

SENECA: You mustn't take these things to heart.

AEMILIA: It's all very well for you to talk, Seneca; you haven't got a son.

SENECA: I would esteem it a privilege to be visited by troubles of this nature. It is only the noblest souls that the gods plague with such disasters in order that, tempered by affliction, the true steel, emerging triumphant from the trial, may serve as an example to mankind.

SERENUS: Not being a stoic, Burrus, I take a different view of the incident. I consider that man is born to enjoy himself, and that the opportunities of enjoyment are rare and far between. Life is monotonous. If your son finds a relaxation from the tediousness of existence in fighting as a gladiator, by all means let him continue to do so. It is a profession which calls forth many of the noblest qualities of man.

206

AEMILIA: But think of the family, Serenus. Think of us, of my sisters, my sisters-in-law, my cousins; think of my husband and the harm that it may do him professionally.

SENECA: Vain thoughts, I assure you, Aemilia. A man's merit depends on the aspirations of his soul and not on the idle gossip of his relations.

SERENUS: All one's relations are liars. It is much better that they should say your son is a gladiator who fights in public – which is true – than that they should say he is a drunkard who drinks in secret, which would be untrue. They would no doubt say that, had they no other food for gossip.

AEMILIA: But Lucius never drinks. He had never given us a day's anxiety until this.

BURRUS: He got all the prizes at school.

AEMILIA: He was working so hard to become an officer.

SERENUS. Ah! Over-education, I see. I assure you the whole matter does not signify.

AEMILIA: It is breaking his father's heart.

BURRUS: I shall never hold up my head in public.

SENECA: Come, Burrus, think of Brutus, and what he had to endure from his son.

SERENUS: Yes, and think of the many Roman sons who have killed their fathers.

SENECA: In every evil, in every misfortune there is always a seed of consolation. You must, of course, deal kindly with him, but firmly, and I am convinced he will listen to reason.

AEMILIA: He wouldn't listen to us at all. We all tried our best to dissuade him – except his cousin Lesbia. Heartless woman! It was entirely her fault.

BURRUS: He shall never cross this threshold again as long as I live.

SENECA: Set a noble example of forgiveness, Burrus, and the world will be grateful to you.

BURRUS: I will never set eyes upon him again. He has disgraced himself and his family for ever. There are certain stains of dishonour which can never be effaced.

*Enter a* SLAVE.

SLAVE: Paulina, the wife of Seneca, is here. She wishes to speak to you.

SENECA: My wife! What can she want?

BURRUS: Show her in.                                 [*Exit* SLAVE.

*Enter* PAULINA.

PAULINA: Forgive me, Burrus, for forcing my way in – they said you were not at home to any visitors – but it is a matter of life and death – and I must speak to Seneca. (*To* SENECA) I have been hunting for you the whole morning, and it's by the merest chance I found out you had come here.

SENECA: What is it?

PAULINA: A terrible catastrophe has befallen us.

SENECA: My Greek vases?

PAULINA: No, it's nothing to do with your horrible collections.

SENECA: Then don't you think we had better go home and discuss the matter in private?

PAULINA: No, I want Burrus's help.

SENECA: What can have happened?

PAULINA: It's Julia.

SENECA: I suppose she's run away with some one.

PAULINA: Oh no; it's far worse than that.

SENECA: You mean——

PAULINA: I don't mean anything. I mean she has disgraced us all.

SERENUS: These little affairs blow over so quickly.

PAULINA: But you don't understand – you will never believe it. The girl has become a Christian.

SENECA: A Christian!

BURRUS: No!

AEMILIA: My poor Paulina!

SERENUS. Curious!

BURRUS: She must have been got hold of by the Jews.

AEMILIA: They are terribly cunning; and people say they're everywhere, and yet one doesn't see them.

SERENUS: But surely there is nothing irretrievable about this. As long as nobody knows about it, what does it signify?

SENECA: You don't understand. It's a matter of principle; I could not possibly harbour a daughter under my roof whom I knew to be a traitor to the State.

SERENUS: It is annoying.

PAULINA: But you don't know the worst: she has gone to prison.

SENECA (*very angry*): Well, I hope you will let her know that she shall never come back to our home as long as she lives. Her conduct is not only immoral, but it is immodest. It is inspired solely and simply by a passion for self-advertisement. It is this modern craze for publicity which is the ruin of our children; she is bitten by this same passion for notoriety which – you will excuse me saying so, Burrus – led your son to be a gladiator. I call it vulgar, tawdry, Byzantine, hysterical, and essentially un-Roman.

SERENUS: But surely, my dear Seneca, nobody can think it amusing to go to prison? Think of the risk.

SENECA: I beg your pardon. People of her class risk nothing. They have got a morbid craze for new sensations.

SERENUS: Rather disagreeable sensations, aren't they? To be eaten by a tiger, for instance?

SENECA: There's no question of that. It's only the worst criminals who are treated like that. Am I not right, Burrus?

BURRUS: Perfectly. A purely religious offender is immediately released on making the mere outward sign of allegiance to the State. An oath is not even required.

PAULINA: Well, that's just what I've come about. The child is in prison, and it appears – it is very foolish and obstinate of her, but Julia always was an obstinate child – that she refuses to fulfil the necessary formality, sacrifice, or whatever it is. So I thought I would come to you, Burrus, and ask you just to say a word to the prison authorities, and then she could be let out – quite quietly, of course. Nobody need know about it.

BURRUS: My dear lady, you know how gladly I would do anything in the world to be of use to you. But in this case – and I am sure you will understand – I cannot see my way; indeed it is quite impossible for me to take any action. You see, Petronius's cousin was released three weeks ago, and smuggled out of the country, and the demagogues got hold of it and complained to the Emperor, who – courting popularity as usual – said it was not to occur again. So you see in what an awkward position we are placed. We can't make these distinctions simply between people of position and others——

PAULINA: But it's always done.

BURRUS: That's just why it can't be done this time. The Emperor is extremely annoyed at people of good family having anything to do with those horrible Christians, and he's determined to stamp this mania out. But all she has got to do is to sacrifice——

PAULINA: But you don't realize how obstinate the girl is.

*Enter* LESBIA, *a lovely gay woman, about 25.*

LESBIA: Good morning, good morning. I've got some places for the Games, and Lucius comes on at three. You *must* see him fight. He's too wonderful. And it's horrible of you not to go and see him, and then they're going to throw *all* the Christians to the lions directly afterwards. so you must come.

CURTAIN.

209

# The Drawback

_____

## (from *Diminutive Dramas*)

SCENE. – *A corner in Kensington Gardens. A summer evening. Discovered, sitting on a seat, a girl, aged 21, pretty and neat, and a good-looking young man, aged 27, dressed in a top hat and a black morning coat.*

HE: But are you quite sure you will not change your mind?

SHE: I never change my mind once it is made up. I often take a very long time to make up my mind, but once I've made it up I never change. Now my sister Alice is quite different. She never knows her mind from one minute to the other.

HE: But your father——

SHE: Papa always does what I want. Besides, directly he knows you it will be all right. And when he knows that you're at the Bar he will be delighted. He always wanted me to marry a lawyer. You see Papa was at the Bar in his young days – I daresay your father was too.

HE (*embarrassed*): No, yes – I mean no. That's to say he is in a way indirectly connected with the Bar; but my father's principal hobby is playing on the harp. He gives himself up almost entirely to that now.

SHE: I see.

HE: Have you told your father yet?

SHE: You told me I wasn't to until I'd seen you again.

HE: Yes, of course. I thought you might have changed your mind.

SHE: As if that were likely.

HE: And then, if you remember, I told you when I, when you, when we settled everything that there was a – er – drawback.

SHE: As if any drawback could possibly make any difference.

HE: I thought it might.

SHE: You mean to say that it is something which might make me wish to change my mind?

HE: Exactly.

SHE: That shows you know me very little – but what is it?

HE: You see it's a kind of confession.

SHE: I know what it is; you want to tell me you once loved some one else.

HE: No, not that, I swear I never did. I may have thought once or twice that I was in love, but until I met you I never knew what love, what real love, was.

SHE: And those other times when you thought you were in love – were there many of them?

HE: It only happened twice; that's to say three times, only the third time didn't count.

SHE: And the first time, who was she?

HE: I was quite young, only a boy. She was a girl in an A.B.C. shop.

SHE: Was she pretty?

HE: Not exactly.

SHE: Did you propose to her?

HE: Yes, but she refused.

SHE: And that's all that happened?

HE: That's all.

SHE: And the second time?

HE: It was the parson's daughter down in the country.

SHE: Did you make love to her?

HE: No, not really, of course, but we were friends.

SHE: Did you kiss her?

HE: Only once, and that was by accident. But it was all years ago.

SHE: How many years ago?

HE: Let me see; two, no, no, it must have been four years ago. I'm not sure it wasn't five. She married the curate.

SHE: And the third time?

HE: Oh! that was nothing.

SHE: Who was she?

HE: She was an artist – a singer.

SHE: A concert singer?

HE: Almost; that's to say she wanted to be one. She sang in a music-hall.

SHE: Oh!

HE: Only a *serious* turn. She wasn't dressed up or anything. She sang 'The Lost Chord' and songs like that. She was called 'The New Zealand Nightingale'.

SHE: And you knew her?

HE: Very slightly. I had tea with her once or twice. And then she went away.

SHE: Back to New Zealand?

HE: Yes, back to New Zealand.

SHE: Now I've made you confess everything. Aren't you glad you've got it off your mind? I don't mind a bit, and I like you for being so honest.

HE: But it's not that at all. It's nothing to do with me.

211

SHE: Then who has it got to do with?

HE: My father.

SHE: You mean he won't approve of me?

HE: Of course I don't mean that. He'd simply love you.

SHE: He's going to marry again.

HE: No, it's not that.

SHE: He doesn't want you to marry.

HE: No, it's nothing to do with me.

SHE: Then I don't understand.

HE: It's something to do with him.

SHE: He's consumptive.

HE: No; his health is excellent.

SHE: He's lost his money.

HE: No; he's very well off. You see it's something to do with his social position. A matter of – I don't quite know how to put it.

SHE: But, Georgie, you don't think I'm such a snob as to care twopence for social position and conventions of that kind? Your father is your father – that's all that matters, isn't it?

HE: I know, I know, but there are prejudices.

SHE: Is it something your father's done? Has he been in the Bankruptcy Court? I wouldn't care a pin.

HE: No, it's nothing he's done. It's something he *is*.

SHE: He's a Socialist!

HE: No.

SHE: Is he a Roman Catholic?

HE: Oh no! He's Church of England.

SHE: I know; he's a Liberal.

HE: No; he says the Liberals are just as bad as the Conservatives.

SHE: Then he's a little Englander.

HE: On the contrary; he's outside politics. He belongs to no party.

SHE: He's a foreigner – by birth, I mean.

HE: Not at all.

SHE: He's not a Mormon?

HE: No. It's nothing to do with politics or religion or that kind of thing. It's his profession.

SHE: His profession! But I thought – as if I cared about his profession!

HE: But you might – there are some professions——

SHE: You see, I know he's honest.

HE: Oh! you needn't have any fear. He's perfectly honest, respectable, and respected.

SHE: Then what is it?

HE: I'd rather you guessed it.

SHE: How absurd you are! I know what it is; he's somebody's agent.

HE: No.

212

SHE: Then he's a schoolmaster.

HE: No.

SHE (*tentatively*): Of course, I know he was never in trade?

HE: No, never. He had nothing to do with it.

SHE: Is he on the stage?

HE: No; he disapproves of actors.

SHE: He's a Quaker.

HE: I told you it's nothing to do with religion.

SHE: Then, he's a photographer. Some photographers almost count as artists.

HE: No.

SHE: Then it is something to do with art.

HE: His profession certainly needs art and skill.

SHE: He's not a conjurer?

HE: Conjurers are scarcely respectable.

SHE: I know, of course. He's a jockey.

HE: No.

SHE: A bookmaker.

HE: No.

SHE: A veterinary surgeon.

HE: No.

SHE: Does he ever give lessons?

HE: Only to his assistants, whom he's training.

SHE: He's a prize-fighter.

HE: Oh no!

SHE: He's an Art-dressmaker.

HE: No. You see it's something some people might mind.

SHE: What can it be? A dentist.

HE: No.

SHE: How stupid of me. He's a literary man.

HE: He's never written a line.

SHE: But you told me. I remember now. He plays the harp. He's something musical; but nobody could mind that. He's a dancing-master.

HE: No.

SHE: A commercial traveller.

HE: No.

SHE: Of course not; it's something to do with art. But what could one mind?

HE: Not exactly art. It's more skill.

SHE: Is he a chiropodist?

HE: No.

SHE: Or a Swedish masseur?

HE: Nothing like it.

SHE: Is it anything to do with officials?

HE: Yes, in a way.

SHE: Then I've guessed. He's a detective.

HE: No.

SHE: He's in the Secret Service.

HE: No.

SHE: It's something to do with the police.

HE: Not exactly.

SHE: With prisons.

HE: In a way.

SHE: He's a prison inspector.

HE: No.

SHE: A prison chaplain.

HE: No; he's not in Orders.

SHE: The prison doctor who has to feed the Suffragettes.

HE: No.

SHE: I've guessed. He's a keeper in a lunatic asylum.

HE: You're getting cold again.

SHE: Then it's something to do with prisons?

HE: Yes.

SHE: He's a warder.

HE: No.

SHE: I don't know who else is in a prison, except the prisoners.

HE: He doesn't live in the prison.

SHE: But he goes there sometimes?

HE: Yes.

SHE: I give it up.

HE: His duty is a disagreeable one, but some one has to do it.

SHE: He's the man who has to taste the prisoners' food.

HE: I didn't know there was such a person.

SHE: You must tell me. I'll never guess.

HE (*blurting it out*): Well, you see, he's the hangman.

    *A pause.*

SHE: You mean he——

HE: Yes, he——

SHE: Oh, I see.

HE: Some people might mind this. He's going to retire very soon – on a pension.

SHE: Yes?

HE: And, of course, he very seldom——

SHE: Yes, I suppose——

HE: It's all quite private, of course.

SHE: Yes, of course. (*A pause. Looking at her watch*) Good gracious! I shall be late for dinner. It's nearly seven o'clock. I must fly. I was late yesterday.

214

HE: Shall I – shall we meet tomorrow?

SHE: No, not tomorrow. I'm busy all tomorrow.

HE: Perhaps the day after.

SHE: Perhaps I had better tell you at once what I was going to write to you.

HE: You think the drawback——

SHE (*indignantly*): I wasn't thinking of that. But I do think you ought to have told me directly about those others.

HE: What others?

SHE: Those women – the A.B.C. shop, the clergyman's daughter, and that music-hall singer.

HE: But you said you didn't mind.

SHE: I minded too much to speak about it. A music-hall singer! The New Zealand Nightingale! Oh! to think that you, that I – Oh! the shame of it.

HE: But——

SHE: There's no but. You've grossly deceived me. You played with my feelings. You led me on. You trifled with me. You've treated me scandalously. You've broken my heart. You've ruined my life.

HE: But let me say one word.

SHE: Not one word. A girl in an A.B.C. shop! A clergyman's daughter! and a music-hall singer!

HE: You really mean——

SHE: I've heard quite enough. Thank you, Mr Belleville. Please to understand that our acquaintance is at an end. Good evening. (*She bows and walks away.*)

CURTAIN.

# 4

## *Russia*

*The old Russia was Maurice Baring's second homeland. In half a dozen books he celebrated his love for its land and people, and if he never saw the new Russia after the end of the 1914 war, his devotion to the constants in the Russian nature and its expressions never left him. Several years before he went to Russia, where his work as a journalist took him, he had already undertaken to learn the Russian language, as his early exercise book in the Beinecke Library at Yale testifies. In his war correspondence, his autobiographical writing, his short stories and sketches, his books on Russian literature, his translations of Russian poetry, he revealed the penetrating sympathy for Russian life and ways which led Sir Bernard Pares to say that he had never known another writer, even a Russian writer, who could write with greater or more profound intuitive comprehension of the Russian peasant, soldier, or worker than Maurice Baring. Any account of his life or survey of his work must devote a generous portion to his Russian experience. I have chosen passages from his journalism, fiction, and literary studies.*

*His small masterpiece of literary history and criticism,* An Outline of Russian Literature, *was composed entire in little more than a month, so swift, certain, and felicitous was his command of the subject. It was written in the very heart of his other country:*

*'In the spring of 1914 I went back to Russia for the last time before the war. I spent over a month by myself at Sosnofka, writing a book, an outline of Russian literature, and bathing every afternoon in the river where the sweetbrier grew on the banks of the willows, and the kingfishers used every now and then to dart across the oily-looking water. It was a wonderful spring. The nightingales sang all day long in the garden and all night long people were singing in the village. Nature was steeped in beauty and calm.' In that summer the war began. He went home to England to serve and never came back to Russia.*

# Russian Land and People

(from *The Russian People*)

## (i) *What Russia Looks Like*

NOT LONG AGO[1] I was staying in a small Russian provincial town where the annual meeting of the County Council for the district was being held. I went out for a walk one afternoon with a Russian friend of mine, and just as we had reached the outskirts of the town, and we looked round on the landscape, we both said simultaneously, 'What a typical Russian scene!' I told my friend that it was very different from what most foreigners who had never been to Russia imagined a typical Russian scene to be.

It was an autumn day in late October. The sky was cloudless and of a light transparent blue, clear and dazzling. So clear was the atmosphere that the distant features of the landscape were as distinct as they are in a kodak photograph. The view had the sharpness of a photograph. We were standing on a wooden bridge which stretched over a narrow and utterly sluggish brown river; the banks were of shelving sand, and you had to go down some wooden steps to reach the bridge on one side and to go up some wooden steps to reach the farther side. On one side of the river, and about thirty yards from it, was the town, standing on level ground; on the other side of it the level country stretched out into the distance, a flat, dark brown plain, cut by a road.

What you saw of the town was, on the right, a large cathedral, the fourth biggest in Russia: the style was Palladian, I suppose, that is to say, it had a front of five large Corinthian pillars supporting a pediment, and a dome; walls, dome, and pillars were all whitewashed. A little farther to the left of it and beyond it was another church, which had a white spire and a round cupola painted ultramarine-blue. Round the church was an open space, and then along the river began the line of houses which formed the limit of the town. They were low, two-storied houses

---

[1] Published 1911.

most of them, some built of bricks and whitewashed, and some built of wood. The corner house of the street, which ended where the open square in which the cathedral stood began, was a barracks, two-storied, of a dun colour and built of stone. The road in front of the house was sandy, dusty, and brown.

On the other side of the river the houses were few and straggling, and belonged to poor people. They had but one story and were built of logs placed horizontally one on the top of the other, and were roofed with iron, but on the right of the road was a larger house, painted white, with a tall chimney, from which smoke proceeded: this was a factory of some kind. Next to it was a tall, wooden windmill; one of its four fans had been broken off and was missing. Right in the distance, on the horizon of the plain, you could see a bare brown wood.

As we leant over the bridge we observed at the foot of the left bank of the river, a raft, and on it, a little wooden house with windows and a flat roof; on the raft a whole bevy of women, in coloured prints, were washing their linen. Five or six soldiers were looking on. The soldiers had got on their dun-coloured, rough-stuff grey coats; some of them were bringing bundles of linen to be washed; others were chaffing the washerwomen.

At our feet, moored to one of the supports of the bridge, was a flat barge, and on it a soldier, in a black tunic and high boots, was washing his linen himself: he must have climbed down the bridge to get there.

There was not a sound in the air, except the splash made by the washing. And then from the plain, along the dusty, rutty road, a whole line of flat carts creaked along, one in front of the other, five of the foremost being without drivers; all of these carts were full of sacks. Alongside of the sixth walked the owner, a bearded peasant dressed in a brown leather and very dirty coat lined with sheepskin. And every now and then he influenced the march of the line of carts by shouting a word or two to the horses. Not long after this, the line of carts crossed the bridge and turned into the town and the creaking died away in the distance; the lazy stillness fell upon the place once more: and so great was that stillness that the whole landscape seemed like a coloured slide of a magic lantern.

Then once more the stillness was broken by the rattling of a carriage; this time it was a *troika* – a *troika* is a carriage drawn by three horses abreast, only in this particular carriage there were only two, one harnessed in the middle and one on the side, so that there would have been room for the third. These were evidently post-horses belonging to the County Council, and in the narrow carriage, just big enough for two, sat two educated men, tidily dressed, one perhaps a doctor, and in front of them on the box, which is on the same level as the carriage seat, the driver in a dark blue peaked cap and a pea-jacket was making a spluttering noise with his lips, which is the way to tell Russian horses to behave gently.

One more the stillness was unbroken; and only now and then the sleepy cry of poultry in the straw of the houses on the roadside accentuated the quiet.

But as we looked towards the town, at the brown street stretching between the river and houses, we saw in the distance, turned to gold in the low sunshine, a cloud of dust, and out of that cloud came a sound of voices and a tramp of feet, and presently we saw a company of soldiers marching, all in their brown-grey coats, without their rifles, and carrying each of them a small white bundle. Presently we heard the rhythm of a large and cheerful song. The verse had ended, and by the time the next verse began the soldiers were much nearer to us. The singing was like this: One soldier, waving his hand as though he were a conductor, sang the opening phrase by himself. Then the chorus joined in with a crash. The four parts were strongly accentuated, but they seemed less like the complementary harmonies of the melody, than successive melodies, imitating the first one and forming a rough counterpoint. The chorus began on a high note, with a high quick phrase; then with a swinging, trotting rhythm, it descended in an answering phrase; it rose again and, broadening, swelled into a great shout, ending in five, slow, sustained notes, when unexpectedly and abruptly, with a sharp clean cry, the chorus ended once more on the high note, leading you to expect it must begin again at once, which it soon did. The soldiers marched on for about two minutes in silence, then the solo took up the song again, and another verse was sung by the chorus, and the process was repeated; and so on, till they reached the barracks gate at the corner of the street; they were still singing as they passed through the open gateway.

These were soldiers coming back from their weekly wash at the *Bania*, the steam-bath, and in their bundles they were carrying their dirty linen.

Soon after they had gone into barracks, we left the bridge and walked up the steps into the street. We leant beside a wooden railing on the top of the steep bank. Behind us was the town, in front of us the straggling houses and the plain. Once more everything had relapsed into an indescribable peacefulness. Two soldiers toiled up the steps carrying a huge sack; a third soldier, interested in the proceedings, strolled from the barracks and asked them why they were hauling up the sacks.

'Because we want to sell them,' they answered, and the joke met with success.

My friend agreed with me that a more typically Russian scene could not be found. The large church, the squat houses, the damaged windmill, the clear, brown plain, the washerwomen, the singing soldiers. You could not see such a thing except in Russia. And the chorus of the soldiers was so strikingly characteristic: the rhythm of the tune, the way it started with a high phrase, and accelerated into a still brisker trot, and then once more slowed down, broadened and opened out, and ended abruptly. Not only was the rhythm characteristic, but the spirit and quality of the tune, the lilting joyousness of it, and the tremendous driving spring and swing of it. As they came to the final note the soldiers swung their arms down. The chorus was so brisk and cheerful that you would have thought they were celebrating some particularly joyful festival or some especially memorable event, whereas they were just coming back from their weekly bath.

There is now appearing in Russia a collected edition of the works of Mr H. G. Wells. He has written a preface to them himself, and in it he tells the Russian public what he imagines Russia to be like: the picture he has made himself of Russia from the books of Russian writers. He then wonders how the Russian reader who has never been to England sees that country in his mind's eye, and he remarks that if the Russian has in mind the England of the manufacturing country, the smoke and the 'grim smile of the Five Towns', that is not the England that he knows.

It would indeed be difficult to give a foreign reader in one or two vignettes the most characteristic sights of England; because in England, as in any other Western European country, there is so much variety. But in Russia the uniformity is so great that if you describe one scene you are describing a million similar scenes. And when you have differentiated between the north and the south – and even here the difference is far less sharp than in other countries – you have practically summed up the whole.

I of course except outlying districts such as the Caucasus and Finland, which are in reality different countries; but between a village in the Government of St Petersburg, a village in the Government of Moscow, and a village in the Government of Tambov, there is practically no difference.

As one travels in the Trans-Siberian Railway from Moscow to the Ural Mountains, one is struck by the absolute monotony and uniformity of the landscape and the physical features of the country. What I have described above is the fringe of a small provincial town. Let us now take a typical landscape in Central Russia.

Let us imagine you are driving, say, twenty or thirty miles through the country. The first thing that will strike you will be the breadth of the road; in summer it will be as dusty as a desert, in early autumn rutty, and in late autumn, if the season has been rainy, a slush of thick, black mud, as black as tar and as thick as paste.

On either side of you stretch limitless plains; fields of wheat, rye, or buckwheat, without any hedges; every now and then in the distance you will see the outline of a wood; sometimes you will drive past the edge of a large stretch of wood where there are oak, aspen, and birch trees. In July everything to the right and left of you will be a golden sea of corn; later this will be bare stubble; and in the autumn the black fields will be a light emerald-green with the growing wheat, which was sown after the harvest, in August or September.

Or you may pass by green meadows, with small sheets of water in them, and here and there broad marshes. Sometimes the road will be lined with willow trees planted at some distance apart. The only features that will relieve the monotony of the landscape are distant woods, windmills, and the spires of churches. The churches are most of them built of wood, but they are painted in light colours, red or green; sometimes they have some gilding, very often a bright ultramarine cupola. Sometimes a village, if it is rich, will boast of an elaborate brick-built church with four cupolas. By the side of the road you will often pass a post about four feet high, which stands supporting two bits of wood forming a triangle; this is a holy image. Or you will see larger ones, a tall post, taller than a man, on the top of which is a little shrine, an oblong cupboard pointed at the top, which holds a holy ikon. These little wayside shrines are called chapels.

You will often come to marshy bits of road, over which planks have been thrown to make a bridge; sometimes the planks will be in such a rotten state that a track has been made round the marshy place: you will avoid the bridge and circumvent it; sometimes you will come to a small river or a pond, and cross it on a bridge whose loose planks will shake and rattle as the carriage drives over it. Sometimes the bridge will be built on the top of a well, or rather a lock whose gates never open.

Then you will drive through a small village: the village street is very wide, often fifty yards in width. The cottages are built of flat logs; they are one-storied and thatched with straw; some of them are crooked and appear to be tumbling down. Behind the houses there is generally a small plot of cultivated ground where vegetables grow, and a shed made of thatch, which looks as if a thatched roof had been taken from a house and put upon the ground, and here and everywhere an immense amount of straw and a great deal of dirt.

Perhaps you will pass through a larger, more well-built village. There you will come across brick houses roofed with iron, and a few houses made of painted wood. These are generally the school, the post office, or perhaps the house of the pope. In the village street there will be quantities of poultry, and of small children in vermilion-red cotton shirts, with straw-coloured hair, growing in thick bunches behind and cropped closely at the edge, over the neck. Here and there you will meet pigs. In the villages also you will see wells from which buckets are lifted by a large pole swinging horizontally over a short pole, the long pole being weighted at one end.

If it is Sunday, you may meet the villagers coming out of church in their Sunday clothes; the men in loose clean shirts, light yellow, red, pink, and blue, but not tucked into their trousers; with their high boots carefully cleaned and having as many creases as possible in them: most of them wearing dark blue peaked caps; and women dressed also in glowing spotless colours, salmon-pink, pale cobalt-green, and pale blue. But if it is a weekday, the women you pass will be dressed in everyday prints, with a white handkerchief on their heads, and the men in darker shirts.

You are sure to meet a whole multitude of carts creaking lazily along, with the driver sitting on some sacks, and his legs hanging over the low sides. If it is cold, he will be wearing his fur cap, and his leather, sheepskin-lined *tulup*, or skirted jacket. You see a good deal of squalor and dirt and straw, but nowhere will you get an impression of bustle and hurry.

But you may be quite wrong if you conclude from the dirty and tumble-down condition of the houses that their inhabitants are necessarily poor. They may be poor, but they may also be rich. Sometimes a peasant who makes money in Russia, will never think of changing his manner of life. This is perhaps less true today than it was some years ago.

Windmills, churches, and distant woods – those are the main features of the landscape. Dirt or dust, mud, squalor, slowness, indolence, and easy-goingness – these are the main characteristics of the manifestations of life that you will meet.

And if you extend your journey, so as to pass through towns, you will notice that they are flat and squat, and that the only tall features in them are the church spires, and the little round cupolas.

I have said that the contrast between the north and the south is not so great as in other countries. This is so; but a difference and a contrast of course exist. The lie of the land is not so very different in the south: you are still in the midst of rolling plains diversified by woods; the main features of the landscape are still churches, windmills, and wayside chapels. The architecture of the churches is exactly the same; so is the shape of the windmills; but where you will notice the main difference lies in the villages and in the appearance of the houses. The villages of South Russia, instead of being uniformly and monotonously brown, are brighter and more cheerful. In Southern Russia small holdings are the rule instead of the exception; the peasant lives in a *hutor* or farm. These little farm-houses are built of bricks, whitewashed or painted pale green or pink, and thatched with straw. They are surrounded by orchards and fruit-trees. They are clean outside and inside. The walls inside are painted red and blue; there are less hens about, and none in the living-rooms.

The national dress of the Little Russian is far more picturesque than that of the Great Russian, but the only place where I have seen it was during the sessions of the first Duma at St Petersburg. When I was in the south of Russia I was all the time in the region of large factories, and the inhabitants there dressed far more like Birmingham or Manchester mechanics than like Little Russian peasants. Their clothes showed the traces of the inroads, but not of the complete conquest, of progress and education. They showed not quite-fulfilled aspirations towards white shirts and collars. Every now and then, however, you came across a picturesque figure, such as a blind beggar playing a real hurdy-gurdy (the German *Leier* which Schubert tells of in his song, 'Der Leiermann', and the French *vielle*). But the whole impression of the south of Russia is cheerful and gay. It is in Central Russia I have seen the most brilliant bits of colouring, but in Southern Russia there is an atmosphere of sunshine and the laziness that comes of *bien-être*: the country smiles at you. In Central Russia it often has a frowning, sullen aspect.

A very beautiful sight in Southern Russia is, in the autumn, the undulating slopes of ploughed fields, which have the appearance of hills, of a rich dark brown, with clouds of mist rising out of them in the rose-coloured sunset.

Among all the sights one can see in Russia, I think the winter is the most striking: when the snow has definitely fallen, and no temporary thaw can any more dislodge it, until the spring, one is tempted to expect a monotony of days, one exactly like the other, until the spring shall return.

This is not so: there is an infinite variety in the aspect of the snow. There is bluish snow, yellow snow, grey snow, gloomy snow, wet snow, soft snow and hard snow; sick snow, cheerful snow, dirty snow, and dazzling snow. The most beautiful of all the winter phenomena is that which occurs when, after a heavy fall of snow, it freezes hard and the sun comes out. Nothing can describe the beauty of the orchards and the woods.

Against an azure sky, whose purity and intensity are increased by the whiteness of the earth, the trees stand out, covered, as it were, with an unearthly blossom, with myriads of delicate flowers and petals, with fairy branches and powdered leaves. It seems as if in this blossoming the world had been changed into an immense orchard and every tree had become a fruit-tree; the stems of the birch trees gleam like silver columns; and the sun, shining on the powdered and petalled branches, produces a hundred iridescent lights; the bushes and the undergrowth stand out in all the beauty of their outline. The whole world is a shimmering fairy-tale; fantastic, strange, and entrancing: one cannot help thinking that it is about to fade and dissolve like a rainbow or a soap-bubble; that it is the sport of a wizard or the dream of a sleeping princess.

When the sunset comes, the trees blush and are tinted with a wonderful hue, like that of almond blossom; add to this the exhilaration of clean dazzling air, and the impression is overwhelming. Even more wonderful is the effect of the sunset on such a clear day, on a hilly slope, for in the flat country there are often clefts and hollows which form hills. The reflection of the sunset spreads over them like a gradual blush, and one seems to be in the world of Shelley's 'Prometheus'. You think this is going to last, and you wake up the next morning and find the world changed: the blossom has left the trees, leaving dewdrops, and sparkling threads, and glistening webs and films hanging from the brown branches. The sun is still shining, and it is still fairyland, but a different fairyland. Then the next day the sun will not shine at all, and the sky will be like a heavy grey curtain with spaces of glinting blue, and, perhaps, a faint pink streak; and the distant woods will be as blue as the deepest blue you can find in a child's paint-box; and far away little brown sledges will give you an idea of the distance and the width of the space in front of you. Then, perhaps, the next day the snow will fall in a whirling blizzard or in a steady shower of flakes. And thus the pageant shifts and changes daily until the winter is done.

As one drives through the snowy plains in a sledge, often the most common and the most disagreeable of the winter phenomena is the *metiel*, a kind of minor blizzard, a dense downpour of whirling and blinding snow and sleet. One instantly loses one's way; one's only guides in the winter, besides the track and ruts made by carts, are the little stumpy posts which are placed at intervals all along the roadside. When the *metiel* covers the tracks the road is obliterated and the posts are invisible. You drive to the right and to the left; at last the coachman thinks he has found the track: you drive straight on, then perhaps, an hour later, he finds that you have come back on your old track, and that you have been moving in a vicious circle. Pushkin has described this in one of his most famous poems, which is called the 'Metiel'. I have been able to check the poet's accuracy by experience, and I have found it only too correct.

The Russian peasant is marvellous in finding a track by the very scantiest evidence and sign: a straw is enough to put him right again when he has lost his way.

The winter is the longest of the Russian seasons. The shortest is the spring. It is heralded by the melting of the snows, the flooding of the rivers, and the overflowing of the meadows. This is also a most wonderful sight: the plains are covered with sheets of water in which the trees seem to float like thin silver shadows; it is fantastic, unreal, and fairylike.

When the spring comes it invades the country with a rush. I arrived once in the country in April and found all the woods bare; a fortnight later everything was green and the bees were booming about the blossom.

In the summer the most striking sights are the immense stretches of ripening corn, the flowering bean-fields, and the warm nights which grow darker as the harvest approaches; then the whole of the land is a sea of golden corn. The heat is often intense. It is too hot to go out in the day-time, and bathing in the river is like bathing in hot tea.

The autumn is longer than the spring; but the period of autumn tints does not last much longer than a fortnight or three weeks. The trees are splashed with gold and crimson. During a week or two the pageant is at its height, then a day of wind will come and fling the tattered branches to the earth. In the south the period of autumn tints last much longer. Everything is hot and dry; the trees remain green and golden; there is little sharpness or moisture in the air, and 'die küsse des scheidenden Sommers' are soft and long-drawn-out. Summer seems to die of excess of warmth and beauty. Sometimes there is an Indian summer after the leaves have fallen – a period of mild and warm weather; a period of stillness and decay, when it seems that the woods are under the influence of an untimely spring:

'Qualche primavera dissepolta'.

But as a general rule the time between the fall of the leaf and the first snow is either cold and raw, or damp and sullen. It freezes hard at night. There is a sharpness in the morning air, a smell of smoke, of damp leaves and of moist brown earth. Then comes the first snow.

It is a tradition that the snow must fall three times before it finally comes to stay. But this tradition is by no means invariably fulfilled. Sometimes the end of the autumn is heralded by three days of heavy snowfall, which never thaws again. But more often there is a slight snowfall which lasts, perhaps, a day, and is succeeded by a thaw, and a period of varying from a fortnight to a month of grey and damp, or frosty and fine, and sometimes even warmer weather. Then a second snowfall followed by a spell of still more frosty and cold weather, and then the third decisive fall of snow, which no subsequent thaw is strong enough to dislodge. Thus the winter, which begins generally towards the end of November, lasts straight on until April and sometimes till the end of April.

The autumn and the spring are trying seasons in the towns, owing to their many and abrupt transitions from heat to cold, and from frost to thaw. The winter is the healthiest season in Russia and, perhaps, the most comfortable. There is no place where you feel the cold so little, because every preparation has been made for it. The houses are warmed evenly and throughout; the passages are as warm as the rooms; and when you go out you are prepared with furs and felt boots to face the cold. I have never felt the cold so keenly as when coming back from Russia to London in winter, from the warm wood-lighted stoves and stove-warmed houses of Russia to the coal chimneys of London, which so insufficiently heat the draughty rooms when it is cold, and overheat them when it is warm.

And even if the winter is not the pleasantest season in Russia – which is after all a matter of taste – it is, perhaps, the most characteristic, and reveals and sets in motion some of the most characteristic and peculiar qualities and customs of the Russian people.

## (ii) *The Russian Character*

IT HAS OFTEN been said that Russia is the country of paradoxes, and it is easy enough to illustrate the point by a hundred examples. In writing on the Russian character I have myself often used the saying to account for seemingly directly contradictory phenomena which the Russian character so frequently affords. But I sometimes wonder whether the application of the phrase is not a convenient way of shirking a difficulty, and whether the impression of a paradox is not sometimes the result of superficial inquiry rather than of an exhaustive investigation into causes and results. Contradictory elements are to be found in the Great Russian without any doubt, just as contradictory elements are found in the Anglo-Saxon, the Celt, and the German; but it is perhaps not sufficient to say paradox and then to pass on. It would be interesting to know whether there is any common cause which must inevitably produce contradictory and twofold results.

In the case of the Great Russian, there is first of all the grain of Finnish alloy in his metal which accounts at least for something twofold. He is first of all Slav – and before going any further let us consider what are the characteristics of the Slav in contradistinction to those of other races. This is certainly no idle or useless question in view of the strange opinions which are current respecting the Slav nature, and which are due to ignorance; since the average Western European is inclined to class the Slav with Mongols, Tartars, and, in general, with barbarous Asiatics.

The Slav is the reverse of barbarous. He is first and foremost peaceable, malleable, ductile, and plastic; and consequently distinguished by agility of mind, by a capacity for imitation and assimilation, and a corresponding lack of originality and initiative. He is deficient in will and character, and superabundant in ideas, understanding, and sympathy.

Well, granted this; and granted not only that the Great Russian is mainly Slav, but affords evidence, by his past history and his daily conduct, that he possesses these essentially Slav qualities, how do we account for his achievements, his conquest and victory over the Oriental dominion, the building up of a great empire, which are obviously the result of qualities of an altogether different character, and the fruits by which he is known? In achieving a work, which stands patent for all the world to see in the shape of the Russian Empire, as it exists today, it is obvious that he has given proof of other qualities besides these which are more or less negative, such as receptivity, plasticity, and assimilation.

Both in the deeds of her great men and in the work of her obscure and unremembered millions, Russia, 'bright with names that men remember, loud with names that men forget', has given evidence of qualities such as energy, sometimes of a frantic kind – as in the case of Peter the Great, who, though an exceptional Russian, was certainly a typical Russian – of laborious patience, endurance, and obstinacy.

If, not content with saying paradox and throwing up the sponge, in face of any attempt at finding an explanation, we investigate the matter more nearly, what do we find?

In the first place there is the alien admixture in the Great Russian, the fusion of the assimilated Finnish element which seems to have made for toughness and energy, and in the second place there is the influence of climate.

With regard to the alien admixture, it certainly must have had some kind of toughening and strengthening result, for in those Slav races which remained entirely pure, without any alien admixture, we do not find this tough element. It is absent in the Poles, for instance, for had it existed among them in a preponderating degree, there would at the present day be a large Poland and a small Russia.

Then we have the question of climate. There is no doubt that the influence of the Russian climate on the Great Russians is twofold and produces two contradictory results. It leads them, firstly, to battle with the hostile forces of nature, for battle with them he must, as far as possible, in order to live, and consequently the struggle develops in him qualities of tenacity, energy, and strength; and secondly, it leads him to bow down and submit to the overwhelming and insuperable forces of nature, against which all struggle is hopeless. Thus it is that he develops qualities of patience, resignation, and weakness. This, again, accounts for that mixture in the Russian which more than all things puzzles the Western European, namely, the blend of roughness and good-nature, of kindness and brutal insensibility. The very fact that he has been hardened by his struggle for existence under desperate conditions has taught the Russian to sympathize with the sorrows and sufferings of his fellow-creatures. Hence his kindness, his sympathy with the afflicted, the desolate, and the oppressed, which strikes everybody who has come into close contact with the Russian people. On the other hand, in the face of obstacles, not a natural hardness, but the stoicism which the bitterness of the struggle has taught him, gets the upper hand. And he applies to an adversary, an enemy, or to any person who has been found guilty of transgressing his code of laws, a brutal treatment, with the same inflexibility with which he would be ready to undergo it, should he be found guilty of an offence calling for a similar punishment. Hence the calm with which a Russian peasant will inflict a tremendous beating – even to death, if it be deemed necessary – on a horse-stealer, which equals the stoicism with which he would himself undergo the beating had he been detected in the crime and condemned to the same punishment. This insensibility, this desperate stoicism, has made people open their eyes when writers speaking from personal experience have affirmed that the Russian peasant is essentially humane, and more humane than other Europeans of the same class. Examples of brutality, whether in real life or in fiction, naturally strike the imagination and stick in the mind more easily than 'little unremembered acts of kindness and love', whose very point is that they are unremembered.

But whereas both these qualities exist side by side, the milder predominates. It is his normal state, and acts of brutality are generally the result of exceptional circumstances. That is to say, the Russian peasant may be said to be naturally a good-natured being, humane and compassionate, but capable of enduring or inflicting suffering, should the circumstances demand it, with unruffled calm. It would be a great mistake to think of him as a being who in his normal state, and in his everyday life, without any rhyme or reason, is constantly swaying between extremes of unaccountable kindness and unaccountable brutality. He is naturally humane, and naturally peaceful and disinclined to fight. To bring his hardness and ruder qualities into play exceptional circumstances are needed, not to mention drink. Even under the influence of drink he is as a rule inclined to be good-natured; but if drink be combined with a pressure of further exceptional circumstances, say an act of punishment or revenge, he will then be capable of committing wild excesses.

Personally in my experience of the Russian peasantry I have never witnessed on their part any single example of brutality; whereas I have come across hundreds of instances of their good-nature and their kindness.

The above tends to show that the gentler and more peaceable qualities predominate in him. This blend, therefore, of human charity and brutish insensibility can be considered not as an unaccountable paradox, but rather as the result of the twofold lesson he learns in the hard school of his life and the bitter war he wages with nature. He learns to suffer, and therefore to sympathize with suffering; he learns to bear suffering with stoicism, and therefore to inflict it with insensibility when the occasion arises.

If we cease to consider the peasant especially, and enlarge our field of investigation so as to include the Great Russians of all classes, we are struck at every turn by a duality, a blend, a mixture of contradictory elements, which is no less striking than the blend of humaneness and insensibility which is so peculiarly characteristic of the peasant. We are struck by a lack of discipline which produces an easy-going *laissez-aller*, happy-go-lucky, 'what does it matter?' spirit. Combined with this spirit, which in Russia goes by the name of *Nichevo*, we find instances of fierce energy and relentless persistence and patience in the face of obstacles: for instance, in the career of Peter the Great and Suvorov; in the manner in which an ordinary Russian workman or peasant will throw himself into a given arduous task; in phenomena such as the defence of Sevastopol, or the transport of troops over the Trans-Siberian Railway.

The Russian workman gives evidence every now and then of a kind of extra flip of energy, a power of accomplishing a little more than the maximum – this is a trait characteristic of young nationalities, of the Americans, for instance.

I was once watching in a village in Central Russia the installation of a steam-engine. An artisan had come from Germany, from Bremen, in order to put it together and to set it going. After the machine had been satisfactorily installed, the German artisan went away, leaving instructions that it should be fed with fuel gradually and carefully and slowly. The fuel was straw; the instructions of the German were carried out, with the result that the heat generated was not sufficient to make the machine work. During the whole day after his departure the machine remained obstinately inert. The next day I visited the machine and found it busily working. I asked one of the workmen how the result had been achieved; he answered, 'We were told to heat it German fashion [*po niemetski*] – slowly and gradually; and that wouldn't do, so we thought we would try to heat it Russian fashion [*po russki*]' – and here he made a gesture with his arm which signified 'go-the-whole-hog' – 'and so we put in a mass of straw and it worked famously'.

This remark struck me as being extraordinarily characteristic. By 'Russian fashion', he meant the extra flip, the superabundant, just more than the maximum touch, which leads men to overcome a difficulty.

A striking instance of this is the behaviour of peasants in a crisis, such as the putting out of a fire, when it is spreading, with the aid of a high wind, through a village. I have assisted at several such scenes. The energy displayed in saving what is possible, in destroying what it is necessary to destroy in order to check and limit the spread of the flames, is fantastic, almost superhuman. I have never seen such energy, such dogged persistence and inspired courage, because it must be borne in mind that the fight is an unequal one; the fire is often on a large scale; the fire-engines are small and inadequate. Everything depends on human energy. And what is peculiarly striking is that the Russians, who often lack individual initiative, have in a high degree that power of co-operative energy. They work altogether naturally without feeling the need of any special leader. I remember a striking instance of this kind in the Russo-Japanese War, in the retreat from Ta-shi-chao, when the retreat of a vast number of transport was effected without any supervising control; it seemed to go in perfect order, automatically. Colonel Gädke, the German War Expert, who was a witness of this, told me at the time that he considered this automatic co-operation very remarkable, and he doubted whether German soldiers would be capable of similar behaviour in similar circumstances.

Another instance of the energy of the Russians in critical circumstances was afforded to the world by the Messina earthquake. Any one who read the correspondence which appeared in the *Daily Telegraph* at the time will remember the almost miraculous energy displayed by the Russian sailors in the work of saving people from the ruins. Eye-witnesses confirmed to me the stories which appeared in the newspapers at the time with regard to the fabulous agility, the perseverance, and the adventurous courage of the Russian sailors.

I have heard from Englishmen who live in Sicily that the Sicilians added the exploits of the Russian sailors to their national legends and classed them with Scylla, Charybdis, Mount Etna, Proserpine, and Pluto. One eye-witness, an Englishman, also told me that he was struck by two things: the tenderness the Russian sailor displayed to the wounded and sick, how he nursed and tended the women and children; and the ruthlessly calm manner in which he disposed of looters and robbers as so much vermin. This illustrates what I have said about the peasants. Any one who has ever witnessed a fire in a Russian village and seen the peasants leap into the dangerous places, hack and hew down what is superfluous and perilous, and save what can be saved, whether persons, animals, or chattels, will not be surprised by the record of the Russian sailors at Messina.

Closely allied to what I called this 'extra flip' of energy is the disposition in the Russian character to go beyond the limit, or rather not to recognize any boundary line. This perhaps proceeds from a lack of self-discipline, but whatever may be the cause, it is a common phenomenon in Russia. The Russian in a hundred ways likes to 'go the whole hog'.

There is a poem of Alexis Tolstoy which expresses this sentiment, and which runs like this:

'Love without slinking doubt and love your best;
And threaten, if you threaten, not in jest;
And if you lose your temper, lose it all,
And let your blow straight from the shoulder fall;
In altercation, boldly speak your view,
And punish but when punishment is due;
With both your hands forgiveness give away;
And if you feast, feast till the break of day.'

Thus, for instance, I have often seen aged men of the professional class, once they began to play cards, continuing to play all night. Only the other day I heard of an instance of some people playing cards for thirty-six hours, without stopping except for brief intervals for food. Nowhere is time, or rather the ordinary prejudices with regard to the limits imposed by time, of so little account as in Russia.

If a Russian company are interested in a card game, they will go on playing until they have had enough; it will not occur to any one to say, 'We ought to stop now because it is too late', or 'It is really time that we should go to bed.' The same thing is true in matters of food and drink. The thought that enough is as good as a meal, the maxim of 'Seek to have rather less than more', is contrary to the Russian temperament. On the contrary, in order to enjoy himself he will aim at having more than less. He is convinced that 'enough' and a 'feast' are two totally different and distinct things, and that for a 'feast' a great deal more than enough is necessary.

Intellectually, this same quality manifests itself to a very remarkable degree. The Russian is adventurous and daring in the domain of thought and of ideas. He is often 'timide par le caractère et hardi par la pensée'. He recognizes no conventional limit or boundary; he will follow his thought to its logical conclusion; and when the conclusion seems to lead to a *reductio ad absurdum* he will swallow the 'absurdum' with a 'Why not?'

For instance, I remember once hearing a Russian argue against marriage; after he had been developing his theory for some time, somebody objected that if it were carried into practice it would mean the end of the world. 'But that's just what I want,' he answered.

In direct contrast to this adventurous audacity, in the region of ideas, the Russian is often distinguished by timidity, prudence, and want of initiative in the affairs of everyday life. He will often display a horror of responsibility and a fear in the face of authority; a dislike of initiative, of striking out a new line; a blend of suspicion and fear of persons who seem ready to take responsibility on themselves and to signalize themselves by any act of initiative or independence. Take any administrative body in Russia, the County Councils, for instance, and one will find that their proceedings are distinguished by an exaggerated spirit of prudence and caution.

The ordinary Russian is essentially a democrat. He is democratic in the good as well as in the bad sense of the word. When I say the bad sense of the word I mean that particular side of the democratic spirit which leads him to fear and to dislike the man who rises above the average, who speaks out and gives proof of moral independence and courage. This contrast between his intellectual audacity and his timidity of conduct corresponds to the contrast between the capacity of violent energy, which he at times displays, and the inclination which he equally often displays towards indolence and happy-go-lucky *laissez-aller*.

So on all sides, and at every turn, we are brought back to something twofold, to a contradiction, and a contrast which tempts one to accept the paradox and to pass on.

Not only do these contradictory qualities exist side by side, but they often manifest themselves in rapid succession, in swift alternatives. There is often something spasmodic here; the Russian will pass rapidly from one mood to another, from despair to a wild gaiety, from apathy to energy, from resignation to revolt, and from rebellion to submission. Again, the Great Russian peasant is convinced above all things that he must make hay while the sun shines, that summer is short, and the time for agricultural labour brief. This leads him to work hard for a short period, to achieve much in a short time, and then to do nothing in the autumn and winter. The result is there is no people who is capable of making so sharp an effort during a short time, and no people with so little aptitude for continuous and regular hard work.

He will also easily be taken with a sudden mania, for a person, a thing, a book, an idea, or an occupation, and equally suddenly drop it.

The system of government has not seldom underlined this propensity by its action. At one time, for instance, it would encourage a certain train of thought; special books and ideals in all the schools of Russia; and at another time it would order these schools to burn what they had adored and to adore what it had burned. M. Leroy Beaulieu accounts for these rapid alternating moods and abrupt contrasts and changes by the influence of the climate. He maintains that these sudden and rapid changes are the reflection of the extremes of climate, the long cold winter, the torrid summer, and the spring and the autumn during which one experiences often from day to day changes from extreme heat to extreme cold. The theory seems plausible, but one might quote instances of other climates which are equally mutable and fickle and equally rich in abrupt changes and sharply contrasted extremes, but which fail to have a similar effect on the inhabitants of the countries to which they belong.

The contrasts of climate, for instance, must be equally sharp in Canada and America, and the Canadians and Americans do not afford such startling examples of mobility and variability of temperament. Whatever may be the cause of it, this mobility is characteristic of the Russian, and closely allied to it is what is probably his most marked characteristic, what is in part the hallmark of all the Slav races.

This is the Russian plasticity – his malleability and ductility, from which proceed his power of comprehension, assimilation, and imitation, and a corresponding lack of originality and creative power; a great deal of human charity and moral indulgence, and a corresponding absence of discipline and a tendency towards laxity; an absence of hypocrisy, and often a corresponding lack of tight moral fibre; a faculty of all-round adaptability, moral and physical, and an unlimited suppleness of mind.

The application of Taine's doctrine of the *faculté maîtresse* has generally the savour of something arbitrary; but whether this group of qualities, which can be best summed up in the word 'plasticity', be the mainspring of the Russian temperament or not, it is certainly one of its most salient features. This plasticity makes at the same time for strength and for weakness, but it is complemented and corrected by something else and something different, which I will come to presently. Let us for the moment discuss the result of this plasticity, which has always been dwelt on by all students of the Russian character and nation, whether Russian or foreign.

Dostoievski, giving it the name of 'all-humanness', said it was the main feature of the Russian nation. M. Leroy Beaulieu is inclined to think it is the *faculté maîtresse* of the Russians.[1] Professor Miliukov, in a book on Russia written especially for Western Europeans, dwells on its importance at the very outset of his work, and in commenting on it adds the profoundly suggestive remark that the Russian lacks the 'cement of hypocrisy' – a saying I have often quoted before, but which is too illuminating to be omitted from any survey of the Russian character. Some critics have questioned the existence of this plasticity among the peasantry. This does not coincide with my experience. I have found the Russian workman quick in understanding what is needed of him, and versatile in his power of being able to turn his hand to different trades.

I know an illiterate peasant who, after having served under a French cook, reproduced, and now still reproduces, to the delight of the richer peasants when they employ his services on festive occasions, the finished simplicity, taste, and excellence of the best French cooking. Among the peasants and the soldiers (who are peasants) I have seen astonishingly versatile men – men capable at the same time of cooking an excellent dinner, of mending a watch, of making fireworks, and of painting scenery for a theatre. In casual conversations with peasants and workmen all over the country, I have never found myself up against a brick wall of obstinate non-comprehension, but I have had rather the experience of being constantly met half-way. Foreign architects and various other foreign employers of labour have told me that they find as a rule the Russian artisan adaptable, and quick to understand and carry out a new idea.

As to the suppleness of mind of the Russian in general, of any class, I have never ceased to be astonished by it. Explain to a Russian something of which he is ignorant, a game of cards, an idiomatic or slang expression in a foreign language, indefinable in precise terms, such as, for instance, 'prig', and you will be astonished at the way in which he at once grasps the point at issue; if it is a game, all the various possibilities and combinations; if it is a word or an expression, the shade and value of its meaning.

Try the same experiment with an intelligent German, and you will be astonished at the result.

Another notable instance of this is the appreciation on the part of the Russians of the comic genius of foreign countries, which so often remains a closed and sealed book to outsiders. Witness the popularity in

[1] 'La souplesse de son intelligence paraît sans limite, et cette aisance à tout s'approprier a pu faire obstacle au développement spontané de l'originalité nationale.' – Leroy Beaulieu, Vol. I. [M. B.]

Russia of books whose whole point lies in the *national* quality of their humour, such as, for instance, the works of Jerome K. Jerome, W. W. Jacobs, the plays of Bernard Shaw, the stories of Rudyard Kipling, the essays of G. K. Chesterton. Translations of Mr Shaw's plays are now popular in Russia, and they are, besides this, being frequently produced; but it is a curious fact that it is the humour of them that pleases, and not their serious import. As long as only such plays as *Mrs Warren's Profession* were produced, and stress was laid exclusively on the serious side of the author (for instance, during the revolution some theatre had the preposterous idea – such was the fanatical state of mind of the intellectual bourgeoisie at that time – of producing *The Devil's Disciple* as a revolutionary political play!), he failed to achieve popularity. Now it is different. Since Mr Shaw's *Caesar and Cleopatra* was produced at the Moscow State Theatre, and a complete edition of his plays obtained a cheap circulation, the public had the opportunity of tasting the full savour of his work, and it was instantly appreciated. And the point is that what pleased and attracted was the Irish wit which is peculiar to Mr Bernard Shaw, and not the problems or the sociology with which the Russians have been sated, not to say glutted, during the last fifty years.

With regard to this faculty of comprehension, there is another point of interest which I have often noticed. An all-round development of faculties is much more common in Russia than in other countries. It is much rarer to find in Russia a man who has certain qualities strongly developed and others utterly non-existent, than a man who is developed at all points and on all sides to a certain extent.

In England, for instance, it is common to find a man who is a brilliant Latin scholar, and at the same time incapable of adding two and two, and equally ignorant of higher mathematics or any kindred sciences. Or again, a man who is fond of literature and tone-deaf to music or vice versa, or a man who has an innate understanding of all the physical sciences, or anything to do with mechanics and engineering, and is at the same time totally uninterested in letters or art. In Russia it is much commoner to meet with the type who possesses the rudiments of mathematics, an outline of scientific knowledge and philosophy, as well as a general groundwork of literature, and a smattering of music and art. This is partly the result of an innate versatility, and partly the result of a bureaucratic and democratic system of education. It cuts both ways; and what is gained in comprehensiveness is lost by a corresponding lack of individual originality and a corresponding superficiality.

I have frequently come across Russians who were ashamed if they were caught ignorant of some new or old manifestation in foreign art, literature, or music; they seemed to feel that they had thereby proved themselves lacking in the necessary amount of 'culture' which every educated man is bound to possess.

Indeed, the Russian word for 'culture' (*obrazovanie*[1]) plays an important part with educated Russians. Several Russian landowners and doctors whom I met during the war, used often to say that they considered a man who had no mathematics could not conceivably be called 'cultivated'. But this so-called culture, although it may in some cases be the rich fruit of a comprehensive mind – if it is allied to studiousness and curiosity – is often the superficial and barren result of a bureaucratic education.

This is one instance of the mixed results of the Russian 'plasticity'. Let us now consider some of the others. I have said the quality made at the same time for strength and for weakness, and that the quality as a whole was complemented and corrected by something of another kind. What are its elements of strength, its positive qualities? In the first place and most important is perhaps the large and warm humanity which proceeds from this all-embracing plasticity. The humanity of the Russian people is rich and generous, and its richness, generosity, and warmth give it a strong driving power.

Somebody once prophesied a few years ago that in the future the Americans and the Russians would carry everything before them because of their sheer warmth of heart.

Closely allied to this quality, so that it is, in fact, a part of it, is their Christian charity, their sympathy, which is by far their most pleasing and attractive trait. It enables them not only to exercise a large tolerance towards the failings and foibles of their fellow-creatures, but to understand people different from themselves, and to extract from them and to assimilate what may be profitable to themselves. The second positive result of the Russian plasticity which makes for strength is this: their power of adapting themselves to foreign people, things, places, and circumstances, to what is new, makes them excellent colonists. This is why it is impossible to prophesy what new developments may arise among the Russian people, what turn its history may take, because their adaptability may expand at any moment to larger spheres, from science to politics and political institutions. It opens a wide field. For Russia and the Russian people there is still a vast stretch of 'fresh woods and pastures new', and the Russian, with his peculiar adaptability, has before him vast fields of exploration in every department of life. The career of Peter the Great proves what the Russian temperament is capable of, when the adventurous and adaptable quality of his nature predominates, and exercises free play.

It is, again, perhaps the absence of limits and bars in his nature which accounts for the quality of his energy, when he is energetic. Just as in the region of speculation he will be ready to push his ideas to their logical conclusion, so in the field of action, when he happens to be adventurous and energetic, he will recognize no obstacles and no limits. He will

[1] *Obraz* means a pattern; 'culture' in Russian practically means education according to pattern and up to sample. [M. B.]

237

accomplish miracles, he will make bricks without straw, with gusto and spirit. This is the strong feature of the Russian genius. This is what distinguishes Peter the Great from all other monarchs of genius, Suvorov and Skobeliev from other generals of genius, Pushkin from other writers of genius, the Russian engineers from other engineers of genius, the Russian dancers from other dancers of genius. A dash, a go, an extra flip of energy, a disregard of the inadequacy of the means at hand, a scorn of obstacles and difficulties, a desperate determination to accomplish the end in view.

I think I have now summed up, as far as it is possible to do in a brief summary, the positive qualities making for strength which are the result of the Russian temperament.

Now let us look at the other side: the weakness and defects of the qualities.

I have already mentioned the superficiality of culture arising from the bureaucratic ideal of an all-round culture. Another facet of the humanity of the Russian which makes for weakness is his indulgence: the frequent absence of backbone which Professor Miliukov so happily calls the 'lack of the cement of hypocrisy'. This, of course, cannot help often resulting in laxity, slovenliness, indolence, waste of energy, waste of time, waste of money, disorder, and anarchy. It means that a lower standard is often acquiesced in, when a higher standard is called for by the circumstances; it means that important questions are often settled by a 'What does it matter?' That discipline is not enforced in circumstances when an exact enforcement of discipline is important. I have dwelt on this subject elsewhere in connection with the war and otherwise, and I will not further enlarge on it; an absence of hypocrisy which leads one man to accept another with all his qualities and defects exactly as he is, and so far from blaming him, to understand his weaknesses and to sympathize with them, relying on finding in others, and being certain of receiving from others, a similar measure of indulgence towards his own failings, cannot help having exactly the same result, as Professor Miliukov said, as the absence of cement has on a building.

The building would fall to pieces were this absence of cement not counteracted by the positive qualities which I have already discussed.

Again, the absence of bars and limits in the Russian nature, while it may account at times for the driving power of his energy, is the cause at others of unbridledness of conduct and ideas, of a lack of balance, of extravagant excesses, of a want of consecutiveness in conduct and opinion, a tendency to extreme reactions of mood, to bouts of energy succeeded by bouts of apathy, of rapid alternatives between enthusiasm and scepticism, and of a tendency to give in, to overrate the enemy, and to underestimate and misappreciate one's own strength and capacities.

I noticed this particularly in the war. The officers fell quickly from unwarrantable hope into an altogether unwarrantable pessimism. They failed to take into account that if their own situation was difficult, there was no reason to assume that that of the enemy must necessarily be altogether satisfactory; that if mistakes were being made on their side, that was no proof that the enemy was infallible; and this unwarrantable pessimism had more than once – and especially in the case of the battle of Liaoyang – a fatal influence on their conduct of the campaign, as well as on the *morale* of the troops.

Another result of the Russian plasticity, which makes for weakness, is the lack of discipline which results from it. The most broadly known fact about the Russian people today is its struggle for political liberty: the despotism which has existed in the past; the various efforts made to destroy it, at first by individuals, then by movements, and finally by a greater part of the educated classes of the nation, culminating in a revolution which lasted sporadically for three years.

Now, the lack of political liberty, or the comparative lack of it, compared with that enjoyed by other countries, and the failure of the Russian people to obtain it, in the measure which they desired, when in great numbers they set about to try and do so, seems to me solely and simply due to the absence of personal discipline in the individual Russian, and especially in the Russian of the educated and professional middle-class, who was the prime factor in the revolutionary movement.

Political liberty cannot exist without discipline; and the average professional middle-class Russian in throwing himself into the struggle for political liberty, refused to sacrifice one jet or atom of the personal liberty, *liberté de mœurs*, which he had enjoyed to a greater extent than the inhabitants of any other European country, and which was not only incompatible with discipline, but strongly conducive to a despotic behaviour as far as his fellow-creatures were concerned. There is no country in the world where the individual enjoys so great a measure of personal liberty, where the *liberté de mœurs* is so great as it is in Russia; where the individual man can do as he pleases with so little interference or criticism on the part of his neighbours; where there is so little moral censorship, where liberty of abstract thought or aesthetic production is so great.

Nobody, for instance, would dream in Russia of calling a man in a public position to task for the irregularities of his private life; such irregularities, whether he is divorced, or whether he has an unofficial family, are matters of profound indifference to him. The censorship of the theatre, such as exists in England, would be incredible to a Russian. Political and religious censure there have existed, and at one time they weighed heavily on the Press, but to forbid a play of Maeterlinck or Ibsen or Bernard Shaw, on the ground that it might have an undermining effect on the morals of the public, would be an unheard-of thing in Russia.

Again, the Press often discusses with the utmost freedom matters which are not mentioned in English newspapers, and as for books, there is no subject which they will fight shy of.

Certain thinkers have agreed that personal liberty – liberty of thought and of manners – always flourishes more freely under a political despotism than under a political democracy. Renan, for instance, cites the régime of Nero in this respect, which he compares favourably, as far as liberty of thought is concerned, with the stringent censorship exercised by the Athenian Government in its prime.

There are certain thinkers who consider such liberty of thought and manners to be a more precious boon than any amount of voting privileges and indirect control over official administration, State legislation, and State expenditure. However that may be, one thing is certain: in order to obtain political liberty, a certain measure of this unlimited freedom of conduct, behaviour, and manners, on the part of the individual, must necessarily be sacrificed. The Russian intellectual bourgeoisie, the Russian proletariat, and, above all, the Russian militant revolutionaries, failed to see the matter in this light; and by their arbitrary conduct, their inability to sacrifice party spirit, personal and class interests and jealousies to the interests of the community; by their failure to act with sufficient discipline to ensure a necessary minimum of order and co-operation; by obstinately refusing to take into account the interests of their fellow-creatures, if they happened to be at variance with the theories they were propounding, they succeeded in estranging, and finally in losing, the support of public opinion at large, which they had had behind them at the outset, and in rendering a revolution, which should change the whole system of government, impossible.

They certainly achieved something, and what they did achieve was the result of temporary co-operation and temporary discipline, which were, however, of short duration.

Disinclination to submit to discipline is one of the negative results of the Russian 'plasticity'; whether it is a fault or a quality I do not pretend to determine. Everybody is at liberty to hold his own views on the subject; but it is certainly the negation of political liberty and the chief obstacle the Russians have to overcome in its achievement.

I think I may be said now to have mentioned the more important weaknesses which accompany, or perhaps are the result of, the virtues of the Russian quality of 'plasticity'. Another element in the Russian character remains to be considered which is the very opposite of plasticity.

There may be a hundred intangible influences and currents which correct this malleability; but in the case of the Great Russian, the quality of an opposite kind to plasticity and malleability which first leaps to the mind, and which is the most salient, is his spirit of positivism and realism. I say the Great Russian, because not only among the other Slav races, but also among the Poles and the Little Russians, this quality is conspicuously absent. It is perhaps the result of the admixture of Finnish alloy in the Great Russian metal; or perhaps it is the result of the severer climate; or, more likely still, of both. It permeates all classes of Great Russians. With the peasants it takes the form of a broad common sense. Shrewdness and common, practical sense are the qualities by which he sets the highest store; great is his scorn for a man 'without a Tsar in his head', as his own proverb says. The Russian peasant has a large store of proverbs which are the apt and often the picturesque expression of a shrewd and practical wisdom. On the other hand, it is difficult to get a Russian peasant to understand an abstract word. I once had a discussion with a peasant about 'distance'. He said, 'I suppose that is what we call *versts*.'

Even in his religion, and especially in the observance of it, the Russian peasant will display a solid matter-of-factness.

This positive quality, this realism, which is solid, substantial, and rooted in the earth, and alien and inimical to what is abstract and metaphysical, is apparent everywhere among the Great Russians: in their songs, in their folklore, in their fairy tales, in their literature, their drama, their art, and their poetry. Compare the most romantic poets of Russia, Lermontov and Pushkin, for instance, with the romantic poets of other countries; it is like comparing pictures of the Dutch School with pictures by Blake. Lermontov is more closely akin in spirit to Thackeray than to Shelley and Byron, and Pushkin to Stendal than to Victor Hugo and Musset. Simplicity, naturalness, closeness to fact and to nature, realism not in any narrow sense of this or that aesthetic school, but in the sense of love of reality and nearness to it, are the main distinctive qualities of all Russian art: from the epic songs of the fifteenth century and the fairy tales handed down from immemorial tradition by word of mouth, down to the novels of Tolstoy and Turgenev, the fables of Krylov, the poems of Nekrasov, the tales of Gorki, and the plays of Ostrovski and of Chekhov.[1]

This positivism, this practical spirit, this innate realism, acts as a powerful antidote to the Slav plasticity and flexibility. It is the hard kernel in a soft fruit. It accounts for the tough element in the Great Russian, his spirit of resource and practical success in dealing with men and things, his tenacity and stubbornness.

Therefore, if I were asked to sum up as briefly as possible the characteristics of the Great Russian, I should do so thus: I will put the positive and negative qualities in parallel tables.

---

[1] 'Selon la remarque d'un de ses écrivains, c'est dans les peines séculaires de la colonisation de la Grande Russie que s'est formée cette disposition à voir en toute chose le but immédiat et le côté réel de la vie. . . . Il règne dans la nation, dans les sphères instruites comme dans les masses ignorantes, un positivisme plus ou moins réfléchi.' – Leroy Beaulieu. [M. B.]

241

| | Positive | Negative |
|---|---|---|
| 1. Plasticity – resulting in: | (a) Humaneness. | Indulgence and laxity. |
| | (b) Assimilation. | Lack of originality. |
| | (c) Suppleness of mind. | Superficiality. |
| | (d) Absence of hypocrisy. | Lack of backbone. |
| | (e) Liberty of thought and of *moeurs*. | Lack of individual discipline and consequently of political liberty. |
| 2. Absence of bonds, bars, and barriers (which may be said to be closely allied to plasticity). | (a) Spasmodic energy. | Extravagance of conduct and a lack of sense of proportion and balance. |
| | (b) Audacity of thought. | Timidity of conduct. Abrupt alternations and transitions from energy to indolence, from optimism to pessimism, and from revolt to submission. Fear of responsibility. |
| 3. Positivism – Realism and common sense. | (a) Patience and unity of purpose. | Lack of individuality, independence, and of civic courage. |
| | (b) Co-operative energy. | |

I think I could substantiate this list by many examples; but when all is said and done, generalizations are unsatisfactory and misleading things, for human nature, and especially the Russian character, is complex and subtle – *ondoyant et divers*.

And yet, although generalizations are misleading, they are, I know from experience, often as welcome to the reader as they are tempting to the writer. For if they happen to be suggestive they give the critic a stone to sharpen his wits on, and they provide the serious with a text and the careless with a catchword. And there is nothing the careless reader likes so much as a catchword. It saves him the bother of reading the book while enabling him to discuss it. It is for this reason that I will close this chapter of generalizations with one final generalization. It is this: If we were asked to name three English types which in English history or fiction, between them summed up the English character, and supposing we said, Henry VIII, John Milton, and Mr Pickwick – what three Russian types, in history and fiction, would correspond to them, and sum up the Russian character?

I for one would answer Peter the Great, Prince Mwyshkin, and Khlestakov. And I would add that in almost every Russian you will find elements of all of these three characters.

I will sum up their characteristics as briefly as possible for those who are unacquainted with them, for Mwyshkin and Khlestakov belong to fiction. Peter the Great I have dealt with at length in a chapter that is to come. Suffice it to say here that he was an unparalleled craftsman, the incarnation of energy; unbridled in all things; humane, but subject to electric explosions of rage; he spoke well, wrote badly, and drank deep. He made bricks without straw; he did everything himself. He was an apprentice to the day of his death, and never an amateur.

Prince Mwyshkin is the hero of one of Dostoievsky's novels. He is a so-called 'idiot', a 'pure fool' only with this difference, that he is not a fool. The weapons and vices of the world fall powerless from off his disinterestedness; his ingenuousness sees through the stratagems of the crafty and the deceits of the cunning; his love is stronger than the hatred of his fellow-creatures; his sympathy more effective than their spite; he is an oasis in an arid world; he is simple, sensible, and acute, and these qualities are the branches of a plant which is rooted in goodness.

Khlestakov is the hero of a famous play by Gogol, 'The Government Inspector', and I cannot do better than quote Gogol's own summary of the character:

'About twenty-three, thin, small, rather silly; with, as they say, no Tsar in his head; one of those men who in the public offices are called "utterly null". He talks and acts with the utmost irrelevance; without the slightest forethought or consecutiveness. He is incapable of fixing and concentrating his attention on any idea whatsoever.'

Besides this he, in some respects, reminds one of the description of Commander Sin in the *Modern Traveller*:

'Lazy and somewhat of a liar;
A trifle slovenly in dress;
A little prone to drunkenness;
A gambler also to excess,
And never known to pay'.

Now as a final generalization I say that in every Russian there is something of Peter the Great, of Mwyshkin, and of Khlestakov.

# The Discovery of Anton Chekhov

(from *With the Russians in Manchuria*)

MOSCOW

*April* 1904

WHEN I started from Moscow for the Far East, everything was going in that city much the same as usual. The most interesting thing in Moscow at the present day, if you have heard the services and the glorious bass-singing at the Cathedral of the Assumption and at St Saviour's, is one particular theatre which is worth mentioning in any book connected with Russian affairs, because it is a sign of the times, not only artistically but politically, and exercises a considerable influence. People are in the habit of saying that in Russia there is no middle class. I cannot conceive what they mean. It exists nonetheless, and it includes the professional class, the world of doctors, lawyers, professors, teachers, artists, the higher and middle merchant class, and besides these (a fact which is not realized), nine-tenths of the officials, and since the introduction of compulsory military service two-thirds, if not three-quarters, of the officers. Most of the generals now in Manchuria, including Generals Kuropatkin and Sakharov, belong to this class. It not only exists, but it is enormously important, since it calls itself the 'intelligentsia', and does in fact number among its constituents nearly all the 'intellectuals' of Russia and all that is most advanced in the world of science, literature, and philosophy. Dostoyevsky belonged to this class; but perhaps its most characteristic and representative spokesman and portrayer is an author who died last year,[1] and whose death was mourned with sorrow by hundreds of Russians even in the wilds of Manchuria, namely, Anton Chekhov. He is famous as a writer of short stories portraying the life of the middle classes in Russia with the same accuracy and insight with which Tolstoy depicted the upper classes and Gogol the officials of a past generation. Some of Chekhov's most successful work was written for the stage; it has been acted with care and exquisite art; the result is that it has been

[1] Written 1905. [M. B.]

244

triumphantly successful; and it has given voice perhaps more than anything else during the last ten years to the feelings, aspirations, disappoint-
ments, the hopes, fears, and disbelieving of the educated Russian people.
For that reason it is important and interesting to any one who is following
Russian affairs at this moment. Chekhov's plays are acted at a theatre
called the Artistic Theatre at Moscow. This theatre was started originally
about four years ago as a company of well-to-do amateurs, under the
leadership of M. Stanislavsky. They began, I was told, by acting Sullivan's
*Mikado* for fun, and continued acting for their pleasure, and resolved to
spare neither trouble nor expense in making their performances as perfect
as possible. They took a theatre and gave performances for nothing or
next to nothing, but their success was so instantaneous and so great,
their public so affluent, that by degrees they were obliged to take a new
theatre, charge higher prices, and at the present time they form what is
certainly the best all-round company of Russia, if not of Europe. It
resembles the *Théâtre Antoine* of Paris, both as regards the quality of
the acting and the kind of plays acted and the extraordinary attention
which is paid to detail.

The acting has an advantage over that of the French School in being
more natural. The character of the plays acted is curious, if not unique,
on the European stage. The clash of events in them is subservient to the
human figure, and the human figure itself is subservient to the atmosphere
in which the figures are plunged.

The *répertoire* of the theatre is varied, and includes *Julius Caesar*,
Gorky's *Lowest Depths*, Hauptmann's *Lonely Lives*, and works of Ibsen
and Tolstoy; but by far the most interesting work produced is that of
Anton Chekhov, because his plays reflect, with far greater fidelity and
less exaggeration than those of Gorky, the soul of the Russian people at
the present day. This is the reason of the great popularity of the plays;
for never did plays contain less action, less 'clash of wills', less *scènes-à-
faire* or any of those things which are supposed to be essential to dramatic
success. They are enough to make Sarcey turn in his grave. And the success,
it must not be forgotten, is substantial, concrete, and financial, and
not one of esteem. It is difficult to get places, even some days beforehand,
for a Chekhov play. His work resembles both in its character and in the
character of its success that of Mr Bernard Shaw, minus the clash of
ideas and the polemics. He is as a dramatist a softened, under-exposed,
Slavonic Bernard Shaw, not without humour, but with the wit, warfare,
and fantasy left out. His importance is, as I said before, more than
artistic; it is political – although politics are never directly mentioned in
his plays. Their importance lies in the fact that no influence can be more
effectual than that of the stage, especially in troublous times. 'Organize
the theatre,' Matthew Arnold said; 'the theatre is irresistible.' Well, the
theatre is almost the only thing in Russia which is organized, and it is

very well organized indeed. Its effect, therefore, can be exceedingly great. Chekhov never mentions politics; but what he leaves unsaid, what he suggests, is far more potent and effectual than any number of harangues or polemical discussion. He shows the Russian soul crying out in the desert; he shows the hopelessness, the straining after impossible ideals, the people who have been longing for the dawn and condemned to the twilight chiefly owing to their own weakness. He shows the difficulty of solving questions and the heart-sickness of those who think about it, in exactly the same way Mr Shaw shows the difficulty of dealing with the Irish question in *John Bull's Other Island*.

I will give a short analysis of one of his most successful plays – *Uncle Vania*. The play deals with scenes of country life, and the thread of action which connects these scenes is of the slightest.

We are introduced into the world of the well-to-do upper middle class, the class corresponding to that with which Ibsen deals. Someone once defined Ibsen's characters as a pack of shopkeepers wrangling over an antimacassar, and his plays as an intolerable mixture of sordid bourgeoisie and hysteria. Chekhov's characters are not sordid; hysterical some of them are, but their hysteria is interesting because there is reason for it. The reason being the profound discontent of the educated people with the manner in which they are governed, a discontent so hopeless and insistent as to lead to hysteria.

The curtain rises on a garden; a well-to-do house with a terrace visible in the background. In the foreground a large table is laid for tea. But something in the aspect of the table leads one to think that the samovar has been waiting long; there is an air of great unpunctuality and vagueness about the whole place. It is three o'clock of an August afternoon, insufferably hot, dull, and sultry, Astrov, a country doctor, has been called to minister to Professor Vladimirov, who is living in the house and suffers from gout. Astrov talks with an old woman servant, and in a few sentences reveals that he is suffering from 'taedium vitae'. Towards the age of forty, said a cynic, men tire of honesty and women of virtue. Astrov is reaching that age. He is overworked and is sickened by the monotony, the labour, the squalor, and the seeming futility of a country doctor's existence.

Great attention is paid to details in this theatre, and by the way the doctor kills flies on his cheek, and other similar trifles, the sultry oppressiveness of the thundery day seems to reach us from over the footlights.

Voinitzky appears next – he is 'Uncle Vania' – after whom the play is named. His position is as follows. His sister was the first wife of Professor Vladimirov. She died leaving an only daughter, Sonia. Voinitzky's father bought the estate in which the action takes place as a dowry for Sonia. Voinitzky renounced his claim to the succession in favour of Sonia, but his father in buying the estate was not able to pay the full sum due, and died leaving behind him a debt of 25,000 roubles (£2,500). Professor

Vladimirov married a second time, a young and beautiful wife, Elena. Voinitzky undertook the administration of the estate, and with the help of his niece Sonia, in the course of ten years, paid off the debt left by his father. These business matters are revealed later on.

The situation at the beginning of Act I is that the professor and his young wife have settled down on the estate. Two facts are plain, that Voinitzky is in a highly strung state of nervous excitement, and that his excitement is due to the professor. We gather that the professor resembles both as to situation and as to character Casaubon in *Middlemarch*. Indeed, throughout the play we are more than once reminded of *Middlemarch*. The professor's presence, Voinitzky tells Astrov, has had a disastrous effect on his manner of living and has introduced a general disorder into the household, for the professor often 'breakfasts at five o'clock tea and dines on the following day'. Yet we guess that it is something more than the professor's irregular habits which have excited Voinitzky to such a pitch.

In answer to Astrov's questions Voinitzky gives his views on the professor. He describes him as a dried-up biscuit, a learned fish, who lives on the estate of his first wife because he cannot afford to live in a town – a grumbler who has been undeservedly lucky, who after writing for twenty-five years is utterly unknown. Astrov suggests that Voinitzky envies him. Voinitzky admits it to the full, pointing to the miraculous way in which this piece of 'diseased egoism' has attracted to it the 'love o' women'. No Don Juan, he says, ever had such success. His first wife adored him, and he inspired his mother-in-law with a lasting veneration verging on idolatry; his second wife gave him her youth and beauty. All have believed in him and slaved for him.

We afterwards learn that Voinitzky slaved for him also, because he believed in him. 'What for?' he asks bitterly, and 'Why?' Elena, Sonia, and Voinitzky's mother make their appearance. The professor is seen walking in the garden in an overcoat and goloshes, in spite of the heat, and from the conversations which take place until the end of the first act we see that Sonia is in love with Astrov, and would make him an excellent wife. We see that Sonia is an admirable character, but unfortunately devoid of beauty and all charm. We see that Voinitzky is in love with Elena, that Elena's interest has been awakened in Astrov, and that she herself is a kind of land mermaid, a middle-class Pagan, not immoral but amoral; a passionless Cleopatra, a good-natured Mary Stuart, a well-meaning Circe; one of those half-sentimental, half-sensuous creatures who give nothing and yet are well content that all who surround them should be spell-bound by the aroma of their personality, while they maintain, even to themselves, the theory that they are intensely harmless and respectable.

Practically nothing happens in the second act. We see quite clearly that Sonia is in love with Astrov, and that he is unaware and careless of the fact; that Voinitzky, more nervous than ever, pursues Elena in vain with his advances; yet in spite of this want of action the attention of the audience is riveted. We are made to feel Astrov's hopelessness at the life of a country doctor in Russia; the ploughing of sands, the physical disgust, and still greater, the moral sickness at the evils which he is powerless to remedy. I often heard the doctors in the war talk exactly in the strain in which Astrov talks in this play. It is not the suffering we encounter which depresses us, they used to say, but the evils which should be instantly remedied, and cannot be remedied, and which are partly inherent in the very character of the people.

We are also made to feel the atmosphere reigning in the house, and emanating from the characters of its inmates. The effect, as Astrov says, is one of suffocation – the professor with his gout and books, Voinitzky a bundle of nerves and hypochondria, Elena who merely eats, sleeps, and walks about, shedding the intoxicating influence of her beauty, languorous and soft, herself as empty of true substance as a sachet.

In the third act Sonia confesses her love for Astrov to Elena, and asks her to find out if her case is hopeless, and if so, to persuade him to cease from visiting the house. Elena reveals the situation to him in a few delicate hints. He looks at her with amazement, and then adopts a tone of cynical brutality. 'If you had told me that two months ago,' he says, 'all might have been different; but now you know very well why, and on account of whom, I have come here day after day: for a whole month I have given up everything for you, and this has delighted you.' Elena plays the part of injured innocence; he takes her in his arms and kisses her violently. At that moment Voinitzky enters and witnesses the scene.

A moment or two afterwards the professor arrives. He has summoned the family to talk business. They all enter and sit down, and the professor makes a speech, prefacing it with the remark that he is not a practical man – a speech in which he proposes that the estate should be sold, and that he should buy a small country house in Finland with the proceeds. Voinitzky interrupts him with violence, and in an ever-increasing crescendo of fury cries out that the professor, who says he is a child in these matters, wishes to turn him out after his ten years of slavery, and to sell Sonia's estate. 'You have ruined my life,' he cries. 'You are my worst enemy; I know what course to take,' and he rushes out of the room. The professor follows shortly. A pistol shot is heard. Voinitzky has fired on the professor. The professor returns, calling on all to stop Voinitzky. Voinitzky enters again, and fires at the professor, but misses him a second time.

The action of the fourth act can be stated in a few words. The professor and his wife leave the house. Astrov goes back to his practice, leaving Voinitzky and Sonia to resume their quiet life of regular work. And yet in saying this I have omitted all that is important in this act, which is the most striking of the four, and impresses the audience the most deeply. It takes place in Voinitzky's room. On one side of the stage is his sitting-room, on the other what serves for the office of the estate. It is an autumn evening. Astrov and Elena take leave of one another. 'I wish to beg one thing of you,' she says to him – 'to respect me.' He smiles derisively. She is just that kind of woman who would like to have what can only be gained by loss of respect and yet be respected.

'If you had stayed here longer,' says Astrov, 'I should have been a ruined man and you . . . would not have improved. Well, you are going. . . . Let me kiss you . . . to say good-bye. . . . Yes? (kisses her). Now . . .' Elena (going to the door): 'I wish you all possible happiness. (She returns and flings herself in his arms; they then hurriedly break away from each other.) It is time to go.' Astrov: *Finita la comedia.*

The professor enters with Voinitzky, Sonia, and his mother-in-law, and bids good-bye. He then leaves the house with his wife. The others go to see them off. Voinitzky and Astrov are left alone. The bells of the horses are heard outside. One after another, Sonia, the mother-in-law, and the old woman servant enter the room saying: 'They've gone!' Described, this appears to be insignificant; seen, acted as it is with incomparable naturalness, it is indescribably effective. In this scene a particular mood, which we have all felt, is captured and rendered; a certain chord is struck which exists in all of us: that kind of 'toothache at heart' which we feel when a sudden parting takes place and we are left behind. The parting need not necessarily be a sad one. But the tenor of our life is interrupted. As a rule the leaves of life are turned over so quickly and noiselessly by Time that we are not aware of the process. In the case of a sudden parting we hear the leaf of life turn over and fall back into the great blurred book of the past, read, finished, and irrevocable. It is this hearing of the turning leaf which Chekhov has rendered merely by three people coming into the room one after another and saying, 'They've gone!'

The intonation with which the old servant said 'They've gone' – an intonation of peculiar cheerfulness with which servants love to underline what is melancholy – was marvellous. Finally Astrov goes. Voinitzky's mother reads a pamphlet by the lamplight, the clatter of the horses' hoofs and the jingling of bells are heard dying away in the distance, and Voinitzky and Sonia set to work at their accounts, and the infinite monotony of their life begins once more.

The play is received at every performance by the audience, although it has been played nearly a hundred times, with boundless enthusiasm.

# The Antichrist

## (from *Half a Minute's Silence & Other Stories*)

IN THE VILLAGE OF X, which is in the government of O, in Central Russia, there were two men: one was called Michael and the other was called Andrew. They were both deeply religious and concerned with the things of a world which is not this world. They spent days and nights in reading the Scriptures and in pondering over the meaning of difficult texts. They had both resolved in their early youth never to marry, for they considered that the human race had something so radically bad about it that the sooner it came to an end the better. They decided, therefore, that it was their duty not to prolong its existence. But when they attained to early manhood the parents of Andrew contracted an alliance for him, and he was wedded to a girl named Masha. Their union was not blessed with offspring, and Michael, who continued to lead a solitary life, with rigorous fasting and uninterrupted meditation, said such was the will of Providence. The young wife of Andrew did not share the views of the mystic, and she yearned to be the mother of a child. Unbeknown to her husband, she sought one night the Wise Woman of the village, who was skilled in finding lost objects, and who was versed in the properties of herbs, and knew the words of power which cured the sick of dreadful disease.

Masha sought the Wise Woman in the night, and told her her trouble. The Wise Woman lit a candle, muttered a brief saying in which the name of King David was mentioned, and that of a darker Prince. She gave her a small green herb, telling her to eat it on the first moonless night in June, and that her wish would be fulfilled.

Masha obeyed the Wise Woman's behest. A year passed by and the wish of her heart was granted. A son was born to her. And Masha and Andrew rejoiced greatly over this. But when Michael heard of it his spirit was troubled. He searched the Scriptures, and the meaning of the event became clear to him. He sought Andrew and said to him:

'This is the work of Satan. You have dabbled in black magic, and you

250

are in danger of eternal perdition. Moreover, the truth has been revealed to me – the child which has been born to you is none other than the Antichrist, of which the Book of Revelation tells. And that is why our poor country is distressful, seething with trouble, sedition, and revolt, and why our Sovereign is vexed, and why evil days have fallen upon Russia, our Mother. We must slay the Antichrist, and immediately the dark cloud will be lifted from our land, and peace and prosperity shall come to us once more.'

That night Michael bade Andrew and Masha come to his house. It was a small, one-storeyed, wooden cottage, thatched with straw. It was swept and clean, and in one corner of the room were many glittering images of the Queen of Heaven and the Saints, before which burned small red lights; and besides this Michael had erected a shrine on which more than a dozen thin waxen tapers were burning. Michael welcomed Andrew and his wife to his house, and the elders of the village also, and they spent an hour in chanting and in prayer, each holding a candle in his hand; but to the priest he said no word of this matter, for he did not trust him nor believe him to be possessed of celestial grace. After they had prayed for an hour, Michael said to Masha:

'Go home and fetch your child.'

Masha obeyed, and returned presently, bearing the infant for whose advent she had so sorely longed, and whose coming had been the cause of great joy to her. Michael took the infant and said:

'In the body of this child is the power of Satan: in the body of this child is the Antichrist of whom the Scriptures tell – this is the cause of the misfortunes which have visited our dear country, and vexed the spirit of our Lord and Sovereign.'

He then blew out all the lights and the tapers in the room: it was pitch dark, and no sound was heard save the muttering of Michael's continuous prayer. Masha trembled, for she was afraid. Michael took the infant. It lay quite still, for it was asleep.

And as Michael took the infant, he said, 'We must exorcise the spirit and slay the Antichrist, who has been born in this child to be the bane of Russia and to vex the heart of our Sovereign!'

And Michael bade the people who were gathered together in the room – there were five men, the eldest in the village, and seven women – be prepared for the great event, and he lifted his voice, and in a wailing whisper he addressed the Evil Spirit.

'Evil Spirit,' he said, 'Antichrist, of whom the Holy Scriptures tell, through the dark dealings of our brother Andrew and his wife, who have trafficked with Satan, thou hast found a way into the body of this child, but it is written that the troubles of Russia and of our Sovereign shall be at their thickest at thy advent, but shall diminish and pass away with thy disappearance. Evil Spirit, I conjure thee, leave the body of this child

251

Then the infant cried plaintively, twice.

'Hark!' said Michael, in a solemn voice, 'the spirit of the Antichrist is speaking. Hark to the cry of Satan, who is leaving the body of the child. Pray, pray with all your might, and help me to slay the Antichrist.'

And fear came upon everybody, nor durst they utter in the stillness, but their spirits were spellbound and seemed to be drawn, tense and taut as stretched wires, in that effort of prayer for the passing of the spirit of Satan and for the slaying of the Antichrist.

The infant cried once again – and then it cried no more! . . .

'The Antichrist has been slain,' said Michael, and a deeper stillness came on the assembly. 'The Antichrist,' said Michael, 'must be buried.' And he walked out of his cottage into the yard where in a shed his horse and cart were kept. He unloosed his horse and said, 'Whither the horse shall lead, thither must we follow.'

The horse trotted slowly down the deserted street. That night there was neither moon nor star in the sky. Beyond the village was a marshy plain. It was just before dawn, and in the thick velvet darkness of the sky there was a glow as of a living sapphire. They reached the marsh, and there the horse stopped, and began to browse.

'It is here that the Antichrist must be buried,' said Michael. And they buried the infant by the reedy marsh. And all this time neither Andrew nor Masha, nor the elders, nor the women who were there, spoke a single word; and when they had finished burying the infant a breeze came from the east, and the dawn, grey and chilly, trembled over the horizon, and the wild ducks swept from the marsh, uttered their cry, and flew away into distance, seeking the fields.

The spell that had kept this assembly mute and speechless vanished with the vanishing darkness. The noises of life began: the creaking of carts was heard from the village, and the cocks were crowing.

Andrew and Masha looked at each other, and a great fear came upon them, and indeed upon all the assembly, for what they had done. They did not speak, but returned severally to their homes; and Masha, when she reached her home, too frightened to cry or even to speak, sat motionless before the swinging cradle which hung from the roof of her cottage, and which was now empty. And Andrew durst not look at her. Presently he left the house and sought the dwelling of the priest. The priest let him in, and there he found Michael, who, likewise overcome with terror and misgivings as to what had been done, had come to tell the story.

The priest reported the whole matter to the local policeman, who in his turn reported it to the police captain of the district, and three days afterwards Michael, Andrew, Masha, and the others were locked up in the gaol of a neighbouring town, and a day after their arrest an old woman of the village sought out the police captain and asked to see him.

'I was present,' she said to him, 'at the slaying of the Antichrist. I held the candle in my hands myself when the evil spirit was exorcised, and the cause of all Russia's trouble was destroyed. They say the Tsar has given money to the others for having destroyed his enemy; and I, who am poor and old, and who was there also, have received nothing. Let me receive my due. Give me the money that the Tsar owes me, for I also helped to slay the Antichrist.'

This story is true. It happened last September, and was recorded in the newspapers, with many more details than I have told. And at the station of Kozlov, as I have already related, in the government of Tambov, between the hours of midnight and 2 a.m., a railway guard told it to myself and a newsvendor, and when he had finished telling it he sighed and bewailed the blindness of his fellow-creatures, the peasants of Russian villages, who, as he wisely said, had so much kindness in their hearts, but were often led through their ignorance to do dreadful deeds.

# Russalka

## (from *Half a Minute's Silence & Other Stories*)

PETER, OR PETRUSHKA, which was the name he was known by, was the carpenter's mate; his hair was like light straw, and his eyes were mild and blue. He was good at his trade; a quiet and sober youth; thoughtful, too, for he knew how to read and had read several books when he was still a boy. A translation of *Monte Cristo* once fell into his hands, and this story had kindled his imagination and stirred in him the desire to travel, to see new countries and strange people. He had made up his mind to leave the village and to try his luck in one of the big towns, when, before he was eighteen, something happened to him which entirely changed the colour of his thoughts and the range of his desires. It was an ordinary experience enough: he fell in love. He fell in love with Tatiana, who worked in the starch factory. Tatiana's eyes were grey, her complexion was white, her features small and delicate, and her hair a beautiful dark brown with gold lights and black shadows in it; her movements were quick and her glance keen; she was like a swallow.

It happened when the snows melted and the meadows were flooded; the first fine day in April. The larks were singing over the plains, which were beginning to show themselves once more under the melting snow; the sun shone on the large patches of water, and turned the flooded meadows in the valley into a fantastic vision. It was on a Sunday after church that this new thing happened. He had often seen Tatiana before: that day she was different and new to him. It was as if a bandage had been taken from his eyes, and at the same moment he realized that Tatiana was a new Tatiana. He also knew that the old world in which he had lived hitherto had crumbled to pieces; and that a new world, far brighter and more wonderful, had been created for him. As for Tatiana, she loved him at once. There was no delay, no hesitation, no misunderstanding, no doubt: and at the first not much speech; but first love came to them straight and swift, with the first sunshine of the spring, as it does to the birds.

254

All the spring and summer they kept company and walked out together in the evenings. When the snows entirely melted and the true spring came, it came with a rush; in a fortnight's time all the trees except the ash were green, and the bees boomed round the thick clusters of pear-blossom and apple-blossom, which shone like snow against the bright azure. During that time Petrushka and Tatiana walked in the apple orchard in the evening and they talked to each other in the divinest of all languages, the language of first love, which is no language at all but a confused medley and murmur of broken phrases, whisperings, twitterings, pauses, and silences—a language so wonderful that it cannot be put down into speech or words, although Shakespeare and the very great poets translate the spirit of it into music, and the great musicians catch the echo of it in their song. Then a fortnight later, when the woods were carpeted and thick with lilies of the valley, Petrushka and Tatiana walked in the woods and picked the last white violets, and later again they sought the alleys of the landlord's property, where the lilac bushes were in blossom and fragrant, and there they listened to the nightingale, the bird of spring. Then came the summer, the fragrance of the beanfields, and the ripening of corn and the wonderful long twilights, and July, when the corn, ripe and tall and stiff, changed the plains into a vast rippling ocean of gold.

After the harvest, at the very beginning of autumn, they were to be married. There had been a slight difficulty about money. Tatiana's father had insisted that Petrushka should produce a certain not very large sum; but the difficulty had been overcome and the money had been found. There were no more obstacles, everything was smooth and settled. Petrushka no longer thought of travels in foreign lands; he had forgotten the old dreams which *Monte Cristo* had once kindled in him.

It was in the middle of August that the carpenter received instructions from the landowner to make some wooden steps and a small raft and to fix them up on the banks of the river for the convenience of bathers. It did not take the carpenter and Petrushka long to make these things, and one afternoon Petrushka drove down to the river to fix them in their place. The river was broad, the banks were wooded with willow trees, and the undergrowth was thick, for the woods reached to the river bank, which was flat, but which ended sheer above the water over a slope of mud and roots, so that a bather needed steps or a raft or a springboard, so as to dive or to enter and leave the water with comfort.

Petrushka put the steps in their place – which was where the wood ended – and made fast the floating raft to them. Not far from the bank the ground was marshy and the spot was suspected by some people of being haunted by malaria. It was a still, sultry day. The river was like oil, the sky clouded but not entirely overclouded, and among the high banks of grey cloud there were patches of blue.

When Petrushka had finished his job, he sat on the wooden steps, and rolling some tobacco into a primitive cigarette, contemplated the grey, oily water and the willow trees. It was too late in the year, he thought, to make a bathing-place. He dipped his hand in the water: it was cold, but not too cold. Yet in a fortnight's time it would not be pleasant to bathe. However, people had their whims, and he mused on the scheme of the universe which ordained that certain people should have whims, and that others should humour those whims whether they liked it or not. Many people – many of his fellow-workers – talked of the day when the universal levelling would take place and when all men could be equal. Petrushka did not much believe in the advent of that day; he was not quite sure whether he ardently desired it; in any case, he was happy as he was.

At that moment he heard two sharp, short sounds, less musical than a pipe and not so loud or harsh as a scream. He looked up. A kingfisher had flown across the oily water. Petrushka shouted; and the kingfisher skimmed over the water once more and disappeared in the trees on the other side of the river. Petrushka rolled and lit another cigarette. Presently he heard the two sharp sounds once more, and the kingfisher darted again across the water: a piece of fish was in its beak. It disappeared into the bank of the river on the same side on which Petrushka was sitting, only lower down.

'Its nest must be there,' thought Petrushka, and he remembered that he had heard it said that no one had ever been able to carry off a kingfisher's nest intact. Why should he not be the first person to do so? He was skilful with his fingers, his touch was sure and light. It was evidently a carpenter's job, and few carpenters had the leisure or opportunity to look for kingfishers' nests. What a rare present it would be for Tatiana – a whole kingfisher's nest with every bone in it intact.

He walked stealthily through the bushes down the bank of the river, making as little noise as possible. He thought he had marked the spot where the kingfisher had dived into the bank. As he walked, the undergrowth grew thicker and the path darker, for he had reached the wood, on the outskirts and end of which was the spot where he had made the steps. He walked on and on without thinking, oblivious of his surroundings, until he suddenly realized that he had gone too far. Moreover, he must have been walking for some time, for it was getting dark, or was it a thunder-shower? The air, too, was unbearably sultry; he stopped and wiped his forehead with a big print handkerchief. It was impossible to reach the bank from the place where he now stood, as he was separated from it by a wide ditch of stagnant water, so he retraced his footsteps through the wood. It grew darker and darker; it must be, he thought, the evening deepening and no storm.

All at once he started; he had heard a sound, a high pipe. Was it the kingfisher? He paused and listened. Distinctly, and not far off in the undergrowth, he heard a laugh, a woman's laugh. It flashed across his mind that it might be Tatiana, but it was not her laugh. Something rustled in the bushes to the left of him; he followed the rustling and it led him through the bushes – he had now passed the ditch – to the river bank. The sun had set behind the woods from which he had just emerged; the sky was as grey as the water, and there was no reflection of the sunset in the east. Except the water and the trees he saw nothing; there was not a sound to be heard, not a ripple on the river, not a whisper from the woods.

Then all at once the stillness was broken again by quick rippling laughter immediately behind him. He turned sharply round, and saw a woman in the bushes: her eyes were large and green and sad; her hair straggling and dishevelled; she was dressed in reeds and leaves; she was very pale. She stared at him fixedly and smiled, showing gleaming teeth, and when she smiled there was no light nor laughter in her eyes, which remained sad and green and glazed like those of a drowned person. She laughed again and ran into the bushes. Petrushka ran after her, but although he was quite close to her he lost all trace of her immediately. It was as if she had vanished under the earth or into the air.

'It's a Russalka,' thought Petrushka, and he shivered. Then he added to himself, with the pride of the new scepticism he had learnt from the factory hands, 'There is no such thing; only women believe in such things. It was some drunken woman.'

Petrushka walked quickly back to the edge of the wood, where he had left his cart, and drove home. The next day was Sunday, and Tatiana noticed that he was different – moody, melancholy, and absent-minded. She asked him what was the matter; he said his head ached. Towards five o'clock he told her – they were standing outside her cottage – that he was obliged to go to the river to work.

'Today is holiday,' she said quietly.

'I left something there yesterday: one of my tools. I must fetch it,' he explained.

Tatiana looked at him, and her intuition told her, firstly, that this was not true, and, secondly, that it was not well for Petrushka to go to the river. She begged him not to go. Petrushka laughed and said he would be back quickly. Tatiana cried, and implored him on her knees not to go. Then Petrushka grew irritable and almost rough, and told her not to vex him with foolishness. Reluctantly and sadly she gave in at last.

Petrushka went to the river, and Tatiana watched him go with a heavy heart. She felt quite certain some disaster was about to happen.

At seven o'clock Petrushka had not yet returned, and he did not return that night. The next morning the carpenter and two others went to the river to look for him. They found his body in the shallow water, entangled in the ropes of the raft he had made. He had been drowned, no doubt, in setting the raft straight.

During all that Sunday night Tatiana had said no word, nor had she moved from her doorstep: it was only when they brought back the dripping body to the village that she stirred, and when she saw it she laughed a dreadful laugh, and the spirit went from her eyes, leaving a fixed stare.

# A Bell is Born

(from *The Puppet Show of Memory*)

... WHEN I ARRIVED AT my destination, Sosnofka, in the government of Tambov, I found the country looking intensely green after a wet summer; the weather was hot, and the nights had the softness and the sweetness that should belong to the month of June.

I found a large crowd at the station gathered round a pillar of smoke and flame. At first I thought, of course, that a village fire was going on. Fires in Russian villages were common occurrences in the summer, and this was not surprising, as the majority of the houses were thatched with straw. The houses were so close one to another, and the ground was littered with straw. Moreover, to set fire to one's neighbour's house used to be a common form of paying off a score. But it was not a fire that was in progress. It was the casting of a bell. The ceremony was fixed for four o'clock in the afternoon, with due solemnity and with religious rites, and I was invited to be present.

'Heute muss die Glocke werden,'

wrote Schiller in his famous poem, and here the words were appropriate. This day the bell was to be. It was a blazing hot day. The air was dry, the ground was dry, everything was dry, and the great column of smoke mixed with flame issuing from the furnace added to the heat. The furnace had been made exactly opposite to the church. The church was a stone building with a Doric portico, four red columns, a white pediment, a circular pale green roof, and a Byzantine minaret. The village of Sosnofka had wooden log-built cottages thatched with straw dotted over the rolling plain. The plain was variegated with woods – oak trees and birch being the principal trees – and stretched out infinitely into the blue distance. Before the bell was to be cast a Te Deum was to be sung.

It was Wednesday, the day of the bazaar. The bazaar in the village of Somotka was the mart, where the buying and selling of meat, provisions,

259

fruit, melons, fish, hardware, ironmongery, china, and books were conducted. It happened once a week on Wednesdays, and peasants flocked in from the neighbouring villages to buy their provisions. But that afternoon the bazaar was deserted. The whole population of the village had gathered together on the dry, brown, grassy square in front of the church to take part in the ceremony. At four o'clock two priests and a deacon, followed by a choir (two men in their Sunday clothes), and by bearers of gilt banners, walked in procession out of the church. They were dressed in stiff robes of green and gold, and as they walked they intoned a plain-song. An old card-table, with a stained green cloth, was placed and opened on the ground opposite, and not far from the church, and on this two lighted tapers were set, together with a bowl of holy water. The peasants gathered round in a semicircle with bare heads, and joined in the service, making many genuflexions and signs of the Cross, and joining in the song with their deep bass voices. When I said the peasants, I should have said half of them. The other half were gathered in a dense crowd round the furnace, which was built of bricks, and open on both sides to the east and to the west, and fed with wooden fuel. The men in charge of the furnace stood on both sides of it and stirred the molten metal it contained with two enormous poles.

On one side of the furnace a channel had been prepared through which the metal was to flow into the cast of the bell. The crowd assembled there was already struggling to have and to hold a good place for the spectacle of the release of the metal when the solemn moment should arrive. Three policemen tried to restrain the crowd; that is to say, one police officer, one police sergeant, and one common policeman. They were trying with all their might to keep back the crowd, so that when the metal was released a disaster should not happen; but their efforts were in vain, because the crowd was large, and when they pressed back a small portion of it they made a dent in it which caused the remaining part of it to bulge out; and it was the kind of crowd – so intensely typical of Russia – on which no words, whether of command, entreaty, or threat, made the smallest impression. The only way to keep it back was by pressing on it with the body and outstretched arms, and that only kept back a tiny portion of it. In the meantime the Te Deum went on and on; and many things and persons were prayed for besides the bell which was about to be born. At one moment I obtained a place from which I had a commanding view of the furnace, but I was soon oozed out of it by the ever-increasing crowd of men, women, and children.

The whole thing was something between a sacred picture and a scene in a Wagner opera. The tall peasants with red shirts, long hair, and beards, stirring the furnace with long poles, looked like the persons in the epic of the *Niebelungen* as we see it performed on the stage to the strains of a complicated orchestration. There was Wotan in a blue shirt, with a spear; and Alberic, with a grimy face and a hammer, was meddling with the furnace; and Siegfried, in leather boots and sheepskin, was smoking a cigarette and waving an enormous hammer; while Mime, whining and disagreeable as usual, was having his head smacked. On the other hand, the peasants who were listening and taking part in the Te Deum, were like the figures of a sacred picture – women with red-and-white Eastern head-dresses, bearded men listening as though expecting a miracle, and barefooted children, with straw-coloured hair and blue eyes, running about everywhere. Towards six o'clock the Te Deum at last came to an end, and the crowd moved and swayed around the furnace. The Russian crowd reminded me of a large tough sponge. Nothing seemed to make any effect on it. It absorbed the newcomers who dived into it, and you could pull it this way and press it that way, but there it remained; indissoluble, passive, and obstinate. Perhaps the same is true of the Russian nation; I think it is certainly true of the Russian character, in which there is so much apparent weakness and softness, so much obvious elasticity and malleability, and so much hidden passive resistance.

I asked a peasant who was sitting by a railing under the church when the ceremony would begin. 'Ask them,' he answered; 'they will tell you, but they won't tell us.' With the help of the policeman, I managed to squeeze a way through the mass of struggling humanity to a place in the first row. I was told that the critical moment was approaching, and was asked to throw a piece of silver into the furnace, so that the bell might have a tuneful sound. I threw a silver rouble into the furnace, and the men who were in charge of the casting said that the critical moment had come. On each side of the small channel they fixed metal screens and placed a large screen facing it. The man in charge said in a loud, matter-of-fact tone: 'Now, let us pray to God.' The peasants uncovered themselves and made the sign of the Cross. A moment was spent in silent prayer. This prayer was especially for the success of the operation which was to take place immediately, namely, the release of the molten metal. Two hours had already been spent in praying for the bell. At this moment the excitement of the crowd reached such a pitch that they pushed themselves right up to the channel, and the efforts of the policemen, who were pouring down with perspiration, and stretching out in vain their futile arms, like the ghosts in Virgil, were pathetic. One man, however, not a policeman, waved a big stick and threatened to beat everybody back if they did not make way. Then, at last, the culminating moment came; the metal was released, and it poured down the narrow channel which had been prepared for it, and over which two logs placed crosswise formed an arch, surmounted by a yachting cap, for ornament. A huge yellow sheet of flame flared up for a moment in front of the iron screen facing the channel. The women in the crowd shrieked. Those who were in front made a desperate effort to get back, and those who were at the back made a desperate effort to get forward, and I was carried right through and beyond the crowd in the struggle.

The bell was born. I hoped the silver rouble which I threw into it, and which now formed a part of it, would sweeten its utterance, and that it might never have to sound the alarm which signifies battle, murder, and sudden death. A vain hope – an idle wish.

# The Pogrom

(from *The Puppet Show of Memory*)

NEAR SMIELO THERE WAS a village which was almost entirely inhabited by
Jews.

It was from this village, one day, that two Jews came to Countess
Bobrinsky and asked if they might store their furniture and their books
in her stables . . . they would not take up much room. When Countess
Bobrinsky asked them why, they said a *pogrom* had been arranged for
the next day. Countess Bobrinsky was bewildered, and asked them what
they meant, and who was going to make this *pogrom*. The two Jews said:
*They* were coming from Kiev by train, and from another town. The
*pogrom* would take place in the morning and *they* would go back in the
evening.

When she asked: 'Who are *they*?' she could get no answer, except that
some said it was the Tsar's orders, some that it was the Governor's orders,
but *they* had been sent to make a *pogrom*.

Countess Bobrinsky told them to go to the police, but the Jews said it
could not be prevented, and that all had been arranged for the morrow.
Both Count and Countess Bobrinsky then made inquiries, but all the
answer that they could get was that a *pogrom* had been arranged for the
next day. It was not the people of the place who would make it; these
lived in peace with the Jews. *They* would come by the night train from
two neighbouring towns; *they* would arrive in the morning; there would
be a *pogrom*, and then *they* would go away, and all the next morning
carts would arrive from the neighbouring villages, just as when there was
a fair, to take away what was left after the *pogrom*. When they asked who
was sending the *pogrom*-makers they could get no answer. Count Bobrinsky
interviewed the local police sergeant, but all he did was to shrug his
shoulders and wring his hands, and ask what could two policemen do
against a multitude? if there was to be a *pogrom*, there would be a *pogrom*.
He could do nothing; nothing could be done; nobody could do anything.

The next morning the peasant cook, a woman, came into Countess
Bobrinsky's room, and said: 'There will be no *pogrom* after all. It has
been put off.'

# The Fascination of Russia[1]

## (from *Russian Essays and Studies*)

FROM 1912 UNTIL THE summer of 1914 I spent the greater part of the year in Russia. I was no longer doing journalistic work, but I was still writing books on Russian life and literature. The longer I stayed in Russia the more deeply I felt the fascination of the country and the people. In one of his books Gogol has a passage apostrophizing his country from exile, and asking her the secret of her fascination. 'What is,' he says, 'the inscrutable power which lies hidden in you? Why does your aching, melancholy song echo forever in my ears? Russia, what do you want of me? What is there between you and me?'

The question has often been repeated, not only by Russians in exile, but by foreigners who have lived in Russia, and I have often found myself asking it. The country has little obvious glamour and attraction. In Russia, as Gogol says, the wonders of Nature are not made more wonderful by man; there are no spots where Nature, art, and time combine to take the heart with beauty; where association, and even decay are indistinguishably mingled; and Nature is not only beautiful but picturesque; where time has worked magic on man's handiwork, and history has left behind a host of phantoms.

There are many such places in France and in England, in Italy, Spain, and Greece, but not in Russia. Russia is a country of colonists, where life has been a perpetual struggle against the inclemency of the climate, and where the political history is the record of a desperate battle against adverse circumstances. Russia's oldest city was sacked and burnt just at the moment when it was beginning to flourish; her first capital was destroyed by fire in 1812; her second capital dates from the seventeenth century; stone houses are rare in the country, and the wooden houses are frequently destroyed by fire. It is a country of long winters and fierce

[1] This essay was used in substantially the same form as the final chapter of *The Puppet Show of Memory* [1922] and was included in a collected volume entitled *What I Saw in Russia* published [1927] in the Heinemann uniform edition.

summers, of rolling plains, uninterrupted by mountains and unvariegated by valleys.

But the charm is there. It is felt by people of different nationalities and races; it is difficult, if you live in Russia, to escape it, and once you have felt it, you will never be quite free from it. The melancholy song, which Gogol says wanders from sea to sea over the length and breadth of the land, will echo in your heart and haunt the corner of your brain. It is impossible to analyse charm, for if charm could be analysed it would cease to exist; and it is difficult to define the character of places where beauty makes so little instantaneous appeal, and where there is no play-ground of romance, and few ghosts of poetry and of history.

Turgenev's descriptions of the country give an idea of this peculiar magic. For instance, the story of the summer night, when on the plain the children tell each other bogy tales; or the description of that other July evening, when out of the twilight, a long way off on the plain, a child's voice is heard calling: 'Antropka–a–a', and Antropka answers: 'Wha–a–a–a–at?' and far away out of the immensity comes the answering voice: 'Come ho–ome, because daddy wants to whip you.'

Those who travel in their arm-chair will meet in Turgenev with glimpses, episodes, pictures, incidents, sayings and doings, touches of human nature, phases of landscape, shades of atmosphere, which contain the secret and the charm of Russia. All who have travelled in Russia not only recognize the truth of his pictures, but agree that the incidents which he records with incomparable art are a common experience to those who have eyes to see. The picturesque peculiar to countries rich in historical traditions is absent in Russia; but beauty is not absent, and it is often all the more striking from its lack of obviousness.

This was brought home to me strongly in the summer of 1913. I was staying in a small wooden house in Central Russia, not far from a railway, but isolated from other houses, and at a fair distance from a village. The harvest was nearly done. The heat was sweltering. The country was parched and dry. The walls and ceilings were black with flies. One had no wish to venture out of doors until the evening.

The small garden of the house, gay with asters and sweet-peas, was surrounded by birch trees, with here and there a fir tree in their midst. Opposite the little house, a broad pathway, flanked on each side by a row of tall birch trees, led to the margin of the garden, which ended in a wooded dip; beyond the dip, on the same level as the garden, there was a pathway half hidden by trees; so that from the house, if you looked straight in front of you, you saw a broad path, with birch trees on each side of it, forming a proscenium; and if anybody walked along the pathway, although you saw no road, you could see the figures in outline against the sky, as though they were walking across the back of a stage.

Just as the cool of the evening began to fall, out of the distance came a rhythmical song, ending on a note that seemed to last for ever, piercingly clear and clean. The music came a little nearer, and one could distinguish first a solo chanting a phrase, and then a chorus taking it up, and finally, solo and chorus became one, and reached a climax on a high note, which grew purer and stronger, and more and more long-drawn-out, without any seeming effort, until it died away.

The tone of the voices was so high, so pure, and at the same time so peculiar, strong, and rare, that it was difficult at first to tell whether the voices were tenors, sopranos, or boyish trebles. They were unlike, both in range and quality, the voices of women I ever heard in Russian villages. The music drew nearer, and it filled the air with a majestic calm. Presently, in the distance, beyond the dip between the trees, and in the middle of the natural stage made by the garden, I saw, against the sky, figures of women walking slowly in the sunset, and singing as they walked, carrying their scythes and their wooden rakes with them; and once again the phrase began and was repeated by the chorus; and once again chorus and solo melted together in a high and long-drawn-out note, which seemed to swell like the sound of a clarion, to grow purer, more single, stronger, and fuller, till it ended suddenly, sharply, as a frieze ends. The song proclaimed rest after toil, and satisfaction for labour accomplished. It was like a hymn of praise, a broad benediction, a grace sung for the end of the day: the end of the summer, the end of the harvest. It expressed the spirit of the breathless August evening.[1]

The women walked past slowly and disappeared into the trees once more. The glimpse lasted only a moment, but it was enough to start a long train of thought and to call up pictures of rites, ritual, and custom; of rustic worship and rural festival, of Pagan ceremonies older than the gods.

As another verse of what sounded like a primeval harvest hymn was sung; the brief glimpse of the reapers, erect and majestic in the dress of toil, and laden with the instruments of the harvest, the high quality of the singing –

'The undisturbed song of pure concent,'

made the place into a temple of august and sacred calm in the quiet light of the evening. The sacerdotal figures that passed by, diminutive in the distance, belonged to an archaic vase or frieze. The music seemed to seal

[1] This lyric episode was used by Maurice Baring as the subject of the XIth example of his *Translations Ancient and Modern* [1925]. Igor Stravinsky, in his *Expositions and Developments* [1962], written with Robert Craft, recalls with nostalgia a similar experience. In 1884, at two years of age, he heard the harvest women singing, and astonished his parents by singing what he had heard – this before he could talk. He wrote later that the voices sounded 'like a billion bees'. Tolstoy, in *Anna Karenina*, part III, ch. 12 [Maude translation], said it was 'as if a thundercloud of merriment were approaching', and then, like a 'wild, madly-merry song, interspersed with screams and whistling'.

a sacrament, to be the initiation into an immemorial secret, into some remote mystery – who knows? – perhaps the mystery of Eleusis, or into still older secrecies of which Eleusis was the far-distant offspring. A window had been opened on to another phase of time, on to another and a brighter world; older than Virgil, older than Romulus, older than Demeter – a world where the spring, the summer, and the autumn, harvest-time and sowing, the gathering of fruits and the vintage, were the gods; and through this window came a gleam from the golden age, a breath from the morning and the springtide of mankind.

When I say that the singing called up thoughts of Greece, the thing is less fantastic than it seems. In the first place, in the songs of the Russian peasants, the Greek modes are still in use: the Dorian, the hypo-Dorian, the Lydian, the hypo-Phrygian. *'La musique, telle qu'elle était pratiquée en Russie au moyen âge'* (writes M. Soubier in his *History of Russian Music*), *'tenait à la tradition des religions et des mœurs paiennes.'* And in the secular as well as in the ecclesiastical music of Russia there is an element of influence which is purely Hellenic. It turned out that the particular singers I heard on that evening were not local, but a guild of women reapers who had come from the government of Tula to work during the harvest. Their singing, although the form and kind of song were familiar to me, was different in quality from any that I had heard before; and the impression made by it unforgettable.

Nature in Russia is, broadly speaking, monotonous and uniform, but this does not mean that beauty is rare. Not only magic moments occur in the most unpromising surroundings, but beauty is to be found in Russian nature and Russian landscape at all times and all seasons in many shapes.

For instance: a long drive in the evening twilight at harvest-time, over the immense hedgeless rolling plains, through stretches of golden wheat and rye, variegated with millet, still green and not yet turned to the bronze colour it takes later; when you drive for miles over monotonous and yet ever-varying fields, and when you see, in the distance, the cranes, settling for a moment, and then flying off into space.

Later in the twilight, continents of dove-coloured clouds float in the east, the west is tinged with the dusty afterglow of the sunset; and the half-reaped corn and the spaces of stubble are burnished and glow in the heat; and smouldering fires of weed burn here and there; and as you reach a homestead, you will perhaps see by the threshing-machine a crowd of dark men and women still at their work; and in the glow from the flame of a wooden fire, in the shadow of the dusk, the smoke of the engine and the dust of the chaff, they have a Rembrandt-like power; the feeling of space, breadth, and air and immensity grows upon one; the earth seems to grow larger, the sky to grow deeper, and the spirit is lifted, stretched, and magnified.

Russian poets have celebrated more frequently the spring and winter – the brief spring which arrives so suddenly after the melting of the snows, with the intense green of the birch trees, the uncrumpling fern; woods carpeted with lilies of the valley; the lilac bushes, the nightingale, and later the brier, which flowers in profusion; and the winter: the long drives in a sledge under a leaden sky to the tinkle of monotonous bells; a whistling blizzard with its demons, that lead the horses astray in the night; transparent woods black against an immense whiteness; or covered with snow and frozen, an enchanted fabric against the stainless blue; or, when after a night of thaw, the brown branches emerge once more covered with airy threads and sparkling drops of dew.

The sunset and twilight of the winter evening after the first snow had fallen in December used to be most beautiful. The new moon, like a little sail on a cold sea, tinged with a blush as it reached the earth, flooded the snow with light, and added to its purity; the snow had a blue glint in it and showed up the wooden houses, the red roofs, the farm implements in a bold relief; so that all these prosaic objects of everyday life assumed a strange largeness and darkness as they loomed between the earth and the sky.

What I used to enjoy more than anything in Russia were the summer afternoons on the river near Sosnofka, where the flat banks were covered with oak trees, ash, willow, and thick undergrowth; and where every now and then, perch rose to the surface to catch flies, and the kingfishers skimmed over the surface from reach to reach. Sometimes I used to take a boat and row past islands of rushes, and a network of water-lilies, to where the river broadened; and I reached a great sheet of water flanked by a weir and a mill. The trees were reflected in the glassy surface, and nothing broke the stillness but the grumbling of the mill and the cries of the children bathing.

Near the village, all through the summer night (this was in June 1914), I used to hear song answering song, and the brisk rhythm of the accordion; or the interminable humming, buzzing burden of the three-stringed *balalaika*; verse succeeded verse of an apparently tireless song, and the end of each verse seemed to beget another and give a keener zest to the next; and the song waxed faster and madder, as if the singer were intoxicated by the sound of his own music.

But the peculiar manifestations of the beauty of nature in a flat and uniform country are not enough to account for the fascination of Russia. Beauty is a part of it, but it is not all. Against these things in the other scale you had to put dirt, squalor, misery, slovenliness, disorder, and the uninspiring wooden provincial towns, the dusty or sodden roads, the frequent grey skies, the long and heavy sameness.

The *advocatus diaboli* had a strong case. He could have drawn up a powerful indictment, not only against the political conditions, and the arbitrary and uncertain administration, but also against the character of the people; he could mention the moral laxity, the extravagant self-indulgence, the lack of control, the jealousy which hounded any kind of superiority; and looked with suspicion on all that was original or distinguished; the dead level of mediocrity; the stereotyped bureaucratic pattern which you could not escape from. The Russians, he would say, had all the faults of the Orient without any of its austerer virtues; Russia, he would say, was a nation of ineffectual rebels under the direction of a band of corrupt and time-serving officials. The indictment was true, but however glaring the faults which Russian moralists, satirists, and politicians used so frequently and so loudly to deplore, the faults that used to make foreigners in Russia so angry at times, they seemed to me the negative results of positive qualities so valuable as to outweigh them altogether.

During my stays in Russia I saw some of the worst as well as some of the best aspects of the country and its people. The net result of all I saw and all I experienced was the sense of an overpowering charm in the country, an indescribable fascination in the people. The charm was partly due to the country itself, partly to the manner of life lived there, and partly to the nature of the people. The qualities that did exist, and whose benefit I experienced, seemed to me the most precious of all qualities; the virtues the most important of all virtues; the glimpses of beauty the rarest in kind; the songs and the music the most haunting and most heart-searching; the poetry nearest to nature and man; the human charity nearest to God.

This is perhaps the secret of the whole matter, that the Russian soul is filled with a human Christian charity which is warmer in kind and intenser in degree, and expressed with a great simplicity and sincerity, than is to be met with in any other people; it was the existence of this quality behind everything else which gave charm to Russian life (however squalid the circumstances might be), poignancy to its music, sincerity and simplicity to its religion, manners, intercourse, music, singing, verse, art, acting – in a word to its art, its life, and its faith.

Never did I realize this so much as one day when I was driving on a cold and damp December evening in St Petersburg in a cab. It was dark, and I was driving along the quays from one end of the town to the other. For a long time I drove in silence, but after a while I happened to make some remark to the cabman about the weather. He answered gloomily that the weather was bad and so was everything else too. For some time we drove on in silence, and then in answer to some other stray remark or question of mine he said he had been unlucky that day in the matter of a fine. It was a trivial point, but somehow or other my interest was aroused, and I got him to tell me the story, which was a case of bad luck and nothing serious; but when he had told it, he gave such a profound sigh that I asked whether it was that which was still weighing upon him. Then he said 'No,' and slowly began to tell me a story of a great catastrophe which had just befallen him. He possessed a little land, and a cottage in the country, not far from St Petersburg. His house had been burnt. It was true the house was insured, but the insurance was not sufficient to make an appreciable difference. He had two sons: one went to school and the other had some employment in the provinces. The catastrophe of the fire had upset everything. All his belongings had perished. He could no longer send his boy to school. His second son, in the country, had written to say he was engaged to be married, and had asked his consent, advice, and approval. 'He has written twice,' said the cabman, 'and I keep silence (*a ya molchu*). What can I answer?' I cannot give any idea of the strength, simplicity, and poignancy of the tale as it came, hammered out slowly, with pauses between each sentence, with a dignity of utterance and a purity of idiom which used to be the precious privilege of the poor in Russia. The words came as if torn out from the bottom of his heart. He made no complaint; there was no grievance, no whine in the story. He stated the bald facts with a simplicity which was overwhelming. In spite of all, his faith in God and his consent to the will of Providence was unshaken, certain, and sublime.

This happened in 1911. I have forgotten the details; but I knew I had been face to face with a human soul, stripped and naked, and a human soul in the grip of a tragedy. This experience, which brought one in touch with the divine, is one which, I think, could only in such circumstances occur in Russia. I wrote this in the year 1913 when I was summing up my impressions on Russian life, and trying to analyse the nature of the fascination the country had for me. When I had finished, I echoed the words which R. L. Stevenson once addressed to a French novelist: '*J'ai beau admirer les autres de toute ma force, c'est avec vous que je me complais à vivre.*'

In the spring of 1914 I went back to Russia for the last time before the war. I spent over a month by myself at Sosnofka, writing a book, an outline of Russian literature, and bathing every afternoon in the river where the sweetbrier grew on the banks by the willows, and the kingfisher used every now and then to dart across the oily-looking water.

It was a wonderful spring. The nightingales sang all day long in the garden; and all night long people were singing in the village. Nature was steeped in beauty and calm. It was a month of accidental retreat before tremendous events and the changes which affected Russia perhaps more than any other country in the world.

# Alexander Pushkin

(from *An Outline of Russian Literature*)

PUSHKIN WAS BORN on May 26, 1799 at Moscow. He was of ancient lineage, and inherited African negro blood on his mother's side, his mother's grandmother being the daughter of Peter the Great's negro, Hannibal. Until he was nine years old, he did not show signs of any unusual precocity; but from then onwards he was seized with a passion for reading which lasted all his life. He read Plutarch's *Lives*, the *Iliad*, and the *Odyssey* in a translation. He then devoured all the French books he found in his father's library. Pushkin was gifted with a photographic memory, which retained what he read immediately and permanently. His first efforts at writing were in French – comedies, which he performed himself to an audience of his sisters. He went to school in 1812 at the Lyceum of Tsarskoe Selo, a suburb of St Petersburg. His school career was not brilliant, and his leaving certificate qualifies his achievements as mediocre, even in Russian. But during the six years he spent at the Lyceum, he continued to read voraciously. His favourite poet at this time was Voltaire. He began to write verse, first in French and then in Russian; some of it was printed in 1814 and 1815 in reviews, and in 1815 he declaimed his *Recollections of Tsarskoe Selo* in public at the Lyceum examination, in the presence of Derzhavin the poet.

The poems which he wrote at school afterwards formed part of his collected works. In these poems, consisting for the greater part of anacreontics and epistles, although they are immature, and imitative, partly of contemporary authors such as Derzhavin and Zhukovsky, and partly of the French anacreontic school of poets, such as Voltaire, Gresset, and Parny, the sound of a new voice was unmistakable. Indeed, not only his contemporaries, but the foremost representatives of the Russian literature of that day, Derzhavin, Karamzin, and Zhukovsky, made no mistake about it. They greeted the first notes of this new lyre with enthusiasm. Zhukovsky used to visit the boy poet at school and

271

read out his verse to him. Derzhavin was enthusiastic over the recitation of his *Recollections of Tsarskoe Selo*. Thus fame came to Pushkin as easily as the gift of writing verse. He had lisped in numbers, and as soon as he began to speak in them, his contemporaries immediately recognized and hailed the new voice. He did not wake up and find himself famous like Byron, but he walked into the Hall of Fame as naturally as a young heir steps into his lawful inheritance. If we compare Pushkin's school-boy poetry with Byron's *Hours of Idleness*, it is easy to understand how this came about. In the *Hours of Idleness* there is, perhaps, only one poem which would hold out hopes of serious promise; and the most discerning critics would have been justified in being careful before venturing to stake any great hopes on so slender a hint. But in Pushkin's early verse, although the subject-matter is borrowed, and the style is still irregular and careless, it is none the less obvious that it flows from the pen of the author without effort or strain; and besides this, certain coins of genuine poetry ring out, bearing the image and superscription of a new mint, the mint of Pushkin.

When the first of his poems to attract the attention of a larger audience, *Ruslan and Ludmila*, was published, in 1820, it was greeted with enthusiasm by the public; but it had already won the suffrages of that circle which counted most, that is to say, the leading men of letters of the day, who had heard it read out in MSS. For as soon as Pushkin left school and stepped into the world, he was received into the literary circle of the day on equal terms. After he had read aloud the first cantos of *Ruslan and Ludmila* at Zhukovsky's literary evenings, Zhukovsky gave him his portrait with this inscription: 'To the pupil, from his defeated master'; and Batyushkov, a poet who, after having been influenced, like Pushkin, by Voltaire and Parny, had gone back to the classics, Horace and Tibullus, and had introduced the classic anacreontic school of poetry into Russia, was astonished to find a young man of the world outplaying him without any trouble on the same lyre, and exclaimed, 'Oh! how well the rascal has started writing!'

The publication of *Ruslan and Ludmila* sealed Pushkin's reputation definitely, as far as the general public was concerned, although some of the professional critics treated the poem with severity. The subject of the poem was a Russian fairy-tale, and the critics blamed the poet for having recourse to what they called Russian folk-lore, which they considered to be unworthy of the poetic muse. One review complained that Pushkin's choice of subject was like introducing a bearded unkempt peasant into a drawing-room, while others blamed him for dealing with national stuff in a flippant spirit. But the curious thing is that, while the critics blamed him for his choice of subject, and his friends and the public defended him for it, quoting all sorts of precedents, the poem has absolutely nothing in common, either in its spirit, style or characterization, with native Russian folk-lore and fairy-tales. Much later on in his career, Pushkin was to show what he could do with Russian folk-lore. But *Ruslan and Ludmila*, which, as far as its form is concerned, has a certain superficial resemblance to Ariosto, is in reality the result of the French influence, under which Pushkin had been ever since his cradle, and which in this poem blazes into the sky like a rocket, and bursts into a shower of sparks, never to return again.

There is no passion in the poem and no irony, but it is young, fresh, full of sensuous, not to say sensual images, interruptions, digressions, and flippant epigrams. Pushkin wondered afterwards that nobody noticed the coldness of the poem; the truth was that the eyes of the public were dazzled by the fresh sensuous images, and their ears were taken captive by the new voice: for the importance of the poem lies in this – that the new voice which the literary pundits had already recognized in the Lyceum of Tsarskoe Selo was now speaking to the whole world, and all Russia became aware that a young man was among them 'with mouth of gold and morning in his eyes'. *Ruslan and Ludmila* has just the same sensuous richness, fresh music, and fundamental coldness as Marlowe's *Hero and Leander*. After finishing the poem, Pushkin added a magnificent and moving Epilogue, written from the Caucasus in the year of its publication (1820); and when the second edition was published in 1828, he added a Prologue in his finest manner which tells of Russian fairy-land.

After leaving school in 1817, until 1820, Pushkin plunged into the gay life of St Petersburg. He wanted to be a Hussar, but his father could not afford it. In default he became a Foreign Office official; but he did not take this profession seriously. He consorted with the political youth and young Liberals of the day; he scattered stinging epigrams and satirical epistles broadcast. He sympathized with the Decembrists, but took no part in their conspiracy. He would probably have ended by doing so; but, luckily for Russian literature, he was transferred in 1820 from the Foreign Office to the Chancery of General Inzov in the South of Russia; and from 1820 to 1826 he lived first at Kishinev, then at Odessa, and finally in his own home at Pskov. This enforced banishment was of the greatest possible service to the poet; it took him away from the whirl and distractions of St Petersburg; it prevented him from being compromised in the drama of the Decembrists; it ripened and matured his poetical genius; it provided him, since it was now that he visited the Caucasus and the Crimea for the first time, with new subject-matter.

During this period he learnt Italian and English, and came under the influence of André Chénier and Byron. André Chénier's influence is strongly felt in a series of lyrics in imitation of the classics; but these lyrics were altogether different from the anacreontics of his boyhood. Byron's influence is first manifested in a long poem *The Prisoner of the Caucasus*. It is Byronic in the temperament of the hero, who talks in the strain of the earlier Childe Harold; he is young, but feels old; tired of life, he seeks for consolation in the loneliness of nature in the Caucasus. He is taken prisoner by mountain tribesmen, and set free by a girl who drowns herself on account of her unrequited love. Pushkin said later that the poem was immature, but that there were verses in it that came from his heart. There is one element in the poem which is by no means immature, and that is the picture of the Caucasus, which is executed with much reality and simplicity. Pushkin annexed the Caucasus to Russian poetry. The Crimea inspired him with another tale, also Byronic in some respects, *The Fountain of Baghchi-Sarai*, which tells of a Tartar Khan and his Christian slave, who is murdered out of jealousy by a former favourite, herself drowned by the orders of the Khan. Here again the descriptions are amazing, and Pushkin draws out a new stop of rich and voluptuous music.

In speaking of the influence of Byron over Pushkin it is necessary to discriminate. Byron helped Pushkin to discover himself; Byron revealed to him his own powers, showed him the way out of the French garden where he had been dwelling, and acted as a guide to fresh woods and pastures new. But what Pushkin took from the new provinces to which the example of Byron led him was entirely different from what Byron sought there. Again, the methods and workmanship of the two poets were radically different. Pushkin is never imitative of Byron; but Byron opened his eyes to a new world, and indeed did for him what Chapman's *Homer* did for Keats. It frequently happens that when a poet is deeply struck by the work of another poet he feels a desire to write something himself, but something different. Thus Pushkin's mental intercourse with Byron had the effect of bracing the talent of the Russian poet and spurring him on to the conquest of new worlds.

Pushkin's years' banishment to his own country place had the effect of revealing to him the reality and seriousness of his vocation as a poet, and the range and strength of his gifts. It was during this period that besides the works already mentioned he wrote some of his finest lyrics, *The Conversation between the Bookseller and the Poet* – perhaps the most perfect of his shorter poems – it contains four lines to have written which Turgenev said he would have burnt the whole of his works – a larger poem called *The Gypsies*; his dramatic chronicle *Boris Godunov*, and the beginning of his masterpiece *Onegin*; several ballads, including *The Sage Oleg*, and an unfinished romance, the *Robber Brothers*.

Not only is the richness of his output during this period remarkable, but the variety and the high level of art maintained in all the different styles which he attempted and mastered. *The Gypsies* (1827), which was received with greater favour by the public than any of his poems, either earlier or later, is the story of a disappointed man, Aleko, who leaves the world and takes refuge with gypsies. A tragically ironical situation is the result. The anarchic nature of the Byronic misanthrope brings tragedy into the peaceful life of the people, who are lawless because they need no laws. Aleko loves and marries the gypsy Zemfira, but after a time she tires of him, and loves a young gypsy. Aleko surprises them and kills them both. Then Zemfira's father banishes him from the gypsies' camp. He, too, had been deceived. When his wife Mariula had been untrue and had left him, he had attempted no vengeance, but had brought up her daughter.

'Leave us, proud man,' he says to Aleko. 'We are a wild people; we have no laws, we torture not, neither do we punish; we have no use for blood or groans; we will not live with a man of blood. Thou wast not made for the wild life. For thyself alone thou claimest licence; we are shy and good-natured; thou art evil-minded and presumptuous. Farewell, and peace be with thee!'

The charm of the poem lies in the descriptions of the gypsy camp and the gypsy life, the snatches of gypsy song, and the characterization of the gypsies, especially of the women. It is not surprising the poem was popular; it breathes a spell, and the reading of it conjures up before one the wandering life, the camp-fire, the soft speech, and the song; and makes one long to go off with 'the raggle-taggle gypsies O!'

Byron's influence soon gave way to that of Shakespeare, who opened a still larger field of vision to the Russian poet. In 1825 he writes: 'Quel homme que ce Shakespeare! Je n'en reviens pas. Comme Byron le tragique est mesquin devant lui! Ce Byron qui n'a jamais conçu qu'un seul caractère et c'est le sien . . . ce Byron donc a partagé entre ses personages tel et tel trait de son caractère: son orgeuil à l'un, sa haine à l'autre, sa mélancolie au troisième, etc., et c'est ainsi d'un caractère plein, sombre et énergique, il a fait plusieurs caractères insignifiants; ce n'est pas là de la tragédie. On a encore une manie. Quand on a conçu un caractère, tout ce qu'on lui fait dire, même les choses les plus étranges, en porte essentiellement l'empreinte, comme les pédants et les marins dans les vieux romans de Fielding. Voyez le haineux de Byron . . . et là-dessus lisez Shakespeare. Il ne craint jamais de compromettre son personage, il le fait parler avec tout l'abandon de la vie, car il est sûr en temps et lieu, de lui faire trouver le langage de son caractère. Vous me demanderez: votre tragédie est-elle une tragédie de caractère ou de costume? J'ai choisi le genre le plus aisé, mais j'ai tâché de les unir tous deux. J'écris et je pense. La plupart des scènes ne demandent que du raisonnement; quand j'arrive à une scène qui demande de l'inspiration, j'attends ou je passe dessus.'

I quote this letter because it throws light, firstly, on Pushkin's matured opinion of Byron, and, secondly, on his methods of work; for, like Leonardo da Vinci, he formed the habit, which he here describes, of leaving unwritten passages where inspiration was needed, until he felt the moment of *bien être* when inspiration came; and this not only in writing his tragedy, but henceforward in everything that he wrote, as his note-books testify.

The subject-matter of *Boris Godunov* was based on Karamzin's history: it deals with the dramatic episode of the Russian Perkin Warbeck, the false Demetrius who pretended to be the murdered son of Ivan the Terrible. The play is constructed on the model of Shakespeare's chronicle plays, but in a still more disjointed fashion, without a definite beginning or end: when Mussorgsky made an opera out of it, the action was concentrated into definite acts; for, as it stands, it is not a play, but a series of scenes. Pushkin had not the power of conceiving and executing a drama which should move round one idea to an inevitable close. He had not the gift of dramatic architectonics, and still less that of stage carpentry. On the other hand, the scenes, whether they be tragic and poetical, or scenes of common life, are as vivid as any in Shakespeare; the characters are all alive, and they speak a language which is at the same time ancient, living, and convincing.

In saying that Pushkin lacks the gift of stage architectonics and stage carpentry, it is not merely meant that he lacked the gift of arranging acts that would suit the stage, or that of imagining stage effects. His whole play is not conceived as a drama; a subject from which a drama might be written is taken, but the drama is left unwritten. We see Boris Godunov on the throne, which he has unlawfully usurped; we know he feels remorse; he tells us so in monologues; we see his soul stripped before us, bound upon a wheel of fire, and we watch the wheel revolve; and that is all the moral and spiritual action that the part contains; he is static and not dynamic, he never has to make up his mind; his will never has to encounter the shock of another will during the whole play. Neither does the chronicle centre round the Pretender. It is true that we see the idea of impersonating the Tsarevitch dawning in his mind; and it is also true that in one scene with his Polish love, Marina, we see him dynamically moving in a dramatic situation. She loves him because she thinks he is the son of an anointed King. He loves her too much to deceive her, and tells her the truth. She then says she will have nothing of him; and then he rises from defeat and shame to the height of the situation, becomes great, and, not unlike Browning's Sludge, says: 'Although I am an impostor, I am born to be a King all the same; I am one of Nature's Kings; and I defy you to oust me from the situation. Tell every one what I have told you. Nobody will believe you.' And Marina is conquered once more by his conduct and bearing.

This scene is sheer drama; it is the conflict of two wills and two souls. But there the matter ends. The kaleidoscope is shaken, and we are shown a series of different patterns, in which the heroine plays no part at all, and in which the hero only makes a momentary appearance. The fact is there is neither hero nor heroine in the play. It is not a play, but a chronicle; and it would be foolish to blame Pushkin for not accomplishing what he never attempted. As a chronicle, a series of detached scenes, it is supremely successful. There are certain scenes which attain to sublimity: for instance, that in the cell of the monastery, where the monk is finishing his chronicles; and the monologue in which Boris speaks his remorse, and his dying speech to his son. The verse in these scenes is sealed with the mark of that God-gifted ease and high seriousness, which belong only to the inspired great. They are Shakespearean, not because they imitate Shakespeare, but because they attain to heights of imaginative truth to which Shakespeare rises more often than any other poet; and the language in these scenes has a simplicity, an inevitableness, an absence of all conscious effort and of all visible art and artifice, a closeness of utterance combined with a width of suggestion which belong only to the greatest artists, to the Greeks, to Shakespeare, to Dante.

*Boris Godunov* was not published until January 1, 1831, and passed, with one exception, absolutely unnoticed by the critics. Like so many great works, it came before its time; and it was not until years afterwards that the merits of this masterpiece were understood and appreciated.

In 1826 Pushkin's banishment to the country came to an end; in that year he was allowed to go to Moscow, and in 1827 to St Petersburg. In 1826 his poems appeared in one volume, and the second canto of *Onegin* (the first had appeared in 1825). In 1827 *The Gypsies*, and the third canto of *Onegin*; in 1828 the fourth, fifth, and sixth cantos of *Onegin*; in 1829 *Graf Nulin*, an admirably told *Conte* such as Maupassant might have written, of a deceived husband and a wife who, finding herself in the situation of Lucretia, gives the would-be Tarquin a box on the ears, but succeeds, nevertheless, in being unfaithful with some one else – the *Cottage of Kolomna* is another story in the same vein – and in the same year *Poltava*.

This poem was written in one month, in St Petersburg. The subject is Mazepa, with whom the daughter of his hereditary enemy, Kochubey, whom he afterwards tortures and kills, falls in love. But it is in reality the epic of Peter the Great.[1] When the poem was published, it disconcerted the critics and the public. It revealed an entirely new phase of Pushkin's style, and it should have widened the popular conception of the poet's

[1] The poem was originally called *Mazepa*: Pushkin changed the title so as not to clash with Byron. It is interesting to see what Pushkin says of Byron's poem. In his notes there is the following passage:
'Byron knew Mazepa through Voltaire's history of Charles XII. He was struck solely by the picture of a man bound to a wild horse and borne over the steppes. A poetical picture of course; but see what he did with it. What a living creation! What a broad brush! But do not expect to find either Mazepa or Charles, nor the usual gloomy Byronic hero. Byron was not thinking of him. He presented a series of pictures, one more striking than the other. Had his pen come across the story of the seduced daughter and the father's execution, it is improbable that anyone else would have dared to touch the subject.' [M. B.]

powers and versatility. But at the time the public only knew Pushkin through his lyrics and his early tales; *Boris Godunov* had not yet been published; moreover, the public of that day expected to find in a poem passion and the delineation of the heart's adventures. This stern objective fragment of an epic, falling into their sentimental world of keepsakes, ribbons, roses and cupids, like a bas-relief conceived by a Titan and executed by a god, met with little appreciation. The poet's verse which, so far as the public knew it, had hitherto seemed like a shining and luscious fruit, was exchanged for a concentrated weighty tramp of ringing rhyme, *martelé* like steel. It is as if Tennyson had followed up his early poems in a style as concise as that of Pope and as concentrated as that of Browning's dramatic lyrics. The poem is a fit monument to Peter the Great, and the great monarch's impetuous genius and passion for thorough craftsmanship seem to have entered into it.

In 1829 Pushkin made a second journey to the Caucasus, the result of which was a harvest of lyrics. On his return to St Petersburg he sketched the plan of another epic poem, *Galub*, dealing with the Caucasus, but this remained a fragment.

In 1831 he finished the eighth and last canto of *Onegin*. Originally there were nine cantos, but when the work was published one of the cantos dealing with Onegin's travels was left out as being irrelevant. Pushkin had worked at this poem since 1823. It was Byron's *Beppo* which gave him the idea of writing a poem on modern life; but here again, he made of the idea something quite different from any of Byron's work. *Onegin* is a novel. Eugene Onegin is the name of the hero. It is, moreover, the first Russian novel; and as a novel it has never been surpassed. It is as real as Tolstoy, as finished in workmanship and construction as Turgenev. It is a realistic novel; not realistic in the sense that Zola's work was mis-called realistic, but realistic in the sense that Miss Austen is realistic. The hero is the average man about St Petersburg; his father, a worthy public servant, lives honourably on debts and gives three balls a year. Onegin is brought up, not too strictly, by 'Monsieur l'Abbé'; he goes out in the world clothed by a London tailor, fluent in French, and able to dance the Mazurka.

Onegin can touch on every subject, can hold his tongue when the conversation becomes too serious, and make epigrams. He knows enough Latin to construe an epitaph, to talk about Juvenal, and put 'Vale!' at the end of his letters, and he can remember two lines of the *Aeneid*. He is severe on Homer and Theocritus, but has read Adam Smith. The only art in which he is proficient is the *ars amandi* as taught by Ovid. He is a patron of the ballet: he goes to balls; he eats beefsteaks and *paté de foie gras*. In spite of all this – perhaps because of it – he suffers from spleen, like Childe Harold, the author says. His father dies, leaving a lot of debts behind him, but a dying uncle summons him to the country; and when he gets there he finds his uncle dead, and himself the inheritor of the estate. In the country, he is just as much bored as he was in St Petersburg. A new neighbour arrives in the shape of Lensky, a young man fresh from Germany, an enthusiast and a poet, and full of Kant, Schiller, and the German writers. Lensky introduces Onegin to the neighbouring family, by name Larin, consisting of a widow and two daughters. Lensky is in love with the younger daughter, Olga, who is simple, fresh, blue-eyed, with a round face, as Onegin says, like the foolish moon. The elder sister, Tatiana, is less pretty; shy and dreamy, she conceals under her retiring and wistful ways a clean-cut character and a strong will.

Tatiana is as real as any of Miss Austen's heroines; as alive as Fielding's Sophia Western, and as charming as any of George Meredith's women; as sensible as Portia, as resolute as Juliet. Turgenev, with all his magic, and Tolstoy, with all his command over the colours of life, never created a truer, more radiant, and more typically Russian woman. She is the type of all that is best in the Russian woman; that is to say, of all that is best in Russia; and it is a type taken straight from life, and not from fairyland – a type that exists as much today as it did in the days of Pushkin. She is the first of that long gallery of Russian women which Turgenev, Tolstoy, and Dostoyevsky have given us, and which are the most precious jewels of Russian literature, because they reflect the crowning glory of Russian life. Tatiana falls in love with Onegin at first sight. She writes to him and confesses her love, and in all the love poetry of the world there is nothing more touching and more simple than this confession. It is perfect. If Pushkin had written this and this alone, his place among poets would be unique and different from that of all other poets.

Possibly some people may think that there are finer achievements in the love poetry of the world; but nothing is so futile and so impertinent as giving marks to the great poets, as if they were passing an examination. If a thing is as good as possible in itself, what is the use of saying that it is less good or better than something else, which is as good as possible in itself also. Nevertheless, placed beside any of the great confessions of love in poetry – Francesca's story in the *Inferno*, Romeo and Juliet's leavetaking, Phèdre's declaration, Don Juan Tenorio's letter – the beauty of Tatiana's confession would not be diminished by the juxtaposition. Of the rest of Pushkin's work at its best and highest, of the finest passages of *Boris Godunov*, for instance, you can say: This is magnificent, but there are dramatic passages in other works of other poets on the same lines and as fine; but in Tatiana's letter Pushkin has created something unique, which has no parallel, because only a Russian could have written it, and of Russians, only he. It is a piece of poetry as pure as a crystal, as spontaneous as a blackbird's song.

Onegin tells Tatiana he is not worthy of her, that he is not made for love and marriage; that he would cease to love her at once; that he feels for her like a brother, or perhaps a little more tenderly. It then falls out that Onegin, by flirting with Olga at a ball, makes Lensky jealous. They fight a duel, and Lensky is killed. Onegin is obliged to leave the neighbourhood, and spends years in travel. Tatiana remains true to her first love; but she is taken by her relatives to Moscow, and consents at last under their pressure to marry a rich man of great position. In St Petersburg, Onegin meets her again. Tatiana has become a great lady, but all her old charm is there. Onegin now falls violently in love with her; but she, although she frankly confesses that she still loves him, tells him that it is too late; she has married another, and she means to remain true to him. And there the story ends.

*Onegin* is, perhaps, Pushkin's most characteristic work; it is undoubtedly the best known and the most popular; like *Hamlet*, it is all quotations. Pushkin in his *Onegin* succeeded in doing what Shelley urged Byron to do – to create something new and in accordance with the spirit of the age, which should at the same time be beautiful. He did more than this. He succeeded in creating for Russia a poem that was purely national, and in giving his country a classic, a model both in construction, matter, form, and inspiration for future generations. Perhaps the greatest quality of this poem is its vividness. Pushkin himself speaks, in taking leave, of having seen the unfettered march of his novel in a magic prism. This is just the impression that the poem gives; the scenes are as clear as the shapes in a crystal; nothing is blurred; there are no hesitating notes, nothing *à peu près*; every stroke comes off; the nail is hit on the head every time, only so easily that you do not notice the strokes, and all labour escapes notice. Apart from this the poem is amusing; it arrests the attention as a story, and it delights the intelligence with its wit, its digressions, and its brilliance. It is as witty as Don Juan and as consummately expressed as Pope; and when the occasion demands it, the style passes in easy transition to serious or tender tones. *Onegin* has been compared to Byron's *Don Juan*. There is this likeness, that both poems deal with contemporary life, and in both poems the poets pass from grave to gay, from severe to lively, and often interrupt the narrative to apostrophize the reader. But there the likeness ends. On the other hand, there is a vast difference. *Onegin* contains no adventures. It is a story of everyday life. Moreover, it is an organic whole: so well constructed that it fits into a stage libretto – Tchaikovsky made an opera out of it – without difficulty. There is another difference – a difference which applies to Pushkin and Byron in general. There is no unevenness in Pushkin; his work, as far as craft is concerned, is always on the same high level. You can admire the whole, or cut off any single passage and it will still remain admirable; whereas Byron must be taken as a whole or not at all – the reason being that Pushkin was an impeccable artist in form and expression, and that Byron was not.

In the winter of 1832 Pushkin sought a new field, the field of historical research; and by the beginning of 1833 he had not only collected all the materials for a history of Pugachev, the Cossack who headed a rising in the reign of Catherine II; but his literary activity was so great that he had also written the rough sketch of a long story in prose dealing with the same subject, *The Captain's Daughter*, another prose story of considerable length, *Dubrovsky*, and portions of a drama, *Rusalka*, The Water Nymph, which was never finished. Besides *Boris Godunov* and the *Rusalka*, Pushkin wrote a certain number of dramatic scenes, or short dramas in one or more scenes. Of these, one, *The Feast in the Time of Plague*, is taken from the English of John Wilson (*The City of the Plague*), with original additions. In *Mozart and Salieri* we see the contrast between the genius which does what it must and the talent which does what it can. The story is based on the unfounded anecdote that Mozart was poisoned by Salieri out of envy. This dramatic and beautifully written episode has been set to music as it stands by Rimsky-Korsakov.

*The Covetous Knight*, which bears the superscription, 'From the tragi-comedy of Chenstone' – an unknown English original – tells of the conflict between a Harpagon and his son: the delineation of the miser's imaginative passion for his treasures is, both in conception and execution, in Pushkin's finest manner. This scene has been recently set to music by Rakhmaninov. *The Guest of Stone*, the story of Don Juan and the *statua gentilissima del gran Commendatore*, makes Don Juan live. A scene from *Faust* between Faust and Mephistopheles is original and not of great interest; *Angelo* is the story of *Measure for Measure* told as a narrative with two scenes in dialogue. *Rusalka*, The Water Maid, is taken from the genuine and not the sham province of national legend, and it is tantalizing that this poetic fragment remained a fragment.

Pushkin's prose is in some respects as remarkable as his verse. Here, too, he proved a pioneer. *Dubrovsky* is the story of a young officer whose father is ousted, like Naboth, from his small estate by his neighbour, a rich and greedy landed proprietor, becomes a highway robber so as to revenge himself, and introduces himself into the family of his enemy as a French master, but forgoes his revenge because he falls in love with his enemy's daughter. In this extremely vivid story he anticipates Gogol in his life-like pictures of country life. *The Captain's Daughter* is equally vivid; the rebel Pugachev has nothing stagey or melodramatic about him, nothing of Harrison Ainsworth. Of his shorter stories, such as *The Blizzard, The Pistol Shot, The Lady-Peasant*, the most entertaining, and certainly the most popular, is *The Queen of Spades*, which was so admirably translated by Mérimée, and formed the subject of one of Tchaikovsky's most successful operas. As an artistic work *The Egyptian Nights*, written in 1828, is the most interesting, and ranks among Pushkin's masterpieces. It tells of an Italian *improvisatore* who, at a party in St

Petersburg, improvises verses on Cleopatra and her lovers. The story is written to lead up to this poem, which gives a gorgeous picture of the pagan world, and is another example of Pushkin's miraculous power of assimilation. Pushkin's prose has the same limpidity and ease as his verse; the characters have the same vitality and reality as those in his poems and dramatic scenes, and had he lived longer he might have become a great novelist. As it is, he furnished Gogol (whose acquaintance he made in 1832) with the subject of two of his masterpieces – *Dead Souls* and *The Revisor*.

The province of Russian folk-lore and legend from which Pushkin took the idea of *Rusalka* was to furnish him with a great deal of rich material. It was in 1831 that in friendly rivalry with Zhukovsky he wrote his first long fairy-tale, imitating the Russian popular style, *The Tale of Tsar Saltan*. Up till now he had written only a few ballads in the popular style. This fairy-tale was a brilliant success as a *pastiche*; but it was a *pastiche* and not quite the real thing, as cleverness kept breaking in, and a touch of epigram here and there, which indeed makes it delightful reading. He followed it by another in the comic vein, *The Tale of the Pope and his Man Balda*, and by two more *Märchen*, *The Dead Tsaritsa* and *The Golden Cock*; but it was not until two years later that he wrote his masterpiece in this vein, *The Story of the Fisherman and the Fish*. It is the same story as Grimm's tale of the Fisherman's wife who wished to be King, Emperor, and then Pope, and finally lost all by her vaulting ambition. The tale is written in unrhymed rhythmical, indeed scarcely rhythmical, lines; all trace of art is concealed; it is a tale such as might have been handed down by oral tradition in some obscure village out of the remotest past; it has the real *Volkston*; the good-nature and simplicity and unobtrusive humour of a real fairy-tale. The subjects of all these stories were told to Pushkin by his nurse, Anna Rodionovna, who also furnished him with the subject of his ballad, *The Bridegroom*. In Pushkin's note-books there are seven fairy-tales taken down hurriedly from the words of his nurse; and most likely all that he wrote dealing with the life of the people came from the same source. Pushkin called Anna Rodionovna his last teacher, and said that he was indebted to her for counteracting the effects of his first French education.

In 1833 he finished a poem called *The Brazen Horseman*, the story of a man who loses his beloved in the great floods in St Petersburg in 1834, and going mad, imagines that he is pursued by Falconet's equestrian statue of Peter the Great. The poem contains a magnificent description of St Petersburg. During the last years of his life, he was engaged in collecting materials for a history of Peter the Great. His power of production had never run dry from the moment he left school, although his actual work was interrupted from time to time by distractions and the society of his friends.

All the important larger works of Pushkin have now been mentioned; but during the whole course of his career he was always pouring out a stream of lyrics and occasional pieces, many of which are among the most beautiful things he wrote. His variety and the width of his range are astonishing. Some of them have a grace and perfection such as we find in the Greek anthology; others – 'Recollections', for instance, in which in the sleepless hours of the night the poet sees pass before him the blotted scroll of his past deeds, which he is powerless with all the tears in the world to wash out – have the intensity of Shakespeare's sonnets. This poem, for instance, has the same depth of feeling as 'Tired with all these, for restful death I cry', or 'The expense of spirit in a waste of shame'. Or he will write an elegy as tender as Tennyson; or he will draw a picture of a sledge in a snow-storm, and give you the plunge of the bewildered horses, the whirling demons of the storm, the bells ringing on the quiet spaces of snow, in intoxicating rhythms which E. A. Poe would have envied; or again he will write a description of the Caucasus in eleven short lines, close in expression and vast in suggestion, such as 'The Monastery on Kazbek'; or he will bring before you the smell of the autumn morning, and the hoofs ringing out on the half-frozen earth: or he will write a patriotic poem, such as *To the Slanderers of Russia*, fraught with patriotic indignation without being offensive; in this poem Pushkin paints an inspired picture of Russia: 'Will not,' he says, 'from Perm to the Caucasus, from Finland's chill rocks to the flaming Colchis, from the shaken Kremlin to the unshaken walls of China, glistening with its bristling steel, the Russian earth arise?' Or he will write prayer, as lordly in utterance and as humble in spirit as one of the old Latin hymns; or a love-poem as tender as Musset and as playful as Heine: he will translate you the spirit of Horace and the spirit of Mickiewicz the Pole; he will secure the restraint of André Chénier, and the impetuous gallop of Byron.

Perhaps the most characteristic of Pushkin's poems is the poem which expresses his view of life in the elegy:

> 'As bitter as stale aftermath of wine
> Is the remembrance of delirious days;
> But as wine waxes with the years, so weighs
> The past more sorely, as my days decline.
> My path is dark. The future lies in wait,
> A gathering ocean of anxiety,
> But oh! my friends! to suffer, to create,
> That is my prayer; to live and not to die!
> I know that ecstasy shall still lie there
> In sorrow and adversity and care.
> Once more I shall be drunk on strains divine.
> Be moved to tears by musings that are mine;

283

And haply when the last sad hour draws nigh
Love with a farewell smile shall light the sky.'

But the greatest of his short poems is probably 'The Prophet'. This is a tremendous poem, and reaches a height to which Pushkin only attained once. It is Miltonic in conception and Dantesque in expression; the syllables ring out in pure concent, like blasts from a silver clarion. It is, as it were, the Pillars of Hercules of the Russian language. Nothing finer as sound could ever be compounded with Russian vowels and consonants; nothing could be more perfectly planned, or present, in so small a vehicle, so large a vision to the imagination. Even a rough prose translation will give some idea of the imaginative splendour of the poem:

'My spirit was weary, and I was athirst, and I was astray in the dark wilderness. And the Seraphim with six wings appeared to me at the crossing of the ways: And he touched my eyelids, and his fingers were as soft as sleep: and like the eyes of an eagle that is frightened my prophetic eyes were awakened. He touched my ears and he filled them with noise and with sound: and I heard the Heavens shuddering and the flight of the angels in the height, and the moving of the beasts that are under the waters, and the noise of the growth of the branches in the valley. He bent down over me and he looked upon my lips; and he tore out my sinful tongue, and he took away that which is idle and that which is evil with his right hand, and his right hand was dabbled with blood; and he set there in its stead, between my perishing lips, the tongue of a wise serpent. And he clove my breast asunder with a sword, and he plucked out my trembling heart, and in my cloven breast he set a burning coal of fire. Like a corpse in the desert I lay, and the voice of God called and said unto me, "Prophet, arise, and take heed, and hear; be filled with My will, and go forth over the sea and over the land and set light with My word to the hearts of the people".'

In 1837 came the catastrophe which brought about Pushkin's death. It was caused by the clash of evil tongues engaged in frivolous gossip, and Pushkin's own susceptible and violent temperament. A guardsman, Heckeren-Dantes, had been flirting with his wife. Pushkin received an anonymous letter, and being wrongly convinced that Heckeren-Dantes was the author of it, wrote him a violent letter which made a duel inevitable. A duel was fought on the 27th of February, 1837, and Pushkin was mortally wounded. Such was his frenzy of rage that, after lying wounded and unconscious in the snow, on regaining consciousness, he insisted on going on with the duel, and fired another shot, giving a great cry of joy when he saw that he had wounded his adversary. It was only a slight wound in the hand. It was not until he reached home that his anger passed away. He died on the 29th of February, after forty-five hours of excruciating suffering, heroically borne; he forgave his enemies; he wished no one to avenge him; he received the last sacraments; and he expressed feelings of loyalty and gratitude to his sovereign. He was thirty-seven years and eight months old.

Pushkin's career falls naturally into two divisions: his life until he was thirty, and his life after he was thirty. Pushkin began his career with liberal aspirations, and he disappointed some in the loyalty to the throne, the Church, the autocracy, and the established order of things which he manifested later; in turning to religion; in remaining in the Government service; in writing patriotic poems; in holding the position of Gentleman of the Bed Chamber at Court; in being, in fact, what is called a reactionary. But it would be a mistake to imagine that Pushkin was a Lost Leader who abandoned the cause of liberty for a handful of silver and a riband to stick in his coat. The liberal aspirations of Pushkin's youth were the very air that the whole of the aristocratic youth of that day breathed. Pushkin could not escape being influenced by it; but he was no more a rebel then, than he was a reactionary afterwards, when again the very air which the whole of educated society breathed was conservative and nationalistic. It may be a pity that it was so; but so it was. There was no liberal atmosphere in the reign of Nicholas I, and the radical effervescence of the Decembrists was destroyed by the Decembrists' premature action. It is no good making a revolution if you have nothing to make it with. The Decembrists were in the same position as the educated élite of one regiment at Versailles would have been, had it attempted to destroy the French monarchy in the days of Louis XIV. The Decembrists by their premature action put the clock of Russian political progress back for years. The result was that men of impulse, aspiration, talent and originality had in the reign of Nicholas to seek an outlet for their feelings elsewhere than in politics, because politics then were simply non-existent.

But apart from this, even if the opportunities had been there, it may be doubted whether Pushkin would have taken them. He was not born with a passion to reform the world. He was neither a rebel nor a reformer; neither a liberal nor a conservative; he was a democrat in his love for the whole of the Russian people; he was a patriot in his love of his country. He resembled Goethe rather than Socrates, or Shelley, or Byron; although, in his love of his country and in every other respect, his fiery temperament both in itself and in its expression was far removed from Goethe's Olympian calm. He was like Goethe in his attitude towards society, and the attitude of the social and official world towards him resembles the attitude of Weimar towards Goethe.

During the first part of his career he gave himself up to pleasure, passion, and self-indulgence; after he was thirty he turned his mind to more serious things. It would not be exact to say he *became* deeply religious, because he was religious by nature, and he soon discarded a fleeting phase of scepticism; but in spite of this he was a victim of *amour-propre*; and he wavered between contempt of the society around him and a petty resentment against it which took the shape of scathing and sometimes cruel epigrams. It was this dangerous *amour-propre*, the fact of his being not only passion's slave, but petty passion's slave, which made him a victim of frivolous gossip and led to the final catastrophe.

'In Pushkin,' says Soloviev, the philosopher, 'according to his own testimony there were two different and separate beings: the inspired priest of Apollo, and the most frivolous of all the frivolous children of the world.' It was the first Pushkin – the inspired priest – who predominated in the latter part of his life; but who was unable to expel altogether the second Pushkin, the frivolous *Weltkind*, who was prone to be exasperated by the society in which he lived, and when exasperated was dangerous. There is one fact, however, which accounts for much. The more serious Pushkin's turn of thought grew, the more objective, purer, and stronger his work became, the less it was appreciated; for the public which delighted in the comparatively inferior work of his youth was not yet ready for his more mature work. What pleased the public were the dazzling colours, the sensuous and sometimes libidinous images of his early poems; the romantic atmosphere; especially anything that was artificial in them. They had not yet eyes to appreciate the noble lines, nor ears to appreciate the simpler and more majestic harmonies of his later work. Thus it was that they passed *Boris Godunov* by, and were disappointed in the later cantos of *Onegin*. This was, of course, discouraging. Nevertheless, it is laughable to rank Pushkin amongst the misunderstood, among the Shelleys, the Millets, of Literature and Art; or to talk of his sad fate. To talk of him as one of the victims of literature is merely to depreciate him.

He was exiled. Yes: but to the Caucasus, which gave him inspiration: to his own country home, which gave him leisure. He was censored. Yes: but the Emperor undertook to do the work himself. Had he lived in England, society – as was proved in the case of Byron – would have been a far severer censor of his morals and the extravagance of his youth, than the Russian Government. Besides which, he won instantaneous fame, and in the society in which he moved he was surrounded by a band not only of devoted but distinguished admirers, amongst whom were some of the highest names in Russian literature – Karamzin, Zhukovsky, Gogol.

Pushkin is Russia's national poet, the Peter the Great of poetry, who out of foreign material created something new, national and Russian, and left imperishable models for future generations. The chief characteristic of his genius is its universality. There appeared to be nothing he could not understand nor assimilate. And it is just this all-embracing humanity – Dostoyevsky calls him πανάνθρωπος – this capacity for understanding everything and everybody, which makes him so profoundly Russian. He is a poet of everyday life: a realistic poet, and above all things a lyrical poet. He is not a dramatist, and as an epic writer, though he can mould a bas-relief and produce a noble fragment, he cannot set crowds in motion. He revealed to the Russians the beauty of their landscape and the poetry of their people; and they, with ears full of pompous diction, and eyes full of rococo and romantic stage properties, did not understand what he was doing: but they understood later. For a time he fought against the stream, and all in vain; and then he gave himself up to the great current, which took him all too soon to the open sea.

He set free the Russian language from the bondage of the conventional; and all his life he was still learning to become more and more intimate with the savour and smell of the people's language. Like Peter the Great, he spent his whole life in apprenticeship, and his whole energies in craftsmanship. He was a great artist; his style is perspicuous, plastic, and pure; there is never a blurred outline, never a smear, never a halting phrase or a hesitating note. His concrete images are, as it were, transparent, like Donne's description of the woman whose

> '. . . pure and eloquent blood
> Spoke in her face, and so distinctly wrought,
> That you might almost think her body thought'.

His diction is the inseparable skin of the thought. You seem to hear him thinking. He was gifted with divine ease and unpremeditated spontaneity. His soul was sincere, noble, and open; he was frivolous, a child of the world and of his century; but if he was worldly, he was human; he was a citizen as well as a child of the world; and it is that which makes him the greatest of Russian poets.

His career was unromantic; he was rooted to the earth; an aristocrat by birth, an official by profession, a lover of society by taste. At the same time, he sought and served beauty, strenuously and faithfully; he was perhaps too faithful a servant of Apollo; too exclusive a lover of the beautiful. In his work you find none of the piteous cries, no beauty of soaring and bleeding wings as in Shelley, nor the sound of rebellious sobs as in Musset; no tempest of defiant challenge, no lightnings of divine derision, as in Byron; his is neither the martyrdom of a fighting Heine, that 'brave soldier in the war of the liberation of humanity', nor the agonized passion of a suffering Catullus. He never descended into Hell. Every great man is either an artist or a fighter; and often poets of genius, Byron and Heine for instance, are more pre-eminently fighters than they are artists. Pushkin was an artist, and not a fighter. And this is what makes even his love-poems cold in comparison with those of other poets. Although he was the first to make notable what was called the romantic movement; and although at the beginning of his career he handled romantic subjects in a more or less romantic way, he was fundamentally a classicist – a classicist as much in the common-sense and realism and solidity of his conceptions and ideas, as in the perspicuity and finish of his impeccable form. And he soon cast aside even the vehicles and clothes of romanticism, and exclusively followed reality. 'He strove with none, for none was worth his strife.' And when his artistic ideals were misunderstood and depreciated, he retired into himself and wrote to please himself only; but in the inner court of the Temple of Beauty into which he retired he created imperishable things; for he loved nature, he loved art, he loved his country, and he expressed that love in matchless song.

For years, Russian criticism was either neglectful of his work or unjust towards it; for his serene music and harmonious design left the generations which came after him, who were tossed on a tempest of social problems and political aspirations, cold; but in 1881, when Dostoyevsky unveiled Pushkin's memorial at Moscow, the homage which he paid to the dead poet voiced the unanimous feeling of the whole of Russia. His work is beyond the reach of critics, whether favourable or unfavourable, for it lives in the hearts of his countrymen, and chiefly upon the lips of the young.

# 5

*Sketches on the Margin of War*

*Maurice Baring saw war in Manchuria as a newspaper correspondent early in the century, and ten years later, as a staff officer in the Royal Flying Corps. If through his extraordinary powers of empathy he felt the sufferings of war as they fell on others all about him he also deeply felt the heroism of war. For he was supremely a romantic, who despite occasions for disillusionment retained his faith in the romantic style. How could horror, stupidity, mindless accident – all the elements of dehumanization – support an idea of glory? And yet they did, and here, as in so many other situations, he seemed to say that life could hardly be worse, while at the same time, man's spirit could triumph over anything, if he could find the dimension beyond himself by which to take his own true measure.*

# War and Illusion

(from *The Puppet Show of Memory*)

I THOUGHT OF ALL the heroes of the past, from the Trojan War onward, and of the words which those who have not fought their country's battles, but made their country's songs, have said about these men and their deeds, and I asked myself, Is that all true? Is it true that these things become like the shining pattern on a glorious banner, the captain jewels of a great crown, which is the richest heirloom of nations? Or is all this an illusion? Is war an abominable return to barbarism, the emancipation of the beast in man, the riot of all that is bad, brutal, and hideous; the suspension and destruction of civilization by its very means and engines; and are those songs and those words which stir our blood merely the dreams of those who have been resolutely secluded from the horrible reality? And then I thought of the sublime courage of Colonel Philemonov, and of the thousands of unknown men who had fought that day in the *kowliang*, without the remotest notion of the why and wherefore, and I thought that war is to man what motherhood is to woman – a burden, a source of untold suffering, and yet a glory.

# An Action in Manchuria

(from *The Puppet Show of Memory*)

A LITTLE BEFORE ONE O'CLOCK a regiment of the First Corps which was in front of us were told to retreat. It was said that the enemy was beginning to turn our right flank. The battery were ordered to fire on a Japanese battery to the south-west, to cover the retreat of a Russian field battery.

The battery went into action at twenty minutes to three. The guns were masked behind the houses of the village, and Colonel Philemonov climbed up a high tree, so as to get a better view. Knowing how ill he was and that he might have a paroxysm of pain at any moment, my blood ran cold. He could not see well enough from the tree, and he moved up the slope of the hill. He began to give out the range, but after two rounds had been fired he fell almost unconscious to the ground, and Kislitski took over.

The Japanese were firing Shimosé shells. We saw a torn mass of a tree or *kowliang* scattered into fragments by the explosion of a shell. But when at three o'clock we left the position we saw it was not *kowliang* nor a tree that had been blown up, but a man. We took up our position on another and higher hill, and the battery fired west, at the farthest possible range, on the Japanese infantry, which we could see moving in that direction against the horizon. This lasted till sunset. At dusk we marched into a village. The infantry was lying in trenches ready for the night attack. Some of the men had been killed by shells, and at the edge of a trench I saw two human hands. The next morning the noise of firing began at four o'clock. We moved into a road and waited for the dawn. It was dark. The firing seemed to be close by. The Cossacks made a fire and cooked bits of meat on a stick. At dawn, news came that the assault of the enemy had been repulsed and that we were to join later on in an attack. The Colonel went to look for a suitable position. I went with him. From the top of a high hill we could see through a glass the Japanese infantry climbing a hill immediately south of our former camp. The Japanese climbed the hill, lay down, and fired on the Russian infantry to the east of them. The Russians were screened from our sight by another hill. The battery fired at first from the foot of the hill, and the enemy answered back from the east and the west. We had to move to a position on a hill farther north, whence we fired on a battery three miles off. The battery went into action at eight. Colonel Philemonov, Kislitski, and I lay on the turf at the top of the hill. Kislitski gave the range. The Colonel had begun to do it himself, but had fallen back exhausted. 'I love my business,' he said to me, 'and now that I get a chance of doing it, I can't. All the same, they know I'm here.' About an hour after the battery had begun to fire, the Japanese infantry came round through the valley and occupied a hill to the north-west of us, and opened fire first on our infantry, which was beneath us and in front of us, and then on the battery. The sergeant came and reported that men were being wounded and horses had been killed: an officer called Takmakov, who had just joined the battery, was wounded. The Japanese infantry were 1,200 yards from us. Three of the guns were then reversed and fired on the infantry. This went on till noon. You could see the Japanese without a glass. With a glass one could have recognized a friend. At noon the infantry retired, and we were left unprotected, and had to retreat at full speed under shrapnel and infantry fire. My pony was not anywhere near. I had to run. The Colonel saw this and shouted to the men to give me a horse, and a Cossack brought me a riderless horse, which was difficult to climb on to, as it had a high Cossack saddle and all a Cossack's belongings on it.

We crossed the river Sha-ho, and just as everyone was expecting a general retreat to Mukden, we were told to recross the river. It began to rain. As we crossed the river, one of the horses had the front of its face torn off by shrapnel. We took up a position on the other side of the river; the first few shots of the enemy fell with alarming precision on the battery, but the Japanese altered the range, and their shells fell wide. Twenty minutes later the enemy's fire ceased all along the line. Afterwards we knew that the reason why it ceased was because the Japanese had run short of ammunition. Kislitski and I walked towards the south to see what was going on. We climbed to the top of an isolated cottage, but could see nothing. Then we came back, and the battery set out for a village south-west by a circuitous route across the river. Nobody knew the way. We marched and marched until it grew dark. The Colonel was in great pain. Some Cossacks and Chinese were sent to find the village. We halted for an hour by a wet ploughed field. At last they came back and led us to the village. We expected to find the transport there. I was hoping to find dry clothing and hot food, as we were drenched to the skin and half-dead with hunger and fatigue. When we arrived at the village I was alone with one of the officers; we dismounted at a bivouac, and the officer went on ahead, expecting me to follow him. I thought he was to come back for me. I waited an hour; nobody came; so I started to look for our quarters. The village was straggling and mazy. I went into house after house, and only found strange faces. At last I got a Cossack to guide me, and, after half an hour spent in fruitless search, we found the house and the officers, but no transport, no food, and no dry clothing. I gave way to temper, and was publicly congratulated by the battery for doing so. They said that it was the first time I had manifested discontent in public.

I spent the night in the Colonel's quarters, and we discussed Russian literature: Dostoievsky, Gogol, and Dickens. He was surprised at a foreigner being able to appreciate the humour of Gogol. I was surprised at a foreigner, I told him, being able to appreciate the humour of Dickens.

At dawn we received orders to hold ourselves ready. Half an hour later we were told to join the First Siberian Corps, which had been sent south to attack.

We marched to a village called Nan-chin-tsa, not far from a hill which the Russians called Poutilov's Hill, and which the English called Lonely Tree Hill. It had been taken in the night by the Japanese. Through a glass you could see men walking on it, but nobody knew if they were Russians or Japanese. Two Cossacks were sent to find out. Wounded men were returning one by one, and in bigger batches, from every part of the field. It was a brilliant sunshiny day, and the wounded seemed to rise in a swarm from the earth. It was a ghastly sight, even worse than at Liaoyang. The bandages were fresh, and the blood was soaking through the shirts of the men. The Cossacks came back and reported that the hill was occupied by the Japanese. We marched back another verst (two-thirds of a mile) and found the corps bivouacking in the plain. All along the road we met wounded and mutilated men, some carried on stretchers and some walking, their wounds fresh and streaming. We marched another verst south again, and the guns were placed behind the village of Fun-chu-Ling, two miles north of the hill to which General Poutilov gave his name. On the way we met General Poutilov himself and the infantry going into action. Colonel Philemonov and I climbed up on to the thatched roof of a small house, whence he gave the range. Kislitski was not there. In front of us was a road; our house was at the extreme right corner of the village; to the right of us was a field planted with lettuce and green vegetables. Infantry were marching along the road on their way into action. A company halted in the field and began eating the lettuce. The Colonel shouted: 'You had better make haste finishing the green stuff there, children, as I am going to open fire.' They hurriedly made off, as if they were to be the target, except one who, greedier than the rest, lingered a little behind the others, throwing furtive glances at the Colonel lest he should suddenly fire on them. The guns were in a field behind us, and immediately under the house where we were perched, two Chinamen, who had been working in the fields, had made themselves a dug-out, and towards tea-time they appeared from the earth, made tea, and then crept back again. The battery opened fire, and the two other batteries shelled the hill, one from the east and one from the west. The enemy answered with shrapnel, but not one of these shells touched us; they all fell beyond us.

A little while later, three belated men belonging to a line regiment walked along the road. Our guns fired a *salvo*, upon which these men, startled out of their lives, crouched down. The Colonel shouted to them from the roof: 'Crouch lower or else you will be shot.' They flung themselves on the road and grovelled in the dust. 'Lower!' shouted the Colonel. 'Can't you get under the earth?' They wriggled ineffectually, and lay sprawling like brown fish out of water. Then the Colonel said: 'You ought to be ashamed of yourselves. Don't you know my shells are falling three versts from here? Be off!' At sunset the battery ceased fire. Soon a tremendous rattle told us the infantry attack had begun. An officer described this afterwards as a 'comb of fire'. We waited in the dark-red, solemn twilight, and later a ringing cheer told us the hill had been taken. Someone who was with us said it was just like manoeuvres. But all was not over, as the Japanese counter-attacked twice. The hill was partly taken, but at what cost we were presently to see.

It grew dark; we sought and found a Chinese house to pass the night in. Men began to arrive from the hill, and from their account it was difficult to tell whether the hill had been taken or not. The Colonel told Hliebnikov to ride to the hill and find out. Hliebnikov said to me: 'He is sending me to be shot like a dog.' We were just lying down to rest when a wounded man arrived asking to be bandaged, then another and another.

The doctor of the battery was with us. The nearest Red Cross Station was eight miles off. Soon the house was full of wounded, and more were arriving. They lay on the floor, on the *K'angs*, on every available place. The room was lit by one candle and a small Chinese oil-lamp. The men had been wounded by bullets and bayonets; they were torn, mangled, soaked in blood. Some of them had broken limbs. Some of them had walked or crawled two miles from the hill, while others, unable to move, had been carried on greatcoats slung on rifles. When one house was full we went to the next, and so on, till all the houses in the street of the village were filled. Two of the officers bandaged the slightly wounded, while the doctor dealt with the severer wounds. The appalling part of the business was, that one had to turn out of the house by force men who were only slightly wounded or simply exhausted. Some of them merely asked to be allowed to rest a moment and drink a cup of tea, and yet they had to be turned ruthlessly from the door, to make room for the ever-increasing mass of maimed and mangled men who were crying out in their pain. As a rule the wounded soldiers bore their wounds with astonishing fortitude, but the wounded I am speaking of were so terribly mangled that many of them were screaming in their agony. Two officers were brought in. 'Don't bother about us, Doctor,' they said; 'we shall be all right.' We laid these two officers down on the *K'ang*. They seemed fairly comfortable; one of them said he felt cold; and the other that the calf of his leg tingled. 'Would I mind rubbing it?' I lifted it as gently as I could, but it hurt him terribly; and then I rubbed his leg, which he said gave him relief. 'What are you?' he said – 'an interpreter, or what?' (I had scarcely got on any clothes; what they were, were Chinese and covered with dirt.) I said I was a correspondent. He was about to give me something, whether it was a tip or a small present as a remembrance I shall never know, for the other officer stopped him and said: 'No, no, you're mistaken.' He then thanked me. Half an hour later he died. One seemed to be plunged into the lowest inferno of human pain. I met a man in the street who had crawled on all-fours the whole way from the hill. The stretchers were all being used. The way in which the doctor dealt with the men was magnificent. He dominated the situation, encouraged everyone, had the right answer, suppressed the unruly, and cheered those who needed cheering up.

Each house was so small, the accommodation in it so scanty, that it took a short time to fill, and we were constantly moving from one house to another. The floor was in every case so densely packed with writhing bodies that one stumbled over them in the darkness. Some of the men were sick from pain; others had faces that had no human semblance at all. Horrible as the sight was, the piteousness of it was greater still. The men were touching in their thankfulness for any little attention, and noble in the manner they bore their sufferings. We had tea and cigarettes for the wounded.

I was holding up a man who had been terribly mangled in the legs by a bayonet. The doctor was bandaging him. He screamed with pain. The doctor said the screaming upset him. I asked the man to try not to scream, and lit a cigarette and put it in his mouth. He stopped immediately and smoked, and remained quite still – until his socks were taken off. The men scarcely ever had socks; their feet were swathed in a white bandage, a kind of linen puttee. This man had socks, and when they were taken off he cried, saying he would never see them again. I promised to keep them for him, and he said: 'Thank you, my protector.' A little later he died.

When we gave the soldiers tea or cigarettes, they made the sign of the Cross and thanked Heaven before they thanked us.

One seemed to have before one the symbol of the whole suffering of the human race: men like bewildered children, stricken by some unknown force for some unexplained reason, crying out and sobbing in their anguish, yet accepting and not railing against their destiny, and grateful for the slightest alleviation and help to them in their distress.

# An Officer's Death

## (from *R.F.C. H.Q.*)

ON JUNE 9TH I received a telegram saying that a great friend of mine, Pierre Benckendorff, the second son of Count Benckendorff, who was Ambassador in London, had been killed in action.

I had seen him off at Moscow station when he started for the Manchurian War. And I had found him in Manchuria when I arrived there. Shortly afterwards he had disappeared in a reconnaissance and had been reported missing. The news of his death was even officially confirmed to me. But somehow or other I did not believe then that he had been killed. This time I had no doubts. A soldier, who was with him, said he had just time to smile and then he fell back.

When I got this news I felt what, alas, one was so often called upon to feel during the war, that the death of a particular person meant the end of a whole chapter of one's life, which was different from other chapters, and could never be repeated.

'All that is ended.' That is what I felt when I heard the news of Pierre's death, and I should like in these pages to pay a small tribute to his memory. He was connected more nearly than anyone else with the happiest days I had spent in Russia. He was one of the most naturally intelligent human beings I have ever met. Completely unambitious, devoted to outdoor life, and shooting, and every kind of outdoor expedition and adventure.

He refused to speak English, although he understood it quite well, and could pronounce it perfectly, and he successfully concealed the fact that he knew French till he was nineteen. He was fond of reading Gogol's stories, Russian translations of Sherlock Holmes, and German translations of Mark Twain. He used to make me read Mark Twain (in German) aloud to him for hours, and laugh uncontrollably, partly at the stories and partly at my un-teutonic rendering, delivery and accent. He had the most satisfactory of all senses of humour, that kind of sense of humour for which nothing is too silly and too foolish. He would riot in the silliest

297

games and occupations. One could spend hours drawing pictures with him that meant nothing, or inventing tunes on the piano. But he was happiest out of doors; shooting duck in the early morning, or waiting for wolves in the snow. The year before the war he was sent to Italy, after a severe illness, and there he no longer concealed his flair and his appreciation for the works of art of antiquity, and all epochs.

The only time he ever went to London I asked him what sights or public buildings or Museums he would like to see, and he said Sherlock Holmes' house. So we drove to Baker Street, and we agreed that Sherlock Holmes' house (according to the story of Colonel Moran in the *Return of Sherlock Holmes*), must be on the right hand side of the street as you drive towards Regent's Park. This is the sort of thing you could discuss with Pierre for hours. We once collaborated in a story I published called 'Sherlock Holmes in Russia', in which most of the subject matter was due to him.

He was a good officer, and once when he asked one of his men why he hadn't cleaned a rifle which was dirty, and the man said he *had* cleaned it, Pierre answered: 'Then you deserve double punishment for cleaning it badly.' He had the eye that sees everything at once, and the mind that understands without any explanation, and need not bother to learn.

In an article on foreign politics, which appeared in a provincial Russian review, discussing the European situation, the writer, a well-known professor, with reference to one of the many Balkan crises before 1914, said: 'The reason why we escaped having to go to war was because we had as ambassador in London the first gentleman in Europe.' Pierre was not unworthy to be the son of a father about whom such a thing could be said from so (as all who know Russia will understand) disinterested a quarter. And he had something also entirely his own, which I have already tried to indicate: a God-gifted naturalness by reason of which it was impossible for him not to understand anything or to strike a wrong note in thought, word or deed, or to be anything other than what he was.

He was more completely devoid of any kind of *pose* than anyone I have ever met. I remember his rollicking amusement when a young lady told him at Nice one day that he was 'beau comme un Dieu'. I was at St Petersburg just before the Japanese declared war on Russia in 1904, and I often saw a troop of his regiment, the *Chevalier Gardes*, riding by over the hard snow; their breastplates and helmets and golden eagles and white tunics glinting in the sunshine under a blue sky, all the brighter for the snow on the ground. One day, a lady told me she was watching this sight, which was as common as seeing the Life Guards ride up St James's Street, and as she was looking at the dazzling troop she noticed one officer younger than the rest and different; and, although she knew Pierre quite well, and was, in fact, his first cousin, she did not at once recognize him 'with his beaver on', but she asked herself who is this apparition? and she told me she thought at once of Shakespeare's description of Prince Harry:

> 'All furnished, all in arms,
> All plum'd like estridges that wing the wind,
> As full of spirit as the month of May,
> And gorgeous as the sun at Midsummer.'

I never saw Pierre with his beaver on; but when he started for the Manchurian War it was difficult to believe that he would ever come back. He seemed to be of those on whom the gods have set their fatal seal. But a nobler fate was reserved to him than to fall in an adventurous war brought about by bungling and intrigue, and alien to the hearts of his fellow-country-men. He was *felix opportunitate mortis*, not only because the circumstances of his death were fitting, but also because, as subsequent events proved, his grief would have, must have, lain onward; his joy behind.

# An Autumn Day in France

## (from *R.F.C. H.Q.*)

LOOKING BACK ON THOSE days at Fère-en-Tardenois, one remembers the time passing in a golden haze. Never was there a finer autumn. And the French landscape, and especially that region of France where we were then, seemed to bask in the richness and the tints of that fine September.

The little gardens were laden with fruit, and the reaped fields were bathed in a calm light. How, one used to wonder, were they reaped, and by whom? The country seemed deserted, save for an old woman here, a child there, and a stray white horse, and yet silently and surely the work was done. In the distance you saw brown ricks, and great long shadows played over the plain.

I remember the heat of the stubble on the Saponay Aerodrome: pilots lying about on the straw; some just back from a reconnaissance some just starting, some asleep, some talking of what they would do after the war; the blazing farmhouses where we used to buy eggs, and chickens, and once a goose. The smell of cider; the courtesy of an old farmer's wife, the proud scorn which lit her face when she said that whatever the Germans might destroy they were incapable by their nature of building a gable or an arch like those of her farm or carving a panel like those in her kitchen. 'Ils n'ont pas de goût!'

There was a château quite close to Fère-en-Tardenois, where we went one day, one of the saddest and most beautiful places I have ever seen. In the garden there were great avenues of trees and a large Renaissance viaduct. Everything was buried in gold and crimson leaves; and Death seemed to be holding a quiet revel there, like a king who commands a private performance in a secluded retreat for a few friends, far away from the theatres of carnage where his public actors were performing daily with so much sound and fury.

In the church at Fère-en-Tardenois, Mass used to be said to a congregation huddled in the chancel, while the aisle was full of wounded and a faint smell of iodoform pervaded the place, and a hospital orderly made the Curé laugh by saying the place would be much better ventilated if the stained glass windows could be broken.

I remember the clucking of the typewriters in our little improvised office, and a soldier singing 'Abide with me' at the top of his voice in the kitchen. And then the beauty of the Henry Farmans sailing through the clear evening, 'the evening hush broken by homing wings', and the moonlight rising over the stubble of the Aerodrome, and a few camp fires glowing in the mist and the noise of the men singing songs of home.

# A Rainy Day in Wartime

## (from *R.F.C. H.Q.*)

IT RAINED ALL THE afternoon. At sunset, about 5.45, a large rainbow appeared in the East. I saw the light suddenly in the office window. I walked down through the garden on to the road and a little way up the hill towards the aerodrome. The sun had set. The west was all a blaze of watery gold, but it was still raining, and the rain drops pattered on the leaves of the trees. The fields on the right of the road were burnished by the sunset. Two white horses were ploughing, but it was too dark to see the ploughman. In the East, against great soft cotton-wool-like masses of white and dull cloud (faintly tinged by the sunset) the little grey town with its red roofs stood out in clear outline, and the cathedral which dominates it, looked like a bird protecting her young. A man in khaki went up the road, whistling. And near the churchyard, on the left of the road, a woman dressed in black was holding a wreath of everlasting flowers. It seemed to me more like sunrise in a dream than like sunset; no, not like a sunset or a sunrise, neither Autumn nor Spring, but the unearthly dawn of a new, strange season. I thought it was perhaps the presage of victory, but victory mingled with tears.

# A Casualty

(The final chapter from *The Coat Without Seam*)

WHEN THE WAR BROKE OUT, Christopher, thanks to Sir Joseph and Dr
Fresham, managed to get out with the R.A.M.C. He wore khaki and a
brassard, and acted as a stretcher bearer with an ambulance. He did not
come into contact with actual war until September 1st, and on that
morning, about eleven o'clock, he found himself at the corner of a road
near a wood with his motor ambulance. The German attack had begun,
and after a morning of shining peace, there was suddenly a tremendous
fire; leaves and branches were falling in the wood. Christopher was with
a trained R.A.M.C. man called Simpson, and a driver called Tuke, who
in peace-time had been a clerk in a Government office.

Towards one o'clock they saw an officer galloping up the road across
which bullets were snapping. He disappeared into the wood. Christopher
and Tuke followed him and when they got there they saw him dismount
and give his horse to someone, and lie down on the ground. He beckoned
to them. He was wounded. Simpson dressed the wound. The firing was
hot. Christopher looked at the man and saw that it was Bruce Lawless.
Lawless recognized him. Just behind them a horse was shot, and Lawless
said:

'You fellows had better go, as you can do me no good, and you will
only be killed or get taken yourselves.'

They put Lawless on a stretcher and gave him morphia. He gave them
his revolver, and at that moment Christopher tripped up over the stump
of a tree and shouted to the others: 'All right, go on, I'm coming.'

A moment later, he was hit himself and must have lost consciousness
for a while; the next thing he remembered was finding himself lying next
to Lawless on the ground.

Lawless said to him: 'You know, these aren't dumdum bullets, they
are allowed by the book, but one can't carry a book about with one to
prove one is playing the game.' He took some bullets out of his pocket,
and threw them into the grass. They could hear German voices. Lawless
said to Christopher:

'I say, I'm for it, and I want to tell you something. I'm sorry about what I did to you. I mean taking Esther from you. They say all's fair in love and war, and I was madly in love with her, but it's been on my mind all my life that I didn't quite play the game. Because I took advantage of your making a fool of yourself just at that moment. I didn't think you loved her – enough. She loved you . . . *then*. Of course it's been all right in a way, and I hope I made her fairly happy. But she gave up her music for me. That was all my fault. I don't believe she would have given it up if she had married you. I wonder if you would mind saying that I can die easy.'

Christopher looked at him, and his life-long bitterness surged up in him and his heart hardened like a stone.

He said nothing.

'You can't?' said Lawless. 'Very well. I suppose I deserve it. I daresay I should do the same.'

At that moment there was a shout of '*Schnell, Kinder*' and swarms of Germans came up and passed them. Lawless had closed his eyes and seemed to be unconscious. Some of the Germans spoke to Christopher. One of them, seeing the red *brassard* on his arm said 'Red Cross!' One of them gave him a coat for a pillow, some water and cigarettes. Another said, 'Why didn't you stay in England? We fought together at Belle-Alliance.' Another said something about the Boers; and another said: '*Verdammter Engländer*'.

Christopher saw the Germans passing as if he were in a dream. He did not know whether he had been given morphia or not. He seemed to lie there for hours. Lawless neither spoke nor moved. Christopher supposed he was dead and felt neither regret nor remorse. After a time some German stretcher-bearers came and carried Christopher to a collecting place for the wounded. They left Lawless where he was, saying he was dead. It grew dark, and in the darkness you could hear the wounded crying like children. Christopher was put in an ambulance and taken to a village. Towards midnight he was carried into the hospital and his wound was dressed. Then he was taken to a shed which was full of English and German wounded. He lay upon the straw, which was covered with blood. Men were moaning and groaning all round him, and one man was raving. The next morning he was taken in an ambulance to another village. The enemy had occupied the village and had only just left it. It was stripped bare, as if a swarm of locusts had devoured its substance. There Christopher found Simpson and Tuke and an R.A.M.C. Colonel. Christopher and the other wounded were put in the Church. It was, Christopher thought, a beautiful church, with stained glass windows. It reminded him of the church at Vernay. A soldier who was lying next to him was telling his beads.

Christopher was half delirious. He had no idea how long he lay in that church; whether it was hours or days. The Curé visited the wounded and did what he could for them. There was a great shortage of bandages. The Curé was an old man. Christopher thought he was the Curé at Vernay, and called him by his name, although he knew he was not the Curé at Vernay, just as in a dream one casts a figure of a person for a particular part and one knows at the same time that the actor is someone else. The Curé asked him whether he was a Catholic. He shook his head and said: '*Autrefois.*' 'Did he not want to make his confession?' 'No,' said Christopher, 'no, no, no.' He relapsed into unconsciousness. When he returned to life, he was told that the Germans had been defeated; they had all gone, and the French had come and gone. Many of the wounded had gone, too. He was still lying in the Church. He had no idea how much time had passed, and when the recent events were explained to him, incoherently by the men next to him, he could not understand. The men were English.

It was a fine September morning. The English soldiers were complaining of the heat and said the Church was stuffy, and that they ought to break the stained glass.

'We asked the Padre to do it,' one of them said, 'but he said it was too valuable.'

Early in the morning the Curé said Mass in the Sanctuary. Many of the wounded followed it. Some of them had rosaries, and told their beads. Christopher watched the Mass from afar like one in a dream. When the bell rang for the Elevation he saw the Church at Vernay, the old Curé whom he remembered was different, or seemed to be different from this Curé. Why were there two Curés? It was all wrong. And where was his *mirliton*? Surely a *mirliton* was necessary at Mass? And where was Mabel? She ought to be there with him. Perhaps she was late, as usual. She was always late. Mademoiselle would scold her, and Mamma would be so cross. Mamma had got on her Sunday gown, the mauve one – and his father had got on his Sunday coat. It was shiny, and his tie was about his collar, and crooked.

He wondered whether the Curé would give him a pear after Mass, a pear and perhaps a *Baba*. Mabel didn't like *Babas* and always gave him hers. Mabel was going to be the Queen of the Gypsies some day and a great singer: Queen Mab. They would take the horses from her carriage and drag her in triumph through the streets of Warsaw. And he was going to be an explorer. He was going to be like Ponce de Leon and discover Eldorado and the fountain of perpetual youth; where was Eldorado? Somewhere near the Fortunate Islands, the Hesperides? Or would he find a forgotten temple and read the inscriptions of a dead language: Etruria, or perhaps it would be in Africa, the caves of Kor; or perhaps he would go to the Holy Land and find a lost relic: the Holy Grail, or the Coat without Seam.

How quickly Mass went by, and yet what a long time it seemed to take. After the Elevation it seemed to last for hours. Christopher wondered what Feast it was. Of course, it was, it must be Sunday. A Sunday after Pentecost. Where was the Chapel with the Holy Coat? It was there, but it was not in its right place. There was the Holy Coat. He could see it distinctly. Reddish brown. Hanging high up, on a pillar. That was the real one. He knew that. That was the *Agnus Dei*. It was not a *Requiem* today. He heard the words, and then the bell again.

### '*Domine non sum dignus*'

The words were distinct, and went straight into his mind, if not into his heart.

There was a long silence.

The Server said the Confession, and Christopher repeated it mechanically. A little girl and a boy and some old women received Communion. Now it was the Blessing. Christopher mechanically made the Sign of the Cross. And then came the last Gospel, and the prayers after Mass. Christopher said them, too, mechanically. He remembered his early instruction and murmured the words *ex opere operato*. '*But whereas the Sacraments of the New Law though they take effect* ex opere operato, *nevertheless produce a greater effect in proportion as the dispositions of the recipient are better, therefore care is to be taken, etc.*' Perhaps, then, even his mechanical prayers were efficacious, but his dispositions had never been good. And ought he to confess that he had killed Mabel? Murder was mortal sin, but it was the intention that counted. Had he meant to kill Mabel? No, but he had meant to bathe, and he knew that bathing might kill her, so he had killed Mabel. It was just the same. Yes, he had killed Mabel. He was a murderer. He would tell M. le Curé, and he would never give him a pear again. He was sure of that. And what would his mother say? She loved Mabel: she did not love him. She had never loved him. Nobody had ever loved him. Esther had never loved him, in spite of what Lawless said. She had loved Lawless. Nobody had ever loved him except Annette: or was her name – Antoinette? And she was dead. Who had killed her? He tried to remember her face, and failed. It was mixed up with Madame Turçin's face, and the face of an actress he had only once seen: Jane Farringdon. Was she dead or had she not married a Hungarian noble? How hot it was! Would not Mass be over by now?

It was over. It had been over for hours. One of the R.A.M.C. men came and spoke to him. It was neither Simpson nor Tuke. It was someone he had never seen. There was a stale smell of blood, iodoform, incense and khaki in the church. Couldn't he be taken out of doors? He asked the R.A.M.C. man. He was an orderly, and he called him

Tuke, although he knew it was not his name. Couldn't he be taken out of doors? He was himself in the R.A.M.C. – his tunic and brassard had gone and he bore no signs of it. The man asked another man, a doctor. They talked to each other, and then presently he was carried out on a stretcher into the courtyard of a small house.

It was a beautiful day. Very still. Cocks were crowing in the distance, the sun shone on the yard. The yard was a square, one side of which was a small house with green shutters and steps leading up to a door; two of the other wings of the yard were stables; the stable doors were open. There were no horses in the stalls, and the remaining wing was a wall with a door that led to the street. The sun shone on the dry white walls. The yard was full of wounded soldiers. There were two Germans lying there on stretchers. They were bandaged and there were veils of thin pink gauze over their faces to keep away the flies. One of them had a purple lump on his forehead as if he had been stung by a wasp. Their faces were like wax. Christopher wondered whether they were dead, but presently one of them said to the other that it was cold.

He heard the doctor say to the orderly that they had telephoned to the . . . what? A string of letters, and *they* had promised to send a lorry and an ambulance to get these men away who were left. The men from the Church had been evacuated. There were no bandages left. Not a scrap of linen or lint. They asked Christopher whether he was all right. He nodded. Did he want any water? No, the last time he had drunk some it had made him sick. Would he like to go indoors? No.

The doctor and the orderly went indoors. Christopher was left with the soldiers, none of whom were badly wounded, and with the two Germans. They were all asleep. He slept too, for a short time or a long time. He did not know which. He was awakened by the sound of a motor horn, and two officers walked into the yard. One of them was an R.A.M.C. doctor. The doctor in charge came out and spoke to them.

Christopher was not only wide awake now, but he had lost all numbness of mind and of body. His wound was hurting him fiercely and his mind had that merciless lucidity which goes with physical pain. Possibly he had been given drugs and their effect had worn off. Christopher listened to the conversation. He heard the newcomers exchange greetings. The two R.A.M.C. men knew each other well. One of the newcomers said:

'Two cars and an ambulance. A Daimler and a Crossley.'

'Splendid,' the doctor in charge said. 'We had better get busy at once and evacuate these cases. None of them are bad. Only three stretcher cases.' He pointed to Christopher and the two Germans.

The newcomers and the local orderly moved towards the Germans. The soldiers began to give vent to complaints. 'It was a shame to take the Germans first.' They then prepared to move Christopher.

'I belong here,' he said. 'I'm in the R.A.M.C., a volunteer stretcher-

307

bearer. At any rate those men must go first.' The new doctor shrugged his shoulders. 'Very well,' he said, 'it's no distance, the cars can come back for the Boches, and for him—' (he pointed to Christopher) 'then there will be nothing for anyone to grouse about.'

They evacuated the men and packed them into the cars, and the men went away whistling and singing. The doctor in charge said to the new-comers: 'Come into the house and have a drink.'

Christopher was left alone with the Germans. They felt cold. One of the officers who had brought the cars came out of the house, and the Germans complained to him of the cold. He fetched some blankets and gave them tea out of a china pot with a spout, and wrapped the blankets round them. During the last few days the heat had been scorching, so Christopher thought, but the Germans complained of the cold. They had marched, they said, for days and nights in the cold.

The officer and an orderly carried them into the stable. 'They will be warmer there, you see,' the officer said.

Christopher shut his eyes and slept once more, but not for long. When he opened his eyes again he saw the Curé talking to one of the officers who had brought the ambulance.

'They rang us up,' said the officer, 'at our H.Q., and said there was a lot of wounded men here, and asked us to lend some cars. We were able to bring a small ambulance and two cars. We have got all the soldiers away now except these two Germans who are in the stable, and that fellow' (pointing to Christopher). 'They are coming back for them presently.' The officer went into the house. Presently there was a noise of shouting and a crowd of villagers, men, women and children, came into the yard shouting, talking and gesticulating; headed by a farmer who was dragging a man in rags.

The Curé asked what it all meant.

'They caught this man,' said the farmer, pointing to the man he was dragging, 'red-handed, signalling to the enemy with this.' The man was holding a tattered red rag and the farmer pointed to it. All the people shouted, 'Spy! Spy!'

The man was wounded and bruised and battered and streaming with blood. His clothes had been torn to shreds.

'It is a lie,' he shouted. 'I am innocent, I swear it. They lie. Save me, *M. le Curé*. They have half-killed me already. I am dying.'

Then the farmer's wife stepped forward. 'He lies, *M. le Curé*,' she said. 'He has been signalling to the enemy. They caught him in the act, and with our *Holy Relic*. He used our Holy Relic to signal with. The Holy Coat: the Coat without Seam that hangs in the Church. He stole it, *M. le Curé*, and used it for his spying. From the steeple, they caught him in the act.'

'They lie,' groaned the wounded man.

'But the man is bleeding to death,' said the Curé.

'Save me,' gasped the wounded man. 'I am innocent. They lie. I am dying.'

The doctors came from the house. The doctor who was in charge and the doctor who had brought the cars. They asked what was the matter.

'There is a wounded man here,' said the Curé, 'and I wanted to know if you had any bandages.'

'We haven't any bandages,' said the doctor. 'Not one. We've used up all the bandages and every scrap of lint. The Germans took away everything. We have sent for some more, but nothing has come. But we will see what we can do for him.'

The crowd became violent and said they would not let the man be treated by the doctors. He was a spy and he must suffer his deserts.

The Curé turned to the doctor and said:

'Leave them to me, *M. le Major*, I will deal with them. Please go back to the house. If you can find some *charpie*, send it.'

'Do you think you can deal with these people?' said the doctor, pointing to the threatening crowd. 'They look to me ugly.'

'Leave them to me, *M. le Major*,' said the Curé. 'Let me be alone with them. I know my people.'

The doctor went back to the house.

The farmer advanced to the Curé and took off his cap. 'With all due respect to you, *M. le Curé*, we know that man is a spy. He was caught in the act and we will see that justice is done at once.'

The wounded man groaned and protested. The Curé spoke with authority.

'My children,' he said. 'You shall leave him to me. He is a dying man. *C'est mon affaire.*'

The farmer protested again, and the crowd snarled. They were like wolves.

'If you take him,' said the Curé, 'it will be across my dead body. Now, *mes enfants*, go home. *All* of you, at once.' There was a silence.

They all went away and left the Curé alone with the wounded man.

Christopher was awake and acutely conscious of what was happening. He took in every detail of the scene as if he were watching a stage-play.

He was lying in the shade. The peace of the afternoon was over everything. The Curé and the wounded man were in the centre of the yard. The man was sitting on the ground and the Curé bending over him.

'Now my child,' said the Curé.

'*M. le Curé*, I am bleeding to death,' gasped the man. 'Bind my wounds. They would have murdered me but for you. I never spied. I swear it. They said it because they hate me. François hates me because he cheated me. His wife hates me. I was already wounded and they have half killed

309

me. I am dying, *M. le Curé*. I swear all this is true. Stop this bleeding. Oh! how I suffer!'

'My child,' said the Curé, 'I have nothing to bandage your wounds with; no *charpie*, not a rag. There is nothing left in the houses. The Prussians took everything away. Every scrap of *charpie* has been used for the soldiers, and I have nothing on me.'

The wounded man held up the crumbling piece of faded red fabric he had been accused of signalling with, and said:

'This will do, *M. le Curé*.'

'Is that the Coat without Seam which belongs to the Church?'

The man nodded.

And in that moment Christopher saw a series of pictures flash past him as distinctly as the slides of a magic lantern: the Roman soldier and his wife, Miriam, and the dying child; the Hungarians on the eve of Mohacs; Sofia about to take the veil; the sale room in London: the actress in powder and lace, Sir Horace Beaufort, her lover, with his coat of velvet embroidered with gold and his waistcoat of cloth of silver: the Abbé.

'How did you find it?' asked the Curé.

'They say I stole it. It is not true. I swear, *M. le Curé*.'

'Do not swear. I believe you already. Where did you find it?'

'I found some children playing with it in the road outside the Church. I swear—. Quick, quick, *M. le Curé*, or I shall die.'

The Curé saw that it was true. The stream of blood seemed to be beyond control. It was a question of seconds. He made the Sign of the Cross and tore the relic into shreds. It was like *charpie*, as thin as a cobweb, and tore easily. The man was now lying stretched out on the ground as on a Cross.

The Curé rolled up a piece of the fabric into a pad, stopped the bleeding, and began to bandage him with other shreds. But as soon as the stuff touched the man, he cried out: 'Stop, *M. le Curé*.'

'What is it, my child?' asked the Curé.

'Wait, I have something to say to you before you bandage me.'

'Let it wait till I have finished. There will be time.'

'No now, now before. Wait a moment, *M. le Curé*! You must hear. What I said just now was not true. Not a word of it. I stole the Coat from the Church after they had moved the soldiers. It is true I wanted to spy. I spied before. I signalled to the enemy with the Coat. They gave me money – but it was not for money. It was revenge. I . . .'

'Patience,' said the Curé, 'my child, till I have bandaged you. Keep still. There, quite still.'

The Curé finished bandaging the man's wounds – there were many on the head, face and arm – with the shreds of the Coat, and when he had finished, he said, 'Now my child, I will hear your confession.'

The man began to whisper, and Christopher felt a sharp twinge of pain, and lost consciousness for what seemed an eternity, but in reality for a short space of time.

When he regained consciousness, the Curé was bending over him. 'And you, *mon enfant*?' he asked.

'How is he?' asked Christopher.

'He is dead,' said the Curé.

'I am dying too,' said Christopher, 'and I want you to hear my confession.'

The Curé heard his confession, and when it was over Christopher said to him:

'I found the Coat without Seam, after all, *M. le Curé*. The real one, you told me about at Vernay, when you gave me the *mirliton*, but I needn't have searched *because it was there all the time*. It was my life that was a Coat without Seam. But I tore it into shreds and now you have mended it. There is no seam in it now.'

'*Oui, oui, mon enfant*,' said the Curé, thinking that Christopher was delirious.

Later, when the ambulance came back, and the doctor and the orderly came to look after Christopher, they saw it was not necessary to send him to the base, for he was dead, but they took back the two Germans.

# 6

## *Poems*

Maurice Baring was ordained as a writer while still a schoolboy. At Eton he wrote his first verses, printed some privately, like many another aspirant to literature, to see how he would look in print, and made determining discoveries for himself in the school library, such as few schoolboys do. 'Dear library, dear musty shelves,' he remembered later, where he saw 'the light of Shelley's song', and heard the tale 'Of his divine desire'. Every literate youth writes poetry, even today, but not all find their lives through the act. Maurice Baring continued to write at Cambridge, and then as a resident in Oxford, and then abroad, forming his style as he outgrew the lyric conventions into which he was born in the eighties and nineties. His poetry forms but a small portion of his large body of work, but it remained a continuing necessity until the late 'twenties, when it served him as elegiac song on the death of his nephew Lieutenant-Commander Cecil Spencer. Sir Edmund Gosse called him 'an English Heredia', and said that his threnody 'In Memoriam: A.H.' – the Lord Lucas to whom he had dedicated Dead Letters in 1909 – lifted him 'to a position among our living poets to which he hardly had a pretension'.

Included in the present selection is a parody of A. C. Benson's poetry which is, as Sir Edward Marsh said, 'a little masterpiece'. It is parody raised above all the usual obvious extravagances, and alternates seriously lovely lines with others soberly idiotic. It belongs here because of its sure command of the English quatrain. As an example of Baring's humour in metrical form at its most blithe, there is here published for the first time, 'Ballade of the Resolution Ward Room'. His translations from the Russian lyric poets exist beyond their faithfulness to the originals for their quality as English poetry.

# Diffugere Nives, 1917

*To J. C. S.*

(from *Collected Poems*)

THE snows have fled, the hail, the lashing rain,
    Before the Spring.
The grass is starred with buttercups again,
    The blackbirds sing.

Now spreads the month that feast of lovely things
    We loved of old.
Once more the swallow glides with darkling wings
    Against the gold.

Now the brown bees about the peach-trees boom
    Upon the walls;
And far away beyond the orchard's bloom
    The cuckoo calls.

The season holds a festival of light; –
    For you, for me,
The shadows are abroad, there falls a blight
    On each green tree.

And every leaf unfolding, every flower
    Brings bitter meed;
Beauty of the morning and the evening hour
    Quickens our need.

All is reborn, but never any Spring
    Can bring back this;
Nor any fullness of midsummer bring
    The voice we miss.

315

The smiling eyes shall smile on us no more;
 The laughter clear,
Too far away on the forbidden shore,
 We shall not hear.

Bereft of these until the day we die,
 We both must dwell;
Alone, alone, and haunted by a cry:
 'Hail and farewell!'

Yet when the scythe of Death shall near us hiss,
 Through the cold air,
Then on the shuddering marge of the abyss,
 They will be there.

They will be there to lift us from sheer space
 And empty night;
And we shall turn and see them face to face
 In the new light.

So shall we pay the unabated price
 Of their release;
And found on our consenting sacrifice
 Their lasting peace.

The hopes that fall like leaves before the wind,
 The baffling waste,
And every earthly joy that leaves behind
 A mortal taste.

The uncompleted end of all things dear,
 The clanging door
Of Death, for ever loud with the last fear.
 Haunt them no more.

The uncompleted end of all employ,
 The wasted store,
The aftertaste of every mortal joy
 Vex them no more.

No more they crave in vain of heedless Fate,
 A last farewell;
No more for them the words: 'No more,' 'Too late,'
 Repeat their knell.

Without them the awakening world is dark
    With dust and mire;
Yet as they went they flung to us a spark,
    A thread of fire

To guide us, while beneath the sombre skies
    Faltering we tread,
Until for us like morning stars shall rise
    The deathless dead.

# Poems from C: *I.M.H.*

## (from *Collected Poems*)

THIS the house we used to know so well;
    This the front door,
And locked. I had no need to ring this bell: –
    Never before.

Where is the sundial with its sphere of gold?
    The vane's bright comb?
All gone! but from the bank the soft black mould
    Still whispers: 'Home.'

Those paths, once cared for, are now choked with grass;
    They've stripped the tower
Of ivy, and exchanged for costly glass
    Our trellised bower.

The old we knew is crumbling in decay;
    The new gives pain;
The soul of home has fled too far away
    To come again.

The door is open: what is this strange face?
    'I'll show you round.' –
'I think I know the way.' Ah! here's the place;
    'Tom Tiddler's ground.'

I walk through empty rooms; she tells her tale:
    'They used to smoke
Here, after dinner. Here, before the sale,
    The walls were oak.'

318

Upstairs. 'Sir, mind the step, – this used to be
  The nursery floor.' –
There is but one thing left that speaks to me:
  A creaking door.

And here, once more I breathe while shadows fall,
  The smell of hay;
The pictures come to life upon the wall;
  My prayers I say.

But hark! what wondrous bird is this that sings
  So sweet a tune?
Now I am borne away on elfin wings,
  Beyond the moon.

The morning sun is streaming through the blind: –
  'They come, they come!
The soldiers! Hark! "The girl I left behind!"
  The fifes! the drum!'

Back to the garden . . . here we used to hide . . .
  Where is the spot,
The summer-house? his garden by its side,
  My rival plot?

A forest now of grass with weeds entwined.
  Ah, there's the mouse!
Ivy! I crawl beneath it, and I find
  Our summer-house.

And here, with buttercups and watering-can,
  We made a brew;
Beneath that tree we called 'Fort Caliban',
  A toadstool grew.

The kitchen-garden. Here's the stagnant tank,
  The floating mole;
The pond with dock leaves and with nettles rank,
  The rat's dark hole.

All is the same. But all is not the same:
  For he is dead.
The well-known cry: 'Hurrah! I've won the game!'
  The curly head,

The laughing eyes, the angry, stammering speech,
    The heart of gold : –
All that is far away beyond our reach,
    Beneath the mould.

He lies not here, but far away beyond
    His native land;
Beneath the alien rose, the tropic frond,
    The burning sand.

His life was like a February day,
    Too warm too soon:
A foretaste of the spring that cannot stay
    Beyond the noon.

As swallows, when September pomps conceal
    A frosty spell,
Fly low about the horses' heads, and wheel,
    To say farewell,

So he, at some sure summons in the wind,
    Or sky, took wing,
And soared to the gold South. He stayed behind
    When came the spring.

They say we'll meet in some transfigured space,
    Beyond the sun.
I need you here, in this familiar place
    Of tears and fun.

I do not need you changed, dissolved in air,
    Nor rarefied; –
I need you all imperfect as you were,
    Here, at my side.

And yet I cannot think that Death's cold wind
    Has killed the flame
Of you, for ever, and has left behind
    Only a name,

That mortal life is but a derelict ship,
    Without a sail;
The soul no stronger than a farthing dip
    Matched with a gale.

I ask, I seek, and to the empty air,
    In vain I cry;
The God they worship, if He hears my prayer,
    Makes no reply.

Lord, give to me the grain of mustard seed,
    That moves the mount:
Give me a drop of water in my need,
    From Thy full fount.

Around me, and above me and beneath,
    Yawns the abyss; –
Show me the bridge across the gulf of Death,
    To banks of bliss.

Cast the dumb devil from my tomb of grief; –
    Help me to say:
'Lord, I believe, help Thou my unbelief.'
    Teach me to pray.

But if the fault be mine, then, Lord, forgive;
    My heart is dry;
So bitter is the world I cannot live; –
    I dare not die.

# *Exile*

———

## (from *Collected Poems*)

THEY with the world would have you reconciled,
Outgrow the impulse of these fantasies,
These rebel storms; and act in grown-up wise.
They know not; in your mother's arms you smiled;

And yet your soul with timeless memories
Was sad; and when old age shall claim you, child,
Your heart with young despair shall still be wild
And childish mirth shall still light up your eyes.

Because a banished spirit in you dwells,
That strayed from lands beyond the unfurrowed sea,
And frets rejecting its captivity;

You hear the horns of the forbidden chase,
The happy ghosts that down the woodland race
And gallop through the trampled asphodels.

# Icarus

*(Translated from the French of Philippe Desportes)*

(from *Collected Poems*)

HERE fell the daring Icarus in his prime,
He who was brave enough to scale the skies;
And here bereft of plume his body lies,
Leaving the valiant envious of that climb.

O rare performance of a soul sublime,
That with small loss such great advantage buys!
Happy mishap! fraught with so rich a prize,
That bids the vanquished triumph over time.

So new a path his youth did not dismay,
His wings but not his noble heart said nay;
He had the glorious sun for funeral fire;

He died upon a high adventure bent;
The sea his grave, his goal the firmament,
Great is the tomb, but greater the desire.

# The Dying Reservist

(from *Collected Poems*)

I SHALL not see the faces of my friends,
Nor hear the songs the rested reapers sing
After the labours of the harvesting,
In those dark nights before the summer ends;

Nor see the floods of spring, the melting snow,
Nor in the autumn twilight hear the stir
Of reedy marshes, when the wild ducks whir
And circle black against the afterglow.

My mother died; she shall not have to weep;
My wife will find another home; my child,
Too young, will never grieve or know; but I

Have found my brother, and contentedly
I'll lay my head upon his knees and sleep.
O brother Death, – I knew you when you smiled.

# 'We Drifted to Each Other'

## (from *Collected Poems*)

WE drifted to each other like two birds,
That meet high in the windy middle air,
Then fly away again; each unaware
That there had passed between us silent words.

Then like two pilgrims, tired and travel-sore
We sought for shelter from the rising tide
Of night, in the dark hollow mountain-side,
And, mutually remembering, met once more.

But when the morning came and we looked down
Upon the glittering cities of the plain,
We lingered in the lonely crag content; –

The world which cannot know the hills will frown; –
But sweet and blissful is the banishment
In the high pinnacles of wind and rain.

# 'We Drift Apart'

## (from *Collected Poems*)

WE drift apart, nor can we quite forget; –
Some link is lost; and that affinity,
That binds us not and will not set us free,
Still tinges all our friendship with regret.

And now I feel our hearts at last have met
In perfect tune; that God made you for me
And me for you; and now that He has set
This veil between us, this mute mystery.

Yet when I wash away the dust of earth,
In the cool kingdoms of celestial dew,
I think that you will meet me with a smile,

The old smile made undying with new birth;
And I'll say this: 'I loved you all the while.'
And you will say: 'I loved you and I knew.'

# Vale

---

(from *Collected Poems*)

I AM for ever haunted by one dread,
That I may suddenly be swept away,
Nor have the leave to see you, and to say
Good-bye; then this is what I would have said:

I have loved summer and the longest day;
The leaves of June, the slumberous film of heat,
The bees, the swallow, and the waving wheat,
The whistling of the mowers in the hay.

I have loved words which lift the soul with wings,
Words that are windows to eternal things.
I have loved souls that to themselves are true,

Who cannot stoop and know not how to fear,
Yet hold the talisman of pity's tear:
I have loved these because I have loved you.

# The Prophet

(from *Russian Lyrics*)

WITH fainting soul athirst for Grace,
I wandered in a desert place,
And at the crossing of the ways
I saw the sixfold Seraph blaze;
He touched mine eyes with fingers light
As sleep that cometh in the night:
And like a frighted eagle's eyes,
They opened wide with prophecies.
He touched mine ears, and they were drowned
With tumult and a roaring sound:
I heard convulsion in the sky,
And flights of angel hosts on high,
And beasts that move beneath the sea,
And the sap creeping in the tree.
And bending to my mouth he wrung
From out of it my sinful tongue,
And all its lies and idle rust,
And 'twixt my lips a-perishing
A subtle serpent's forkèd sting
With right hand wet with blood he thrust.
And with his sword my breast he cleft,
My quaking heart thereout he reft,
And in the yawning of my breast
A coal of living fire he pressed.
Then in the desert I lay dead,
And God called unto me and said:
'Arise, and let My voice be heard,
Charged with My Will go forth and span
The land and sea, and let My Word
Lay waste with fire the heart of man.'

A. S. PUSHKIN

# *Elegy*

(from *Russian Lyrics*)

I've lived to bury my desires
And see my dreams corrode with rust;
Now all that's left are fruitless fires
That burn my empty heart to dust.

Struck by the storms of cruel fate
My crown of summer bloom is sere;
Alone and sad I watch and wait
And wonder if the end is near,

As conquered by the last cold air
When winter whistles in the wind,
Alone upon a bough that's bare,
A trembling leaf is left behind.

A. S. PUSHKIN

# 'I Loved You'

## (from *Russian Lyrics*)

I loved you: and perhaps my love today
Has not yet died away.
Howbeit, that shall no more trouble you;
I would not have you rue.
I loved you utterly remote and dumb,
Jealous: o'ercome;
I loved you with so true a tenderness –
God grant another may not love you less!

A. S. PUSHKIN

# 'Do You Remember'

(from *Russian Lyrics*)

Do you remember, Mary,
A house of bygone times,
And round a pond that slumbered
The immemorial limes?

The overgrown old garden,
The silent walks and trees,
The lengthy row of portraits
Beneath the halls' high frieze?

Do you remember, Mary,
The sky at eventime,
The endless level landscape,
The distant village chime?

The bank behind the garden,
The river's quiet flow,
The shimmering of the cornfields
Where coloured cornflowers grow?

The wood where we the first time
Went wandering, you and I?
Do you remember, Mary,
The days that have passed by?

COUNT ALEXIS TOLSTOY

# *Troparion*

## (from *Russian Lyrics*)

WHAT joy does earthly life possess
That hath no part in earthly sorrow?
What joy that proves not false tomorrow?
Where among men is happiness?
Of all that we through toil obtain
Nothing is lasting, all is vain –
What glories on the earth are sure
And steadfast and unchanged endure?
All is but shadow, dream, and sand,
And like a whirlwind blows away,
And face to face with Death we stand
Unarmed in helpless disarray.
The right hand of the mighty one
Is nothing, naught the king's command –
Lord, now Thy servant's life is done,
Receive him in Thy blessèd land.

Death like a warrior hot with pride
Waylaid and like a robber felled me,
The grave its jaws hath opened wide,
From all that liveth hath withheld me.
Be saved my children and my kin,
From the grave hear my warning knell,
Brothers and friends be saved from sin
So you escape the flames of hell.
Life is but vanity throughout
And, at the scent of death's decay,
Like unto flowers we fade away –
Why do we vainly toss about?
The grave is what was once a throne,

## Troparion

Our palaces a heap of sand –
Lord, now Thy servant's life is done,
Receive him in Thy blessèd land.

Who midst the bones in rotting heap
Is warrior, judge, or king or slave?
Who shall be numbered with the sheep,
Who the rejected evil knave?
Where is the silver and the gold,
O Brothers, where the hosts of slaves?
And who among the nameless graves
The rich and poor beneath the mould?
All is but smoke and dust and ash,
A dream, a shade, a phantom flash –
Lord, but in Thy bright paradise
Our refuge and salvation lies.
All that was flesh beneath the sun
Shall fade, our pomps shall rot in sand –
Lord, now Thy servant's life is done,
Receive him in Thy blessèd land.

And Thou who for the world dost weep,
Thou, Advocate of the oppressed,
We cry to Thee, the Holiest,
For him our brother here asleep.
Pray to Thy God-begotten Son,
Pray, O most pure of womankind
That now our brother's life is done
He leave his sorrow here behind.
All is but smoke, and dust, and wraith,
O friends, in phantoms put no faith!
When we upon some sudden day
Shall scent the breath of death's decay,
We shall be stricken everyone,
Like corn beneath the reaper's hand –
Lord, now Thy servant's life is done,
Receive him in Thy blessèd land.

I travel on a road unknown,
Half hopeful, half in fear I go.
My sight is dim, my heart a stone,
My lids are sealed, my hearing slow,
And motionless, bereft of speech,
I cannot hear the brethren wail,

333

And out of sight and out of reach
The censer's blue and fragrant veil;
But till in endless sleep I fall,
My love shall never pass away,
And by that love I, brethren, pray
That each thus unto God shall call:
Lord, on that day when moon and sun
Shall vanish at the trump's command –
Now that Thy servant's life is done,
Receive him in Thy blessèd land.

COUNT ALEXIS TOLSTOY

# *Informes Hiemes Reducit Jupiter*

(a parody of A. C. Benson, from *A Number of People,*
by Sir Edward Marsh)

The busy sun, laborious, large,
  Above the trees is sinking slow;
The chilly fields from marge to marge
  Are white with complicated snow.

Above the towering, tumbled hills
  Shy grey clouds wander near and far;
The impatient ravens bite their bills
  Awaiting the unpunctual star.[1]

And hidden by the selfish reeds
  The imperial moorhen sits alone,
Like some great priest that counts his beads,
  Unconscious of the pontiff throne.

Along the hard and dinted road
  The frost is muttering words of fear,
And strives with bitter shot to load
  The unsubstantial atmosphere.

Six months ago the hopeful plains
  Were starred with spiky bits of bloom;
The subtle cowslip taking pains
  Forgot the hints of distant doom.

[1] This anticipates the 'vague unpunctual star' in *Grantchester*; but I am pretty sure
Rupert Brooke never saw the piece. [E. M.]

335

And where today the teal blaspheme,
  And huddled widgeon curse the cold,
Red berries dyed the timorous cream,
  And wasps with liveries of gold,

Like anxious footmen, buzzed about,
  And tender maggots glimmered green,
While in the yard with dreaming snout
  The hog lay wistful and serene.

What means the sudden change, the glimpse
  Of leafless tree and barren sky?
How comes it that the pheasant limps
  And stupid starlings starve and die?

Alas, 'tis vain to catechize
  The airy plans of Providence;
Perchance in some far-off assize
  We'll know the wherefore, why and whence.

What though we miss the goal, the good,
  And fringe the nearer, sullen base,
And dare not utter as we would, –
  Two straight lines cannot hold a space.

# Ballade of the Resolution *Ward Room*

I can't drink whisky with a grin,
And soda cocktails make me sick,
And bitters bore a hole through tin,
And brandy neat has too much kick;
I think this ship is far too quick,
But since you summon me to quaff,
For once I don't mind giving in –
I think I'll have the other half.

I have drunk Han-Shen at Pekin,
And shandygaff at Eton Wick;
Deep draughts of Pilsner at Berlin,
And Viking's Mead at Reykjavik,
And Benedictine made from brick
And vodka with a Russian staff.
You say there's something in the bin?
I think I'll have the other half.

My head will soon begin to spin;
My utterance is growing thick;
I've sprained my thumb and bruised my shin,
And broken someone's walking stick;
I cannot see the flickers flick,
I cannot read the barograph –
But just to drown the sense of sin,
I think I'll have the other half.

### ENVOI

Prince, though I hate the taste of gin, –
I can't think why that makes you laugh –
I'm feeling very well within: –
I think I'll have the other half.

# *Stop-Shorts* [1]

(from *Selected Poems*)

THE lake is growing grey: the lotus flower
Remains yet roseate with the sunset hour.
The moon has climbed above the mountain's rim:
The water shines: the lotus flower is dim.

•

The mist is on the sky and sea, a veil:
And in the silver stuff a russet sail.

•

I waited for you all the dark night long,
And listen lonely to the sky-lark's song.

•

The twilight is not darker than the day,
And pipes are playing somewhere far away.

•

Here once a thousand men in battle died,
Where the red clover grows by the wayside.

[1] 'Stop-shorts are Chinese poems in four lines. They are called Stop-Shorts because the sense goes on when the sound stops.' – M. B., in *The Puppet Show of Memory*.

338

# Cecil Spencer

## (from *Selected Poems*)

*Lieutenant Commander Cecil Spencer[1] died at Malta on 14 February
1928 from injuries received while riding. He gained the D.S.C. and Bar
and Legion of Honour for gallantry in action at Zeebrugge on 23 April,
and Ostend on 10 May 1918.*

'Lieutenant the Hon. Cecil E. R. Spencer, D.S.C., R.N. This officer
was in command of a coastal motor-boat (No. 23) and escorted *Vindictive*
close inshore and kept touch with her until she gave the "last resort"
signal, on which he laid and lit the flare, which greatly assisted the
operation, drawing heavy fire, previously directed at the *Vindictive*, on
to himself.' (*From Sir Roger Keyes' despatch, 24 July* 1918.)

> IT was the feast day of St Valentine,
> And turbulent and fine;
> And the wind tossed the high clouds through the blue;
> The dust in eddies flew,
> Round and round,
> On Marsa Polo Ground;
> The game was fast that day;
> You were not there to watch it, nor to play;
> For you were racing Death in Bighi bay.
>
> Down in the sheltered harbour it is dark.
> The lights are twinkling. Hark!
> The noise of carnival!
> The band! the singing and the stamping feet!
> The boats are taking dancers to a ball,
> And masqueraders flitting through the street.
> The wind has rattled over Bighi bay,

[1] He was Maurice Baring's nephew.

339

Knocked at the windows of the hospital
Throughout the day,
And made them shake.
Heedless, you would not wake;
For the last race was being run,
The struggle not yet ended, the labour still undone.

Now all is ended and now all is done.
No labour more for you on land or sea,
Adventure, sorrow or felicity,
No fighting, and no riding, no disaster, and no fun,
For all is ended now and all is done.
And all has ended well;
For us, but not for you, the sharpness of farewell.

Now through the darker air,
A more tremendous flare
Than that which with its million-candle power
You took to Zeebrugge, to draw the fire,
Is rising for you like a sun;
A still more wondrous hour,
Most secret, most supreme, your heart's desire:
As you would say:
'Swift Death and no long dalliance with decay.
When life is at its fullest and its best,
Then let the signal come in the midst of the game!'
The signal came.
The boat is called away.
And you go west.

Rest, grant him rest, the lapping waters sighed;
Rest, everlasting rest, the wind replied;
The anchorage of immortality;
The light and dew of dawn throughout eternity.

The noise of festival came from the bay,
Heedless you lay;
Hardly breathing, slowly dying,
While the ships in the harbour lying,
Under the starry skies,
Watched you with sleepless eyes.

And Ceres and Calypso and Bryony
All kept you company.

The last notes of the Last Post sounded and died.
You seemed to know
The time was now at hand for you to go.
More gently and more softly came your breath,
For the Angel of Death
(Oh! noiselessly he called away the boat!)
Saluted you and saw you over the side,
And safe afloat,
Upon the eternal tide.

The sun was shining in an azure sky,
When Queen Elizabeth went proudly by,
Through the grand harbour bound for Hagiar Khim,
And bugles sounding the salute
(Whole ships were at attention stiff and mute)
Rang like the trumpets of the Seraphim.
Destroyers, submarines raced through the blue,
And overhead the roaring seaplanes flew;
Resolution, Valiant, Warspite were under way;
(Their firing was that day).

Good visibility, a little swell;
All the fleet's business which you knew so well.

Upon the quarter-deck, which was your pride,
On the port side,
A space was set apart;
Elsewhere the work proceeded, noiseless, smart;
And there in a steel coffin strong and sure,
You lay secure,
And over it the Union Jack outspread.
With arms reversed and bended head
A sailor at each corner mourned the dead.
Assistance sacrificed her 'make and mend',
And worked all night so that your journey's end
Should happen thus on board, and here at sea,
As you (they knew) and they, would have it be.

Then we reached Hagiar Khim, and there,
Facing the rocky headlands, where
Phoenicians built huge temples to strange suns,
And where perchance Ulysses watched the foam
(For this they say was once Calypso's home)
Between this high and haunted coast,

And a rock used as target for the guns,
There where a hero welcomes you for host,[1]
They gave you to the wave.
And there you lie with all the sea for grave.

The firing party fired its rounds of blank,
The last note of the Last Post sounded and died.
The wreaths thrown over the side
Drifted upon the tide,
And sank.
And now the band
With pipe and clarion
And the gay quickstep summoned every hand
To carry on.

[1] Sir Walter Congreve, V.C. was buried at sea in the same place.

Rome, February 27th, 1928. [M. B.]

# In Memoriam A.H.

(from *Selected Poems*)

Auberon Herbert, Captain Lord Lucas, R.F.C.,
killed 3 November 1926

Νωμᾶται δ' ἐν ἀτρυγέτῳ χάει

THE wind had blown away the rain
That all day long had soaked the level plain.
Against the horizon's fiery wrack,
The sheds loomed black.
And higher, in their tumultuous concourse met,
The streaming clouds, shot-riddled banners, wet
With the flickering storm,
Drifted and smouldered, warm
With flashes sent
From the lower firmament.
And they concealed –
They only here and there through rifts revealed
A hidden sanctuary of fire and light,
A city of chrysolite.

We looked and laughed and wondered, and I said:
That orange sea, those oriflammes outspread
Were like the fanciful imaginings
That the young painter flings
Upon the canvas bold,
Such as the sage and the old
Make mock at, saying it could never be;
And you assented also, laughingly.
I wondered what they meant,
That flaming firmament,

Those clouds so grey so gold, so wet so warm,
So much of glory and so much of storm,
The end of the world, or the end
Of the war – remoter still to me and you, my friend.

Alas! it meant not this, it meant not that:
It meant that now the last time you and I
Should look at the golden sky,
And the dark fields large and flat,
And smell the evening weather,
And laugh and talk and wonder both together.

The last, last time. We nevermore should meet
In France or London street,
Or fields of home. The desolated space
Of life shall nevermore
Be what it was before.
No one shall take your place.
No other face
Can fill that empty frame.
There is no answer when we call your name.
We cannot hear your shout upon the stair.
We turn to speak and find a vacant chair.
Something is broken which we cannot mend.
God has done more than take away a friend
In taking you; for all that we have left
Is bruised and irremediably bereft.
There is none like you. Yet not that alone
Do we bemoan;
But this: that you were greater than the rest,
And better than the best.

O liberal heart fast-rooted to the soil,
O lover of ancient freedom and proud toil,
Friend of the gipsies and all wandering song,
The forest's nursling and the favoured child
Of woodlands wild –
O brother to the birds and all things free,
Captain of liberty!
Deep in your heart the restless seed was sown;
The vagrant spirit fretted in your feet;
We wondered could you tarry long,
And brook for long the cramping street,
Or would you one day sail for shores unknown,

344

## In Memoriam A.H.

And shake from you the dust of towns, and spurn
The crowded market-place – and not return?
You found a sterner guide;
You heard the guns. Then, to their distant fire,
Your dreams were laid aside;
And on that day, you cast your heart's desire
Upon a burning pyre;
You gave your service to the exalted need,
Until at last from bondage freed,
At liberty to serve as you loved best,
You chose the noblest way. God did the rest.

So when the spring of the world shall shrive our stain,
After the winter of war,
When the poor world awakes to peace once more,
After such night of ravage and of rain,
You shall not come again.
You shall not come to taste the old Spring weather,
To gallop through the soft, untrampled heather,
To bathe and bake your body on the grass.
We shall be there, alas!
But not with you. When Spring shall wake the earth
And quicken the scarred fields to the new birth,
Our grief shall grow. For what can Spring renew
More fiercely for us than the need of you?

That night I dreamt they sent for me and said
That you were missing. 'Missing, missing – dead':
I cried when in the morning I awoke,
And all the world seemed shrouded in a cloak;
But when I saw the sun,
And knew another day had just begun,
I brushed the dream away, and quite forgot
The nightmare's ugly blot.
So was the dream forgot. The dream came true.
Before the night I knew
That you had flown away into the air
For ever. Then I cheated my despair.
I said
That you were safe – or wounded – but not dead.
Alas! I knew
Which was the false and true.

And after days of watching, days of lead,
There came the certain news that you were dead.

You had died fighting, fighting against odds,
Such as in war the Gods
Aethereal dared when all the world was young;
Such fighting as blind Homer never sung,
Nor Hector nor Achilles never knew;
High in the empty blue.

High, high, above the clouds, against the setting sun,
The fight was fought, and your great task was done.
Of all your brave adventures this the last
The bravest was and best;
Meet ending to a long embattled past,
This swift, triumphant, fatal quest,
Crowned with the wreath that never perisheth,
And diadem of honourable death;
Swift Death aflame with offering supreme,
And mighty sacrifice,
More than all mortal dream;
A soaring death, and near to Heaven's gate;
Beneath the very walls of Paradise.
Surely with soul elate,
You heard the destined bullet as you flew,
And surely your prophetic spirit knew
That you had well deserved that shining fate.

Here is no waste,
No burning Might-have-been,
No bitter aftertaste,
None to censure, none to screen,
Nothing awry, nor anything misspent;
Only content, content beyond content,
Which hath not any room for betterment.
God, who made you valiant, strong and swift,
And maimed you with a bullet long ago,
And cleft your riotous ardour with a rift,
And checked your youth's tumultuous overflow,
Gave back your youth to you,
And packed in moments rare and few
Achievements manifold
And happiness untold,
And bade you spring to Death as to a bride,
In manhood's ripeness, power and pride,
And on your sandals the strong wings of youth.
He let you leave a name

## In Memoriam A.H.

To shine on the entablatures of truth,
For ever:
To sound for ever in answering halls of fame.

For you soared onwards to that world which rags
Of clouds, like tattered flags,
Concealed; you reached the walls of chrysolite,
The mansions white;
And losing all, you gained the civic crown
Of that eternal town,
Wherein you passed a rightful citizen
Of the bright commonwealth ablaze beyond our ken.

Surely you found companions meet for you
In that high place;
You met there face to face
Those you had never known, but whom you knew;
Knights of the Table Round,
And all the very brave, the very true,
With chivalry crowned;
The captains rare,
Courteous and brave beyond our human air;
Those who had loved and suffered overmuch,
Now free from the world's touch.
And with them were the friends of yesterday,
Who went before and pointed you the way;
And in that place of freshness, light and rest,
Where Lancelot and Tristram vigil keep
Over their King's long sleep,
Surely they made a place for you,
Their long-expected guest,
Among the chosen few,
And welcomed you, their brother and their friend,
To that companionship which hath no end.

And in the portals of the sacred hall
You hear the trumpet's call,
At dawn upon the silvery battlement,
Re-echo through the deep
And bid the sons of God to rise from sleep
And with a shout to hail
The sunrise on the city of the Grail:
The music that proud Lucifer in Hell
Missed more than all the joys that he forwent

347

You hear the solemn bell
At vespers, when the oriflammes are furled;
And then you know that somewhere in the world,
That shines far-off beneath you like a gem,
They think of you, and when you think of them
You know that they will wipe away their tears,
And cast aside their fears;
That they will have it so,
And in no other wise;
That it is well with them because they know,
With faithful eyes,
Fixed forward and turned upwards to the skies,
That is is well with you,
Among the chosen few,
Among the very brave, the very true.

# 'Alone When Pride Lies Dying'

(from *Robert Peckham*)

ALONE when pride lies dying in the dust,
And living dreams are trampled under foot,
And scotch'd like a dead snake lies earthly lust,
And sweet desire is torn up by the root;

Alone when busy aims are cast away,
And glory tested shows as false alloy,
And fortune's prize but as a brittle toy,
The world's rewards but garlands that decay;

When every tie that strongly bound the heart
To mortal heart than life itself more dear,
Is cut in twain, however sharp the smart,
And howsoever bitter be the tear;

Alone when all that wealth is sunk and drown'd
Can that which is beyond all price be found.

> *Written | as by Robert Peckham | at
> Loreto on Palm Sunday*, 1569.

# 7

## A Novel

*Maurice Baring's two masterpieces in the novel are* C *and* Cat's Cradle, *and the latter seems to me the more beautifully achieved in form, style, and the sense of life retained in art. Both are very long books – over three hundred thousand words in the telling and both required this scale to give us the sense of complete lives woven together. Limitations of space in this volume made it impossible to reproduce either book entire; but for a moment I thought to make a sizeable extract from either which would sustain a thread of story and yet be short enough for this collection. As I read for the purpose of finding the suitable thread, I realized what I had not known so clearly before – that long as they are, and seemingly shapeless, as most of life seems shapeless, the novel in each case was so tightly constructed that it was impossible to detach any of its parts from the rest. I was reminded then that Maurice Baring's novels are all like separate chapters, some long, some short, out of an extremely copious chronicle; and that to show him as a novelist I had only to find one of his shorter novels.*

*His penultimate one, here presented, gives us in smaller compass examples of the virtues which keep his works moving off the page into our own possession as experience. He tells the story here at one remove – someone has told him something, and he tells it to us: 'This is the story, or rather, what I have made of it.' He thus frees himself to use his familiar technique of offhand narration which is so convincing, and he gives us a parable of loveliness, the most true delicacy of an exquisite woman, thrown away for love which summons her through the body of vulgarity. She sees beauty and finds that it encloses insensibility. The mystery, and Baring's usual compounded love stories whose lines cross, give the book a shimmer of feeling far beyond what the words so directly say. He published only one more novel – Darby and Joan, in 1935.*

# The Lonely Lady of Dulwich

(*complete*)

## To B. and C.

*Post tempestatem magna serenitas.*

*Thomas à Kempis.*

### CHAPTER I

IN THE SUMMER OF 1919 I spent a fortnight at Haréville taking the waters. There I met an old lady whom I will call Mrs Legge. I was living at Dulwich at the time.

Mrs Legge hearing this, asked me if I had met a Mrs Harmer who lived there. I had not. In the course of the fortnight I spent at Haréville, Mrs Legge told me Mrs Harmer's story; this is the story, or rather what I have made of it.

Oliver Mostyn, half Irish, with a dash of French blood, educated in Germany and Paris and widely travelled, had been an adventurer in the best sense of the word. He had been adventurous, and adventures had come to him. In some ways he had been like Dryden's famous portrait of Buckingham: everything by starts and nothing long, nearly successful in so many enterprises and undertakings but never quite: he made a discovery just too late, someone had just made it; he had nearly won the Grand National, riding the horse that had come in fourth; he had three times almost been elected to Parliament; he had once practically made a fortune, but had lost it immediately. He wrote a play which was produced and was almost a success, but the same play was soon after written by someone else, and was a success. He was a handsome, gay, popular man, good-humoured, friendly and easy. The one thing in his life which was not a failure was his marriage. His wife was an American from the South, who had been brought up in a French convent: Dolores Foyle. He had met her in Paris. This all happened a long time ago, and

353

he was married before the days of the Second Empire. In her youth she was beautiful: transparent, fair, blue-eyed, and ethereal; the dazzle of her looks and her complexion passed quickly; but the radiance of her good humour and of an inexhaustible vein of fun remained. She had three daughters, and her whole life was spent in an arduous and, in the end, successful effort to make both ends meet. That they did meet, in spite of her husband's irrepressible and spontaneous extravagance, was due to her unobtrusive cleverness as a manager and to her unostentatious talent for housekeeping. She had been poor in her youth; she had done the housework and the cooking herself, and nobody could make a more appetizing salad or a lighter omelette. Her daughters grew up extremely good-looking; and she hoped they might marry well. She took them out in London, where her husband would take a house for the season. He had to live in London sometimes – he explained – because of the racing; he was obliged to race, not for pleasure, of course; he didn't care for racing, he would say, 'unless you go for the day with a pal, and even then it's a damned bore'; but he had to race from economy so as to meet his expenses. His wife never contradicted him when he said this, but merely hoped he would not lose quite as much money as at the last meeting. On the whole, he was lucky, and didn't lose much; but he certainly made nothing; for what he did win on the race-course he lost at the clubs, playing cards.

Dolores pinned her hopes on her daughters.

The eldest was rather too like a waxwork for real beauty, and exaggerated like a child's picture of a beauty; she was born in the wrong age, and would have been perfect for the screen; nevertheless, she attracted everybody's attention and arrested the devotion of an English nobleman, Lord St Alwyn, and all seemed well. He was wealthy and of good lineage, had possessed estates and a London house. Unfortunately, soon after the marriage he lost all his fortune on the Turf. Everything had to be sold; things went badly in every way; discord at home was the first result, and finally separation. His wife, Teresa, went abroad and settled in a pension at Florence; there was no divorce, as the Mostyns were Catholics. There were no children. Teresa was given an allowance by her husband's trustees, and he lived on cheerfully in debt, as before, and in grave sin with a respectable-looking widow. Everyone said he had behaved badly.

The second daughter, Agnes, a dark Juno-like figure, married a respectable but obscure Italian diplomat: one of those diplomats who seem to be sent only to the uninteresting places. She was, however, quite happy, whether at Berne, or Rio, or Cettinje.

Then there was the third daughter, Zita. Her mother, who had been in her youth better-looking than all her three daughters put together, said with a sigh that Zita was not going to be so good-looking as her sisters. She would not, in fact, hold a candle to them.

But Oliver Mostyn, who was a great connoisseur of female beauty, said that Zita would be first, and the rest nowhere, and that she would marry a millionaire. When Zita was eighteen, and just about to come out, after having spent five years at a convent, she was, in spite of her mother's dismal prognostications, a lovely creature. There was a softness and a radiance about her that made you at once think of the dawn and doves, of apple-blossom and lilac and lilies-of-the-valley.

But just as she was ready to be taken out in London, Oliver Mostyn died of a cold caught at a race-meeting, much to the regret of a number of friends, especially those who played whist with him at his club, where he managed to lose everything except his temper.

Oliver's death altered the whole situation. He had left little; there was little to leave. Dolores sold what she could and migrated to the South of France, taking a cheap little apartment at Cannes, whence, after a short time, she migrated to a cheaper pension at San Remo. The first year, being in deep mourning, they spent in comparative seclusion. The next year Dolores did the best she could for Zita, who was greatly admired, but in spite of her beauty – perhaps because of it – had no success. It seemed, in fact, to keep people aloof and at a distance, until Robert Harmer appeared on the scene. It was Easter-time, and Dolores and Zita were at Nice; it was the last gay winter season of the Second Empire.

Robert Harmer was in business, a North-country Englishman, a banker, successful and well-to-do. He fell in love with Zita at first sight, and determined to marry her. Before the end of a fortnight he had spoken to Dolores and had proposed to Zita. Dolores was, of course, enchanted. Did he mind Zita being a pauper? Not a bit. Did he mind the difference of religion? Not at all; not even if the children——? No, for in those days the sons of mixed marriages could still be brought up in the religion of their father, the daughters in their mother's. Robert Harmer had no objection; he thought it did not matter what the religion of women was, and not very much what that of men might be, unless it made things inconvenient.

Zita was not in the least in love with him. So far there had been only a fleeting shadow of a romance in her life. She had been attracted by a good-looking but unsatisfactory young man who was said to be undesirable, reckless, unscrupulous, and a spendthrift. He acted on the theory that every woman is at heart a rake, and that, if you make it quite clear at once that you are yourself a rake, heart, body and soul, you are certain to find favour. The more aloof, difficult and remote a woman might seem to be, the more ardent and persistent were the advances that he made. He was generally successful, People seemed shy of Zita, and said they could not get on with her. Not so Rupert Westrel, for such was his name; he treated Zita with familiarity and ease;

disguising nothing, and paying her the most outrageous compliments. Dolores was a little bit uneasy, but Rupert attracted her, and she could never resist a sense of humour, which he had in an eminent degree. He proposed to Zita, and she accepted him at once; but, as neither of them had a penny, they agreed to wait. While they were waiting, Rupert made the acquaintance of a luscious and lively American heiress. Soon, with an air of resigned martyrdom, he broke off his engagement with Zita, deeply against his will, as he explained, and shortly afterwards he was engaged to the heiress and married her. They both, it may be said, lived to regret it. Zita was not heart-broken, but she was disappointed. Rupert had been charming to her, and nobody else spoke to her at all.

Zita refused Robert Harmer's first proposal, but six months later he renewed it.

This time she consented, much to the delight of her mother. In accepting Robert, Zita had simply followed the dictates of common sense. 'If I fall in love with anyone, he is sure to be undesirable, impossible, in fact,' she reasoned, 'because those are the people one falls in love with; and if I don't marry it means hanging around my mother's neck like a millstone, while she drags me round from pension to pension and denies herself everything. She has done that all her life. She had hopes of her other daughters; they disappointed her, and now I have the chance of making all right by marrying a man who may not be a Romeo or a Prince Charming, but is desirable, honest, kind, and well-off.'

Marriage was a shock to Zita, a much greater shock than she had expected. She not only discovered when she had married someone that she had married someone else, but all the facts of marriage, major and minor, were a shock and a surprise to her. They lived in the country, in a house called Wallington. Robert was as kind as possible, and wanted her to have her way in everything. There was no mother-in-law; such relations as he had were either dead or at a distance. She had nothing to complain of. He made no difficulty about her religion, and she was driven to Mass every Sunday. Zita was not particularly religious, but fulfilled her duties as a matter of course. But it was chiefly the want of any interchange of ideas or interests that surprised her. She knew less about her husband and his doings than if he had been living at the South Pole. Every Monday morning, except at Christmas, Easter, Whitsuntide and in August, he went up to London and stayed there till Friday evening, sleeping at his club, where he had a permanent bedroom. He never mentioned his affairs. He was never cross or ill-tempered. He was anxious that Zita should enjoy herself and have everything she liked. He would beg her to invite her friends to the house. She had none. Her sisters were both abroad, so was her mother; and she did not wish for the searchlight of Mrs Mostyn's all-seeing glance to be thrown on the situation.

She saw quite a number of people; there were neighbours. Robert often asked them to luncheon on Sundays, and for visits during the shooting season, in the autumn, or at Christmas. Five miles off there were Lord and Lady St Eustace, who lived childless in their historic house, where Queen Elizabeth had slept and Charles II had hidden, which was, nevertheless, often full of people, young and old, and where luncheon was laid for fourteen every day, whether there were guests or not. Then a little nearer there were Colonel Gallop and his wife, Lady Emily. He was a great deal younger than she was; they had sons and daughters. Emily Gallop was full of energy, and flattered herself she knew about almost everything on earth – the sports of men, the traditions of the army and the navy, as well as the feminine accomplishments of women; the arts as well as the crafts. She would inspect Zita's needlework and criticize it, and make her play duets with her on the pianoforte or accompany her while she herself sang. She had a robust contralto voice, and sang a little out of tune when tired; at other times she would insist on inspecting the bedrooms and the stables at Wallington, or spend an evening going through Zita's household books with her, seeing what might be reduced with advantage. She would come with her husband, whose high spirits were almost excessive, and one felt that in spite of all her energy, Emily Gallop was a little fatigued by her husband's youth. Sometimes Robert and Zita would go and stay with the Gallops. Visits in those days seldom lasted less than a week, and sometimes ten days, and even when Robert was too busy to go himself, Zita used to go by herself to long shooting-parties, or in the summer to cricket-weeks.

But on the whole, she did not mind these visits, for both the Gallops and the St Eustaces were friendly. Then there were many other neighbours who did not entertain, but who came for the day or for a meal: the Anglican Bishop of Easthampton, a cultivated, charming, and paradoxical divine, suspected of having leanings towards the Greek Church; and his wife, who was a mass of erudition and militant philanthropy. They never appeared on Sundays; they were too busy, but they sometimes came to dine. Then there was the local parson who lived in the village, rubicund and old-fashioned, fond of partridge-shooting and port; and his next-door neighbour, Charles Baxter, who was in the city, in Baxter and Coles's firm, and a great friend of Robert's. He was a bachelor, and used to come to Easthampton at Easter and Christmas, and sometimes for a week or two in September and October. He was middle-aged, but he liked the young. He was fond of racing, coursing, and Homer and Horace. His first two hobbies he was able to share with Robert Harmer; not the third; indeed, the only books at Wallington were a whole series of bound volumes of Ruff's *Guide to the Turf*; and the only instrument of culture, and indeed the only outstanding ornament in the encircling leather and rep, was a barrel-organ that imitated an orchestra and made a deafening noise.

In the autumn of the first year of her marriage Zita gave birth to a little girl, but, after a long confinement, during which her sufferings were great, the baby was still-born. The doctors said Zita could never have another baby. Robert took the news calmly, as if he had always expected it. Another year passed in the way which has been described. Zita never went to London; neither her mother nor her sisters came to see her. Mrs Mostyn had settled down to live with her eldest daughter, Teresa, at Florence. Business then made it necessary for Robert to go to Buenos Aires; Zita went with him. She enjoyed the journey and the new sights and sounds, and the colour; but life was not different. The only people they saw were business friends of Robert, who smoked large cigars, and occasionally the British Minister or one of the secretaries from the Legation. Zita made no friends, and the climate did not agree with her. They lived there two years.

And then one day Robert told her suddenly they were going to Paris for good, at least for some years.

They settled in Paris. Robert Harmer took the apartment and engaged the servants. He did all that. It was taken for granted Zita was incapable of any practical action. Zita thought that a new life was about to begin for her. She had not enjoyed living in the country in England; she had liked South America still less. Altogether marriage had been a shattering disillusion to her, little as she had expected. Now she was looking forward to Paris. She had never lived there, but she had been through it and heard a great deal about it from her father.

'I expect we shall get to know a lot of French people,' she said to Robert the day they arrived there.

'French people keep to themselves,' said Robert.

'My father used to say he knew a lot of people,' she said, 'such interesting people – writers.'

'I don't care for Bohemians,' he said, 'frowsty sort of sportsmen.'

'But he knew all sorts of people – doctors, lawyers, and soldiers.'

'They would be too clever for me,' said Robert.

'But Papa used to go racing a great deal.'

'Yes, he did,' said Robert, rather grimly.

After this conversation, Zita suspected the worst.


## CHAPTER II

Zita's fears were realized. Their life in Paris was just the same as it had been in England and in Buenos Aires. Robert invited either his partner or a business friend to luncheon or to dinner; they talked business and smoked large cigars. Robert went to the races when he could. They knew no French people; they left cards at the Embassy, and went to one garden-party at the end of the summer. The theatres were shut. Once or twice they dined at a café chantant out of doors. Robert took Zita to the Opera once, but slept through the performance. Zita spent much time by herself. She drove in the Bois in the afternoon, and sometimes went to picture galleries with her maid.

Zita had only one friend, Flora Sutton, the wife of a stockbroker, a friend of Robert's, who often came over for the races, or just for pleasure. Robert had let Wallington for five years, and in August he took a shooting lodge in the north of Scotland and invited three men friends beside Wilfred Sutton and his wife.

To the outward world Zita appeared to be neither happy nor unhappy; she had for the moment lost the radiance she had had as a girl – it had been drenched and saturated in tears – but this was not surprising, after her sojourn in the trying climate of South America. People said the elements of beauty were still there undiminished, though temporarily eclipsed. She and her husband had arrived in Paris at the end of one summer; a year passed and then another, when they again went to Scotland and entertained the same guests, and things might have gone on for ever had it not been for the advent of a new Second Secretary at the British Embassy. His name was Cyril Legge. He was forty-two years old: he had been already to Paris, Berlin, Buenos Aires, Rome and Constantinople. He had a literary vein and was slightly Bohemian, but he was thought to be a good man of affairs, in spite of that, and a successful diplomat. He was popular; foreigners liked him. When he was thirty and *en poste* at Rome he had met Amelia Foster, Robert Harmer's first cousin, and married her; they had two children. They were poor, but Amelia was clever and practical, and Cyril was a good manager, too; they were devoted to each other and got no end of fun out of life.

Cyril arrived at Paris late in July to take up his duties. It was his first morning at the Chancery, and he was sitting in the little room which was his by right, he being head of the Chancery, when the Chancery servant brought him a card bearing on it the name of Robert Harmer. The name conveyed nothing to Legge, but the Chancery servant explained that the visitor said he was a cousin of Madame's.

'I suppose I must see him,' Legge said, with a sigh. 'Show him in.'

In walked a tall and large middle-aged man with an open-air complexion and shrewd eyes. Legge greeted him as if he had been awaiting his arrival with impatience.

'I am Amelia's first cousin,' said the visitor. 'I only heard yesterday that you had arrived.'

'Of course,' said Legge, who had no idea which cousin he might be, and knew nothing about him. 'Amelia hasn't arrived yet. I'm alone.

We've taken a flat, a little apartment, but we can't get into it until the end of the month, so Amelia has taken the opportunity to stay with her mother. The Ambassador is very kindly putting me up till she comes. She won't be here for another month.'

There was a pause.

Harmer evidently had some subject on his mind which he found some difficulty in broaching.

'I think you know Sutton,' he said, 'he's on the Stock Exchange. He's been staying here; he came over for the Grand Prix.'

Cyril recollected a prosperous, cultivated and rather sleek young man whom he had sometimes seen at the St James's Club.

'Well, he knows all about pictures and furniture and all that . . . and he was saying that Zita . . . that my wife ought to be painted. The question is, who is to do it? It would have to be done here, you see, because I spend any holidays I get shooting in Scotland. He advised me to consult you, and when he mentioned your name, knowing, of course, you were Amelia's husband, I thought you wouldn't mind.'

'Of course I'd do anything to help,' said Legge. 'Sutton would know far more about it than I do. I haven't been here long, and it's ten years since I was here *en poste*. That was before the war.'

'If we were in England,' said Harmer, 'it would be easy to get a fellow who's in the Academy; but who could do it here?'

Harmer talked as if they were on a desert island.

'I think there are still plenty of painters,' said Legge, inwardly amused. 'What did Sutton think?'

'He told me of a fellow called Bertrand.'

'Ah,' said Legge.

He knew Bertrand's work; he wondered what Mrs Harmer was like, and whether she was to have a voice in the matter; so far it did not seem as if she were.

'You've never met my wife,' said Harmer, 'but I think you know her sister, Lady St Alwyn.'

'Oh yes, we met at Rome; she was very kind to us.'

Legge now understood who Mrs Harmer was. He was at once interested.

'I believe Bertrand is thought to be one of the coming men,' he said. 'He hasn't quite arrived yet, but I think he will, and that has the advantage of making him less expensive,' he said, with a twinkle.

'It's not so much the money I mind,' said Harmer, 'but I want, you know, the kind of picture one can hang on one's walls at home without having to explain to everyone who and *what* it is.'

'I think his pictures are thought like,' said Legge.

'Is he in Paris now?'

'We can easily find out.'

Legge soon discovered where he lived. Harmer still looked helpless. Legge thought he saw the difficulty.

'I know a friend of Bertrand's,' he said, 'would you like me to get him to get Bertrand to make an appointment with us, and we could go together to his studio? We should see some of his work there, and if you liked it you could arrange for sittings.'

Harmer said that would suit him exactly. Legge supposed that Mrs Harmer would accompany them, or, at any rate, be consulted.

'Then I will let you know what he says,' was all he said.

'Thanks most awfully,' said Harmer. 'As soon as Amelia arrives you must let me know, and come and have a meal in my house. I want her to know – my wife.'

Harmer went away. Legge arranged the meeting with Bertrand through an old French friend of his, a connoisseur of pictures and a friend of artists, and a few days later he was able to write to Harmer telling him of the date and hour of an afternoon appointment suggested by Bertrand.

Harmer wrote that he would call for Legge in his carriage half an hour before the time mentioned. Legge was curious to see, when the time for the appointment came, whether Harmer would bring his wife with him or not. He arrived at the appointed time by himself. They drove to the studio, which was on the other side of the river.

Bertrand received them. He at once made a favourable impression on Harmer; firstly, because he was dressed neither in a blouse nor in black velvet, but just like anyone else; his hair was of the ordinary length. Secondly, he spoke English. He had lived in England at various periods of his life. Thirdly, he was utterly unaffected.

On an easel there was the portrait of an English lady, the wife of a well-known statesman. She was painted in an evening gown of pale yellow satin. Legge recognized the original of the picture at once.

'Mrs H,' he said, 'I think it's wonderfully good.'

Bertrand did the honours of his studio and offered Harmer a glass of Madeira and some cakes. Harmer sipped the Madeira, which he hated doing between meals. He said he thought the studio must be convenient, that he knew nothing about art himself, but that he liked a portrait to be like: that of Mrs H was a speaking likeness. Bertrand showed them a few landscapes he had done, and apologized for showing landscapes to an Englishman, as 'the English are the masters of us all', he said, 'in landscape'.

Harmer was surprised at finding that Bertrand was so young – he was not more than thirty-five – and he had an idea that all successful painters were at least fifty years old. They talked about England: Cambridge, where Bertrand had lived for a term; the Norfolk Broads, Scotland, the Yorkshire Moors, English gardens, and the Thames, and then suddenly

Harmer looked at his watch and said he must be going, and as they went to the door he mumbled to Bertrand:

'I wonder, Monsieur Bertrand, whether you would paint me a portrait of my wife?'

Bertrand said he would be charmed. 'But perhaps,' he said, 'Madame Harmer would not care for my style of painting.'

'Oh yes, she would,' said Harmer.

'When could she come and sit?'

'She can come any time, and you must make the picture any size you like.'

A date was fixed. Nothing was said about the price. That matter had already been dealt with through the good offices of Legge and his friend, the connoisseur, and Harmer was perfectly satisfied with the sum that had been mentioned.

But Legge wondered more than ever what Mrs Harmer's attitude was, and would be, and he wrote that night a long letter to his wife, whom he justly considered the most sensible person in the world. He wrote describing Harmer's visit in detail.

## CHAPTER III

When Harmer told Zita that he had arranged for her to sit to Bertrand for her portrait, she was less surprised than she might have been, because Wilfred Sutton had reported to his wife what Harmer had told him, and Flora Sutton had told Zita. She had seen a picture by Bertrand at an exhibition, and had liked it; but she told Flora Sutton she was quite indifferent who should paint her, and was only pleased with anything that satisfied Robert. Robert took his wife to the studio on his way to his office, and left her there. He would send his carriage to fetch her.

Bertrand was astounded when he saw her; Legge had told him that she was supposed to be good-looking, and that she was one of three beautiful sisters; but he expected something large, British, a full-blown Romney, or else a haggard Pre-Raphaelite – too tall and too thin. But Zita was neither.

She was beautiful, in spite of looking listless and pale at the moment. Yes, she was beautiful, more than beautiful, he thought, and he wondered why she was so particularly beautiful; and he wondered for the millionth time at the mystery of mortal beauty. What was it? That is to say, what was it when you could not define it, when you could enumerate no special outstanding attributes? When you could point to speaking eyes and chiselled features, majesty, perfect proportions, exquisite finish, it was simple enough. If Bertrand had seen Zita's sisters, he would have had no difficulty in defining their quality and pointing out their assets and what was lacking. But here there were none of these things in a high enough degree to account for the whole effect. There were no obvious assets: soft eyes, yes; a well-cut face, a good line, a charming expression . . . and yet you looked, he did, an artist, that is to say . . . spellbound. He could not take his eyes off her. There was nothing marvellous, no obvious perfection, and yet there was something in the whole of her appearance, something that emanated from her texture, line, movement and expression like a phrase of music, or the light on a cloud, or the unexpected sight of a branch of blossom, or the sudden scent of a hyacinth, something in the *substance* beyond the accidents of flesh and bone, shape and colour; and that substance was celestial.

'She is beautiful. Yes,' thought Bertrand, 'but what is her impalpable quality, that is, as it were, outside beauty and beyond it?'

He asked her how she would like to be painted.

'Just as you like,' she said. 'Paint me just as I am. Only I suppose I had better take off my hat?'

'Why?' said Bertrand.

'It will be out of fashion next year,' she said.

She was wearing a small straw bonnet tied under her chin with a black ribbon.

'It is a great mistake,' said Bertrand, 'to be afraid of the fashion when one is painting a portrait, or to try and neutralize it. Nothing dates so quickly and so sharply as fancy-dress, and when people have their portraits painted and try to make the clothes of the day look of no date, but as much as possible like fancy-dress, the picture dates quicker than one which accepts the fashion and doesn't mind; the hair always betrays the date, even when the model is dressed as Cleopatra or Mary Stuart.'

'I expect you know best,' said Zita. 'Paint me just as you like, but without my bonnet.'

'Just as you are,' Bertrand said, laughing, 'but with the bonnet, a profile. It will be perfect. I promise you in ten years' time your coiffure will have become far more old-fashioned than your hat.'

'Very well,' said Zita, with a sigh, 'with the bonnet.'

And so the sittings began. And with the sittings began a new life for Zita. Bertrand did not talk much while he worked, but he talked unlike anyone she had met hitherto. He was a slow worker, and Zita did not make him feel inclined to work faster. They talked on general topics, and the more often Bertrand saw Zita the less he felt he knew her; she was so young, and yet she seemed so old for her age; so inexperienced and yet (so he felt) disillusioned, with possibilities of gaiety all locked up in a box.

And then she seemed so utterly aloof; to know nobody, either here in Paris or in England; and she talked of her mother and of her sisters as if they belonged to another world.

Bertrand was married and he told his wife about this strange Englishwoman who was so unlike any of the English women he had ever seen or heard of. One evening Bertrand and his wife received a visit from his wife's brother, Jean de Bosis, who stayed to dinner. Jean de Bosis was only twenty-seven years old. He had literary ambitions and had written some verse; some of it had been printed in reviews, but as yet he had not published a book. Jean asked Bertrand whether he was busy.

'I am doing a portrait of an English lady.'

'What is an English woman doing in Paris at this time of year?' asked Jean.

'She is living here: her husband is in a bank. They stay here all the summer and take their holiday in autumn or winter, not to miss some kind of sport – I forget which.'

'I see,' said Jean, 'she is *sportive*.'

'Not at all. It is her husband, who is much older than she is.'

'Then she is young and pretty?'

'Young, yes; pretty is not the word. She is . . . she is interesting to paint . . . and difficult – very difficult.'

'Is she one of those English women who are as tall as poles and flat as boards?'

'No, she is not like that. She looks to me like a flower that is pining for want of sunlight.'

'What flower?' asked Jean.

'A branch of lilac,' he said, 'but on a day when there is no sun. If there were only sunlight, one feels she would be dazzling. That is by the way. I don't know what she will suggest to you, but to me she is like something dazzling that for the moment is undergoing a soft eclipse.'

'Perhaps she is like the Sleeping Beauty in the wood?'

'Perhaps; I don't think so. I think she is wide-awake, so wide-awake that she can never get to sleep; but if you would like to see her, all you have to do is to come to my studio tomorrow between ten and twelve – she will be there.'

'And the husband?'

'An Englishman . . . clean and sensible – likes racing.'

'He loves his wife?'

'He would be capable of being jealous – he wouldn't be easy.'

'Does he come with her?'

'He brings her always, but he never stays.'

The next morning – it was a hot morning in July – Jean de Bosis went to Bertrand's studio. He found Bertrand hard at work painting Mrs Harmer. She was dressed in muslin and wearing her little straw bonnet.

'Talk as much as you like,' Bertrand said, after he had introduced them, 'but forgive me if I am rude and absent-minded. I am in the middle of something difficult.'

Jean sat down. Zita seemed to be interested in him at once; his features were a little rough: his eyes, dark and grey and trustful, and full of understanding and gentleness. They were talking of people going away, of the heat, the crowd.

'Personally, I like Paris in July, one feels so much freer,' he said.

'I used to feel like that in London in August, when it was supposed to be empty. It was just as full really, only the five or six people you *didn't* want to see were away, and that made all the difference.'

'That's just it,' said Jean. 'You miss London, madame?'

'Oh, no. I lived in London very little after I was grown up – only a month. My husband lived in the country, and my mother lives abroad.'

'The English country is so lovely,' said Jean.

'You know it?'

'Only from Bertrand's descriptions and from books.'

'You speak English?'

'Not at all, and I only read English books in translation. But I have read Shakespeare, Byron, Dickens, and Ouida. You are a great reader, madame?'

'I read novels, and I forget them.'

'French novels?' asked Jean.

'French, English, and even Russian novels translated – Tauchnitz, mostly. It passes the time.'

'You must be homesick for England.'

'Not at all,' Zita smiled. 'I like Paris and I like French people; they are so civil, and then they notice that one exists.'

'Did you escape notice in England?' Jean asked, with an accent of good-humoured irony. 'That would, I think, be difficult to believe.'

'But it is true, nevertheless.'

'English people must be very absent-minded.'

As he said this he looked at her with such undisguised admiration that she felt shy and blushed.

'Do you read novels?' she said, to change the subject.

'I have read all the novels everyone has read. One has to do that once, and then one need never do it again.'

'Jean de Bosis is a poet,' said Bertrand. 'He has published sonnets in the *Revue Blanche*.'

'That is the sad truth,' said Jean.

'Why sad?' asked Zita.

'Because if they had been really good they would have been refused.'

'They were accepted,' said Bertrand, 'because they prove that he has something in him: whether he will write verse or not, is another affair. I am sure he will write something.'

365

'I often wonder,' said Jean, taking no notice of what Bertrand had said, 'whether things in life ever happen as they do in a novel. Do you think they do?'

'When you are reading a novel,' said Bertrand, 'you oughtn't to feel it has really happened. A novel must not be too life-like, or else where does the artist come in?'

'If a writer,' said Jean, 'invents a whole story and means you to think it like life, and you *do* think it like life, I consider he is a good artist. But life seems to me so badly constructed, as if the author were constantly forgetting what he had meant his characters to do.'

'He never forgets what he means his characters to be,' said Bertrand; 'people remain themselves.'

'I don't agree,' said Jean. 'I think people are continually changing. They say that every seven years one has a totally new body. I am quite certain that every seven years one has a totally new mind. One has become a different person. And think of one's friends. Every seven years one wants a new set of friends.'

Bertrand laughed.

'What are you laughing at?' asked Jean.

'I was wondering how you could possibly know. Seven years ago you were a schoolboy.'

'I wasn't; I was a soldier. I don't have to wait seven years to change,' said Jean. 'I can't look at the books I adored three years ago.'

'And the people?' asked Zita.

'Oh people – people are all alike. The more they change the more they stay the same.'

'That's exactly what I said just now, and what you contradicted,' said Bertrand.

'I meant, we always see the same people here, we never see anything new, different, never hear anything original, fresh, except . . .' he stopped.

'Except when?' asked Zita.

'I stopped just in time; I was just going to pay you a banal compliment, madame, and then I remembered that English people don't like compliments.'

'Don't they?' asked Zita, with serious expression.

Jean laughed.

'Why are you laughing?' she asked.

'It is you who are laughing at me.'

'Oh! No! I assure you.'

'Bertrand,' said Jean, 'you should paint Madame Harmer just as she was just now, when she laughed at me with her serious face; it would be marvellous. May I see?'

He walked towards the easel.

'No, not yet, wait till the end of the sitting. I shall not be a moment.

I have done all I can today. There is little more I can do at all. The truth is, madame, you are too difficult – no, painters don't pay compliments. There is something intangible; it is as if there were a curtain of gauze between you and the world, and then every day you are different. But it is more than that. It was as if you had the gift of making yourself almost invisible; of closing your petals. I feel there is something to see which I could paint, but you will not let me see it. You are wearing an invisible mask; or perhaps it is that I don't know how to paint – how to look. What a trade! There now, I've finished for today.'

'May we look?' asked Zita.

'Yes, you may look now.' He walked back himself and looked at the canvas critically.

'It seems to me wonderfully painted,' said Zita; 'of course I can't judge.'

'Yes,' said Jean, 'it's good; it's very good; *mais il y a quelque chose qui manque*, the touch of mockery, the malice.'

'Ah! that was not there last time,' said Bertrand.

'You think I am mischievous, wicked?' asked Zita.

'Not wicked, but I think if you liked you could be very——'

'Very what?'

But at that moment Bertrand's servant announced that monsieur was awaiting madame below.

## CHAPTER IV

The sittings went on for a month, and Jean de Bosis attended them often, but the picture did not seem to advance. These sittings made a great difference to Zita's life: they brought something new into it, and something gay.

Zita never met either Bertrand or Jean de Bosis anywhere except at the studio, and this situation might have continued unchanged but for the arrival of Legge's wife, Amelia. She arrived, although the apartment was not ready, feeling that if she did not come it never would be ready. Perhaps she was right.

Amelia Legge was not pretty, but everybody said she had a nice face. She arrived in Paris with her two little boys . . . she was only just over thirty; practical, shrill, plaintive, energetic, shrewd, inquisitive, and brimming with human interest. She stayed at an hotel one day only; the next day she and her husband moved into their apartment which, although it looked then as if it could not be finished for months, was, after they had once got into it, practically finished in forty-eight hours.

They dined together on the night of their arrival, at their favourite restaurant out of doors, near the Rond Point. And they had hardly finished their melon when Amelia said: 'Fancy Robert being here!'

'Yes,' said Legge, 'and established for good, at least I suppose for the next four or five years, or perhaps for ever; he's a partner in the Bristol Bank. But what really interests me is his wife; what is she? I asked the young men in the Chancery, and all they know is that she has been here since the summer before last. He goes to the races regularly, and she goes *nowhere*.'

'Well,' said Amelia, 'if I may say a word, darling, I can tell you quite a lot about her. In the first place, she is Teresa St Alwyn's sister.'

'I know, your cousin told me that.'

'The youngest. Robert met her at Nice. They were married the year before we were married, and then they went to England and lived, I think, in the country, at Robert's house, Wallington, near Easthampton, a dreadful place, a regular "Bleak House". She's good-looking, but nothing like so good-looking as the sisters, so they say.'

'Well, I'm not sure you're right,' said Legge. 'Bertrand says she's a dream.'

'Artists!' said Amelia, 'they always admire what other people don't admire. They like discovering something nobody else sees; in fact, they like what they can paint.'

'But he says she's unpaintable.'

'You haven't seen her?'

'No. I left cards, but your cousin made it plain he didn't want to do anything till you came.'

'Poor child; she must be lonely,' said Amelia. 'But we will change all that; I've written to Robert already.'

Two days later Robert asked the Legges to luncheon.

'Amelia would like,' he explained to his wife, 'a lot of jabbering Frenchmen to meet her, but she won't get that here.'

'I think she sounds rather alarming,' said Zita.

'No,' said Robert, 'Amelia's all right really; she's a sensible woman, but she's restless, and she likes to have a finger in every pie.'

She arrived the next day at one. She was unlike what Zita had expected. Zita had expected something gaunt and spare, and tall and hard; Amelia Legge was soft and fair, essentially comfortable. She was warm in her manner. Cyril Legge was affable, buoyant and gay. Amelia greeted Robert affectionately, and then said:

'So this is Zita. I used to know your mother a little. You are like her and like your beautiful sisters. You didn't tell me, Robert, she was the most beautiful of the lot. I remember your elder sister, Teresa, coming out; it was the year I came out; she made a sensation, but there. . . .'

There was not a shadow of doubt that Amelia admired Zita. The Suttons and Wilmot, his partner, whom Robert had asked, arrived, and they went in to luncheon.

Sutton asked after the portait, and Zita said it had been almost finished when Bertrand had painted out everything he had done and started afresh.

'I must see it at once, dear,' said Amelia, 'I admire Bertrand's work *enormously.*'

'I've got a sitting tomorrow,' said Zita, 'if you would like to come.'

'I should like it above all things.'

'Then you can bring Zita back,' said Robert, 'and have luncheon with us.'

'Does Robert always take you to and from the studio?' asked Amelia.

'Always to,' said Zita, 'and sometimes from.'

'He's damned slow painting the thing,' said Harmer; 'nearly a month now, and he's hardly begun.'

'Bertrand is always like that,' said Sutton. 'He is a slow starter; he'll work for six weeks and throw away everything he has done, then start again and finish it off in forty-eight hours.'

'I hope it will be worth looking at when it's finished,' said Harmer. 'I wish we could have had it done in London by Millais, or someone like that.'

'You're lucky to have got Bertrand,' said Amelia; 'you will never regret it.'

They talked of other things. When the party broke up Amelia stayed behind with Zita.

'You must tell me at once,' she said, 'when you want to get rid of me, but as I am Robert's cousin and have known your sister, I can't feel that you are a stranger.'

Zita thought Amelia original, lively, and comfortable. On the other hand she did not feel that anybody so intensely interested in human nature and in other people's affairs as Amelia obviously was, could help being indiscreet.

Amelia spoke a great deal of Paris, the Paris that she had known as a child, and that was now so changed, but where she still had a great many old friends – friends of her parents.

After asking Zita whether she knew so-and-so and so-and-so, Amelia realized that Zita knew no French people at all.

'So you know no French people?' she said.

'Not one, except Mr Bertrand who is painting me, and there is another man who has been once or twice while I have been sitting.'

'Who's that?' asked Amelia.

'His name is Jean de Bosis; he writes.'

'I will ask Madeleine if she knows him. You must know Madeleine Laurent, she is a great friend of mine. She doesn't write herself, but she knows all the writers. She likes English people, too – sincerely. She has even been to England, once. Fancy Bertrand painting you! Whoever put that into Robert's head? Robert's a dear, and I'm devoted to him, but the arts are not his strong point.'

'It was Mr Sutton who suggested it,' said Zita, 'and your husband approved.'

'I suppose you've been to the Embassy?'

'We went to a garden-party.'

'But, my dear child, why live like a hermit? Why not make friends?'

'Foreigners bore Robert,' said Zita, 'and I am rather shy too. I am quite happy as I am.'

'Seeing no one; going nowhere?'

'I see a great deal of Robert's English friends.'

Amelia Legge needed to hear nothing further. She divined the tenor of Zita's life with perfect accuracy. And she was appalled.

'Unless something is done,' she said to herself, 'this will end in disaster.' And Amelia Legge was one of those people who, when they resolve that a thing is to be done, set about to do it.

She drove back to her apartment. She wrote a few letters and then drove to keep an appointment with her friend, Madeleine Laurent. Madeleine Laurent lived in a small apartment in a street leading into one of the new avenues. She was expecting Amelia Legge, and greeted her warmly with a wealth of kisses and exclamations. They each gushed at each other for a time. They both had warm, expansive, exuberant natures. Madeleine Laurent was a widow. In her youth she had done a little professional painting, but now she had given it up. Her husband had been dead some years. She lived for her friends, of whom she had a great number, both in France and England.

She was small, dark, but not at all semitic-looking; her nose turned up a little; her eyes were full of observation and fun. There was something electric about her, but the electricity was in her expression; her movements were calm and rare.

She led Amelia to a divan in a room almost entirely furnished with high bookcases and without pictures, except the portrait of a man on an easel, and bombarded her with pertinent questions. She commented briefly, sometimes only by a nod of the head, on Amelia's answers.

'I've found a cousin here,' said Amelia, 'who is married.'

'What cousin is that?'

'Nobody, my dear, you would know, a middle-aged *homme d'affaires*; but the point is he has now married the daughter of people I knew, a girl whom I had never set eyes on till yesterday, and she's a real beauty, and charming.'

'*Quel genre?*' asked Madame Laurent.

'I don't know. I have never seen anybody like her. You would notice her anywhere. She has got a lovely smile and wide apart eyes; but she is celestial – like a tune played on muted strings or on a piano with the *sourdine*.'

'Tall?'

'Not really, I think, but she made me feel even smaller than I am.'

'And how long have they been married?'

'Seven years.'

'Then she is much younger than her husband?'

'Oh, much; she is only about twenty-seven.'

'And children?'

'There was one – still-born. She can have no more.'

'And any *roman*?'

'Ah, that I don't know. It is the first time I have seen her. I know Robert, her husband, very well. Apart from his being my first cousin and having known him all my life, we have always been great friends. I like Robert immensely and I admire him. I think he is remarkable in many ways besides being, everyone says, a first-rate man of business. I'm not surprised at his being attracted by a girl like that, but I do rather wonder whether it was wise to marry someone so much younger than himself and so different.'

'So different?'

'Oh! yes. One can see that at a glance. You see my cousin is a north-country man, shrewd and practical, fond of outdoor life and sports, but quite capable of giving them up for a time if necessary; fond of horses and racing, but all the artistic side of life – art, literature, music, painting – is a sealed book to him.'

'And she?'

'Ah, she . . . I don't know what she likes, but nothing could be more different. She was brought up in a convent, and when the father died they lived at Cannes and Nice, anywhere, in pensions; so you see. I suppose she must have been in love with Robert to have married him. I don't know what she's really like, nor what she thinks, but I'm certain of one thing, that between her and Robert there cannot be one idea in common. I knew her mother – a sensible, amusing American, who they say was a beauty; and her father, a charming adventurer, half Irish, and cosmopolitan. The sisters were beautiful, and they married, but I think Zita is the best-looking of all of them. She is being painted here.'

'Who by?'

'Bertrand.'

'Ah!'

'And, by the way, there is a man apparently who goes to the studio to look on, Jean de Bosis. Do you know him?'

'Yes, I know him well. His mother is my greatest friend.'

'He will be able to tell you all about Zita Harmer. But I shall soon know more myself; in the meantime, can I bring her to see you?'

'Of course; bring her tomorrow, it's my *jour*. Does she like seeing people?'

'I think she might, but I don't believe my poor cousin has ever given her the opportunity. You see he goes to the races, and he never asks anyone to the house except business friends.'

'Is he jealous?'

'That would be the obvious explanation, and had occurred even to me.' Madeleine laughed.

'But, but,' Amelia went on, 'I don't think it's the right one after all.'

'No?'

'Well, you see Robert is in many ways an odd man, and it's quite possible he may be jealous of *everybody*, but he's very *fair*, and I am quite certain he is not jealous of *anyone*.'

## CHAPTER V

The next morning Amelia Legge went with Zita to the studio. Mrs Legge admired the picture, and she made the acquaintance of Jean de Bosis, who was there as usual. She took Zita in the afternoon to see Madeleine Laurent. There were not more than four or five people there – there never were. Madeleine Laurent took an instant fancy to Zita and admired her.

'She is a *belle de nuit*,' she said to Amelia.

The arrival of the Legges entirely changed Zita's life. Cyril Legge's apartment soon became an agreeable centre of a group of literary and artistic people, French, English and foreign. They asked Zita and Robert as often as they could to their house, and at first it was not difficult to get them to come, but Robert suddenly urged Zita to go without him to the Legges. He distrusted foreigners, it is true, but he thought she was safe among the literary, and just at that time he made friends with a handsome American widow, a Mrs Rylands, who was to play an important part in his life. She was about the same age as himself – a practical, sensible woman of great and ripe experience. It was thought by some to be a liaison, by others not. Robert Harmer admired her immensely and took everything she said for gospel. He found it more and more convenient for Zita to go out by herself to houses of intimate friends.

Bertrand finished his picture, and it was exhibited in the spring at the Salon. It attracted a great deal of attention. It was the year of the Exhibition. There were many foreigners and many English people in Paris. Cyril Legge had persuaded Robert, without difficulty, to go to the Embassy, and the English people who saw Zita there, hearing her picture, 'Portrait de Madame——', talked about, and behaving, as usual, like sheep, began to admire her, having said before, without having seen her, that she could not hold a candle to any of her sisters; the catchword which was now handed about was that she was the best-looking of the whole family.

She had certainly blossomed into something ravishing. She was lovely because she was happy, and she was happy because she was admired. That spring and summer, Sarah Bernhardt, who had just appeared as Doña Sol in *Hernani*, and Zita and her portrait were the two main topics. But it was neither the catchwords of the fashionable nor the admiration of the man-in-the-street that affected Zita, but the admiration of one person: Jean de Bosis.

And now I come to the moment of the story when Amelia Legge says she was probably to blame, although she never was prepared to plead guilty. The facts are these: when Bertrand finished his picture, Zita could, of course, no longer see Jean de Bosis at the studio. At first the only place where they met was Madeleine Laurent's, where there were seldom less than four other people. Zita never asked him to her apartment, and Madeleine Laurent was not at home to visitors except on her day. By this time Zita had got to know Mrs Legge intimately; intimately for her, that is to say. Zita was not a person who allowed people to become intimate with her; she was veiled and reserved, and generally rather silent. Amelia thought her a puzzle. She liked her immensely, but she did not pretend to understand her. She was startled sometimes by the things that Zita would say. For instance, one day they were talking of her sister, Teresa, and Zita said she thought she was one of the most fortunate people in the world. Amelia asked why, and Zita said she was fortunate because if her husband hadn't left her she would have led a miserable life; she simply hated wealth and everything that appertained to it. Now Amelia thought she knew Teresa well. She had known her as a girl, and met her since her separation at Rome, where Teresa had stayed at the Embassy, and she knew that Teresa detested poverty and moreover felt lonely; that she had been devoted to her husband in spite of all; also that she was extravagant, pleasure-loving, and born with expensive tastes, which she was obliged to forgo, and she made no secret of this. But Amelia reflected that people rarely understood their brothers and sisters; they knew them too well and not well enough.

Then there was another occasion; Zita and Robert were to dine with the Legges one evening, and the day before Amelia, in reminding Zita of it, said: 'By the way (Amelia was greedy and knew all about cooking), does Robert like *langouste*, or can't he eat it?'

'Oh!' said Zita, 'Robert likes anything. He doesn't know what he is eating.'

This remark opened a door for Amelia on all sorts of things, and it amazed her, or rather it puzzled her more than ever – as Robert had told her that he ordered dinner himself and saw to all that . . . and indeed the food at the Harmers' flat was delicious; and did Zita think that it all came from Heaven by accident, or was entirely the doing of the cook, who had been engaged by Robert, so he said, after a thorough investigation and a searching cross-examination, and a great deal of trouble? It also threw light on Robert and his behaviour to Zita. It was obvious that he never made any fuss about any domestic or kitchen details, and Amelia, who knew how particular he was, thought that he deserved credit. It amazed her that Zita should be so blind, but then she reflected – perhaps women are blind when their husbands are concerned. Or was she wrong? Was Robert blind? Were they both blind and was Zita right?

Did Zita really do everything?

Another time they were discussing a common acquaintance, Hedworth Lawless, who was at that time Minister at Copenhagen and was staying in Paris on his way through. Hedworth Lawless was good-looking and was thought to be a great charmer; they were talking of him and Zita said: 'Lady Lawless is so sensible, she is never jealous; I suppose she thinks there's safety in numbers.' Now Amelia knew that so far from its being a question of numbers, there was only one person who counted in Hedworth Lawless's life, an Italian who had married a diplomat, and that, so far from not being jealous, Lady Lawless would have been jealous even had she ceased to love; she would have had toothache even after losing all her teeth. Then she reflected – Lady Lawless is a clever woman, and Zita is ingenuous. But when one day, talking of Jean de Bosis, Zita said she thought he had an essentially happy nature; that he was entirely domestic, devoted to his mother; that he would marry, have a large family and not stir from his fireside, his garden and his farm in Normandy, then Amelia said to herself: 'Zita isn't stupid, but she has no more perception than a rhinoceros, which is curious, considering what a sensitive creature she is in some ways.' And the more she saw of her and the better she got to know her, the more she was convinced that this was the truth.

'Zita is either unperceptive or deep,' she said to Madeleine Laurent.

'Oh,' said Madeleine, 'she is deep, but not in the sense you mean: she could be a well of suffering, and it is partly because she is unperceptive. Any French person could see she is unperceptive at once. *Elle ne sait pas même s'arranger.* Which for a woman with her beauty is a pity.'

But to get back to why Amelia thought herself to blame; Zita had got into the habit of dropping into the Legges' apartment at any time; and the visits of Jean de Bosis began to be more frequent. Cyril Legge liked him and always pressed his wife to invite him, which she did, seeing no reason why she shouldn't. At first Robert used to come with his wife, but as his intimacy with Mrs Rylands increased and it became a matter of seeing her every day, he found it more convenient to let Zita go out by herself.

Then Zita started having a day. Jean de Bosis used to attend it regularly. Sometimes he would stay a little while after the other guests had gone. Zita would sometimes ask him to dinner. Things went on like this till the spring of the next year, and Amelia was unaware of there being anything unusual or perilous in the situation until some of those little things happened that leave you perplexed and guessing, and not a little uneasy; little incidents that give one the tantalizing feeling that the right key is in the lock and just about to be turned, and yet cannot be turned, or that there is a rift in the firmament and that you could look through the clouds and see what you want to see, only it closes again too soon.

Two little incidents of this nature occurred.

This was the first.

The Legges arranged a small party one night to go to the *Théâtre français*. There was a revival of *Ruy Blas*; Sarah Bernhardt was playing the part of the Queen of Spain. Cyril had taken a box, one of those boxes in which people sit in twos: two in front, then two behind, and then two behind those. The party consisted of the Legges, Bertrand and his wife, Jean de Bosis and Zita. Robert had dined with the Legges on condition that he might be spared a play in verse.

In the box the party was arranged like this: Madame Bertrand and Zita were in front – Zita on the side of the box nearest to the stage; then Amelia and Bertrand, and then Jean de Bosis and Legge. Jean was on the extreme left, at the greatest distance from Zita, so that she could see him, and he, looking at the stage, could look straight at her.

When Sarah Bernhardt came to the lines:

> 'Qui que tu sois, ami dont l'ombre m'accompagne,
> Puisque mon cœur subit une inflexible loi,
> Sois aimé par ta mère et sois béni par moi!'

which she sighed like an Aeolian harp, Zita, who was looking at the stage and had tears in her eyes, turned her head in the direction of Jean de Bosis. You could not have said their eyes had met, because she had turned her head back and he was looking at the stage once more. It happened in a second; it was a mere nothing; and yet Amelia noticed it, and in noting it she felt that something electric and significant had brushed past her.

During the entr'acte they walked in the foyer. Zita walked arm-in-arm with Bertrand and Amelia with Jean de Bosis. Jean discussed the play with Amelia and said it needed a genius to make one swallow so absurd a story: 'but, after all,' he said, 'the plots of all the greatest plays are absurd. It is absurd to think Oedipus could have lived for twelve years without mentioning the past; that, after being told he was to kill his father and marry his mother, he should have killed an old man and married a woman much older than himself without suspecting anything might be wrong, is frankly incredible. But I am ready to accept the *donnée* of any story the dramatist likes to set before me on condition of not thinking it out. What could be sillier than the plot of *King Lear*? What could be more wildly improbable than the conduct of Othello? *Ruy Blas* isn't a sillier story than any of these, and it is dramatic, and Sarah Bernhardt makes the Queen seem as true as Desdemona or Cordelia.' Cordelia somehow or other made Amelia think of Zita, because she felt that Zita might have behaved like Cordelia, but she couldn't have behaved like Desdemona.

'Bertrand,' she said, 'told me at dinner that he wants to paint another picture of Zita; what do you think?'

'He can always try,' said Jean, 'but nobody but Velasquez could have painted her.'

'Velasquez?' said Amelia, surprised.

'Yes, because of the small head,' he said, pensively.

That was the second of the little things. Amelia wondered. When the play was over the Legges dropped Zita at her apartment.

On the way they talked about the play and the acting.

'Bertrand wants to paint you again,' said Amelia, 'but Jean de Bosis says there is only one painter who could have painted you, Velasquez!'

'Velasquez!' said Zita, with a slightly artificial laugh. 'What an idea! I wonder what made him think that?'

'He thought that,' said Amelia, 'because you have got such a small head.'

Zita said nothing, but Amelia thought in the darkness that Zita had blushed, and she wondered once more. She was left guessing.

## CHAPTER VI

the month of August that year Robert took a moor in Scotland in he same remote spot in the north. He asked some of his friends, the only ther woman besides Zita being Flora Sutton. He asked Mrs Rylands ut she had been ordered by the doctors to take waters. He asked the Legges, but Cyril could not leave Paris. The Legges stayed in Paris all through August and September. Jean de Bosis went to stay with his mother in Normandy. But he came to Paris often, and every time he came he visited the Legges and talked about Zita. When the Harmers came back from Scotland, Bertrand asked permission to paint Zita again, this time for himself. Robert was delighted. Bertrand painted her in an evening gown this time: cream coloured satin and tulle, with a tea-rose near her heart. The picture is now in the Luxembourg, and is thought to be

Bertrand's masterpiece. Amelia went often to the sittings now; Jean de Bosis suddenly gave up going altogether, nor did he any longer pay visits to the Legges; nor was he seen at Zita's day – he had disappeared.

Amelia mentioned his name one day to Zita and she said:

'We never see him now at all. I think he is living in the country with his mother.'

Talking it over with her husband, Amelia said to him:

'I believe I was wrong after all about Zita and Jean de Bosis.'

'Yes?'

'I don't believe she cares for him, and he never goes to the studio now, or here, as to that, and he never goes near Zita.'

'I expect he found it was useless,' said Cyril. 'Or perhaps Robert noticed it?'

'No,' said Amelia, decisively, 'Robert could never be jealous of a Frenchman. As far as Zita is concerned, he thinks foreigners don't count. In his eyes they belong to a different category. He could never imagine Zita being attracted by a foreigner.'

'But supposing,' said Legge, 'cousin Robert knew for certain Zita was attracted by a foreigner, what then?'

'Ah! then I don't know.'

It was in the spring, shortly after the opening of the Salon, when everyone was talking of Bertrand's new picture, and the English people in Paris were raving about Zita's portrait, and Robert seemed to be enjoying their admiration, that Jean de Bosis published his first book, a small book of verse called *Stances*. It attracted little attention and few copies of it were sold.

Amelia heard of the publication from Madeleine, who was interested.

'He is not a poet,' she said to Amelia, as they sat together late one afternoon in Madeleine's flat, the day of her *jour*, when the visitors had gone, 'but he has got talent certainly, and I expect he will write something, but not verse.'

'Are there any love poems in it?' asked Amelia, who was interested more in the personal than in the artistic side of poetry.

'No,' said Madeleine, 'nature poems and landscapes. There are one or two love poems – the wreaths on the already faded tomb of a dead love. He was unlucky for the time being.'

'Why unlucky?'

'He loved someone who didn't love him and who never could love him?'

'Zita?'

'Yes.'

'You think she didn't – doesn't?'

'I am sure.'

'And he?'

'Oh, he *did* . . . but when he saw it was useless, that there was nothing to be done, he gave it up.'

'It is all over then?'

'It has been over for a long time now. There are only a few pale reflections of it in the book. There it is, you can take it if you like. Jean has been in the country getting over it. It was like a bad illness, but it is all over now, and soon it will be someone else. He has a *coeur à louer* and it will not stay long vacant.'

'Has it always been occupied before?'

'Always more or less, but never by anyone who mattered – till this.'

'This was serious, you think?'

'Very. He took it badly.'

'And she?'

'She was quite indifferent.'

'You think she is——'

'*Un glaçon*, yes.'

'Well, I don't believe she was ever in love with Robert.'

'Of course not.'

'But her mother——'

'Her mother – that was *autre chose*. Her mother was nothing but temperament.'

Amelia sighed.

'It's just as well,' said Madeleine.

'What?'

'Well, that nothing happened.'

'I suppose so. May I take this book?'

'Do. You will see he has talent.'

Amelia took the book home with her. She opened it and chanced on a poem about ploughed fields, and then on another about autumn woods and ponds, and felt she had read enough. Had she read the book more carefully she would have come across a poem that might have interested her. It was called *L'Exilé*, and it told of a lovely princess with a small head, and of the hopeless passion she inspired in the heart of an alien wayfarer.

That evening the Legges dined with Robert and Zita. The first thing that Amelia noticed on one of the small tables when she arrived was Jean de Bosis' poems with a written dedication on the cover.

'Have you read Jean de Bosis' poems?' she asked Zita.

'He sent them to me,' she said; 'so kind of him, but I don't really care for French poetry. It's to me like oil poured on smooth water.'

Robert, who was listening, took up the book and glanced at it, cut a few pages with a paper-cutter, and put it down again.

After dinner there was music. Flora Sutton sang some English sentimental songs – English ballads with tunes by Tosti, and Legge, who had a pleasing baritone, sang some Schumann. Robert, who was not musical sat in the corner of the room near the table, and Amelia noticed that he took up Jean de Bosis' poems and read them as if absorbed. She wondered how much he understood of them. Not much, she thought; but perhaps he enjoyed the poem about the wild ducks in the dawn. He was a lover of nature, if inarticulate.

The guests went away early. Zita and Robert were left alone. Robert lit a cigar.

'That fellow writes quite well,' said Robert, after a time.

'Who?' asked Zita.

'Bosis.' (Robert pronounced the word 'Bossis'.)

Zita said nothing.

'He describes wild duck getting up from a marsh very well.'

'I haven't had time to read them yet,' said Zita. 'I must read them soon.'

'You must be quick if you want to read them before we go away.'

'Are we going away?' said Zita.

'Yes,' said Robert, with a sigh, as of infinite relief, 'for good. They want me in London.'

'When did you settle this?'

'I heard from our people in London this morning, but I didn't make up my mind till this evening.'

'Oh!' said Zita.

'Do you mind?'

'Oh no, of course not. I shall be sorry to go in some ways. We shall miss the Legges.'

'Yes, we shall miss the Legges.'

There was a long pause. It was broken by Zita, who said:

'Where shall we live in England?'

'At Wallington, as soon as the tenant goes.'

'Just as before?'

'Yes, just as before.'

'And how soon shall we go?'

'Tomorrow fortnight, but I am going over to London the day after tomorrow for two days.'

'I see. I am sleepy,' said Zita, 'I am going to bed.'

'I am not going to bed yet. I have a letter to write. Good night, my dear.'

'Good night, Robert.'

As Zita went through the little ante-chamber into her bedroom, she saw a letter for her on the table. She opened it. It was from Madame Bertrand. They had asked a few friends to come to the studio the next afternoon between five and seven. If they were doing nothing better and happened to be anywhere near, she would meet some friends – Madeleine

379

Laurent, and they were asking the Legges. There would be a little music . . . etc.

Zita went to bed and stayed awake a long time after she heard Robert go to bed. She was thinking of Wallington.

Next day Zita went to the studio with Madeleine Laurent. Robert had encouraged her to go but would not take her himself, because he could not stand musical parties in a studio, and as he was starting for London the next morning he wanted to have tea with Mrs Rylands. The Legges were not at the studio, there were only French people there; among others Jean de Bosis. Zita thanked him for sending her his book, and told him they – she and her husband – were leaving Paris.

'For a while?' he asked.

'No, for good,' she said, looking straight in front of her at a large unfinished picture on the wall at the other end of the room.

'To London?' he asked.

'No, not to London; at least, my husband will be a lot in London, but I shall be in the country.'

'And how soon?'

Zita told him what had been arranged, and then their conversation was interrupted, as someone began to sing – a contralto. She sang a song of Godard's.

Zita had no further talk with Jean, but the Bertrands heard the news of her coming departure, and were loud in their regrets. Robert started for London the next morning.

'I shall be back in three days,' he said. 'I have written to Amelia and told her to look after you.'

'But I'm coming with you to the station,' said Zita.

'No, don't bother,' said Robert. 'I hate good-byes at stations, and there won't be time.'

'But I'm ready,' said Zita. She had on her hat. 'I am quite ready.'

'No, dear,' said Robert. 'I would rather you didn't come.'

'Very well,' she said.

This was the first time she had not accompanied him to the station. It is true he had seldom gone away by himself.

Robert then said good-bye to Zita and left at once. He liked being in good time for the train.

'You'll have a long time to wait,' Zita said, looking at the clock.

'I don't mind waiting, and I hate being rushed.'

He had been gone about five minutes when a clerk from the bank arrived, much flustered, saying he had brought an important letter for M. Harmer, which it was essential he should take with him to London. He had been delayed and he had not thought M. Harmer would have started so soon, but, no matter, he would go straight to the station.

'I shall have time to catch him,' he said.

'I will take it,' said Zita; 'there is something I have forgotten to tell him.' She had still got on her hat.

She took the letter from the slightly-reluctant clerk, and rang for a fiacre.

She arrived at the Gare du Nord in plenty of time. She caught sight of Robert standing on the platform smoking a cigar. He was surprised to see her. She told him what had happened, and gave him the letter.

'And I forgot to tell you I want you to bring me back a cake of spermaceti soap. This is where you can get it.'

She gave him a piece of paper. He kissed her and said good-bye. There was still nearly ten minutes before the train was to start, but she thought it would irritate him if she stayed. As she walked down the platform she met Mrs Rylands arriving with a lot of hand luggage and engaged in voluble explanations to a porter and a maid. When she saw Zita she stopped.

'I'm going to London,' she said, 'by the same train as your husband. I'm going to see about getting a house. My niece whom I'm looking after is bent on living in London.'

'You'll find Robert farther up,' said Zita, 'we have said good-bye, and I must go home.'

They said good-bye amicably. Zita drove back to her apartment in a fiacre.

It was a lovely May morning; the chestnuts were in flower. Paris was radiant and gay.

Zita was not jealous of Mrs Rylands, but it irritated her that her husband should treat Mrs Rylands with reverence. It irritated her that he had said nothing about her going to London, although she had heard she was going to London some time or other. When she got home she found a letter waiting for her on the table of the ante-chamber. She recognized the handwriting at once. It was from Jean de Bosis. So far she had only received brief notes from him, and these rarely – answers to invitations. This was a long letter – eight pages and more – in his sloping, clear and sensitive handwriting. It turned out to be longer than she had thought, more than eight pages. After reading the first page she sat down in an arm-chair. It was a love-letter, a declaration. He told her that he had always worshipped her from the very first moment he had seen her, but had not dared say anything; he just thought it hopeless. He had believed in her profound indifference. But gradually he had begun to have hopes. He had thought, after the night they went to *Ruy Blas*, that she cared a little. When she had left Paris for Scotland this last time he had nearly gone mad. Never had he been through anything like that. Never had he known a man could suffer what he had suffered. Then, when she came back, he thought she was so little pleased to see him that everything he had dreamt about her feelings had been a mistake: he was certain she did not care for him. He decided to go away. He would cure himself. He had ambitions – he wanted to be a poet, to do something with his life, to be someone; why should he waste his life, throw it away for someone who did not even know whether he was alive or dead? Then that day when they had met at Bertrand's studio and she had said she was going away for good, he knew that he had looked into her soul and read the secret of her heart. She *did* care; she *did* mind going. She was unhappy. She was more than unhappy. She was desperate. He knew now that she loved him. He understood what she was feeling and what her life would be if she went to England with her husband now. He had a practical plan to suggest. She should leave her husband and go with him to Algiers. He had a little house there; it was all ready waiting; he was independent; they would have plenty to live on.

He knew she loved him as much as he loved her. Why should she sacrifice herself? What for? and for whom? She would have no remorse about her husband. She knew only too well that he was fully occupied. When they got tired of Algiers they would go elsewhere. Would she mind the *qu'en dira-t-on*? He thought not. If they loved each other, what did all the rest matter? What did anything matter?

He, at any rate, could not live without her. He was not threatening her. He would not do anything melodramatic, but he would simply cease to live. It would not be necessary for him to do anything. Nature would do it for him. It would just be impossible for him to go on living.

He would be at Bertrand's studio that afternoon at three. Bertrand would not be there. Would she come and leave the answer there for him? He begged her to come, whatever the answer was to be, even if it was to say good-bye to him for ever.

Zita read the letter through twice. Jean's words lit up her face. She sat down and wrote a letter. This is what she wrote.

'You have guessed right. It is true. I will do what you ask me to do. I have thought about it and made up my mind. It is perhaps selfish what I am doing, perhaps bad for you. I love you too much to say "No". I will have no deception of Robert. Robert and I are by way of leaving for London tomorrow week. It is all settled beforehand, as is always his habit. The night before that I will start with you for Algiers. All I ask you to do is to send me a telegram with the name of the station and the hour the train starts. I will be there and I shall leave a letter for Robert telling him, but till then I will neither see you nor read any letters from you. Please do not try to meet me in anyone else's house.'

She took this letter to the studio and left it there. That same evening she received a telegram telling her the name of the station and the hour at which the train started for the south.

## CHAPTER VII

The afternoon following the day of Robert's departure Zita had tea with Amelia, and after they had been talking of various things, she said:

'I have got a piece of news for you, but you may have heard it already. Robert is going back to England for good.'

She said this in a colourless, matter-of-fact way, as if it did not concern her. Amelia had not heard it. She had not been to the Bertrands, and Madeleine Laurent had left Paris for St Germain, where she was spending a few days. Amelia asked when they were going, and Zita told her all she knew. Amelia remembered afterwards that Zita had spoken throughout of Robert, and never of herself. Zita left. Amelia was bewildered. As soon as her husband came back that evening she talked it over with him.

'I can't understand Zita,' she said. 'I should have thought she would be miserable at the idea of leaving Paris just now that she has made friends and is having such fun, and going back to Wallington, of all places.'

'Will they go there?'

'Zita will, unless Robert takes a house in London, which is unlikely. But instead of being miserable she seemed to me not only indifferent, but to be stifling excitement like a child that has been told it is going to be taken to the play.'

'Will Jean mind?' said Cyril.

'No,' said Amelia, 'that is all over. But, do you think,' she asked after a while, 'that Robert could possibly have been jealous, a little green-eyed?'

'I think Robert is a *shrewd* man,' said Cyril.

'Yes, one can't take him in, he can see through a brick wall, but I don't imagine Zita trying to, do you?'

'Then you think she never was in love with Jean?'

'No, never. I did think so for a moment; I was sure about it; but I think I was wrong, at least, I suppose I was wrong. Madeleine is sure she never cared for him. I think Jean got tired – Madeleine thinks Zita is an icicle, and I don't know whether she isn't right. I don't know what to think.'

'I wonder why she married Robert?'

'Oh, that is simple,' said Amelia, 'it was the result of a first love affair that went wrong, and the wish not to disappoint her mother as her sisters had done, and to get away from pensions and hotels. And then I daresay she liked him. I think she does still like him.'

'They never seem to me to speak to each other,' said Cyril. 'I often wonder what on earth they talk about.'

'I forgot to tell you – the other night when we dined there and you and Flora were singing after dinner, what do you think Robert was reading . . . ?'

'What?'

'Jean de Bosis' poems?'

Cyril laughed.

'He understands French,' said Amelia, 'although he says he doesn't, and I believe when we are not there he speaks it.'

'I am sure he wouldn't understand those poems,' said Cyril.

'I suppose not,' said Amelia, 'although he's fond of nature; and the poems are about ploughed fields.'

'I believe,' said Cyril, 'he puts Zita on such a pedestal that he simply couldn't imagine her giving a thought to anyone in the world.'

'Whatever he thinks, he's probably certain to be wrong, because men always are wrong.'

'Are they, darling? I'm sure you know,' said Cyril, laughing.

'We must have a farewell dinner for them,' said Amelia, 'and ask Jean.'

'Of course; Jean and the Bertrands.'

Robert came back from England. Everything, he said, had been arranged. Wallington would be ready for them in September. The lease on which the present tenant held it came to an end then, and Robert would not extend it.

The Harmers were to start on a Wednesday, and on the Sunday morning Zita went to Mass at Saint Philippe du Roule. Zita was not, or had not been until now, a religious woman. She was just *pratiquante*: that is to say, she went to Mass on Sundays and abstained on Fridays. She fulfilled her Easter duties. But that was all.

The church was crowded and stuffy. Zita was a prey to distractions till a Dominican got into the pulpit and began to preach. She found it was impossible not to listen to him, although she tried. He was eloquent and forcible, and he seemed to be speaking to her personally and individually, as if he was aware of her private difficulties and secret thoughts. He pointed out among other things how necessary it was that the individual should cheerfully accept sacrifice for the good of the community. The Church might seem hard on the individual; the hardness must be faced and accepted. He had spoken, too, of the stern necessity of duty, of the danger of illicit love. Zita listened to this eloquence unmoved. His words applied to her. They might have been directed at her personally and individually, but they did not affect her. She was determined to leave Robert; determined to go away with Jean. It was not that she was overwhelmingly swept away by passion for Jean; she could not say that. She was not really sure she loved him. But she was going. She said to herself that the eloquence of the Dominican's words had no effect on her whatsoever.

The Legges' farewell dinner came off that evening. They had asked the

Bertrands, Madeleine Laurent, Mrs Rylands, one of the secretaries from the Embassy and his wife. Jean de Bosis was asked, but excused himself.

The guests could not take their eyes off Zita, as if they had been seeing her for the first time. She was dressed in black lace. On Amelia she made exactly the same impression as she had made when she had first told her Robert was going home. She was still like a child suffering from suppressed excitement, and so afraid of losing the coming treat that it does not dare even mention it.

Robert, on the other hand, seemed in rather forced good spirits; he was not like a schoolboy going home for the holidays, but like a schoolboy going back to school and pretending to like it.

When the guests were gone Amelia said to her husband:

'Well, how do you think it went off?'

'Robert doesn't seem so pleased at going as I should have expected,' said Legge.

'He will miss Mrs Rylands,' said Amelia.

'She told me she was going to London soon.'

'How lovely Zita looked!'

'It's extraordinary. She oughtn't to be lovely on paper. Mrs Rylands said it was a pity she didn't dress better.'

Amelia laughed. 'She knows what suits her. She is independent of fashion. She looks like a princess in disguise.'

'It's her expression that's half the battle,' said Cyril.

'Oh, it's everything about her,' said Amelia; 'the men's faces were a study at dinner.'

'And Robert seemed to be so proud of her.'

'Oh yes, he is.'

'I wonder what she feels?'

'What about?' he asked.

'About everything.'

'I doubt if we shall ever know that.'

'Well, you've known her for how many years? Four. Don't you feel you know her?'

'Not a bit better than the first day I set eyes on her.'

When the Harmers got back to their flat that night the appearance of the apartment was depressing. The pictures were off the walls; the room was full of packed and half-packed packing-cases and trunks; the table strewn with old papers and old music, magazines, newspapers and every kind of junk. Near a half-packed box, Robert's Airedale terrier, Tinker, was keeping a sullen watch. The door of the sitting-room opening into Robert's study was open, and Robert's study, Zita noticed, was bare. A waste-paper-basket was near the writing-table overflowing with papers and photographs he had destroyed: among these she noticed at once a photograph of a group which had been taken of him and herself and her

385

mother when they were engaged, at Nice. It had always been on his writing-table wherever they had been. It had been taken the day they were engaged. Robert had always been particularly fond of this photograph.

She was on the verge of saying, 'They've thrown away the Nice group,' but she reflected he must have done it himself. Why?

Robert read a letter which he found waiting for him, and then said to Zita:

'I shall have to start tomorrow.'

'Oh!' she said. 'Tomorrow morning?'

'Yes; tomorrow morning.'

It was on Tuesday evening that she was to meet Jean at the station. Zita had not changed her mind.

'But there's no reason why you should come,' he went on, 'you won't have time to pack; and you had better stay on a few more days,' he said. 'You could stay on another week if you like, and I can come back and fetch you. That will be the best arrangement. I have sub-let the apartment, but it is ours till the end of the month, and Amélie and Joseph can stay on another week.'

Zita said nothing.

'You can think it over and settle tomorrow,' said Robert. 'But I'm sure you won't want to hurry.'

At that moment the dog, Tinker, came and put his paws on her lap and looked her in the face in an appealing manner, as if to say, 'Don't go away.' The dog was fond of her, and she loved him.

'Tinker knows,' she said to herself.

'Tinker will miss you,' said Robert, and as he looked at her his eyes seemed to see right through her. Zita could say nothing. 'He must come with me tomorrow,' he added, as if explaining the remark and making it natural. 'Did you write and thank Jean de Bosis,' Robert said, 'for sending you his book?'

'No,' she said truthfully.

'Well, you had better write to him tomorrow; he is going away: to Algiers.'

Zita was startled.

'I know because Williamson heard him order his tickets at Cook's.' Robert stressed the plural. 'He ordered,' he went on, 'two sleeping-compartments with a place for his servant. So he is not going alone. He is taking either his mother . . .'

'Or?' repeated Zita mechanically.

'Or his mistress.'

At that moment Zita, who was not, as a rule, a perceptive woman, knew, and knew for certain, that Robert knew. Knew that she meant to leave him; to go away with Jean de Bosis. How, she had no idea; but she had absolute faith in this sudden fit of lucidity. He not only knew, but he was making it easy for her; helping her; making it unnecessary for her to lie to him, or enabling her to lie as little as possible. She still felt no twinge of remorse, and no prick of conscience, but now, when Robert stood there in front of her looking at her with his far-seeing honest eyes, when he said the word 'mistress', revealing to her what she took to be his certain knowledge, the categoric imperative swept by her like a spirit. She knew she could not go away.

'I shan't want any more time for packing,' she said. 'I shall be quite ready to come with you tomorrow. All my things are packed.' This was true.

'Good night, Robert.'

'Good night,' said Robert, lighting a cigar. 'You must think over it, and don't forget to write to Jean de Bosis.'

## CHAPTER VIII

Zita left Paris the next morning with Robert Harmer, and before starting she wrote two letters; one to Jean and one to Amelia Legge. To Amelia she said that they had been obliged to start a day earlier than they had expected, and she begged her to make her excuses where it was necessary.

To Jean she wrote that she had found at the last moment she could not leave her husband; she had not changed, and did not think she would change, but she knew she would only make him, Jean, unhappy if she left Robert.

A few days later Amelia Legge heard from Zita, who said that she had arrived safely in London. About a fortnight later still Madeleine burst in on Amelia one morning and said she had things of importance to tell her. Jean was ill. At one moment his life had been despaired of. His mother was nursing him in his apartment. She, Madeleine Laurent, had been away during the last fortnight at Fontainebleau, and had only just heard the news. Madame de Bosis had been to see her. It had been brain-fever, apparently. Now he was out of danger.

'Was it because of Zita?' Amelia asked.

'His mother says so,' said Madeleine. 'He seems to have been stunned by her departure, then demented, then ill.'

'But how extraordinary!' said Amelia, 'he had stopped going near her.'

'He had probably given it up as hopeless, but that did not prevent him feeling what he felt. Madame de Bosis says he was in love with Zita, and that she led him on and then left him. She is furious with her, of course. And she says that is how all English women behave, that she is a cold-hearted flirt: cold-hearted and hot-blooded. We had a long discussion, and I tried to make her admit that Zita's going away was the best thing that could have happened. But all she said was: "You don't know Jean. He's not like the others. He will never get over it." I said they would have been equally unhappy whatever else had happened. Suppose she had run away with Jean, I said. "God forbid," Madame de Bosis had answered. "Well, then, what?" I asked, "an ordinary *liaison*?" . . . "Whatever they did, the mischief was done," she said. "My son has been poisoned by that woman." '

'And what do you think, Madeleine?' asked Amelia.

'I think,' said Madeleine, 'that she did not love him and that she never did love him. I think Jean loved her and saw it was hopeless. That he left off seeing her, thought he was cured, and found when she went away that he was not cured at all. Of course, I do not pretend to understand *vous autres*.'

'But it is just as difficult for me,' said Amelia plaintively. 'I don't pretend to understand Zita; and the more I see of her, and the longer I know her, the less I feel I understand her.'

'And Harmer?' asked Madeleine, 'did he perhaps play a part?'

'I wonder,' said Amelia, 'Robert is by no means a fool.'

'If he was jealous it might explain everything,' said Madeleine.

'He couldn't have been jealous of Jean,' said Amelia, 'Zita has not set eyes on him for weeks.'

'That is of no consequence,' said Madeleine, 'it is not what people do that make men jealous, but what they are. It is the instinct of the male that leads men to be jealous of the right person. That is why it's not the cleverest men who are the least easily deceived, but often quite ordinary men who have the male instinct. I imagine Mr Harmer had it.'

'Quite possibly,' said Amelia, 'but there was nothing to have it about.'

'Who knows?'

'Oh! if it comes to that, we know nothing! Did Jean tell his mother anything?'

'Not a word, and in his delirium he raved the whole time about someone called Marie.'

'Well, you see! Zita was never called Marie.'

'It was fatal for Jean to meet your Zita,' said Madeleine. 'She was fated by her beauty, her peculiar beauty, which would not be admired by everyone, still less by every Frenchman, to inspire a passion in a man like Jean, and she was equally destined by her nature and her circumstances to be incapable of satisfying it. It is a great pity.'

'Perhaps it is just as well for both their sakes,' said Amelia. 'Why shouldn't Jean marry someone and be happy?'

'Because he is one of those people who are not born for happiness.'

'Poor boy!' said Amelia, with a tearful voice, 'I should like him to be happy,' (and then petulantly) 'He ought to be happy.'

Jean recovered slowly. He told his mother nothing. He left Paris and retired to her house in Normandy, where he started to write a novel.

The Legges saw nothing of him, neither did the Bertrands.

Amelia Legge heard from Zita from time to time. Robert had taken a house at Wimbledon, where they were to live until the tenant who had taken Wallington left. But when the time came for him to leave, the tenant proposed renewing the lease for five years, and Robert consented. The truth was that while nothing would persuade Robert to take a house in London, Zita had suddenly made it clear to him that nothing would persuade her to live at Wallington. She had her mother, who was in England, to back her up. She told Mrs Mostyn that sooner than live at Wallington she would leave Robert for good, and Mrs Mostyn persuaded Robert that she meant this. Robert did not greatly care if he lived at Wallington or not so long as he did not live in London. Living at Wimbledon enabled him to drive up to London every day. He resolved to take a shooting lodge in Scotland every autumn. He easily could go racing from Wimbledon, and he could always sleep at the club when he wanted to; moreover, Mrs Rylands had taken a house in London for three years, so everyone was satisfied.

A new life began for Zita. After her brief hour not of fame, but of notice, for she had not only been admired by the French in Paris, but her beauty had been a topic of discussion among English visitors, she passed once more into obscurity and permanent eclipse. She lived as one in a dream. She saw few people; she hardly ever went out in London, except every now and then to some small dinner-party or perhaps to a musical evening given by one of Robert's city friends. She seemed not to care; to be neither happy nor unhappy; just listless, like a person who had been drugged. It was the truth. She had been numbed by what had happened, and was like a person who has taken a narcotic.

Robert was attentive and devoted to her as before, and did everything he could to please her, but all his efforts were of no avail. Nothing he did seemed to rouse her. She walked amiable and beautiful through life like someone in a trance.

She seemed to have no interests. She had no real friends, and few acquaintances. Her mother died soon after they came back to England; her sisters both continued to live abroad.

She was not a reader; when she had first married she read every novel that came her way, and now, as if suffering from all that surfeit, she never opened a book. She was not wrapped up in her religion; she fulfilled her duties and no more. She knew no priests. But she had one engrossing hobby, and that filled her life. It was perhaps more than enough. It was her garden. She had suffered at Wallington from not being able to create a garden. There was one already, a large one; large, but irremediable, and under the eye and relentless hand of a competent North-country man who was not going to change anything: so Zita did not even enter the lists with him. But when she came to live at Wimbledon there was a large garden and a tame gardener, and she set about to create a garden such as she wanted, and Robert was delighted that she should have an occupation. It filled her life, and the garden which she created was, if people could have seen it, one of the sights of England.

It was a masterpiece of taste and design, a riot of cunningly devised and arranged colour. A feast to the eye, a rest to the body; the shade and the light were in the right place. As it was, few people saw it except Robert's business friends. And all they said was 'Quite a nice lot of flowers you've got, Robert. I suppose *you* do all that, you always were a clever gardener. Those chrysanthemums are doing well,' pointing to the bergamots.

It is a surprising, but not an uncommon, thing that a woman as beautiful as Zita (and as time went on she became more rather than less beautiful – she was twice as beautiful now as she had been when she had first come out), should, after having been recognized as a beauty in Paris by the French and the English, have lived for nearly ten years in the suburbs of London, now and then paying visits in the counties of England, without attracting more attention than she did. She was the reverse of a professional beauty. She had been forgotten and was never rediscovered.

There is not one single portrait extant of her by an English artist. The only two pictures that exist of her are the two that Bertrand painted: one of which is at Wallington and the other at the Luxembourg in Paris. She was photographed once or twice on a seaside pier or at a fair, but never by a photographer of note. She went to no large entertainments and took part in no public functions. She was unknown to the general public and unnoticed by any public. She lived alone, content, apparently, in her garden, and looked after her husband.

He seemed to be happy. Zita fitted in with his ideas of comfort. He liked ordering dinner, but he liked someone to see that his orders were carried out in the way he liked. That is just what Zita did. She did more: much more. She appeared to do nothing, but she did everything: she always had, and Amelia and others had been deceived and wrong about her.

Robert was happy in his business. He did well. He got richer and richer. Every year he spent one month in Scotland in the shooting-lodge he took, and later in the autumn he would stay for a week with friends for the pheasant-shooting. He attended the Derby regularly, also the Grand National, the St Leger, and at least one autumn and one spring meeting at Newmarket. He entertained his city friends at Wimbledon. The cooking was good and the wines excellent. In addition to everything else, he saw Mrs Rylands every day. She now lived permanently in London, originally to look after a niece, but, now that the niece was married, because she had become so fond of England that she would feel a stranger or an exile were she to go back to Paris, and still more so were she to go back to America.

What were their relations? Nobody ever knew. Mrs Rylands was a handsome woman about the same age as Robert, possibly younger than he was and looking older than her age, or possibly older than he was and looking younger than her age. She was large, smooth and blonde, with a short Greek nose and magnificent shoulders and rather lustreless eyes, one of those women who are born handsome. She was sensible and universally liked. Whatever their other relations might be, Robert venerated her opinions on every subject in the world, and believed in her absolutely.

She, in this delicate situation, behaved with tact and did all she could not to annoy Zita or interfere with her. Mrs Rylands disliked women as a rule, but she did not mind Zita. Secretly, in her heart of hearts, she probably thought it was a great shame that Robert Harmer had married such a wife. He ought to have married a woman of the world with a great deal of character who would have pushed him on and helped him and been a real companion, whereas Zita was hopeless, mooning about in a suburban garden and not knowing a soul. . . . She may have thought such thoughts, but if she did she did not express them. She never made things difficult for Zita; she was far too naturally shrewd.

Zita, on the other hand, seemed to be delighted that Robert should be friends with her, and accepted her as a matter of course. The unwritten rules of the game were observed on both sides with the greatest punctilio. Robert stayed two nights a week in London for dinner – it was called dining at the club. Once a month Robert and Zita gave a small dinner-party, to which Mrs Rylands was invited. She never dined by herself at 'The Birches', the name of Robert's house, but she sometimes, though rarely, had tea with Zita when Robert was not there.

Sometimes she gave a dinner-party, to which Zita and Robert were both invited. It was small, and meant going to the play. They drove home in a brougham. Zita accepted one of these invitations once a year and declined the others, and Robert went by himself.

Robert took Mrs Rylands to the races with a party of other friends, and she always stayed in Scotland at the Lodge.

During the next few years Zita never went abroad, except one Easter, when they spent a week in Florence and a week in Rome. Robert Harmer went often to Paris on business, and for the Grand Prix and other meetings, and once to Monte Carlo. He suggested that Zita should accompany him, but she declined. They heard little from or of their Paris friends.

The Legges had been appointed to Tokio soon after the Harmers left Paris, and they stayed there four years, at the end of which time they went to Stockholm.

The year after the Harmers left Paris, Jean de Bosis published a book,

391

which made him famous. It was in prose this time, and startlingly different in tone and subject from his volume of verse. It was a short novel dealing with contemporary life: bitter, cynical, rather crude, extremely vivid; and it surprised, shocked, and captivated the public. In the Press it was praised by some and attacked by many. It was discussed by everyone; translated into many languages, but not into English. Jean de Bosis did not send Zita a copy of the book, and she never read it, although echoes of its notoriety reached her through Mrs Rylands, who said 'it was disagreeable, although, of course, very well written'.

A year later Jean published a second book. Fantastic this time and full of colour and sensuality, and some people said the crudest coarseness. This book had a definite success of scandal, and was banned by libraries or booksellers in some countries. Jean came in for a torrent of abuse in France, and he excited the anger of the best and serenest critics, who burst into a chorus of frenzied vituperation; they all agreed that this time he had gone too far. But his sales grew larger than ever. His book was dramatized, turned, that is to say, into a long and crude melodrama. This was extremely successful, too. Then, as if in defiance of criticism, Jean set about to exaggerate the faults which the critics had complained of. His next book read like an imitation of his own manner in which the faults were exaggerated and the mannerisms caricatured. This often happens with writers whose work at the same time excites the vituperation of the critics and wins the favour of the public – the author tends as a result to abound in himself. Not two hours after writing these lines I came across in a book just published a passage referring to Bulwer Lytton, in which the author[1] said that a 'combination of readers' enthusiasm and critics' brutality always worked on Bulwer's peculiar temperament in such a way as to bring out the worst of his many mannerisms'. This sentence exactly fits Jean de Bosis, and might have been written about him.

The new book was more successful than ever with the public. The critics had little left to say. They had already used all their powder and shot. They contented themselves by saying that Jean de Bosis was 'finished' and written out.

After that he produced a new book every year: 'the same book', his enemies said, 'slightly deteriorating year by year'.

The year his second book appeared he married a singer. Her name was Emilia Altenbrandt. She was the widow of an Austrian. Her own nationality was mixed. 'She might have been a Russian, French, or Turk, or Prussian, or perhaps Italian,' but what she exactly 'remained', it was difficult to say: not French certainly, and not English. She spoke most languages and could be silent in none. She was handsome, dark, and flamboyant, exhausting and exacting. She sang *Lieder* in French, German,

[1] M. Sadleir. [M. B.]

392

and Italian, and sometimes in Russian, all over the Continent. She was more than successful among the musical publics of Europe. They went mad over her, but she had not been to England. It was not for want of being asked by the concert managers, but she refused to come; the climate, she said, would kill her, and she was a woman who knew her own mind.

Mrs Rylands told Zita all about her and her marriage, all about Jean's success and Emilia Altenbrandt's success, of the triumphs they were both enjoying all over Europe: at Vienna, St Petersburg, Berlin, Rome, Milan, Madrid; of their great happiness, and of the wild ecstasy of their double world-wide fame.

Zita listened with calm as to a story that happened a long time ago.

'A great while since, a long, long time ago.'

## CHAPTER IX

It was not until nine years after they had left Paris, the year of the next great Paris Exhibition – that of the Eiffel Tower – that Zita Harmer for a second time came in contact and in touch with her old Paris friends.

Robert was ordered by his doctor to take the waters at Haréville, and he obeyed his doctor's orders. They went there in the middle of July.

Robert took the waters. Zita merely looked on. The first person she met the morning after her arrival, as she strolled through the *Galeries* looking at the shop windows, was Amelia Legge, not much changed; a little bit greyer, perhaps, and perhaps even more voluble and plaintive than before. She told Zita all her news in the first five minutes of their meeting. Cyril was now Councillor at Paris; he was arriving the next day, or as soon as he could; he had not to drink the waters. She had to drink the lighter, not the stronger, waters for her eyes. They were back again in Paris, but not, alas, at their old apartment; they had taken one on the other side of the river.

'It's wonderful to see you again, Zita,' said Amelia, 'and looking not a day older; on the contrary, more beautiful than ever. Madeleine Laurent is alive and flourishing, and Jean de Bosis is married and famous, even more famous than his wife. We never met her, but we heard her at Berlin. He writes too much . . . and it is a great pity. I found his last book fearfully interesting, in fact, I think all his books are interesting. Cyril says I am wrong, and, of course, I know they shock a great many people. They are shocking, there's no denying it, but they don't shock *me*, so few books do,' she said, with an apologetic sigh.

'I haven't read any of them,' said Zita. 'I never seem to have time to read now; I'm always busy.'

'Busy at what?'

'Oh, lots of things – gardening chiefly.'

'Ah, you've got a garden now, at Wimbledon. You don't live at Wallington?'

'Wallington is still let.'

'I think that is sensible of Robert. Wallington wasn't a possible place to live in, it was too dark, bleak, too cold, too large, and too uncomfortable.'

'I sometimes wonder whether Robert doesn't miss it.'

'Oh! nonsense, Zita; don't think such things. If he missed it he would live there. Men, you know, don't do what they don't want to. Here is Robert,' she said, as Robert strode towards them in white flannels and a straw hat. He looked, Amelia thought, considerably older and rather ill. No wonder he was taking the waters. He looked infirm, grey and thin, and slightly care-worn. He greeted his cousin warmly.

That was the first of many meetings, and the more Amelia saw of her cousin and her cousin-in-law, the more she wondered, and the more she wondered the more impossible she found it to come to any conclusion.

Mrs Rylands was not at Haréville, but after the Harmers had been there for some days it turned out that the doctor at the watering-place where she was staying, which was ten miles off – a long distance in those days – told her that the waters were not strong enough for her, and that she had better try those of Haréville, which he was sure would suit her better. She obeyed her doctor, and almost at the same time Cyril Legge arrived from Paris, and with him Jean de Bosis, without his wife. Jean de Bosis had been ordered a course of the waters, but his wife said she could not endure the monotony and the dullness of Haréville, and he was to meet her at Venice, where they had taken the first floor of a palace, for later on, as soon as he should have finished his cure.

Jean de Bosis met and talked with the Harmers with the utmost ease and friendliness. Zita thought he was altered; Amelia thought not. It was not that he looked much older – he was thirty-nine and looked younger – but his expression was, Zita thought, different. It had hardened. She wondered what had happened to him, and what he felt. He was a new man to her, as if she had never known him. But to Jean de Bosis, Zita seemed no different. There was no doubt about that. She seemed to him just as beautiful, perhaps more beautiful than she had been ten years ago. Amelia noticed this, and commented on it.

'He admires you just as much as ever,' she said one morning to Zita, while they were sitting in the park listening to the band.

'Oh! I don't think so,' said Zita.

'It is perfectly obvious, and if you're not careful he'll be in love with you. I used to think he was in love, or going to be in love, with you in Paris in old days.'

Zita laughed.

'Did you think that?'

'Yes, I did. I think he *was* at one time, for a moment, only you were so . . . well, I suppose you didn't care for him and gave him no encouragement.'

'His wife is beautiful, isn't she?'

'Not exactly beautiful, but handsome. And a remarkable woman, and her singing is wonderful. You've never heard her?'

'No, she's never been to England. Is he very fond of her?'

'He certainly was at first, they say, but I think they both have bad tempers. She's obviously the woman he described in his book, well, in all his books, but chiefly in *Le Philtre*.'

'I must read it. He isn't musical, is he?' asked Zita.

'Oh no! He hates music, and she hates literature. That was one reason, I suppose, they were attracted to one another.'

'Is she much younger than he is?'

'No, older, she was a widow when she married him.'

'And are there no children?'

'There was one; it died.'

But soon Zita was able to get first-hand impressions of Jean de Bosis. Robert got up early in the morning, and drank his first glass of water at half-past six. Owing to this he felt tired in the afternoon, and he took a long siesta. Jean did not begin his cure until much later, and it was of a much milder nature. The day after his arrival, at two o'clock in the afternoon, he found Zita sitting by herself under the shade of a tree in the park. She always sat in the same chair under the same tree doing needlework. The Legges had gone out driving, so Jean took a chair and sat down next to Zita. It was the first time in his life he had been able to talk to her completely by himself, that is to say without the presence of witnesses or of observant friends, who, although they might not be listening, were there.

'Why did you do it?' were his first words.

'Do what?'

'Say you would come with me and not come?'

'Robert knew,' she said.

'What did he do?'

'He did nothing, and said nothing; that was just it.'

'How did he know?'

'I don't know, but he knew, and he was making things easy for me. He was helping me out; helping me not to lie; it was terrible.'

'Did he read my book?'

'Which book?'

'The book of poems I sent you.'

'Yes, he did, some of it, with some trouble.'

'Then of course he knew.'

'Why?'

'Because there was a poem about you in it.'

'Robert would never have thought that. He liked something about wild ducks; but that would never have occurred to him; that poem might have been about anyone. It never occurred to anyone that it was meant for me – nor to Amelia or Madeleine Laurent – they would have told me at once.'

'It would not have occurred to them, but it would to your husband. There are some things that only men understand; just as there are some things that only women understand. That is one of them – one of men's things.'

'But Robert doesn't know what poetry is about.'

'He knew what that poem was about – that one and the one about the wild ducks.'

'You think so?'

'I know. You know I was ill.'

'When I went away?'

'Yes, when you went away. So ill – I nearly died. You knew what my illness was?'

'Yes, I knew. I could do nothing. I could have run away with you, and I couldn't do that, so I could do nothing.'

There was a long pause.

'But now are you happy?' Zita asked, not looking at him.

'Happy?' he said, with a slightly harsh laugh.

'At any rate, you are famous.'

'Oh yes.' His laughter was harsher and more bitter. 'That's just it.'

'You are not pleased with your books? I have not read one of them.'

'Thank God! But it's your fault.'

'What?'

'That my books are what they are. If you had come with me they would have been different; they would have been like my first book; like what I wrote for you. Perhaps you saved your soul, but you lost mine.'

'Don't say that. Whatever I did wrong I have paid for, I assure you. After all, life is like that. Who is happy?'

'You may well ask. I believe my wife is. She is happy in her art, in her success, and, most of all, in the society of the band of *cabotins* who surround her wherever she goes.'

'I believe,' said Zita, 'that work is the secret of happiness. I have got no work, but I have an occupation; I have made a garden.'

'How lovely it must be,' said Jean, with dreamy eyes.

They talked of the Bertrands; they talked of Madeleine Laurent; they talked of the Legges; of Jean's travels, and as they talked the time rushed by. The band in the kiosk began to play a selection from *La Mascotte*, and Zita got up abruptly and said she must fetch her husband; it was time for her to wake him.

That night they all dined together at the same table. Robert was friendly with Jean. The next day exactly the same thing happened. The routine continued to be the same every day. Robert took his long siesta and the Legges went for a drive, because Amelia liked sketching. Zita sat in her chair. Jean joined her. They talked of everything under the sun, easily and without sense of effort or of time. Like Krylov's two pigeons, they never heeded how the time flew by. Sadness they knew; they were never anything but sad, but they never tasted the weariness of satiety – what Shelley calls 'love's sad satiety'.

For Jean did not make love to Zita. They seemed to be living in a dream. They lived, as it were, in the past, and not in the present. Every night they sat at the same table. A fortnight passed like this before they noticed it. Robert's cure was to last three weeks.

There is a fragment of a Greek poem which tells of the pause that occurs midmost in the winter month, when, the poet says, Zeus brings fourteen days of calm, and mortals call it the sacred windless breeding-time of the many-coloured halcyon. So in the lives of Zita and Jean came a brief interval of halcyon days.

Never had life seemed more peaceful and uneventful to Zita, Robert, and Jean; and yet never had fate been more busy weaving the irreparable for all three of them.

It was at the end of their fortnight that Amelia said at dinner that she had written to Madeleine and told her all the news. Madeleine was at the time at Versailles – and going backwards and forwards between Versailles and Paris. She had told her in her letter, among other things, that Jean de Bosis was at Haréville, and seemed to admire Zita more than ever. The day Madeleine received this letter she met Madame Jean de Bosis at a déjeuner. She talked of Jean, said she knew that he was at Haréville, and added, 'He will have met some old friends – an Englishman and his wife whom he used to know ten years ago in Paris.'

'Oh,' said Madame de Bosis, 'that will be nice for him.' She was not interested.

'Yes,' said Madeleine, slightly nettled at her want of interest. 'Harmer and Mrs Harmer. She is beautiful – Bertrand painted her twice.'

That was enough for Emilia de Bosis. She left for Haréville the next day. She arrived in the evening. She had announced her arrival by a telegram, and she made no objection when her husband told her that they would dine at the same table with the Legges and the Harmers – that is to say, with the Legges and Mrs Harmer, because those who drank stronger waters – Mr Harmer and Mrs Rylands – dined at the *table d'hôte* at six, where a special diet was served them.

Emilia explained her arrival by saying that her husband's presence at Haréville had been noised abroad, and she had been asked to sing for charity at the concert which was to take place at Haréville on the following

Sunday. On Monday, she said, she and Jean were going to Venice. Jean had told Zita he was staying another week, as long, in fact, as she and Robert were staying; but that was all changed now.

Emilia de Bosis made herself the centre of the group, as she was in the habit of doing in any group anywhere. She ate heartily; she drank sparingly; she talked a great deal; she sometimes smiled, but she never laughed. When dinner was over and they were drinking coffee outside, she said they must all go to the theatre; she wished, she said, to feel the atmosphere of the house, as she was to sing in it on Sunday. Zita and the Legges consented, but Mrs Rylands and Robert said they would go to the Casino.

At the table next to them sat a young man by himself, who watched their whole party with absorbed interest. He was a journalist, Walter Price by name, a British subject, although he had lived and worked for some years in America, and still wrote for American newspapers as well as for an English one. He was strikingly good-looking; big, well-made, and hard to place at first sight. He did not look like an Englishman, but neither did he look particularly like anything else; his face was square, with straight features and a low forehead, and he reminded Zita, who noticed him directly, of a bust, Classic or Renaissance, she had seen somewhere, either one of the Roman Emperors or an Italian *Condottiere*, she thought.

Just as the Harmers and their friends were leaving the little table where they had drunk coffee outside on the veranda and were preparing to go into the Casino, Price, who had a great deal of quiet assurance, and did not know what shyness meant, walked up to Jean and talked to him. Jean did not for the moment recall him or place him . . . as I have said, he was hard to place . . . but in a moment he recollected having met him several times at first nights, or on other artistic or maybe sporting occasions in Paris.

'I want Madame to give me an interview for the *Planet*,' he began.

'I don't think she . . .' Jean said, so as to be on the safe side, but his wife overheard the conversation, and interrupted him:

'Good evening, Mr Price,' she said, giving him her hand. 'We are old friends,' she explained to Jean. 'Come to my salon tomorrow at eleven. I have things I want to ask you about this concert.'

Price was delighted; all the more so because Madame de Bosis, although he had twice been presented to her before, had never recognized him when they had met on subsequent occasions; but this wasn't what he wanted now. He wanted to be introduced to Mrs Harmer, and as they walked towards the theatre he asked Jean to introduce him.

'With pleasure,' Jean said, and he introduced Walter Price to the Legges and to Zita.

## CHAPTER X

The concert came off on Sunday night, but Emilia de Bosis did not sing at it because she received, so she said, an urgent summons to go to Venice at once from an impresario who had come all the way from Vienna to meet her. Jean and she left the morning after her arrival, and Jean had no conversation alone with Zita from the moment his wife arrived.

The Harmers and the Legges and Mrs Rylands stayed on another week. Walter Price stayed, too, and he saw a great deal of them. By degrees he attached himself to them, and ended before the week was over by becoming an integral part of their little group.

At the end of the week the Harmers went to Gérardmer on the advice of Robert's doctor, who wished him to have an after-cure. The Legges went with them, and Walter Price. Mrs Rylands said she felt as comfortable with Walter Price as she did with a real American. Robert Harmer said he thought he was not a bad fellow, but it was a pity he spoke with an American accent. Cyril Legge said it was catching. Amelia liked him, and so did Zita. She got on with him without any trouble. She felt as if she had always known him. They went together on the lake: they all went together for expeditions near and far. They spent an enjoyable week, at the end of which the Harmers and Mrs Rylands went back to England and the others to Paris. Walter Price announced his intention of visiting London later on. He came to England in the winter. The Harmers followed their regular routine; in August they had spent a month in Scotland shooting with Wilfrid Sutton and his wife, and one or two others as guests; later on they paid a few visits in the north of England, and by November they settled down once more at Wimbledon.

Walter Price came to London soon after this. He had got himself permanently transferred to London, and he was making a name for himself in journalism as a writer of clever impressionistic articles and interviews – he was an all-round journalist, and seemed to be able to turn his hand to anything: sport, the stage, books, nature, social events, political meetings, occasions, and personages; he was smart and superficial as a writer, and unhampered by distinction or refinement. He came to Wimbledon as often as he could, but that was not often, as he was a hard-worked man, and his work took him all over the country; one day he would be attending a football match in the north of England and the next at a political meeting in South Devon, or interviewing someone in Dublin or Glasgow. Notwithstanding the comparative rarity of his visits, he came to know Zita well. He admired her, looked up to her, and was happy in her society. He poured out to her haphazard and without choice or discrimination his adventures, thoughts, troubles, joys, cares, hopes, ambitions . . . everything, in fact. He talked exclusively about himself, and she liked it. Never had she felt so much at her ease, so comfortable with any human being. So matters went on until the spring, when Walter Price was sent by his newspaper to America. He was away the whole summer, and Zita missed him, seldom as she had seen him while he had been in England. Without knowing it she had become used to him, and he had brought something into her life that hitherto had been absent, something she had never known before – namely, companionship and gaiety: because Walter was gay; he had an un-English buoyancy and quickness he had caught in America; he was appreciative, and had an infectious laugh, and he thought Zita funny, and roared with laughter at some of her remarks. This was the first time anything of this kind had happened to her.

When July came again, Robert Harmer was advised by his doctors to repeat his cure at Haréville. He arranged to go there at the same time as the Legges. The day before the Harmers were to start, Walter Price came back from America and went straight down to Wimbledon. When he heard their plans he told them by an odd coincidence he had also been ordered to Haréville. His decision to go there was taken on the spur of the moment. He had on his arrival applied for and been granted three weeks holiday, but until he saw the Harmers he had no intention of going to Haréville.

Both the Harmers were delighted. Walter Price amused Robert.

Mrs Rylands was to join them in a few days. They would find the Legges at the hotel. All was the same as it had been last year, but Zita was aware that everything was different. Life to her was now a different thing, different from anything it had ever been. It was lined and shot with a curious excitement. She was anxious as she had never been before as soon as one day was over for the next day to begin.

It was when Walter arrived at Haréville that she first faced the situation, and said to herself: 'What has happened to me?' She thought of any answer except the true one, which she refused to give herself. 'I am forty; he is not thirty. I am almost old enough to be his mother . . . and yet there is no doubt that since he has come back from America life has been different; but quite different.' She knew she had, when she was with him, the feeling of timelessness; that she felt she could go on talking and listening to him for ever. She never wanted their intercourse to stop.

As for Walter Price, he seemed to enjoy it, too; but he never appeared to wish to be alone with Zita; he was just as happy if Robert or the Legges were there, nor did he ever resent a *tête-à-tête* with Zita being interrupted. He seemed to be happy with all of them, as if he were a part of their family or group, something essential and integral which belonged to them and could not live without them.

He paid just as much attention to Mrs Legge, and to Mrs Rylands when she arrived, as he did to Zita.

One or two mornings after Zita had arrived at Haréville she was sitting in the park talking to Amelia Legge when Amelia said to her:

'Do you ever hear anything of Jean de Bosis?'

Zita said he had sometimes written to her, but she had heard nothing of or from him for some months.

'Well, I can tell you a little about him,' said Amelia. 'He's written another book, as you probably know, a fearfully interesting book, but rather shocking, only, as usual, it don't shock me! I suppose I'm hardened. And his wife has been singing all over the world, just as usual. They went to Russia in the winter. I saw them sometimes in Paris this spring, but not often. I don't think he's at all happy. He told me the last time I saw him some months ago that he would come here in the summer.'

'Oh!' said Zita.

'Yes, and he asked after you.'

Zita smiled. Jean de Bosis seemed to her to belong to something infinitely far away, both in space and in time.

'He's not happy,' Amelia went on, 'his wife's friends bore him and his friends bore her. They can't really live together and they can't do without one another.'

'She's still fond of him?' asked Zita.

'Oh yes, and desperately jealous. She has never looked at anyone else. He would have if he dared, but he doesn't dare! She has a tremendous hold over him. She's a wonderful woman, in a way. She's not only a great artist – and she is, without doubt, a really great artist, and the best concert-singer alive, I suppose, and that's a rare thing – but she is a remarkable woman as well, and that's rarer still.'

'They never come to England,' said Zita.

'No, she doesn't like England, or rather the thought of it, because she doesn't know it. He looks much older than he did. He is tired with all that writing, and all the wrangle of their domestic life, and all that travel.'

'It must be very tiring,' said Zita.

It was clear during all this conversation that she was only faintly interested in Jean de Bosis, but she was not entirely conscious of the fact. She was conscious of it two days later, when the manager of the hotel announced to her that Jean de Bosis was arriving.

'Is Madame de Bosis coming too?' she asked.

The manager said no; not at present, at any rate.

He arrived the next night by himself.

He went straight to Zita and asked if he might sit at her table. They dined together that night: Zita, the Legges, Jean de Bosis and Walter Price. Robert Harmer and Mrs Rylands had dined at the *table d'hôte*.

He said that he had been ordered to take the waters. His wife was at the Mont Dore for her throat. She was with a party of musical friends.

'They didn't want me,' he said, 'and I doubt whether I could have supported the Mont Dore and so many musicians for all that time. Anyhow, the matter was settled by the doctor, who said I was to come here.'

He looked, indeed, as if he needed a cure somewhere; ten years older than he had looked the year before. After dinner they sat out in the garden until it was time to go to bed.

The next day in the early afternoon Jean de Bosis walked into the park, expecting to find Zita at the usual place in her chair. She was there, but Walter Price was there too. He did not go away when Jean de Bosis came, but stayed until Zita went to fetch her husband, and talked incessantly.

The evening was spent like the preceding one, except that they went to see a play in the Casino. Before they went to bed Jean managed to say to Zita:

'I must have a talk with you alone some time tomorrow. Let us go for a little walk in the park after *déjeuner*.'

Zita nodded. She had no wish to go for a walk with Jean. She realized this, but she did not know how to refuse. It was at that moment that the truth began to break upon her, but not wholly. She knew that she did not want to see Jean de Bosis. She did not want to see anyone but Walter Price, and she wanted to see him every day and every moment of the day, but yet she did not put the question to herself: 'Am I in love with him?' She only knew that nothing like this had happened to her before. She slept badly that night. She did not know what to do about Jean.

'I suppose I must see him,' she said to herself, 'but what shall I say to him?'

And at the same time she wondered how she could still manage to see Walter. The matter was settled for her. M. Carnot, the President of the Republic, was passing through Nancy for some ceremony or inauguration, and Price's editor telegraphed to him to attend the ceremony, and if possible to obtain an interview with anyone of importance with regard to the relations of the Royalist and any other parties who had been intriguing with General Boulanger, now utterly discredited. Price had to catch a train early in the morning. There was no escape for Zita. Jean found her in her usual place just after *déjeuner*.

'I have been waiting for this moment the whole year,' he said.

'Really?' said Zita. She wanted to appear as friendly as possible. 'I am very glad to see you again.' This phrase, with its all too-friendly accent, its accent of a friendliness, that is to say, that could only mean indifference, was like a knell to Jean.

'I see,' he said, 'it is all over.'

'What?'

'All that used to be, and all that might have been.'

'I did not know there *was* anything.'

'You have forgotten last year?'

Zita felt she might well have said that it was surely he who had shown least signs of remembrance, since she had only heard from him once or twice since the past year, but she did not wish to seem to have a grievance. He voiced her thoughts.

'You think because I made so few signs of life that I had forgotten?' he said. 'I have forgotten nothing. I could do nothing because of Emilia. She guessed at once, and was fearfully jealous. We had scenes and reconciliations, terrible scenes! and even more terrible reconciliations! over and over again. I once nearly killed her. I tried to kill myself. I know I was weak and despicable, and I do not deny she had real, complete power over me. She dominated me altogether, but now that is over . . . at least it might be over if you would help me. I could be free at last for the first time. She knows why I have come here. She knows the truth, that I hate her and that I love you, and that I cannot live without you.'

'Oh, don't—' said Zita frightened.

'Then it is all over?' said Jean, savagely, 'and I know why – I knew why at once, directly I saw you, but I tried to deceive myself.'

'What do you mean?'

'You are in love with that vulgar reporter, Price. But I warn you you're making a mistake; he's not a *real* person.'

Zita blushed scarlet, and, like a blinding flash, the truth came to her fully for the first time. She knew that this was true; that she loved Walter; that she had loved him from the first, from the moment she had first set eyes on him. She had, when she had first seen Walter, been struck with fatal lightning, which is always the herald of a real passion and never of a passing fancy, but which, unfortunately, so rarely happens at the same time to both parties concerned.

'I think you are mad,' she stammered.

'I am not mad, and you know I am not mad. Emilia's instinct must have somehow told her this had happened, otherwise she would never have let me come here by myself. She was right. She had nothing to fear. I will go away tomorrow. I can't stay here and see this going on.'

'It is all too absurd,' said Zita. 'I am almost old enough to be his mother.'

'As if age had anything to do with those things,' said Jean.

Zita knew that however vehemently she might deny and dispute what Jean was saying, she could not find the accents which would make her words sound true. She took refuge in tears, which came all too easily.

Jean melted at the sight.

'My poor child,' he said, 'it's not your fault that you love him; you can't help it, but I wonder whether he loves you. Not as he ought to in any case; he will make you unhappy. There is nothing to do except for me to go away.'

'Don't go away,' she said, but there was no real conviction in her voice.

Jean would have given worlds for her to deny the whole thing in accents that he would have believed, but this was just what she did not, what she could not, do.

The band began to play a selection from *Le Petit Duc*.

'I must go and wake Robert,' she said, 'he told me to wake him directly the band started playing.'

Walter Price stayed that night at Nancy, and the next morning Jean left Haréville for the Mont Dore.

## CHAPTER XI

Watering-place life leads to intimacy, and Zita and Walter Price reached, during their stay at Haréville, a pitch of great intimacy, although they were seldom alone together. This did not seem to affect Walter. He was always busy; he always had something to do, and always seemed happy to be a part of the group. He appeared not to want more. Zita did want more, but she could not express her desire, nor do anything to bring it to pass.

As the year before, they took an after-cure at Gérardmer, and then they went home in time for Scotland and the grouse shooting. Robert Harmer invited Price to shoot; he stayed in Scotland a week with them.

After that the lives of the Harmers fell into the old rut; so did Walter's, except that he was sent to Constantinople for several months towards the end of the year. The next year he was in London on and off, but constantly on the move. He managed, nevertheless, to find time to be at Wimbledon. He was getting on in his career, and was often sent on special missions to interview important people or to be on the spot where stirring things were happening. In spite of this, his name had not definitely emerged from the ruck; he was not known outside Fleet Street. Sometimes he would go as far afield as Lisbon or St Petersburg, and sometimes no farther than Manchester or Plymouth.

Between these journeys he would find time to go down to Wimbledon, and so a year passed. The following year the lease on which Harmer had let Wallington came to an end, and he made up his mind to live there again. He let the Wimbledon house, took one in Regent's Park, and settled to spend his holidays at Wallington.

Had anyone told Zita two years previously that when this should happen she would not only not mind it, but positively welcome the change,

she would not have believed them. But such was the truth, and the cause
of it was that she knew she would see more of Walter. She was blissfully,
radiantly happy, and life seemed to begin again for her once more.

When Robert Harmer told Mrs Rylands of the move, she said:

'I am afraid it will be a dreadful blow to Zita to leave that beautiful
garden, which is her creation.'

'I am afraid it will,' said Robert, and he hardly dared broach the topic
for a time; but when at last he did so, and stammered something about the
garden, all that Zita said was:

'Oh! the garden! We will make one at Wallington. I always thought
we could make something wonderful there, but in those days I didn't
know enough. I know better now.'

Robert Harmer was immensely relieved.

They moved into their London house in the spring and stayed there
all the summer. Robert did not go to Haréville that year. Zita went to
Wallington in July. She wished to get everything ready for the autumn.
Walter Price happened to be in the neighbourhood 'covering' a bye-
election, and she saw something of him. Robert had given her *carte
blanche* to do what she liked with the house, and she managed to improve
it a little and to make it a little less gloomy and bleak, and she also set
about introducing reforms in the garden, and silently undermining the
obstinacy of the gardener. Altogether she was ecstatically happy.

They did not go to Scotland that year, but they asked friends for the
partridge shooting in September, and a party for the pheasant shooting
in November that lasted a week. Mrs Rylands came, and Walter Price
was there for a day and a night, which was all he could spare from his
work.

Zita stayed at Wallington all the autumn. They paid two visits and
came home for Christmas, which the Legges, Mrs Rylands, the Suttons,
and Walter Price spent with them.

In January they went to London and stayed there till July, when Robert
Harmer, who had not been so well, was told he must do a proper cure
at Haréville this year; so they went there in July, accompanied, as usual,
by Mrs Rylands, and meeting the Legges there, as usual, again. Walter
Price was busy in London, but he hoped, he said, to be able to put
in ten days at Haréville; the doctor had told him it would be unwise
not to, and like Robert Harmer, he had missed a year and paid for so
doing.

They had been a week at Haréville.

Zita was sitting in the park one morning near the band kiosk talking
to Amelia Legge.

'I had a letter from Madeleine this morning,' said Amelia. 'She
says that Jean de Bosis is dangerously ill. They are all anxious about
him.'

'What is it?' said Zita, frightened at her own indifference.

'They don't quite know. He seems to be wasting away – it's a kind of fever.'

'Is his wife with him?'

'Oh, yes! Madeleine says she is distracted and nursing him wonderfully. His mother is there too. Poor Jean! They say he worries over his last book, which was not such a success as usual. He has come to think all his books were bad, in spite of his great fame.'

'Do you know I have never read one of his books,' said Zita, 'except that little book of poems, and not all of those.'

'It's impossible to get that book now, and not many people have ever heard of it,' said Amelia. 'I'm sorry he is so unhappy,' she added, with a plaintive voice.

'Has he been unhappy?' asked Zita, not looking up.

'Yes, really unhappy. *She* made him unhappy. You see she was too like him, in a way. It was a case of Greek meeting Greek. He ought to have married a quiet, humdrum girl; someone gentle: but the last person he should have chosen was an artist, especially a singer. And Emilia has a terrible temper and Jean is a bundle of nerves. Still, what can one expect? Things so rarely go right. I often think I am not grateful enough having found such a perfect husband as Cyril. When I was younger I used to complain of having to live abroad and go from place to place, but now I know better. I shall never complain. I know how rare perfect husbands are, and I know that I shouldn't have enjoyed a humdrum life in England nearly as much as I've enjoyed our life of travel and bustle and change and interest. I have loved all of it. And you, Zita dear, you ought to be thankful, too. You are a happy woman and you have a perfect husband; you couldn't have found a better one. I used to think when you first married that Robert wasn't the right person for you. I know better now. You have a lot to be thankful for.'

'Oh, yes,' said Zita. 'I know I have, and I hope I am grateful.'

That morning Zita received a telegram from Walter Price saying he was arriving the same evening. As she read the telegram her heart beat. She had not seen Walter for several months. He had been, on behalf of his newspaper, spending the spring and early summer months in Berlin. He wired from Paris. She would see him that evening. She had never felt so sharp a pang of joy in her life. She was conscious of never having loved him so much. Her whole being seemed to be rushing out towards him. She was ready for anything, any act of sacrifice: she wanted to give everything; to offer – to sacrifice – to surrender.

He arrived before dinner and joined Zita and the Legges.

'You have heard, I suppose,' were his first words, 'that Jean de Bosis is dead.'

They had not heard it.

'Yes; he died early this morning, at four o'clock, of malarial fever, which he caught in Italy. I've got to write his biography, not only for my paper but for America, and I thought you might help me,' he said, looking at Zita and Mrs Legge. 'I cabled a story this morning. The funeral is to be in the country, and quite quiet – only relations. They are making a big hullabaloo about him in Paris; and the Americans are cabling like hell; his name is popular in the States, he is one of the few European writers that are known there.'

'You will be able to help Mr Price,' Zita said to Amelia.

'I haven't seen him lately,' said Amelia. 'I hardly ever saw him after the last time he was here; that was three years ago, when he went away in such a hurry, called to Mont Dore by his wife, who never could leave him out of her sight for five minutes – a genius shouldn't marry a genius. Be careful whom you marry, Mr Price. Don't marry anyone who cares for journalism, or news, or newspapers, or Fleet Street. Find out your opposite.'

Walter Price laughed.

'I shall certainly make a wise choice,' he said.

Zita quaked inwardly at the thought of his possibly marrying.

'The Americans,' said Walter, 'want personal stuff about his life. She is well known in America, too.'

'Yes,' said Cyril, 'they went for a long tour there, she sang, and he gave one or two lectures in English. He told me he hated it, but they made a lot of money, and people were kind to them.'

'Yes,' said Price, 'and they were personally popular. Madame de Bosis has, you see, the international touch; that's what Americans like. They don't like someone who is just all French or just all British – that freezes them.'

'Do the Americans like his books?' asked Cyril.

'They have never really read them; but he's a popular personality, on account of his wife. And then some of his books were thought to be scandalous, and they were forbidden in some States, and that all helps from a news point of view.'

'Do you think his books will live in France?' asked Cyril.

'Oh, no!' said Walter, 'but they are having a good innings and the top of the boom is now, and I am doing my best to boost it more. I'm sorry he's dead, of course, but he has died just at the right moment for me; he couldn't have chosen a better time.'

'Poor Jean!' said Amelia.

'He was a white man, and he'll be missed. There was no pretension about him,' said Walter.

The next day there were races in the neighbourhood, and Robert Harmer insisted on going. He wanted everyone to go: Mrs Rylands and the Legges consented, but Walter Price did not appear in the morning; he was too busy writing; and Zita said she had a headache. She did not come down in the morning. The others went by train to the races directly after *déjeuner* without her.

After luncheon Zita felt better. She came down and sat in the shade in the park, which was deserted. She sat working, wondering at the fate of Jean de Bosis, and what Walter Price was doing. He answered her question by appearing in person and sitting down next to her.

'I thought you had gone to the races,' she said.

'I'm far too busy,' he said. 'I have roughed out a story, but what I want is the personal touch, and that's just what I can't get.'

Zita laughed a little sadly.

'I could supply that,' she said, at last.

'You?'

'Yes. I was connected with an odd episode in the life of Jean de Bosis, a long time ago, more than ten years.'

'Could I use it? Could it be published?'

'Oh, no.'

'Not even in America?'

'Just imagine what Robert would feel!'

'He needn't see it.'

'He might, and then . . .'

'It's a pity, because I suppose it's interesting?'

'It is, or was, interesting to me.'

'Is it a love story?'

'Yes.'

'Then you had better not tell me. It's too rough. It would have made my whole career.'

'Would it?'

'Yes.'

'Well, I will tell it you.'

'Don't; if you tell it me I shall use it; I shan't be able to flog myself off it.'

'Well, you *can* use it; I don't care; I will risk it,' she said triumphantly.

The opportunity had come to her at last to make just such a sacrifice as she was longing to make – the supreme sacrifice. Yes, she would face all the consequences, even if it meant leaving Robert. It would prove to Walter how much she loved him.

'I am very fond of you, Walter,' she said, almost in a whisper.

'And I am very fond of you,' he said, reverently.

'Are you?' she asked, not really understanding the quality of his intonation.

'Yes,' he said.

He meant it, but he meant a different fondness from hers. She loved him with passion. He had put her on a pedestal, to worship in a way, but he had never thought of loving her as she dreamt of being loved. She seemed to him quite outside the range of all that.

'Yes,' she said, hesitatingly, 'I am fond of you. I will prove it you by giving you this story, and you can do what you like with it. After all, you can leave out the names – my name.'

And then she began to tell him the story of what had happened long ago in Paris; the story of her early life, of her marriage, her life at Wallington; how she and Robert went to Paris, and how Bertrand had painted her picture, and how she had met Jean de Bosis.

'I was young, and very lovely in those days,' she said.

'They say you are still better-looking now,' said Walter.

Zita knew she was still beautiful, but she knew there was no longer the bloom of youth about her. It had gone for ever. She smiled, and went on.

She told him how she had settled to run away with Jean de Bosis, and how at the last minute she had been unable to.

'I suppose the real reason was I didn't love him. I didn't know then what real love meant; I never knew that till much later.'

'And he – was he sore?' asked Walter.

'Yes, he was unhappy and then ill; he nearly died.'

'And when did you meet again?'

'Ten years later; the year I first met you here.'

'And he loved you still?'

'He said he did.'

'And you?'

'It was like a dream to me; I was glad to see him, but I couldn't begin that again, and then. . . .'

'And then what?'

'Well, something happened. I became different; I woke up.'

'It's a wonderful story,' said Walter. 'I can make something big out of it.'

'Do you think you can?' she said, feeling an exaltedly secret and fearful joy.

'Sure,' he said, 'it will make my whole career. There's not a soul who knows it, either?'

'Not a soul. Amelia once had an inkling that something of the sort might happen, but she never knew.'

'I must get busy,' said Walter, and he went up to his room, leaving Zita by herself.

She spent the rest of the afternoon alone, till the others came back from the races in time to drink their afternoon glass of water. Zita felt rather like one who has been walking in her sleep and is half aware of having done something tremendous, but does not know what it is.

## CHAPTER XII

At dinner that night Walter Price announced that he would have to leave Haréville the next morning. He had received orders to go to Paris immediately. The Legges were going to the play, as usual, and Harmer and Mrs Rylands spoke of a mild game of *petits chevaux*. Zita said she was tired. And as the party got up to separate, after drinking their coffee on the veranda outside the hotel, Zita said to Walter:

'I shall be in my sitting-room if you have time to come and have a little talk before you go.'

'I think I'd better say good-bye now,' he said. 'I shan't be able to get to bed as it is; I shan't be through with my writing till the morning. I've got the whale of a story on hand,' he said, with a glance of gratitude to Zita, 'so I'll say good-bye now, Mrs Harmer, and I hope you and Mr Harmer will have a lovely time, and I do thank you from my heart for your great kindness.' As he said this he advanced to Mr Harmer, who was just a little bit ahead. Then coming back a step he said, 'Good-bye, Mrs Harmer,' and he added in a lower tone, 'you have done more for me than you know. We shall meet in London in the autumn.'

'Yes,' said Harmer, 'and you must come to Wallington and shoot some partridges.'

'Sure,' said Price, gaily. 'I must say good-bye to Mrs Legge and Mrs Rylands; I shan't see them in the morning.' And he left Zita and Harmer, and caught up Mrs Rylands and the Legges, who had gone on ahead, and said good-bye to them.

Zita went up to her room and waited. She still hoped that Walter Price had spoken as he had done for the benefit of the public, and that he still meant to come and bid her a more private and more intimate good-bye, even if it was only one word. She waited up till eleven, but he never came, and soon after that her husband came in and she went to bed.

She did not see Walter Price again, and when she came down in the morning she was told that he had gone by the earliest train.

The Harmers stayed only another ten days at Haréville, and a week at Gérardmer, and then they went to Wallington.

The day after they arrived, a lovely August day, when the garden was shimmering with heat and there was a pleasant noise of mowing-machines on the lawn, Zita came down early to breakfast, which was at 9, and found awaiting her a letter which she saw at once was in Walter Price's handwriting. She was glad that Robert was not yet down. She opened it. It was a long letter. This is what she read:

# The Lonely Lady of Dulwich

———— *Club, London.*

*Adorable 'Queen Guinevere'.* (This name was a joke between them. Walter Price had christened her Queen Guinevere because one day she had said to him: 'Robert's name is Arthur as well as Robert, but he can't bear the name, and he can't bear being called Arthur, even in fun', and Walter had said: 'That's because he doesn't want you to be Guinevere.')

*I have not had a moment to write since I left Haréville. Things have been humming and a rare lot has happened. I owe all to you. I reckon you know all I have felt for you, although men are pretty dumb when it comes to saying anything they mean or feel, but God, fortunately, made women cute enough to make things square. I'm not much good at saying things, things that I really feel, but I suppose you must have some hunch of what I have always felt for you. I have always, ever since the first moment I saw you, put you above everyone and everything else I have known or seen in the world. You have for me always made the rest of the world look like thirty cents, as the Americans say. You have been my good genius, my guardian angel, and have even replaced in my heart and in my life the place that my sainted mother once held, and might have held still had she not been cut away untimely by a cruel disease.*

*You crowned all you did for me by giving me that story the other day at Haréville. I worked it up, and gave all my heart to it. Of course I handled the story with the greatest reverence and reserve, and was careful not only not to mention your name, but not to say anything which would betray you to the most cute, nor offend the most sensitive. I pride myself that it is all in good taste. Well, the U.S.A. Editor – A. L. Scarp – ate it, and on the strength of it I have got a permanent post on the 'Illustrated Weekly Moon', the largest illustrated paper in the States, and the best selling paper. Thanks to this I am now able to realize what up to now has been but a shadowy dream and a teasing mirage. I have for over two years been engaged secretly to Sylvia Luke, the daughter of Cuthbert Luke, the great genre painter. She is one in a thousand; a jewel of the first water. I need not describe her, as you may have seen her pictures in the shop windows. We have loved each other long, but marriage seemed up to now an impossible dream. To make things easier, Sylvia went on the stage and earned a pittance by playing small parts on tour in vaudeville. She got some good notices, and folks liked her, but the competition was too great, and her father thought she would do better on the concert stage than on the stage, and lately she has been singing at concerts in the provinces with success – she does imitations. But that is all over now. She need no more work for her living. I have enough for both, and besides a handsome salary, one of the swellest positions in the modern Press. And this is thanks to you, Queen Guinevere – great, generous and noble Fairy Godmother. How we both bless you! Sylvia is longing to know you. I have told her so much*

411

*about you and talked of you so often that she feels she already knows you intimately. We are to be married at the beginning of September, and in a fortnight's time we sail for the States. We shall live there, but I shall come over to England every summer when things are quiet over there, and I shall not forget the old country, nor Wallington. What more can I say, except that we are grateful to the Fairy Queen who, with a touch of her golden wand, has changed the world for two love-sick mortals? Please give my kindest regards to Mr Harmer.*

Zita read the letter twice. As in a blurred dream, certain odd sights seemed to rise obstinately before her: the first was a small party at Cuthbert Luke's house in St John's Wood. It was an elaborate house – a house furnished as with stage properties. There were a great many palms and brass warming pans, and some of the rooms were so low you could hardly stand up in them. It was, she remembered, a musical party that night: Robert had refused to go, and she had been by herself. Luke had welcomed the guests in his velvet jacket, and pointed out what he was exhibiting at the Academy – a picture called 'After Long Years', and another called 'The Patrician's Daughter'. The painter's technique was admirable.

A pianist had played Hungarian dances; a violinist had played *Simple Aveu*; a tenor had sung 'I'll sing thee songs of Araby'; and 'Maid of Athens', and, finally, the daughter of the house had stepped on to the platform. There was no pressing, because she regarded herself as a professional. She was overwhelmingly blond – what would now be called a 'platinum blonde', but the word had not then been invented. She had light grey eyes and a dazzling row of teeth. She did a few imitations – some with music, some without – of Letty Lind, Florence St John, Marie Lloyd, Violet Cameron, Arthur Roberts, and Ellen Terry. She caught and reproduced the accent of the stage and the mannerism of the originals exactly, but there was not a spark of fancy or of humour in her impersonations.

And then Zita remembered walking down the Burlington Arcade one day and seeing in a shop window a photograph of the same dazzling blonde with flashing teeth, and under it was printed: Miss Sylvia Luke. This was rare in those days, unless the sitter was an actress or a singer of note, and Sylvia Luke as an artiste was unknown to the public; but she was known as a beauty, well-known enough to have her name printed on the photographs that were for sale in the Burlington Arcade.

The third snapshot that floated across Zita's memory was one day at Brighton; she was shopping, and looking at the window of a second-hand jeweller's shop full of pretty silver and quaint ornaments, when she caught sight of Sylvia Luke and her father, who were looking at the same shop window.

She only heard Sylvia say two words before she and her father walked on. They were:

'They're false.' And in these two words she managed to instil the maximum of contempt with the minimum of refinement.

Then one day, when Wilfrid Sutton was having tea with her, and the subject of Cuthbert Luke's pictures happened to crop up, Zita asked Wilfrid whether he knew Sylvia Luke, as he knew most people in the theatrical and Bohemian world.

'Oh, yes,' he said, 'she's a good girl. Good-hearted and respectable; no use on the stage. She can't act for nuts, and she can't sing. She has a gift of mimicry, and she can reproduce the sound of some people's voices exactly, but she isn't funny, and she has no sense of humour, so she can't make it amusing, and it ends by being rather a bore; but she's good-looking and a good sort, and she's greatly admired and liked. Lots of people have wanted to marry her.'

That conversation had taken place a year ago, and now. . . .

She walked to the sideboard and she noticed that in Robert's place there was a large roll that might contain an illustrated newspaper.

'Perhaps,' she thought, 'that contains Sylvia Luke's picture.' And she helped herself to eggs and bacon. Robert was late; so late that she rang the bell and asked whether he was not yet up.

The butler said that he had had breakfast early, and had gone out riding; he would be back presently. Zita finished breakfast; looked at a newspaper; saw the cook; ordered dinner, that is to say, checked the bill of fare that had already been glanced at by Robert; answered some letters and walked into the garden as far as the gardener's house, which was at the end of the kitchen-garden. She wanted to see the gardener. She found him and discussed one or two matters, cut some flowers for the house, and then strolled back to the house.

'What a lovely day,' she said to herself, 'even Wallington is beautiful today.'

When she got back to the house she was met by Clark, the butler, who had been with them ever since they were married. Mr Harmer had been obliged to go suddenly to London, he said. He had gone by the ten forty-five. He wanted her to follow by the five o'clock train. He had ordered the carriage, and her things were being packed. The caretaker had been informed by telegraph.

'Did he tell the kitchen-maid to go?' Zita asked.

'Yes, madam. He said that she was to go tomorrow.'

'Didn't he leave a letter or a message for me?'

Clark shook his head, and said 'No' – sadly, thought Zita. A curious feeling as of a nightmare began to creep over her.

'Mr Harmer said he would explain everything in London; he had only just time to catch the train, and as it was he nearly missed it, so Charles (the coachman) said.'

'Oh, that accounts for everything,' said Zita; but she thought it accounted for nothing.

Before luncheon the second post arrived, and with it a large illustrated newspaper in a roll for her. That's just like the one which came for Robert this morning, Zita thought. She opened it, and her eye fell at once on an article called 'The Life Romance of Jean de Bosis'. There was the story, exactly as she had told it to Walter, with every particle of emphasis, accentuation and vulgarity that headlines, captions, and all the artifices of publicity, as far as they went at that epoch, could give. The captions were terrible: 'Lovely bride homesick in Parisian home': 'Thwarted poet meets his soul-mate': 'Famous painter throws starving souls together': 'Scared wife jibs at the last fence'.

Zita read through the article from beginning to end. The whole story was there. Her name was not mentioned, but short of that everything was said, and her picture by Bertrand was produced as an example of his art – as though by accident. There was the story of her life, trumpeted to the world on the loudest of brass instruments, and blazoned in letters of limelight.

'Well, had she not foreseen this might, this *must* happen?' Not quite like that; and then at that moment she had been prepared not to mind because she thought that Walter loved her, or might love her, but now. . . .

'Robert has seen this,' she said to herself; 'he will turn me out of the house.'

She went into his study. In the fireplace there was a litter of envelopes which had been thrown away, and among other rubbish she saw the charred remains of the wrapper that had held the *Illustrated Weekly Moon*.

Zita found that her maid had received instructions to pack and go to London with her. She arrived in London at seven o'clock and found the caretaker waiting for her.

Mr Harmer, she said, was staying at the club; but dinner was ready. The caretaker had cooked a chicken and rice-pudding. There was also a letter awaiting her that had been sent by hand. It was from the family solicitor, Mr Hanson, saying Mr Harmer wished him to see her the next morning at his office, and would she kindly call at Lincoln's Inn at eleven o'clock.

Zita arrived punctually at Mr Hanson's office at eleven o'clock the next morning. Mr Hanson received her like a father and plunged gently into the matter, talking in a soothing diminuendo. He did not refer to the reason, the why or the wherefore; he just stated the fact that Mr Harmer had suggested a separation by mutual consent, and was willing to make his wife an adequate allowance. Mr Harmer had no wish to divorce, and he supposed she would not wish it either. Would she be willing to agree to this arrangement? Oral consent was sufficient, but it was more usual to draw up a deed, and that was the course Mr Harmer preferred. If she was willing, all that she would have to do would be to sign the deed when it was drawn up. There were certain minor questions of detail as to chattels to settle.

Zita said at once she was more than willing. Mr Hanson gave a sigh of relief. Mr Harmer was anxious for her to live in the London house until she should find a house that suited her. He had even arranged for a kitchen-maid to come up to London from Wallington to cook for her and to stay as long as should be necessary. He himself would be returning to Wallington as soon as the deed was signed.

'You understand,' said Mr Hanson, 'the separation will be immediate.'

Zita said she quite understood. A further appointment was made for the signing of the deed, and the interview came to an end. Zita was determined to find a house as soon as possible. She found one the next day in Dulwich Village: a furnished cottage with a small garden, and in a fortnight's time she had moved in. Robert Harmer had told her, through Mr Hanson, that he would send her all her personal effects, but she refused to keep any of the jewels or anything that he had given her, and she had few things of her own.

She never saw Robert again. He died two years later during an epidemic of influenza. Before he died he had sold both his London house and his house at Wimbledon. He left Zita the same allowance she had received during his lifetime. He left a legacy to Amelia Legge, and Wallington went to the next of kin, a nephew who had settled in Canada, and who died five years later, leaving a son. This boy, Kenneth Harmer, became a cadet in the navy, and was a midshipman in 1914. He did well in the war and after. He used to go and see Zita when he was on leave, and she must have liked him, as she left him the small patrimony she had inherited from her mother, and the works of Tennyson.

Zita Harmer lived at Dulwich for the rest of her life, and died at the age of seventy, in 1920. She made her little garden beautiful, but she seldom saw anyone, and she never met Walter Price again. He settled down in America for good. The Legges used to visit her when they were in England. Legge died, an ambassador, a few years before the war: Amelia lived till the end of the war, but mostly abroad. She died the same year as Mrs Harmer.

Zita was a beautiful old lady. Her hair was white and there were many tiny wrinkles on her lovely skin; but in her carriage, her movements, and her walk were the authority that only great beauty and the certainty of having possessed it confer, and her smile still lit up a whole room. People who would see her walking in Dulwich Village and Dulwich Park would wonder who she was, and what her story had been – that is to say, if she had had a story, which they thought unlikely.

They called her the 'Lonely Lady'.

I was at Dulwich when the effects of Mrs Harmer were being sold by auction in her cottage. The effects were mostly ordinary Victorian furniture, which was of no interest or importance, and went for little. There were a great many books, but with the exception of an odd collection of novels, they were mostly about gardening and technical at that. Mrs Harmer must have been a serious gardener.

There were no pictures in the house except one or two early Victorian engravings by Landseer and Frith, which she had found there when she had taken the house. She had changed nothing in the furniture or the decoration, and had introduced no furniture of her own.

There was an early Broadwood pianoforte, which made a wheezy tinkling noise like a spinet. I should have liked to have bought that, had I known what to do with it. I went all over the little house before the sale, and visited the garden. It was a small garden, but it had been evidently planted and tended by a master hand and a loving mind.

The sale took place towards the end of June, and the Madonna lilies were out; and the garden was curiously aromatic with verbena and sweet-scented geranium, cherry-pie and stocks, and sweet-william and pinks. The cottage walls were smothered in roses. It was an unpretentious garden, and yet there was something special about it; something rare and intensely individual. This was odd, because in the house there was nothing that gave one the slightest indication of anything individual or personal. In the bedroom there was a cheap crucifix and a large coloured lithograph of the Holy Family.

I bought two lots at the sale: a French book and an old-fashioned leather work-box or writing-desk – I don't know which, for it contained reels of silk, tapestry needles, a crochet-hook and a half-finished kettle-holder with 'A Merry Christmas' begun but not finished on it, as well as pens, pencils, an inkpot and a little note-book, and some sealing-wax and a seal.

The French book was an old one, published in 1880. It was tattered, but only half cut; it was a little book of verse called *Stances*. On the title-page there was an inscription in violet ink: '*à Madame Harmer, avec les plus respectueux hommages de Jean de Bosis, Paris, le 3 Mai,* 1880.' One day I was looking at the writing-desk or work-box, and I took out the little note-book. I found it contained three entries in pencil. One was headed:

'New Year's Day, 1894.
'So far, that my doom is, I love thee still.
Let no man dream but that I love thee still.'

Underneath this was written 'Guinevere'.

Further on in the book was another entry:

'Good Friday, 1900.
'Amor meus crucifixus est.'

There was a third entry, dated 'May, 1920'. It must have been written just before she died. It was to this effect: 'Kenneth came to tea.'

'Secure for a full due.'

I took out the small gold seal from the box, but I could not distinguish the image nor decipher the superscription. Out of curiosity, I took an impression. The image was that of a face enclosed in a heart, from which a flame arose, and the inscription was:

*Saignant et brûlant.*

# 8

## *Good Things*

*Maurice Baring was fond of the small quotation which could give pleasure while standing apart from its context. As one who loved to hear 'good things' – those felicities of notion and word which outlast their casual utterance – he could also say them. It seems appropriate to include in this book a small anthology – he delighted, too, in making small anthologies of brief extracts – drawn from scattered sources throughout his whole range of work. I have grouped them loosely under two headings – 'Society and Character', and 'Arts and Style'.*

# Good Things

## (i) *Society and Character*

[Conformity is] the worst form of snobbishness, that is to say, of cowardice.

'High-Brows and Low-Brows', in *Lost Lectures*.

If we knew the future . . . we could not endure it.

*Robert Peckham.*

'He's mysterious – mysterious about nothing.'

*Cat's Cradle.*

'I was in love with her once, five years ago, when I was a boy, and I created a scandal by giving her a family emerald – an heirloom. Such a lovely thing! What fun it was to give it away!'

*Cat's Cradle.*

' "Querelle de moine," Leo X said when he heard of the Reformation. I think he was right. Sensible man.'

*Cat's Cradle.*

He pointed out, too, how difficult it would be to break off the engagement at the eleventh hour.
'But that's just the beauty of the eleventh hour. That's what it's there for, surely,' she said.

*Cat's Cradle.*

'The French put things so well – so clearly. They are not afraid of platitude.'

*Cat's Cradle.*

She wasn't pretty, but she had one of those faces that make you happy:

421

grey eyes, a turned-up nose, and a way of letting out funny things, as if she couldn't help it, and she was always making disastrous mistakes – moral malaprops which were just to the point.

*Cat's Cradle.*

She heard the voice of Truth speaking within her without the noise of words.

*Cat's Cradle.*

Mr Crowe was an invalid without an illness.

*Cat's Cradle.*

'Nothing is more nauseating than praise from people one dislikes.'

*The Grey Stocking.*

Every now and then C. would send her poems that he wrote, and she ended by treating them like bills; they got lost almost before she looked at them.

*C.*

She was very simply dressed in black . . . her clothes seemed to grow on her.

*C.*

'I believe that Nature never repeats herself; and that every note that is struck in the universe is struck once only, and for ever.'

*C.*

'The point of life is – I think – its imperfection.'

*C.*

La Fontaine found nothing in life but *un vain bruit et l'amour*, but then *l'amour* went a long way.

*French Literature.*

'Jenny,' said Teresa, '. . . has a fatal gift for intimacy with almost everyone she meets.'

*Comfortless Memory.*

'That Mrs Childs is a charming woman; and how good-looking!'
'Her mother was affected,' said Mrs Cantillon.

*Darby and Joan.*

'But Lady Jarvis knows him.'
'She's seen everybody once . . .'

*Daphne Adeane.*

[The way a Queen talks]:

'You live in Ireland,' said the Queen. 'I have been to Ireland, too. It was in the year before the war, and we travelled incognito, but sometimes we had to say who we were. Everyone was very kind, especially Lord Kiltarlity; no, that was in Scotland. The Scotch gardens are so beautiful. I am very fond of gardens, but it is difficult here. Nothing grows. I should like to have a Scotch gardener. But the King does not care for sweet-smelling flowers. They give him hay fever. It's dreadful.

'Presently we shall have tea, and my sister-in-law is coming. She wants to know you. *She* is very clever. I am not clever.' The Queen laughed, and indicated by a slight bend of the body that the conversation was at an end. And she passed on to another guest.

*Friday's Business.*

The Ambassador, Sir Edmund Monson, was academic with a large swaying presence and an inexhaustible supply of polished periods.

*The Puppet Show of Memory.*

There is a greatness in things light as well as in things heavy.

*French Literature.*

She was, in spite of an exemplary piety – which was genuine – fundamentally non-moral.

*Cat's Cradle.*

When we read in Cicero's letters of the oppressive presence of Julius Caesar at a dinner-party, or in Pliny's letters how often a sentence in a letter creates a false impression which a word of conversation (were the correspondents to meet) would put right, we say 'How modern!' What we mean is, 'How human!'

*French Literature.*

[Talk between lovers] . . . that conversation that never began nor ended.

*Daphne Adeane.*

'One has to *accept* sorrow for it to be of any healing power, and that is the most difficult thing in the world. . . . A Priest once said to me, "When you understand what *accepted* sorrow means, you will understand everything. It is the secret of life." '

*Darby and Joan.*

*In a letter to Ethel Smyth during the war,* 20 *September* 1916: 'I am mortally tired – tired morally, not physically. . . .'

*Ethel Smyth, A Biography* by Christopher St John.

The Englishman likes privacy; the American detests it.
*Round the World in Any Number of Days.*

Russia and America are the two most hospitable countries I have ever visited. I think the Russians and the Americans are the *kindest* people in the world, and their countries the most really democratic (whatever their respective governments may be). (They may be both perhaps *vile*.)
*Round the World in Any Number of Days.*

The intonation with which the old servant [in *Uncle Vania*] said, 'They've gone' – an intonation of peculiar cheerfulness with which servants love to underline what is melancholy – was marvellous.
*The Puppet Show of Memory.*

The fields and trees had that peculiar deep green they take on in the twilight, as if they had been dyed by the tints of the evening.
*Overlooked.*

Aston said, '. . . I believe people like myself . . . are the last branches of a dying tree, or rather a dead tree; the tree is the old country gentry. Soon there will be none of us left, and the tree will be cut down and thrown away, and a damned good job, too. We're not wanted any more.'
I said that the new class which was taking the place of the old country gentry was hardly an improvement.
'Give them time,' said Aston, 'and they'll get just as old and rotten and useless as we are.'
*A Triangle.*

*Singleton:* You see, when I do admire someone, I can't look at anyone else. Some women put everyone out, like candles.
*Lady Lawless:* I know they do. It's very disagreeable for the candles, I assure you.
*Singleton:* But it must be nice for the woman. I often wonder if beautiful women know *how* beautiful they are.
*Lady Lawless:* They know, exactly.
*His Majesty's Embassy.*

Beauty has almost always proved the bane of the very beautiful.
*Have You Anything to Declare?*

She spoke most languages, and could be silent in none.
*The Lonely Lady of Dulwich.*

Whenever one came to France from England one seemed to step from a dark room into a bright one.
*R.F.C. H.Q.*

[Seneca, in the parody play, *The Stoic's Daughter*, has just been told that his daughter has become a Christian. A character exclaims]: 'She must have been got hold of by the Jews.'

*Diminutive Dramas.*

[War diary, 20 May 1917] . . . Someone has written to me asking to suggest a Latin motto for the Tanks. I suggested *Nihil Obstat*.

*R.F.C. H.Q.*

The culture imbibed from the air is the best culture.

*Have You Anything to Declare?*

Just as in the art of writing, and in fact all the arts, the best style is where there is no style, or rather where we no longer notice the style, so appropriate and inevitable, so easy the thing said, sung, or done is made to appear, so in diplomacy the most delightful diplomats were those about whom there was no diplomatic style, nothing which made you think of diplomacy.

*The Puppet Show of Memory.*

## (ii) *Arts and Style*

'I always think that all the great things, the greatest things, are simple. It is the second-best things that are so complicated.'

*The Coat Without Seam.*

'Rostand!' exclaimed Miss Tring, in disgust; 'he writes such bad verse – *du caoutchouc* – he's so vulgar.'
'It is true,' said Wilmott, 'he's an amateur. He has never written professionally for his bread, but only for his pleasure.'
'But in that sense,' said Giles, 'God is an amateur.'

'A Luncheon Party', in *Half a
Minute's Silence & Other Stories.*

A story told by Maurice Baring, quoted by Enid Bagnold in *The Times*, 14 November 1962:
One doctor to another: 'About the termination of pregnancy – I want your opinion. The father was syphilitic. The mother tuberculous. Of the four children born the first was blind, the second died, the third was deaf and dumb, the fourth was also tuberculous. What would you have done?' – 'I would have ended the pregnancy.' – 'Then you would have murdered Beethoven.'

*Vernon Lee, Violet Paget, 1856–1935,
by Peter Gunn.*

'Italians seldom are *really* musical; they only care for *their* music.'

*Cat's Cradle.*

Someone was playing the piano – playing Chopin with so much expression that he was scarcely audible.

*C.*

I remember . . . a recital of Paderewski where he played Liszt's arrangement of the *Erlkönig*. When he came to the end of it, the impression was that he himself had experienced the ride in the night; that he had battled with the Erl King for the life of the child, and that it was he and not the child who was dead.

*The Puppet Show of Memory.*

[In Racine's play] Sarah Bernhardt 'embodied the sumptuous malignity of Athalie'.

'Sarah Bernhardt' in *Punch and Judy and Other Essays.*

I think it was 1896, I was present at a performance of *Magda* in Paris at the Renaissance by Sarah; in her own phrase, le Dieu était là. . . .

*The Puppet Show of Memory.*

In the Drury Lane pantomime . . . Dan Leno played a harp solo, which I think is the funniest thing I ever saw on the stage. He had a subtle, early Victorian, Byronic way of playing, refined and panic-stricken. . . .

*The Puppet Show of Memory.*

The city of Florence appeared to them in the evening light like a fabric of the same texture as flowers. Brunelleschi's Dome seemed ethereal; Giotto's Tower looked like a lily.

*Darby and Joan.*

I have nothing against modern art, but I want to know exactly what people mean when they talk of modern art. If they mean the products due to the fresh impressions and to the ardent vision of the young, I am with them; but if they mean that modern art must have no roots in the past, and no connection with anything that has gone before, I think they are talking nonsense.

'High-Brows and Low-Brows', in *Lost Lectures.*

[To become immediately old-fashioned is the fate of all works of art that] 'startle more by the modernity of their ideas than by their truth to nature'.

'Sarah Bernhardt'.

426

The portrait was as life-like as it was lifeless.

*C.*

Somebody once defined an artist . . . as a man who knew how to finish things.

*Have You Anything to Declare?*

[Of a World War I aviator]: Like all great artists, he seemed to do nothing at all, and to let the machine fly itself.

*R.F.C. H.Q.*

It frequently happens that when a poet is deeply struck by the work of another poet he feels a desire to write something himself, but something different.

*An Outline of Russian Literature.*

'Why is it,' asked Christopher, 'that one cannot bear to talk about anything one really knows something about, even if it is only a little?'

'I think it is because people are always striking wrong notes, and wrong notes matter when one has an ear for anything.'

*The Coat Without Seam.*

Catullus . . . gives one the impression of a man almost inarticulate, so much has he to say.

*Have You Anything to Declare?*

Every great man is either an artist or a fighter.

*An Outline of Russian Literature.*

'A novel must not be too lifelike, or else where does the artist come in?'

*The Lonely Lady of Dulwich.*

His next book read like an imitation of his own manner in which the faults were exaggerated and the mannerisms caricatured. This often happens with writers whose work at the same time excites the vituperation of the critics and wins the favour of the public – the author tends as a result to abound in himself.

*The Lonely Lady of Dulwich.*

Art was Flaubert's religion; he served it with all his might; and, although he wrote but little, he died of overwork.

*French Literature.*

Whether Montaigne coined the word 'essay' or not, it is certain that he created the thing.

*French Literature.*

In all countries and in all languages writers who can succeed in writing their language as it is spoken, purely and without slovenliness, racily and yet with elegance, are rare.

*French Literature.*

*In a letter to Ethel Smyth, 2 September 1922*: One of the greatest, the supreme pleasures in life, is, I think, to take up a book, saying to oneself, it is no use reading that now as I know and remember it too well, and then beginning it to find that you have forgotten so much of it that the second or third reading is better than the first.

*Ethel Smyth, A Biography* by Christopher St John.

'Writing is planchette, only before you can get the planchette to work mechanically, some sharp-pointed instrument must wound and stab you – that is to say, some experience or impression. . . . When the wound is healed, the writing begins.'

*Daphne Adeane.*

The University is not a stimulating place for aspiring writers. The dons have seen it all so many times, and heard it all so often; the under-graduates are so terribly in earnest and uncompromisingly severe about the efforts of their fellow-undergraduates; so cocksure and certain about their judgements. . . .

*The Puppet Show of Memory.*

Few writers think before they write, or even when they are writing; they let their pen guide their thoughts. And I am certain that those writers who write too much suffer from a disease of the fingers and not of the brain.

*Round the World in Any Number of Days.*

[In the nineties] Dickens was little read, except by the public.

'The Nineties', in *Lost Lectures.*

One afternoon while I was at the Acropolis I met a peasant and had a little talk with him. I had with me in a little book Sappho's 'Ode to Aphrodite', and I asked him to read it aloud, which he did, remarking that it was in *patois.*

*The Puppet Show of Memory.*

The ideal bookcase would be that in which you could plunge a hand into in the dark and be sure of extracting something readable.

*The Puppet Show of Memory.*

Pushkin is Russia's national poet, the Peter the Great of poetry, who out of foreign material created something new, and Russian.

*An Outline of Russian Literature.*

She said she could never read the books she possessed, only other people's.

*Daphne Adeane.*

Goethe was a great man and poet as well; Victor Hugo, although he was more than a mere poet, was not a great man.

*Goethe and Victor Hugo*, in
*Punch and Judy and Other Essays.*

'The English see no difference between Voltaire's plays and Racine's; they don't see why lines like

*J'ai voulu devant vous exposant mes remords,*
*Par un chemin plus lent descendre chez les morts*

are the lines of a great poet, that they are as good as they can be. They talk rot about it not being Greek. It isn't; it's French. Phèdre is a practising Catholic Christian, slightly tinged with Jansenism, and she talks the language of Versailles. But she is a living being, and the language she talks is quite perfect.'

*C.*

Lord Saint-Edith said he couldn't understand people thinking Bacon had written Shakespeare's plays. If they said Shakespeare had written the works of Bacon as a pastime he could understand it.

*Passing By.*

Nothing is so futile and so impertinent as giving marks to the great poets, as if they were passing an examination.

*An Outline of Russian Literature.*

There is no amount of praise which a man and an author cannot bear with equanimity. Some authors can even stand flattery.

From the dedicatory letter of *Dead Letters.*

# 9

## *Maurice Baring Parodied*

*One of the awesome and sometimes unnerving honours bestowed upon public figures during roughly the first half of the twentieth century was to be noticed by Max Beerbohm in drawing or writing. Maurice Baring figured in both. He was depicted in various Beerbohm caricatures and – supreme accolade – he was expertly victimized in the second (1950) edition of Beerbohm's volume of matchless parodies,* A Christmas Garland, *along with such leading literary figures as Henry James, John Galsworthy, Arnold Bennett, Rudyard Kipling, Thomas Hardy, Bernard Shaw, and Joseph Conrad. Beerbohm's verbal caricature of his novelistic style delighted Baring, for in the prefatory note to the second edition Beerbohm wrote that 'it amused and pleased my old friend', and added that 'had he not liked it, I would not include it in this later edition'.*

*Beerbohm touches the nerve in Baring's essential themes, kinds of characters, and habits of style. With the title itself, he nudges Baring's Catholic piety, and again in the reference to an aunt who 'had been a devout Catholic, but there was some kink in her, and she was now a Presbyterian'. The pessimism of Baring's heroes, his devotion to governesses, his cult for foreign ladies with their endless fascinating talk, all are drolly hit off. We are given one of those catalogue passages of personal history, and in a wonderful echo of Baring's habit of making narrowly nice distinctions, we hear that Madame Yakovlev is 'a very agreeable woman, but I don't think she's amiable'. Professor Jorton is one of Baring's cosmopolites to the life, for 'no capital city was complete without him'. Romance dawns and is extinguished.*

*Really good parody, as critics have long admitted, has critical value. Beerbohm's parody does not destroy the serious value of Baring's fiction for us – but it does let us remember much that is so peculiarly flavoursome in the original that we can afford to recognize it, in the imitation, with a smile.*

# All Roads . . .

(from *A Christmas Garland* by Max Beerbohm)

## CHAPTER V

MICHAEL FORSTER REACHED ROME in the first week of December and drove straight to the Embassy. Every one there was very kind to him. It was rather like being a new boy at a public school and not being bullied. All the same, he could not help wishing himself back at Copenhagen, or at Berne, where he had felt life-sized. Rome dwarfed him. She seemed to say to him, 'If you want monuments, look around you! You will then know that though you are twenty-five years old you are nobody – and never will be anybody, though you live to be a hundred.' But at any rate he was not dreading the advent of Christmas.

Year after year, he had dreaded it ever since his childhood. When he was five years old, his parents had had the usual Christmas-tree party at the Grange, but his German governess, Fräulein Schultz, had a sick headache and could not come down for it. To most people she was just a German governess like another, but she was not so to Michael. To him she was a winged Angel, and there was none like her, and he worshipped her. And now she was ill, and he believed she would die. He did not want to cry during the party, but he cried all the time, hating the presents that were given him; and though Fräulein Schultz was quite well next day, and though he forgot all about her soon after she went to be a governess somewhere else, he never lost his dislike of Christmas.

Because they make less of that festival in Latin countries, he was glad to be transferred to Rome. Not that he had yet felt any definite wavering in regard to the Church in which he had been baptized and confirmed. He was still a Protestant. But he had long since ceased to protest day in, day out, and the prospect of seeing a Christmas passed over lightly was one of the things that cheered him on his journey south. He forgot that embassies are on neutral territory, and it was a blow to him when one day Sainson, the Second Secretary, said, 'Of course, the Chief will be giving the usual beano dinner on Christmas night.'

Michael, at this news, wished more than ever that he had been born with a *real* vocation for diplomacy, but he did manage to think out a plausible excuse, and on Christmas night, after he had dressed, he slipped out and dined in an obscure little restaurant in the Via Golfango. It had been recommended to him by a friend of his family, Pierre de Frénard, who had spent ten years over a treatise on the geology of the Campagna. It was known to Frénard and to a very few other people because of its special dish, *tagliatelli coi fichi*. It was kept by a very old man who did the cooking and waiting and had helped Garibaldi to escape from Vallenza.

When he was half-way through his meal, Frénard himself came in and joined him at his table. Later, while they sat over their coffee, Frénard said he thought of going on to Mme Yakovlev's.

Michael asked, 'Who is Mme Yakovlev?'

Frénard laughed and said, 'Oh, she's one of those women who know everybody. Fancy anyone not knowing *her*! You had better come with me. This is one of her *Soirs*. She has two a week. *Un seul ne suffirait pas à cette gourmande.*'

'Tell me about her,' said Michael.

'There's not much to tell,' answered Frénard, blowing a puff of cigarette smoke. 'Her father was very poor, an Irish landowner, living mostly at home in a tumble-down castle, but sometimes travelling. From one of his journeys, he brought back a bride – a young Turkish lady, a niece of Mustapha Pasha. There was one child of the marriage, a daughter; she was christened Clara. Both parents died when she was twelve years old. She was then brought up by an aunt in Scotland. The aunt had been a devout Catholic, but there was some kink in her, and she was now a Presbyterian. The girl was not at all happy with her. She ran away when she was sixteen and became a postulant in an Ursuline Convent near Glasgow. But she found she had no real vocation. She again disappeared and nothing was known of her till she became the wife of Freiherr von Ostach, who was Hofmarschall to the King of Saxony. He died four years later. His wife was then twenty-one years old. She left the Saxon Court and went to Brazil, where she formed an immense collection of butterflies and married a Spanish diamond merchant, whose name I forget. He died, leaving her very well off. She came back to Europe. Sergius Yakovlev, her third husband, was a trusted adviser of Alexander the Third, and was Gouverneur of the Corps de Pages. She and he are said to have been quite happy while he lived. Anyhow, she never married again. She settled in Rome. She used to go out a great deal, but now she never goes out. She is always to be found in her apartment in Palazzo Triforna. She is a very agreeable woman, but I don't think she's amiable. She was seventy-three last June. She knows a great deal, but seldom says very much. What she says has point. Paul Bourget once said of her,

"*Je ne trouve pas qu'elle est vraiment* witty, *mais elle a beaucoup d'esprit.*" At one time she wore a brown wig. She has very small feet. She plays cribbage for three hours every Tuesday afternoon with Oliveira, the Portuguese military attaché.'

Michael was not much attracted by this description; but it was clear that there was nothing Christmassy about Mme Yakovlev, and he willingly agreed to accompany his friend to Palazzo Triforna.

The *salone* was a vast octagonal one of grey stone, with an enclaved ceiling. There was only one picture in it – a Martyrdom of Sta. Vestina, by Murillo, almost black with age. Below it stood a pianoforte. This was the only piece of furniture. Had there been chairs or tables, there would not have been room enough for the multitude of guests. Michael was piloted by Frénard to Mme Yakovlev and presented to her. Somehow he had expected her to be tall, but she was quite short. She repeated his name in a rather harsh mezzo-soprano voice, and asked if he were a relation of *un tel Monsieur Septimus Forster* whom she had known in Algiers.

Michael said he thought that he wasn't.

Mme Yakovlev shrugged her shoulders and said, '*Eh bien, on ne peut pas être parent de tout-le-monde.*'

Before he could think of an answer, he had to make way for another fresh arrival. He felt that he had not made a good impression. But afterwards Frénard told him that Mme Yakovlev had liked him very much.

In one of the groups nearest to him he saw a young woman whose face was familiar to him, though he was sure he had never seen her before, and though she was unlike any one he had ever seen. She was like a spray of jasmine that had taken the semblance of human form and yet was still only a flower. She seemed utterly remote from the group she stood in. It was as though she had cleared a great space around her, and were visible through a silvery twilight of her own making. How was she here? Who could she be? That she was a musician, and an exquisite one, Michael was sure. Her eyes and her hands proclaimed that. But for the rest. . . .

While Michael gazed and wondered, the vast bulk of Professor Jorton suddenly interposed itself between him and the unknown, and he was affectionately hailed in the booming voice of the famous Alpine climber and Egyptologist, who was an old friend of his family and was one of his Godfathers. That Jorton should be here was natural enough, for in spite of all his peaks and papyri he was the most social of men, and no capital city was complete without him. Michael felt sure he could learn from Jorton something about the identity of the young woman.

'Yes, yes,' said Jorton in reply to his appeal. 'I don't wonder that you're struck by her. Eleanor d'Urutsias don't grow on every bush. Her father was Owen Prescott, one of the Canons of St Paul's, a most interesting fellow. She married out of the schoolroom, as it were. She was only sixteen when young Fernand d'Urutsia came over to London. He was attached to a Special Mission that had been sent over from Madrid. He was quite poor, and so was she, but they were ideally happy. He died on the first anniversary of their wedding, at Qualva, a fishing-village near Biarritz. It was feared that she would lose her reason. But she is "of the stuff that can affront despair". She withdrew into complete solitude for three years – no one knows where. Probably in some conventual institution, for she had become passionately *dévote* when she was received into the Roman communion. She is now twenty years old. Tonight is her *rentrée dans le monde. Endlich ist Sie uns wieder erschienen. Ben' tornata.* She is very musical. She used to sing charmingly. She plays her own accompaniments. I hope she will sing tonight. Shall I present you to her?'

'Ah, not tonight,' said Michael. 'Not here, in this crush.'

With his eyes fixed on her again, he knew in his heart that somehow, mysteriously, not yet, but not a long while hence, his life would be linked with hers.

Presently Jorton moved away, and Michael found himself talking with other people whom he knew – the James Corvelts, of Boston, Monsignor Olbretta, full of the persuasive wisdom that had already begun to affect him so deeply, the Raymonds, Miss Travers, and others.

Then he was aware that something was happening. There was a movement in the group around Mme d'Urutsia, and a murmur of excitement throughout the room, and then a deep hush, as she passed slowly to the pianoforte.

Michael had known that if she sang it would be unlike any singing that he had heard. But he had not known how utterly unlike it would be. The song itself was one he had often heard, and had not cared for – Weber's setting of Béranger's 'Noël'. She transported it into some sphere of unconjectured beauty in which one could only hold one's breath, and marvel as best one might.

> *'Noël s'en va,*
> *Patati et patata.*
> *Vois-tu, Noël passe,*
> *Hélas.'*

The notes came and went without melancholy as one knows it, without gaiety as one could recognize it, but with an ethereal mingling of both these moods. And they seemed to come not from within the room. One seemed to hear them wafted from a great distance, across the waters of a great lake. They made Michael all the more certain in his heart that his future was indissolubly one with the future of Eleanor d'Urutsia. As it happened, he never saw her again. But she had entirely conquered his dislike of Christmas. He was destined to love it ever after.

# 10

*A List of Principal Books by Maurice Baring*

# A List of Principal Books by Maurice Baring

1899    *Hildesheim*, quatre pastiches
1902    *The Black Prince*
1903    *Gaston de Foix*
1905    *With the Russians in Manchuria*
1906    *Desiderio*
1906    *Sonnets and Short Poems*
1906    *Thoughts on Art and Life of Leonard de Vinci* (translation)
1907    *A Year in Russia*
1908    *Proserpine*
1909    *Russian Essays and Stories*
1909    *Orpheus in Mayfair*
1909    *The Story of Forget-Me-Not and Lily of the Valley*
1910    *Landmarks in Russian Literature*
1910    *Dead Letters*
1910    *The Glass Mender*
1911    *Diminutive Dramas*
1911    *Collected Poems*
1911    *The Russian People*
1912    *The Grey Stocking and Other Plays*
1913    *Letters from the Near East*
1913    *What I Saw in Russia*
1913    *Palamon and Arcite*
1913    *Lost Diaries*
1914    *The Mainsprings of Russia*
1914    *An Outline of Russian Literature*
1916    *English Landscape: An Anthology*
1916    *Translations (Found in a Commonplace Book)*
1919    *Round the World in Any Number of Days*
1920    *R.F.C. H.Q. (1911–1918)*

1921 *Poems 1914–19*
1921 *Passing By*
1922 *The Puppet Show of Memory*
1922 *Overlooked*
1923 *His Majesty's Embassy*
1923 *A Triangle*
1924 *C*
1924 *Punch and Judy and Other Essays*
1925 *Half a Minute's Silence and Other Stories*
1925 *Collected Poems*
1925 *Translations Ancient and Modern* (with originals)
1925 *Cat's Cradle*
1925 *The Oxford Book of Russian Verse* (Editor; introductory essay)
1926 *Daphne Adeane*
1926 *Last Days of Tsarskoe Selo* (translation)
1927 *French Literature*
1927 *Tinker's Leave*
1928 *Comfortless Memory*
1928 *Algae*
1929 *Algae. Second Series*
1929 *The Coat Without Seam*
1929 *Fantasio* (translation)
1930 *Robert Peckham*
1931 *In my End is my Beginning*
1932 *Lost Lectures*
1933 *Friday's Business*
1934 *The Lonely Lady of Dulwich*
1935 *Darby and Joan*
1936 *Have You Anything to Declare?*
1943 *Russian Lyrics*

# 11

*Acknowledgements*

# Acknowledgements

WITH ALL THANKS I must note my indebtedness for the sources of my work on this book.

First, in directly personal acknowledgement, I offer my gratitude to Mr Michael Wheeler-Booth for suggesting that I attempt a book dealing with Maurice Baring; and for giving me profitable suggestions for the improvement of my introductory essay.

I am grateful to my American editor, Mr Robert Giroux, of Farrar, Straus and Giroux, for sound guidance and strong support throughout every stage of the development of this book, over a period of several years. Sir Rupert Hart-Davis favoured this undertaking from the beginning, and I thank him for excellent suggestions concerning both substance and style. My English editor, Mr W. R. Smith, of Heinemann, contributed much to the final form of the book.

Otherwise, I am indebted for assistance, whether in terms of enthusiasm or critical advice, to my sister, the late Rosemary Grant, Professor Leon Edel, Mr Edmund Wilson, the Very Reverend Father Martin C. D'Arcy, S.J., the late Mr Daniel Longwell, the Reverend Austin McCurtain, S.J., and Mrs Roger Williams Straus, Jr. I have enjoyed the generous help of Mr Herman Liebert, director of the Beinecke Rare Book and Manuscript Library of Yale University, who granted me access to the Baring collections there, notably that one catalogued as under the former ownership of Lady Diana Cooper. From the Houghton Library at Harvard also I obtained otherwise inaccessible material. The hitherto unpublished 'Ballade of the *Resolution* Ward Room' appears in Section VI by kind permission of Lady Maclean of Strachur House, Argyll. Mr Keith Hutchison of Durham, Connecticut, assisted me greatly in procuring out of print editions of Baring's books. In early drafts, my introductory essay was given in lecture form, first at Georgetown University as an incident of the University's Centennial celebration, and later at Saybrook College, Yale, during my visit there as Hoyt Fellow, and again, at Fairfield University as a visiting lecturer. All my work in connection with this

ACKNOWLEDGEMENTS

text was done at the Center For Advanced Studies of Wesleyan University, in whose Fellows and faculty colleagues I read abbreviated excerpts of my essay. I thank Mrs Tania Senff for her expert help in giving final form to the manuscript.

I acknowledge with respect my debt to books which contributed details to my essay and notes: *A Number of People* by Sir Edward Marsh; *The Rainbow Comes and Goes, The Light of Common Day* and *Trumpets from the Steep* by Lady Diana Cooper; *Maurice Baring, A Postscript* by Laura Lady Lovat; *The Journal of Arnold Bennett*; *Vernon Lee* (*Violet Paget*) by Peter Gunn; *Ethel Smyth* by Christopher St John; *Around Theatres* by Max Beerbohm; *Maurice Baring, Impressions that Remained, As Time Went On* and *What Happened Next* by Dame Ethel Smyth; *Live was Worth Living* by W. Graham Robertson; and *Expositions and Developments* by Igor Stravinsky and Robert Craft.

'An Officer's Death', 'An Autumn Day in France' and 'A Rainy Day in Wartime' from *R.F.C. H.Q.* are reprinted in Section 5 by kind permission of William Blackwood Ltd. 'All Roads . . .' from *A Christmas Garland* by Max Beerbohm is reprinted in Section 9 by kind permission of William Heinemann Ltd. Alfred A. Knopf, Inc., kindly added their permission for the inclusion of *The Lonely Lady of Dulwich* (Section 7), 'Alone When Pride Lies Dying' from *Robert Peckham*, and the final chapter of *The Coat Without Seam*.

P. H.